STEPHEN J. VOORHIES

CONNECTICUT RAILROADS

. . . An Illustrated History

By Gregg M. Turner & Melancthon W. Jacobus

Edited, and with a Foreword, by Oliver Jensen

ONE HUNDRED FIFTY YEARS OF RAILROAD HISTORY

A Publication of
THE CONNECTICUT HISTORICAL SOCIETY
1986

Designed by Edward J. McLaughlin and set in Times Roman type.

Printed in the United States of America by Allied Printing Services, Manchester, Connecticut.

Typography by Southern New England Typographic Service, Inc., Hamden, Connecticut.

[FRONTISPIECE] A set of Amtrak rail diesel cars glides into Hartford, 1985. From the collection of Tom Nelligan.

Jacket/cover illustration: *The 9:45 Accommodation, Stratford, Connecticut* (detail) by Edward Lamson Henry, 1867. Oil on canvas. Courtesy The Metropolitan Museum of Art, Bequest of Moses Tanenbaum, 1937.

Table of Contents

Melancthon Williams Jacobus

The Connecticut Historical Society suffered a great loss when, on April 6, 1984, Melancthon W. Jacobus died. "Chick," as he was known since his undergraduate days at Princeton, was identified with this book from its conception as co-author and prime advocate. His death has, we regret to say, naturally delayed the publication beyond the previously announced date.

After a distinguished teaching career at the Kingswood School in West Hartford, Connecticut, Chick became curator of prints and photographs at The Connecticut Historical Society and in that capacity gave generously of his time in assisting the public to know and use the Society's archival collections. How many people he helped will never be known; he was modest and unassuming as befitted a gentleman of the old school. In addition he made himself an authority on steamboating and wrote the authoritative work on that topic, *The Connecticut River Steamboat Story*. Fascinated since boyhood by trains, he also became a careful student of Connecticut railroad history.

In 1983 Chick delivered at the Society a highly successful lecture on the state's railroads, complete with slides and a superb photographic exhibition. This in part was the springboard for this book, a project in which he was joined by fellow Connecticut railroad historian Gregg Turner. Unfortunately, while the project was still in the early research stage, Chick's health failed and he was hospitalized. To the end of his life the completion of this book weighed heavily on him, so much so that in his will he left, among other gifts to the Society, funds which have helped make an expensive project possible.

KINGSWOOD - OXFORD SCHOOL

The Society remembers him with deep affection and is also most grateful to Gregg Turner for writing the entire text and carrying the project to a successful conclusion.

Ellsworth Grant
President
The Connecticut Historical Society
1985

Acknowledgements

The author is grateful to the persons and organizations cited throughout this book, and in particular to those named below. Without their contributions, cooperation, and skills, the research and preparation of this book would not have been possible.

First among them is my late friend and collaborator, Chick Jacobus, a tribute to whom the reader will find elsewhere in this book. Other members serving on our advisory panel who have made a variety of contributions include: Robert Bell, owner of the Train Exchange model railroad emporium in Manchester, Connecticut; Charles Gunn, a former official photographer of the New York, New Haven & Hartford Railroad Company; Oliver Jensen, senior editor of *American Heritage Magazine* and board chairman of the Valley Railroad Company in Essex, Connecticut; and Peter Malia, former managing editor of The Connecticut Historical Society.

Numerous organizations cheerfully responded to inquiries arising from this project, and a word of appreciation is owed to: The Railway & Locomotive Historical Society; The California State Railroad Museum Library, Walter P. Gray, curator; The National Museum of American History, Smithsonian Institution, William Withuhn, curator, Division of Transportation; The New Haven Railroad Historical & Technical Association; The New Haven Colony Historical Society, Lucinda Burkepile, curator of photographs; The Steamship Historical Society of America, Laura Brown, researcher, University of Baltimore Library; Baker Library at Harvard Business School, Robert Lovett, curator of manuscripts and archives; The Connecticut State Library; The New Hampshire Historical Society, Stephen Cox, manuscripts curator-editor; The American Heritage Publishing Company Picture Library, Patrick Bunyan, librarian ; and to Professor David Roth of The Center for Connecticut Studies at Eastern Connecticut State University and Professor Richard Ruth of Mitchell College in New London.

Invaluable assistance was freely given by many libraries and historical societies located throughout Connecticut, from answering questions to providing materials cited herein. Their spirit and depth of response were noteworthy.

Many railroad enthusiasts generously provided materials from their private collections. I am grateful for their assistance, especially to Thomas McNamara, inheritor of the famous Kent Cochrane photographic collection of the New Haven Railroad; Francis Donovan, Patrick Goedert, Scott Hartley, Oliver Jensen, Clifford Lund, James McFarlane, Max Miller, Tom Nelligan, Douglas K. Patterson, Alice Ramsdell, Karl Stieg, Jack Swanberg, James M. S. Ullman, Donald Valentine, Jr., and Philip Wooding.

I wish also to express my gratitude to both the Publications Committee of The Connecticut Historical Society for undertaking the publication of this book and to these Society staff members: Diana McCain, who guided the book through editing and production; Martha Wojan, who oversaw the typing revisions of the text; Elizabeth Abbe, librarian, for her help from the very start; and Kate Steinway for assistance with photographic research.

Special thanks are owed to Edward J. McLaughlin, art director; Lawrence Hill, cartographer; my typist and secretary Edwina Curtis; and to my wife, Nancy, who encouraged the pursuit and completion of this pleasant task.

I conclude, perhaps apologetically, that it is not possible to name the scores of railroaders who have contributed something to my own knowledge of railroading. Few professions have employees so knowledgeable of their daily occupations. I am grateful to them.

Gregg M. Turner
Mansfield Center, Connecticut

NOTE TO READER: Photographic materials not otherwise credited in this book are from the collections of The Connecticut Historical Society. Credits bearing the initials "R & LHS" refer to the Railway & Locomotive Historical Society, while those marked "SHSA" indicate The Steamship Historical Society of America.

Editor's Foreword

It is no use arguing that Connecticut is a large state; the map is against you. But as anyone with even the sketchiest acquaintance with history is aware, size has nothing to do with importance. With ability, ambition, and inventiveness, Connecticut was from the beginning bountifully endowed. It produced America's first written attempt at representative government, the Fundamental Orders; it gave birth to many men of mark; and it witnessed many of the first stirrings of the industrial revolution in the young republic. The wheels of early factories were already turning in millraces along such rivers as the Quinebaug, the Shetucket, and the Naugatuck when enterprising men in the 1830s commenced laying down the first little sections of a railroad system. They were separate, independent, frail affairs, but their purpose was to bring the products of all this inland enterprise to a larger market, chugging down to seaports along Long Island Sound, that convenient, sheltered waterway to the outside world.

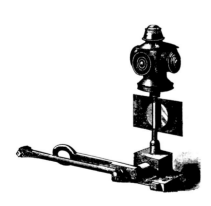

To some people of the time, however, Connecticut was not small but too large. For those who wished to travel between the growing cities of Boston and New York it was simply a long, tiresome obstacle on the journey by land. On the Commercial Overland Stage, for example, advertised as the speediest way in 1815 — via Worcester, Stafford Springs, Hartford, Middletown, and New Haven — it took a hard, bumpy thirty-nine hours and considerable endurance on the part of the six passengers accommodated. The age of steam was just beginning, however, at first on the rivers and sounds, and it was not long before the hustlers between cities could travel in new comfort by steamboat to Providence, where a railroad was soon installed to take the travellers on to Boston. The flaw in this route was that the boats had to pass out of the quiet waters of the Sound through open ocean around stormy Point Judith, with poor effect on delicate stomachs. It was not long before entrepreneurs perceived their opportunity and extended the railway line down to Westerly, Rhode Island, and on for another six miles into Connecticut, to Stonington, the easternmost port on the Sound. And so railroading began in this state.

Out of that tender concern for sufferers from *mal de mer* — and with, to be sure, motives of profit — grew in time a busy network of tracks throughout Connecticut. Readers in large states may smile indulgently at the phrase "throughout Connecticut," but it was probably the densest system for its area in the country. Just to cite a few facts, no fewer than seven lines of steam railroads (not counting ten of intercity trolley cars) once steamed out of Hartford, radiating like spokes from a wheel hub. There were six out of New Haven, six out of Waterbury, six out of Willimantic, five out of Middletown. Middletown? Sneer not at Middletown: the famous *Air Line Limited* stopped at Middletown's busy station but didn't even hesitate as it ran through New Haven at speed.

It is hard to make people believe the service once enjoyed all over the state, but the old timetables reproduced in this book may give one the idea. There were, for example, four trains a day each way from little Farmington to smaller New Hartford, four trains up to Litchfield, four through trains west from Hartford to Canaan and Millerton, New York. There were eight from New London to Norwich merely on the east side of the Thames River, and more on the west side; there were eleven for commuters from Branchville to Ridgefield; six from Saybrook to Hartford up the Valley Division; six from Amston on the 3.6-mile branch to Colchester; seventeen between Middletown and Berlin. No trains run on these lines today. On a line that still carries passengers, the Northeast Corridor, five trains a day serve the Old Saybrook—New London run against twelve in New Haven Railroad days. But perhaps the best way to dramatize the difference between then and now is to use one little statistic from the massive Connecticut Railroad Commissioners' report for 1911. The state's railroads that year had 2,610 passenger cars in use. The fleet with which Amtrak today struggles to serve the whole United States numbers 1,633.

Amtrak, of course, would dearly love to have more cars; it could fill them and increase its profitability if it had enough to furnish more service and get people to leave their cars at home, but government keeps it on short rein and constant threat of extinction. The subject comes up only because the situation of Amtrak today is almost the direct opposite of the New York, New Haven & Hartford Railroad in its imperial days, sixty, seventy, and eighty years ago. By the turn of the century, almost all the railroads in Connecticut and adjoining areas, not to mention the steamboat lines and trolley companies, had been gathered into that huge monopoly, one by one. It had an imperial fleet to operate an imperial system, and as the new century began it acquired an emperor, the great banker J. Pierpont Morgan, who collected railways as Queen Victoria collected colonies.

Morgan despised competition as wasteful and untidy. Through force of personality rather than his own money he brought vast sums into play to achieve his objectives; he and his henchman, Charles S. Mellen, stalk through this book like kings on a stage. To Morgan, before it became his final undoing, the New Haven road was a plaything and, in the panic of 1907, an emergency cash box. In its palmy days in the 1880s and 90s, it had been famous not only for its great deluxe expresses and palace steamers but also for its stock, sound as bedrock, selling at around $200 a share and paying a steady 10 percent, the prudent investment of widows and orphans. The railroad's revenues were thrice the state's; its power swayed legislatures — or simply bought them — in southern New England. In Connecticut alone, the New Haven in 1911 employed 34,767 men (no women are mentioned), and carried more than eighty-four million passengers; its fleet of steamboats outnumbered most navies. (One of them, the giant *Commonwealth*, once collided with an American battleship, and it was the man-of-war that was badly dented.) The triumphs, and scandals, of Connecticut railroads were front page news, especially when Morgan extended his railroad empire into neighboring New York and even into northern New England.

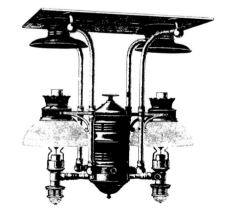

The story ends, as all such moral tales must, in collapse, the death of the emperor, and the long, slowly accelerating decline of the New Haven Road, but not without many good years for what some latter-day railroad men referred to disdainfully as "the passenger element." There is much more to the narrative than this, however. The rise of the automobile could not help but put much local railroad service out of business, and the truck, with its convenience, wiped out much freight service.

Government favored and still favors Detroit. Interstate highways went up, over $450 billion worth, next to railroad arteries. If you rarely see a freight train these days — let alone have to stop at a country crossing and watch a long one roll by, and perhaps even enjoy the romantic, picturesque names on the box cars — you know why. The train is on the highway, speeding by on all sides, each "box car" or "tank car" with its own engineer, each with a mind of its own, which has taken a lot of the old-time joy out of "motoring." You never see a caboose, because this train has no end.

To bring this whole story together has been a labor of love for the author, Gregg Turner, made the more difficult by the untimely death of his original collaborator, the late Melancthon Jacobus, with whom he originally planned the book. It has been volunteer work, too, for others at The Connecticut Historical Society, which is proud to have put forth the first comprehensive history of railroads in this state. Between them, Messrs. Turner and Jacobus went through the extensive collections of the Society, and then sought more in likely other depositories in Connecticut and throughout the country, a task in which I had the pleasure of joining. The great majority of the illustrations come from Mr. Turner's own files, of several thousand, gathered over many years and now generously donated to the Society. For all the clichés uttered on the subject, pictures do greatly illuminate and enliven a serious work of history, so that one can see really how it was, or as the German historian's phrase goes, *wie es eigentlich gewesen*. To organize photographs, timetables, maps, engravings, and other evidences of the past and present is not an easy task, and all of us are pleased with the general plan followed by Mr. Turner and the art director, E.J. McLaughlin, a railroad enthusiast and artist in his own right.

There is already one generation in existence, perhaps more than one, to whom the story of railroading in Connecticut will come as something of a surprise. Indeed, some young people know nothing about railroading whatever, and have never seen or ridden on a train. So they tell me when they look for the first time at the panting steam engines at the Valley Railroad in Essex, breathing steam at every crack and crevice. Then they peer in the parlor car. "Was it really like this?" Yea verily, it was. So little has survived the bankruptcies and break-up of the New Haven, and the even more disorderly collapse of Penn Central. There appears no sign that anyone is planning, come November, 1987, to celebrate that first little train which puffed out of Stonington 150 years ago, or all that railroads accomplished for Connecticut, or still may in a happier future for travellers. But, celebration or not, laid up here and there "where neither moth nor rust doth corrupt," this book will help preserve their memory.

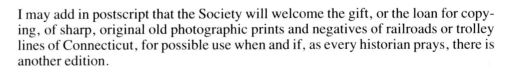

I may add in postscript that the Society will welcome the gift, or the loan for copying, of sharp, original old photographic prints and negatives of railroads or trolley lines of Connecticut, for possible use when and if, as every historian prays, there is another edition.

Oliver Jensen
Fenwick, Old Saybrook,
Connecticut
January, 1986

Author's Introduction

There is something marvellous in the development and progress of the railroads! Their construction commenced under great difficulties, and by parties who had neither the experience or the opportunities to profit by the example of others.

— Connecticut's railroad commissioners, Annual Report, 1868

As a boy I grew up in the Quaker Hill section of Waterford, Connecticut, within earshot of the Central Vermont Railway and not far from the upstream finish line of the Yale-Harvard Regatta. At this point, called Bartlett's Cove, the railroad hugs the western bank of the Thames River. Seventy-five years ago the palatial black steam yacht *Corsair* would be anchored here—just for a day—allowing its notable guests to witness once again the colorful rowing spectacle. America's greatest banker and financier would be the host, a man who also controlled at that moment the great New Haven Railroad empire. That was J. Pierpont Morgan.

The Central Vermont was the first railroad I can remember, and in the early 1950s the steam engine was still king. Several roads crossed the railroad track just north of here, and the skilled engineers of the Central Vermont could be counted upon—just as they can be today—to ably announce their approach. Their reverberating locomotive whistles made a powerful impression, and I can still hear the echoing effect as they played over the Thames to Gales Ferry and finally drifted upriver.

After much pestering of my parents, I finally got to see the Central Vermont trains up close. That was memorable. You first heard the staccato exhaust crackling in the distance. Then the train would suddenly round the bend: whistle screaming, headlight aglow, and the bell madly ringing. I'd reach for their hands then—not scared—but bracing myself for that climactic moment when the mass of steam and speed would hurtle by. Immediately after, the hypnotic clickety-clack would begin as the freight cars paraded past—different colors, all shapes and sizes. Bobbing along at the end would be the orange-red caboose, and on its side was painted the grand maple-leaf insignia of the Central Vermont Railway. Where this train was ultimately heading, and the destinations of her countless sisters, were too much for a chap of four. But I did know I had fallen in love with trains.

Needless to say, that affair grew and grew. Thirty years later the railroad history of Connecticut became the center of my interest. Since relatively little on the subject existed, I was inspired to do some research and writing, and this brought me into contact with Melancthon Jacobus, the curator of prints and photographs of The Connecticut Historical Society. Together we began this illustrated history of Connecticut railroads. Both of us believed that this kind of book was not only needed but also might give some pleasure to that perceptive portion of mankind that enjoys trains, railroading, and history.

Our state's railroad heritage can be divided into three contrasting periods: the era of local enterprise, when the state's principal railway lines were built and operated as separate companies; the era of consolidation and monopoly, which primarily focused on the acquisitions, growth, and demise of the vast New York, New Haven & Hartford Railroad system; and our modern era of change and uncertainty, characterized thus far by abandonments, reorganization, government intervention, rehabilitation of certain lines, and a shifting restructure of ownership among both large and small operators.

Each of these periods has its share of absorbing moments, particularly the New Haven Railroad* narrative, some of which still lies in human memory. But it is a century and a half since the steam locomotive made its startling appearance on Connecticut soil and began knitting together the coastal and interior centers. Thrust upon our ancestors—almost overnight—was an unparalleled dose of social and economic growth. It was an era filled with dreams and folly, accomplishments and failures, and a fair amount of charm.

That era of both private and local enterprise commenced in 1832 when the first railway charters were granted, although it was five years before the first train moved in Connecticut. These early lines were built on easy terrain, terminated at Long Island Sound or at river ports, and avoided geographic hazards. Later the more challenging routes beckoned. Some went directly through Connecticut on their way from Boston (or Providence) to New York. Many were built out of civic pride. Overall, railroads planned north to south were in harmony with the uplands of the state, while most of the east-west routes had to negotiate severe grades and curves, river crossings, and deep valleys.

Great railroad experimentation and improvement occurred throughout the nineteenth century, coinciding with America's industrial age, whose waves of booms and panics, inventions and new technologies, greatly affected railway operations. Locomotive efficiency was increased, interiors of passenger cars became more comfortable, and freight cars grew larger. Advances in engineering provided stronger bridges and better track installations, while jobs and train operations became safer.

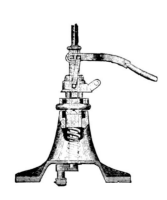

Dozens of Connecticut railroads were chartered back then. Many were justified, some were not, and a few never saw the light of day. Where once the Connecticut legislature looked coldly at the iron horse, "it later inclined to smile upon him," reported the *Hartford Courant*, "and gave him free course over the State." The railway network grew dramatically. Our railroad commissioners remarked in 1861 that "no town within the state is more than 14 miles distant from these important highways," suggesting that construction was about to crest. Eight years later, however, they admitted that "in no state has the limit of their construction even been approximately reached." Fewer than fifty miles of track existed in Connecticut in 1837; by the 1890s there were more than one thousand. Except for several minor projects, all of the principal steam railway lines of Connecticut were completed in this era.

The historical foundations of any Connecticut railroad can be traced to that most coveted of all documents, its charter. Interestingly, the language contained in those early documents was often extracted from ancient canal and turnpike charters, businesses with which the legislature had prior experience. Frequently a railroad had the conventional turnpike right "to establish gates, erect toll houses, and demand toll upon the road." Other forms of locomotion were sanctioned, including

---

*The name New Haven Railroad, or the Consolidated, refers throughout this book to the New York, New Haven & Hartford Railroad Company. A full-fledged corporate history of that firm this book is not, nor does it fully cover the company's activities outside the state's borders.

the "power of horses." The Danbury & Norwalk Railroad, for instance, was conceived of as a horse railway and included an inventory of "six passenger carriages, fifteen wagons for burdens, and thirty horses with stables, harnesses, etc." The Norwich & Worcester Railroad, however, proudly reported that "the only power used is by locomotive steam engine, the great expense of horse power being entirely avoided." The novelty of being hauled by a steam "animal" in the 1830s amused the *Connecticut Herald and Journal*: "Gentlemen will keep their own steam coaches, and find it cheap, pleasant, and convenient to travel, and not at the slow rate of twenty miles to the day in their private vehicles. Stables will cease to be an annoyance; steam carriages will be patient animals, never kicking for flies, nor whisking their tails in men's mouths, nor sending out noisome odors. When a gentlemen would take a ride, he has only to direct John to put the kettle on and whisk away in a jiffy."

Other charter sections named incorporators; specified routes, width and number of tracks, and legal obligations; and authorized set amounts of stocks or bonds that could be issued. The charter also gave railroads the governmental right of eminent domain as a help in acquiring private property along the proposed route. To check that privilege, however, Connecticut wisely appointed three land commissioners to each system, to oversee just recompense to property owners. Land that was not sold at market values was often given to a particular railroad or sold cheaply in order to attract it to a certain area.

Funds for construction usually were raised through sale of stocks and bonds—some even being sold on credit. Delinquent stock payments were frequent during the initial decades of Connecticut railroading, especially when the nation was gripped by financial panics. Erratic payments interrupted construction or bankrupted projects. Towns, cities, and banks subscribed to these issues in addition to private investors. Tax abatements were granted. Public spirit soared, and many towns and cities became financially overextended in the day of railway fever. As a result, by 1875 such railroad indebtedness in Connecticut stood at $5,561,000. Two years later Connecticut's railroad commissioners found that not one of the original railway companies was even earning the interest on its bonded debt. The legislature responded by forbidding any town or municipality to invest further in railroad stocks and bonds.

Each company was required to compile fiscal data and forward it to the secretary of the state. Returns were later enforced by the Connecticut railroad commissioners, whose published annual reports were valuable resources, enlightening investors and helping to curb illegal profiteering. Connecticut's infamous exception was the Schuyler stock defalcation upon the New York & New Haven Railroad in 1854, only one year after the Railroad Commission was organized. This enormous swindle shook the country and cast suspicion upon railway officers everywhere.

As patronage increased so did the amount of trackage. Several early Connecticut railroads actually used wooden rails at first with iron straps (or bars) fastened at the top. Later they bought ones made completely of iron, and still later, of steel. Orders for iron rails were initially placed with British mills until their economical manufacture in America became common. It was not until the late nineteenth century, however, that track and superstructure were able to withstand the severest weather and use.

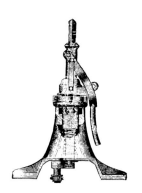

The task of surveying and constructing a railroad route properly was demanding and complex, but professional engineers were few and far between when railroading in the state first began. Connecticut companies occasionally looked outside the region for trained engineers to locate routes and instruct local figures in the science of creating secure roadbeds and laying the rails according to elaborate requirements of track geometry. Talent and expertise were often found in the topographical engineering officers of the United States Military Academy. Major George

Washington Whistler and Captain William Gibbs McNeill were distinguished West Pointers who worked on several Connecticut railroads. Professor Alexander Twining of Yale had also studied engineering at West Point and later surveyed one after another of the state's lines. The New York & Boston Air Line was located in Connecticut by Erie Canal apprentice Edwin Ferry Johnson, while contractor Sidney Dillon, famous for his part in the Union Pacific Railroad, engineered the Western Division of the New York & New England Railroad over the difficult terrain between Waterbury and the Hudson River.

The scientific achievements of the industrial age also brought progress to rail operations. The telegraph, telephone, and electric signalling apparatus made their appearance. Unfortunately, the adoption of safety equipment was not always uniform, or even trusted. The Stonington Railroad once actually advertised that no trains were run by telegraph, as if this aid in dispatching trains were something to be avoided.

The state's hundreds of waterways provided a challenge to railroad engineers on virtually every line. Influenced by such notable New England bridge builders as S. H. Long, Ithiel Town, and William Howe, Connecticut men undertook a number of engineering feats, including the impressive Lyman Viaduct on the Air Line Railroad in East Hampton, and a huge drawbridge for the Shore Line Railway at the mouth of the Connecticut River at Old Saybrook. Growing engineering expertise was displayed at Windsor Locks in 1846 when the Hartford & New Haven Railroad replaced the large Howe truss bridge across the Connecticut River in only forty-five days. The former one had been blown off its piers by a strong gale. But the state's greatest engineering feat did not occur until 1889, when what was then the world's largest steel drawbridge opened on the Thames River at New London, built by the Stonington Railroad.

Various kinds of steam engines hauled early Connecticut trains. Some had no cabs, forcing the "engine driver" to stand on a platform exposed to nature, flying cinders, and thick smoke. Eventually bells, headlights, cowcatchers, and cabs for the engine driver appeared. Engines and tenders were often painted in vivid colors, lined with ornate script in gold leaf, and named for virtually every conceivable personality, place, or thing of importance to Connecticut. One prominent builder was William Mason of West Mystic, Connecticut. He established himself at Taunton, Massachusetts, and built engines noted for precision, beauty, and interchangeable parts. Thomas Rogers, a Connecticut native and student of locomotive building, became a partner in the famous New Jersey firm of Rogers, Ketchum, and Grosvenor. William Slater of Norwich was once president of the Rhode Island Locomotive Works. Connecticut railroads placed dozens of orders with these and other firms, in addition to building engines in their own shops.

Another evolution unfolded in passenger car design. An early coach on the Stonington Railroad was no more than a suspended stagecoach body with passengers often both inside and on the top. Other companies used cars with center aisles and reversible seats and ordered them from such firms as Davenport and Kimball of Boston, Wason of Springfield, and Bradley of Worcester. Demand was so great that the Norwich & Worcester Railroad established the Norwich Car Manufactory and turned out hundreds of units a year. Connecticut's Naugatuck Railroad experimented with the first vestibuled passenger car in America. George Mortimer Pullman and Webster Wagner capitalized on yet other designs: the sleeping car, the dining car, and the luxury parlor car.

Perhaps the most famous Connecticut train of the nineteenth century was the New York & New England's *New England Limited*, whose Pullman cars were at one time painted cream white and lined with gold script. Steam piped from the locomotive eventually provided heat to the cars, while toilets and washbasins added immeasurably to the comfort of passengers. Sleeping cars improved overnight schedules, pleasing at least the *New York Tribune*, which in 1846 was critical of overnight accommodations. "The Housatonic Railroad in Connecticut is requested by a correspondent to run their trains in the course of a day or stop them where passengers can find beds. We think this perfectly reasonable. He says he was among a number who could obtain no accommodation at New Milford where the train stopped for the night, several ladies having to lie on the floor of the station without beds."

The railway safety movement in America brought in a new series of appliances. The Miller Platform of last century raised the floors of adjoining cars to the same level, George Westinghouse made unprecedented advances in braking systems, and the Janney coupler replaced dangerous link and pin couplings with a movable knuckle. Even though the Master Car Builders Association vigorously pressed for the adoption of such devices, individual company response was sluggish because of high initial costs and the availability of the older devices. But to equip an engine, tender, and three passenger cars with the life-saving Westinghouse Air Brake actually cost less than $1,000, according to our state's railroad commissioners in 1877. In 1882 the legislature considered an act to forbid the dangerous link-and-pin car couplings, so often responsible for maiming trainmen or crushing them to death. The *Hartford Courant*, critical of the New York, New Haven & Hartford Railroad for not completing such a humanitarian program, said sarcastically, "We can imagine opposition to such a bill from just two sources—the railroad, which objects to the expense, and the undertakers, who would naturally look with quiet disapproval on what goes to curtail their legitimate industry."

Stations on Connecticut railways varied widely in their appearance and accommodations. Flag-stop shelters and small frame depots were the most common, though occasionally architectural splendor infiltrated some metropolitan stations. Architect Henry Austin designed New Haven's first Union Station as well as the ones at Collinsville and Plainville; Henry Hobson Richardson conceived the building at New London; Shepley, Rutan & Coolidge drafted plans for the stations at Hartford and Norwich; while McKim, Mead & White brought Italian flair to their monumental work at Waterbury. One of the nation's most historic stations—continuously operated since 1873—still stands in Canaan and is used by a tourist railroad.

Railway prosperity in Connecticut in the last century brought along with it a corresponding increase in train schedules and speeds. But the accident rate unfortunately soared, with wrecks often attributed to disregard for rules, poor construction, or lack of safety appliances. In 1850 the state legislature considered a railroad commission to investigate wrecks, but it was not until one of the country's first great rail tragedies occurred, at South Norwalk in 1853, that one was organized. At South Norwalk, a speeding passenger train of the New York & New Haven Railroad careened through an open drawbridge because the engineer failed to acknowledge a stop signal. Grisly details of the wreck were distributed to the legislature which then happened to be in session. The Connecticut Railroad Commission was promptly organized "to prevent injuries and destruction of life upon railroads, and by railroad trains." Its three members were to inspect the railways of the state, to regulate speeds of trains and standardize signals, and to implement directives for safer operations. In response to South Norwalk, they forbade any engineer to bring his train across a drawbridge without first coming to a full stop. Later the order was rescinded whenever protective signalling and derailing apparatus were installed in advance of the drawspan.

Logic and accumulated experience contributed much to the commission's success in the field of railway safety. The commissioners' first report of 1853 ordered "that a lantern shall be lighted and furnished with a reflector of not less than ten inches in diameter, and placed in front of the engine on all trains running in the night season." Three years later they learned a better way to test wooden bridges. One had collapsed under a Naugatuck Railroad train at Derby in 1857. Previously the commissioners had approved the bridge's condition, powerful blows with a heavy sledge hammer along its length sounding bright and sound. During the investigation, however, they decided to drill a hole into one of the suspect members. The timber, made of western oak, revealed the cause: a yellowish decay and disease common to this species.

The commissioners were to have "due regard to the character and income of each road" and to publish their findings annually. In no way whatsoever could they be connected with any railway of the state. Later the body became part of the state's Public Utilities Commission. As much as its commissioners tried to eliminate hazardous practices, they could never fully curb injuries and fatalities to railway trespassers—especially those of drunkards. Their journals were peppered with violations similar to a post-Civil War entry that noted: "September 5th—Edwin Pendigast, drunk, came to an untimely end by getting on the track of the Norwich & Worcester Railroad near Grosvenordale station. He was using the road for a bed and the rail for a pillow. *He sleeps his last sleep*."

Beyond safety, the commissioners addressed other railway matters such as excessive locomotive whistling, the merit of color blindness tests for certain employees, Sunday trains, and transmitting correct time. The running of trains on Sundays excited more than one pious pilgrim. A typical letter of complaint, published in the commissioners' annual report of 1881, came from the clerk of the First Congregational Church in East Hartford: "This church notices with regret and concern, the increasing desecration of the Lord's Day in our town by the New York & New England Railroad Company; not only in running trains, but in switching cars, and making up trains at all hours of the day thereby hindering and endangering the people on their way to and from church, and disturbing public worship, and destroying the peace and quiet of the New England Sabbath." Stopping an industry from working just one day was not the province of the railroad commissioners, who then referred the problem to the legislature. Nothing was done.

The commissioners did however strongly endorse a system of transmitting correct time to the state's railroads, so vital to train movements, schedules, and timetables. Then, as now, railroads required "correct" time even if trains were occasionally not "on time." Two years before standard time zones were established in America, the commissioners noted that, in 1881, no fewer than three time zones existed east of the Connecticut River to Boston, and two west thereof to the Hudson River. This calculated into an eight-minute difference between the eastern and western borders of the state. Confusion was held to a minimum thanks to a unique arrangement with Yale University. Professor Leonard Waldo, astronomer in charge of Winchester Observatory, arranged to have a correct signal, based on New York City time, transmitted daily through Western Union telegraphic instruments and over lines of the New York, New Haven & Hartford Railroad. Thus the remotest railroad station clock could be calibrated to the accuracy of the observatory's chronometers. Railroaders then had only to compare and correct their own pocket watches.

Certainly one also must note that many Connecticut railroad builders were often engaged for projects outside their home state. Much of Joseph Sheffield's fortune, acquired while building the Lake Shore & Michigan Southern and the Chicago, Rock Island & Pacific railroads, was given to establish a scientific school at Yale University. Collis P. Huntington of Harwinton, Connecticut, spearheaded the building of the Central Pacific. His famous art collection was bequeathed to the Metropolitan Museum of Art in New York. In addition he aided black education by endowing Hampton Institute in Virginia and Tuskegee Institute in Alabama. Henry B. Plant of Branford founded the Plant System of some fourteen railroads, as well as steamship lines, hotels, and the city of Tampa, Florida. Charles Morgan of Killingworth organized the Morgan Line of steamers and ran several Texas railways. From Brookfield came Philo Hurd, who rose through executive positions with the

Hudson River and Harlem railroads. Connecticut's Eleazar Lord gave up the ministry and became the first and only pious president of the great Erie Railroad; Gordon Lester Ford of Lebanon was a president of the Brooklyn, Flatbush & Coney Island Railroad. Southbury's Horace F. Clark was a director of the New York & Harlem, president of the Lake Shore & Michigan Southern, the Northern Indiana, and also of the Union Pacific railroads. Chauncey Rose of Wethersfield organized and built the Terre Haute & Richmond Railroad, while William P. Burrall of Canaan was once president of the Illinois Central. And from Bridgeport hailed the greatest of them all, Theodore P. Judah—"Crazy Judah"—to whom belongs the credit for helping locate the route of the first transcontinental railroad, which linked the oceans.

Railroads play an important part in Connecticut history; they were America's first big business. At least one local historian of the last century captured how great our debt to railways really was. That was Ellen Larned, who completed her impressive double volume history of Windham County, Connecticut, in 1880. Miss Larned observed that "modern Windham County dates its birth from the first whistle of the steam engine. That clarion cry awoke the sleeping valleys. Energy, enterprise, and progress followed its course. At every stopping place, new life sprung up." She was, of course, speaking for all of Connecticut. The text and pictures here recall some of that marvelous legacy.

Gregg M. Turner

Central Vermont Railway's Yale-Harvard Regatta "Boat Train" standing at Bartlett's Cove in Quaker Hill, waiting for shells to cross the finish line, 1913.   COLLECTION OF JAMES R. McFARLANE

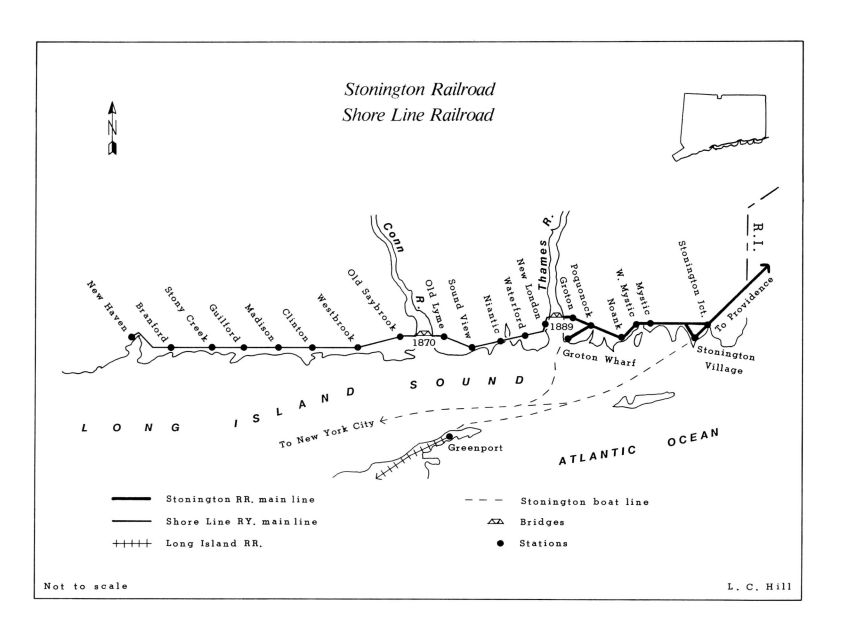

Stonington Railroad
Shore Line Railroad

New Haven · Branford · Stony Creek · Guilford · Madison · Clinton · Westbrook · Old Saybrook · Conn. R. · 1870 · Old Lyme · Sound View · Niantic · Waterford · New London · Thames R. · Groton · 1889 · Poquonock · Noank · W. Mystic · Mystic · Stonington Jct. · To Providence · R.I. · Stonington Village · Groton Wharf

LONG ISLAND SOUND

To New York City ← · Greenport · ATLANTIC OCEAN

―――― Stonington RR. main line
―――― Shore Line RY. main line
+++++ Long Island RR.

– – – Stonington boat line
△△ Bridges
● Stations

Not to scale

L. C. Hill

Steam engines changed the face of America, then disappeared. They were once symbols of speed, technology, and sometimes beauty, as this Civil War era engraving suggests.

Chapter One

Stonington and the
Shore Line Route

The successful completion of the Stonington Railroad is a matter of national concern. It is undoubtedly the ne plus ultra *of communication between Boston and New York City unless a swifter and safer flight can be projected above the surface of the Earth.*

—*New York Journal of Commerce, July 1833*

There is no better place to start an excursion through Connecticut railroad history than in seafaring Stonington Village. Not far from the borough proper is Evergreen Cemetery. You can meander through its old section and still see the stone shaft marking the burial plot of Major George Washington Whistler. This eminent engineer built Connecticut's first railroad. If alive today, he would no doubt be pleased to see seventy-mile-per-hour Amtrak trains roaring over his beloved route—now boasting concrete ties and welded steel rails. In the borough you can ponder a bronze tablet almost on the front lawn of the Congregational church; it marks the spot where Whistler first built his track to the dock from Providence. It might have been amusing to hear the clergy of the last century expound on the scene when belching iron horses were eventually allowed to go hard by the church on Sundays—especially at sermon time. That was all part of the Stonington railroad story.

George Washington Whistler
R & LHS

Nothing was more important to New England transportation history than the completion of a railroad route from Boston to New York City by way of the Connecticut shore line. The route, constantly interrupted in Connecticut by rivers, coves, and inlets, required the building of bridges both longer and stronger than any hitherto contemplated. Thus the line was not built all at once. Through the mid-nineteenth century it emerged slowly from the linkage of separate railroad companies. Two Connecticut firms that helped forge the route were the Stonington Railroad (Providence to Stonington, and later Groton) and the Shore Line Railway (New London to New Haven). By the end of the century the New York, New Haven & Hartford Railroad Company fully acquired the Shore Line Route of original companies, and over its tracks ran a roster of distinguished and still-remembered trains, including the *Gilt Edge*, the *Yankee Clipper*, and the *Merchants Limited*. It is interesting to note than many of these evocative names have been kept alive with almost religious fervor ever since, first by Penn Central, now by Amtrak. Despite vast outlays on track and equipment, however, they are slower. In 1985 the *Clipper*, for instance, was scheduled to take one minute longer from New York to Boston and the *Merchants* four minutes more than their steam-hauled predecessors required some forty years earlier.[1] All Shore Line Route trains today are as alike as peas in a pod and equally plebeian, and it adds a twist to the knife of nostalgia to recall that these were once crack trains. The *Merchants*—extra fare, of course—carried the swells to Boston in nine parlor cars, a club car, and a diner with gleaming silver on white table linen. Not a lowly coach in the consist.

The steamboat Rhode Island *chugged between Stonington and New York in the 1830s, connecting with our first railroad.*
SHSA

2

The early engine Roger Williams *had but one pair of driving wheels and, until it was rebuilt, no protective cab for its crew.*

R & LHS

The traveler with time to spare had only to frequent the Wadawanuck Hotel, owned by the Stonington line, for food or lodgings.

COLLECTION OF HENRY R. PALMER, JR.

The New York, Providence & Boston, known locally as the Stonington Railroad, was actually the first rail line to open on Connecticut soil, although on a very small piece of it. Its trains ran between Providence and the dock at Stonington Village where connecting steamboats took passengers overnight to New York City. The line's history began in May 1832, when Connecticut chartered the New York & Stonington Railroad "to locate, construct, and finally complete a railroad in Stonington to the eastern boundary of this State, on Pawcatuck River."[2] One month later Rhode Island created the New York, Providence & Boston Railroad to continue the line from the Connecticut border at Pawcatuck to Providence. The two companies merged in 1833 and retained the name of the Rhode Island enterprise. The Stonington Railroad connected at Providence with the Boston & Providence Railroad to reach Boston proper. The Boston & Providence also ran steamboats to New York City from Providence, but with the drawback that its vessels had to round stormy Point Judith, Rhode Island—the Cape Hatteras of New England. In substance, the Stonington Railroad extended the railway portion of such a journey and eliminated "the disagreeable matter of going around Point Judith, bringing the whole steamboat passage under cover of Long Island Sound."[3]

Officials broke ground for the Stonington line on August 14, 1832, at both

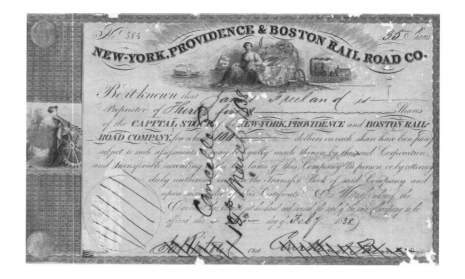

Stonington and Westerly, Rhode Island. An account related, with spare Yankee humor, that:

> Governor Francis of Rhode Island drove down from Providence in a coach drawn by four white horses driven by a negro coachman. He met Governor Edwards of Connecticut, and they broke ground at Stonington Point. They came to Westerly [Rhode Island], and again broke ground, Gov. Edwards at Stonington and Gov. Francis in Rhode Island close to the river in Westerly. He (Governor Francis) had a small wheelbarrow that would hold about a peck and a spade that seemed well fitted for the use of a small boy. The barrow was very highly painted and the spade beautifully polished. He loaded his barrow and wheeled it to the river's bank and there dumped it. Speeches followed this great feat of dirt moving. Governor Francis put up at Benj. Frink's tavern. The bar took $110 that day.[4]

The eminent West Point graduate Major George Washington Whistler had surveyed the proposed railroad route from Providence to Stonington Village. (Many years later his artist son, James McNeill Whistler, would paint the portrait so widely known as "Whistler's Mother.") Previously, the father was chief engineer of the Proprietors of the Locks and Canals on the Merrimack River in Lowell, Massachusetts. After the Stonington project Major Whistler surveyed and built the Western Railroad in the tough Berkshire Hills of Massachusetts. Thereafter he left for Russia to engineer the imposing Moscow & St. Petersburg State Railroad, for which accomplishment Czar Nicholas II bestowed upon him the Order of Saint Anne. Whistler died of heart complications in Russia but was later interred at Evergreen Cemetery in Stonington. He is recognized as a founding father of American civil engineering.

Stagecoach-type cars were used by the Stonington and other early U.S. railroads.

The telegraph, first used on American railroads in 1851, found little favor at first; the Stonington line even boasted of not using it.

A Shore Line Railway train crosses on the long covered bridge at Fair Haven, moving on to New London, a ferry across the Thames to Groton, and the Stonington road.

Whistler and his brother-in-law, Captain William Gibbs McNeill, another West Point graduate, undertook construction of the railroad from both ends, Providence and Stonington. To accommodate patrons at Stonington the railroad erected the plush Wadawanuck Hotel, which stood on the spot now occupied by the public library. The single main-line track ultimately stretched from Providence to Stonington via East Greenwich, Kingston, and Westerly. Some people along the route opposed the railroad's coming and forced Whistler to lay down his tracks away from centers of such towns as Kingston and Wickford.

Resistance was also encountered at the railroad's home base in Stonington. Dissidents forced the borough's warden and burgesses to have the railroad reveal its "exact location within the limits of the Borough"[5] Believing that it would disturb the tranquil setting of the town, they adopted a law "preventing the passing within the limits of this Borough of locomotive engines propelled by Steam, and to affix

TIME TABLE, NO. 71.

STONINGTON AND PROVIDENCE RAILROAD.

Monday, January 22, 1866.

No Train will be allowed to leave a station before the time specified in this Table, as regulated by clock at Providence Station.

| From Groton and Stonington to Providence. (Upward.) | | | | | | | | | MILES | STATIONS | From Providence to Stonington and Groton. (Downward.) | | | | | | | | |
Sunday Mail	Mail Train	Boston Freight	Local Freight	1st Accommodation Passenger Train	Passenger Train	Express Passenger					Passenger Train	Express Passenger	Local Freight	Providence Freight	1st Accommodation Passenger Train	Express Freight	Steamboat Train	Mail Train	Sunday Mail
P.M.	A.M.	A.M.	A.M.	A.M.	P.M.	P.M.					A.M.	P.M.	P.M.	P.M.	P.M.	P.M.	P.M.	A.M.	P.M.
10.00	1.40	.....	.....	7.00	2.00	5.15				Dep. New London, Ar.	9.55	2.45	.....	.....	.....	6.53	.....	12.20	10.20
10.20	1.55	5.00	.....	7.12	2.15	5.30				" Groton, "	9.45	2.30	.....	5.48	.....	6.43	.....	12.05	10.05
10.25	2.02	5.09	.....	7.20	2.23	5.36			3	" Poquonnock S., "	9.36	2.23	.....	5.36	.....	6.33	.....	11.58	9.58
10.34	2.12	5.20	.....	7.32	2.35	5.44			7½	" West Mystic, "	9.27	2.16	.....	5.14	.....	6.18	.....	11.48	9.48
10.36	2.14	5.28	.....	7.34	2.38	5.49			8½	" Mystic, "	9.24	2.14	.....	5.07	.....	6.15	.....	11.46	9.46
10.43	2.22	5.40	.....	7.43	2.48	6.00			12	"Stonington Stat'n,"	9.15	2.05	.....	4.49	.....	6.03	.....	11.39	9.39
10.44	2.23	4.31	5.42	6.07 7.44	7.49 2.49	6.01			12½	"Stonington Junc.,"	9.13	2.04	4.26	4.44	5.20 5.51	6.01 6.59	8.57	11.38	9.38
.....	.....	4.30	5.45 6.05	7.45 7.48						" Ston. Stb't L'd'g,"				5.22	5.57	7.00	8.58		
10.54	2.35	4.44	6.32	8.03	3.03	6.09			17½	" Westerly, "	9.02	1.54	4.06	5.09	5.40	6.45	8.48	11.28	9.28
11.03	2.45	4.56	6.56	8.15	3.15	6.16			22½	" Charleston, "	8.50	1.45	3.43	4.58	5.29	6.32	8.37	11.19	9.19
11.11	2.54	5.06	7.14	8.26	3.26	6.22			26½	"Richmond Switch,"	8.41	1.39	3.26	4.48	5.20	6.22	8.29	11.11	9.11
11.16	3.00	5.14	7.27	8.35	3.32	6.26			28½	" Carolina, "	8.35	1.35	3.10	4.43	5.14	6.05	8.25	11.06	9.06
11.28	3.14	5.38	8.18	8.53	3.52	6.39			35	" Kingston, "	8.18	1.24	2.42	4.30	4.58	5.47	8.13	10.54	8.54
11.41	3.29	5.58	8.39	9.11	4.10	6.50			42	" Wickford, "	8.00	1.07	2.12	4.10	4.39	5.20	7.54	10.40	8.40
11.53 A.M.	3.43	6.14	8.58	9.27	4.25	7.02			48	" Greenwich, "	7.45	12.57	1.50	3.48	4.25	5.00	7.41	10.28	8.28
12.02	3.54	6.27	9.18	9.40	4.42	7.12			53	" Warwick Switch, "	7.30	12.49	1.23	3.35	4.10	4.42	7.33	10.18	8.18
12.10	4.03	6.37	9.30	9.49	4.52	7.25			57	" Junction, "	7.21	12.43	1.12	3.26	4.01	4.22	7.25	10.10	8.10
12.20	4.15	6.50	9.45	10.00	5.05	7.33			62	Ar. Providence, Dep.	7.10	12.35	1.00	3.15	3.50	4.10	7.12	10.00	8.00

Trains meet at Stations indicated by heavy figures.

In his private railway car, Cornelius S. Bushnell, New Haven banker and kingpin of the Shore Line Railway, sits at the head of the table for a dinner. Polished brass lamps, mirrors, and ornate roof braces grace the scene. He was also a director of the great Union Pacific, a friend of its chief, Thomas Durant, and had attracted Oakes and Oliver Ames into its controversial affairs. The Bushnell car showed up for the Golden Spike ceremony at Promontory in 1869.

penalties."[6] Orders to this effect were served on Whistler, who then merely elected to use horses to draw trains through town. Eight days after the railroad's grand opening even the speed of the horses was limited by the borough to five miles per hour. For exceeding such a breakneck pace the railroad would be subject to a $2 fine. The engine house and turntable, originally planned to be located near the steamboat dock, were built on the borough's outskirts near Orchard Street. Years later the laws were rescinded, and steam locomotives chugged to the dock past the Congregational church.

Construction costs, including land payments, several engines, depots, and rolling stock, came to the tremendous sum of $2,600,000. It was raised through the sale of thirteen thousand shares of stock at $100 a share, and by a bond issue of the same amount. Two years after the line opened, however, trustees of the bond mortgage took possession of the Stonington Railroad as a result of financial reversals brought about by the panic of 1837. New York City investors owned the majority of the stocks and bonds, and they themselves largely suffered the embarrassments.

The Lowell, Massachusetts, firm—previously employing Major Whistler—built the first locomotives for the Stonington Railroad. They had a 4-2-0 wheel arrangement—that is, four wheels under the pilot, one pair of large drivers, and nothing under the driver's platform. They cost $7,000 each and burned wood. There were no covering cabs for the engineers because "if stage coach drivers could stand the weather then so could engine drivers."[7] Fast-burning yellow pine was used for fuel; it was brought from the South to Stonington in schooners. The first coal-burning locomotive, *Matthew Morgan*, did not arrive until 1859. Engine-operating costs amounted to 15¢ per mile with wood and were later reduced to 11¢ with coal. Boiler pressure was measured by spring balances and varied from eighty-five to one hundred pounds per square inch. The first passenger cars were merely stagecoach

A wood-burning locomotive of the New Haven, New London & Stonington, an ancestor of the Shore Line Railway. It was named for the town of Madison as the boiler nameplate attests. A portrait adorns the side of the headlight, a practice of that era.

bodies suspended with leather straps and springs over four-wheel trucks. In summer the adventurous often rode topside, though they had to dodge volumes of smoke and flying sparks. Longer cars later provided for more seating, safety, and comfort. Coaches were painted olive green, while yellow distinguished cars of the steamboat express trains. The cars were originally connected by iron chains, resulting in much bumping when slowing down and stopping.

The grand opening of the line occurred on November 10, 1837. Early that morning the steamer *Narragansett* arrived at Stonington from New York City with the New York directors and President Courtland Palmer. There were also about one hundred people, "several of whom were gentlemen." A cannon salute was fired, after which a marching band led the procession to the Wadawanuck Hotel for a breakfast "prepared in a style which satisfactorily showed that the host well understood how to cater for the appetites of his guests."[8] After breakfast the party returned to the dock, where two highly decorated trains awaited them. The trains moved under horsepower as far as Orchard Street, where the horses were replaced with the steam engines *Little Rest* and *Stonington*. The first railway trains in Connecticut history were under way! The Providence-bound trains returned to Stonington around six o'clock, and the delegation converged again on the Wadawanuck Hotel for supper. More than thirty toasts were proposed, including salutes to Whistler, his associates, the railroad officers, and, of course, to the fair ladies of Stonington: "May the

An open drawbridge beckons Connecticut River traffic at the first bridge between Old Lyme and Old Saybrook, erected in 1870. A newer span has since replaced it.

railroad, the completion of which we are this day caused to celebrate, more extensively introduce their charms and virtues to their fellow citizens from Maine to Georgia."[9]

Cornelius Vanderbilt

Service began the following day with one train in each direction. The steamboat *Narragansett* by contract left every other night from Stonington for New York City, taking a full night, while the 47$^{1}/_{2}$-mile rail trip from Stonington to Providence required only two hours and twenty-five minutes. Later joining *Narragansett* to provide daily departures were *Rhode Island* and *Massachusetts*. Their specifications were similar and all burned wood. *Narragansett*, 576 tons, was 212 feet long and was equipped with a three-hundred-horsepower steam engine. The more luxurious *Massachusetts* had copper boilers and cost $100,000. In 1839 Commodore Cornelius Vanderbilt and Daniel Drew, buccaneers of the steamboat age, assumed ownership of the boat line. Each even briefly served as both a director and president of the Stonington Railroad in the late 1840s.

In 1838 President Palmer prophetically remarked that the railroad probably could not meet critical loan payments due before the company's next annual meeting. He was proven correct. The following year the road's assets were attached by the superior court in New London, and the property was transferred to the mortgage trustees. William Lewis, cashier of the Girard Bank in Philadelphia, assumed control. The trustees instituted a new debt structure and returned the road to stockholders in 1843. A new bond was floated, reducing the standing debt of $1,900,000 by almost two-thirds. Lewis and his colleagues saved the road, but the real financial loss was suffered by the old bondholders, "who made a heavy sacrifice by giving up 50% of their principal and accumulated interest."[10] Solvency was restored, and the road began to prosper.

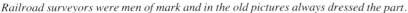

Railroad surveyors were men of mark and in the old pictures always dressed the part.

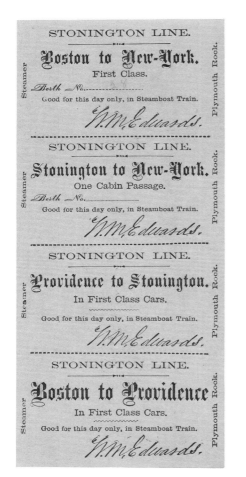

[RIGHT] *An exchange of stock erased the last vestiges of the Shore Line Railway. The road was already leased to the larger line.*

New steamboats arrived in the 1840s, including *C. Vanderbilt*, *Commodore*, *Oregon*, and *Knickerbocker*. Gross revenues of the Stonington Railroad had now passed the $200,000 mark. The annual report of 1848 noted a rolling stock inventory of six locomotives, sixteen passenger cars, nineteen box cars, and twenty-two flat cars. In the next ten years schedules were increased, additional depots were erected, and other locomotives were purchased. The Wadawanuck Hotel in Stonington was sold—though still used—and profits realized from the sale were applied to current debt. Further stock capitalization was authorized, and in 1857 sixteen thousand new ties were installed as well as three hundred tons of iron rails. A total of twenty-two miles of track had now been re-laid or repaired. [11]

For many years no railroad existed west of Stonington to New Haven, but during the 1850s promoters sought to complete such a link. In 1848 the New Haven & New London Railroad was chartered to build a fifty-mile line via the towns of Fair Haven, Branford, Madison, Clinton, Old Saybrook, Lyme, Niantic, and Waterford. To locate the route the new company retained Professor Alexander Twining of Yale; his previous experience embraced the teaching of mathematics and philosophy. Like Major Whistler and Captain McNeill, he had studied topographical engineering at West Point, the institution *par excellence* at which to learn it. [12] It opened two years later, though its traffic proved small and the line became encumbered with debt. A huge timber trestle carried the track from New Haven over the Quinni-

9

Steamer Stonington *in an early lithograph.*

piac River to Fair Haven,* whence the line closely hugged the shore to New London. A ferryboat shuttled cars and engines across the Connecticut River from Old Saybrook to Old Lyme, where trains were reassembled for the final segment of the route to New London. The road was cheaply built, and many wooden trestles were required to traverse the numerous inlets and miles of marsh lands.

The missing link from New London to Stonington came next. In 1853 the New London & Stonington Railroad was chartered, only to fail within four years from lack of financial patronage. Directors of the New Haven & New London road were crestfallen; they needed the little thirteen-mile road to connect with the Stonington Railroad. The New Haven & New London pleaded its case before the General Assembly in Hartford, absorbed the defunct line in 1856, and reorganized everything as the New Haven, New London & Stonington Railroad. The Groton to Stonington link opened in 1858 with a ferryboat working the Thames River crossing. Although three mortgages financed the new company, the road was not able to

*This structure and fourteen grade crossings through the heart of Fair Haven were eliminated in 1894 when the New Haven Railroad opened a cutoff via the present-day East Haven tunnels.

Distance from New Haven	STATIONS
0.00	New Haven..........N
9.13	Branford.............
11.40	Pine Orchard..........
12.48	Stony Creek..........
13.98	Leete's Island.........
16.81	Guilford.............D
18.90	East River............
20.91	Madison.............
24.59	Clinton..............D
29.09	Westbrook...........
32.97	Old Saybrook........N
34.70	Conn. River S. S. 104.N
38.45	Sound View..........
43.83	East Lyme...........
44.63	Niantic River S. S. 108.N
47.57	Waterford S. S. 110...D
50.78	New London..........

Engine Westerly *was built for the Stonington Railroad by the Taunton Locomotive Works of Massachusetts in 1850.*

10

The frequency and quality of steamboat service on Long Island Sound last century amazes the modern generation. The Stonington Line was extremely popular.

A mixed train of freight and passenger cars passes Fort Rachel in Mystic, en route Stonington to Groton. Stereo slide, 1867.

COLLECTION OF AMOS HEWITT, SR.

meet interest payments, and bond trustees had to foreclose. In 1864 they sold the eastern portion of their line between Groton and Stonington to the Stonington Railroad for $410,000—the latter calling the addition its "Groton Extension." The western section between New Haven and New London was reorganized as the Shore Line Railway. A new debt structure solved the line's financial problems, and the Shore Line Railway began to prosper. In 1870 it financed and built a huge drawbridge over the Connecticut River, but only after overcoming a great deal of maritime and political opposition. In that same year the directors also leased their entire property to the wealthy New York & New Haven Railroad at an attractive rental, giving the latter a strategic thrust towards Boston.

As an interesting aside, before the drawbridges were built at the Connecticut and Thames rivers, visiting author Charles Dickens travelled over this very route in the 1860s, and reported that "two rivers had to be crossed and each time the whole train is banged aboard a steamer. The steamer rises and falls with the river which the railroad don't do, and the train is banged uphill or banged downhill. In coming off the steamer at one of these crossings yesterday, we were banged up to such a height that the rope broke and the carriage rushed back with a run downhill into the boat

Factory-fresh from the big Manchester Locomotive Works and bearing a name to stir the blood, the Stonington engine Earthquake *of 1873 had wheels 66 inches in diameter.*

Departing New York City, the wooden sidewheeler Connecticut *heads for Stonington.*

A six-axle heavy Stonington coach of later days contrasts strongly with the glorified stagecoach shown at the start of this chapter.

A page from the New Haven timetables of 1893. Note the routing of these through trains, requiring a steam ferry transfer from Newark to the Harlem River Station of the New Haven road. No tunnels existed then under the Hudson and the East rivers.

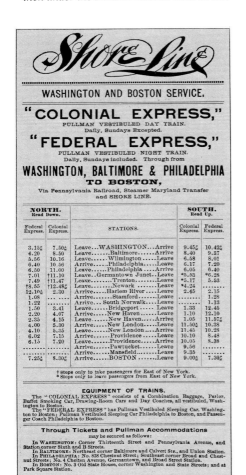

again. I whisked out in a moment, and two or three others after me, but nobody else seemed to care about it."[13]

Citizens of Stonington Village did not relish the "Groton Extension" purchase, since it meant the busy Stonington steamboat terminal would be moved to Groton, and that its convenient New York City connection would be lost. But on a bitter night in December 1865 the steamer *Commonwealth* burned at its pier in Groton,* destroying the Stonington Railroad's new dock, depot, surrounding buildings, twenty freight cars, and all the company's fixtures. The terminal was immediately relocated back to Stonington, much to the delight of its citizens. Acres of land were filled in, extensive docks were built, a twelve-hundred-foot sea wall was constructed, a new depot appeared, and new company offices were erected, along with a new brick engine house and turntable. The switching yard soon became one of the busiest in New England.

After losing *Commonwealth* and experiencing a suspension of steamboat service, the railroad petitioned the Connecticut General Assembly for the right to organize its own Stonington Steamboat Company[14] rather than contract the boat services. Approval was obtained, nearly $255,000 was invested in the firm, and an order was placed for two new steamers, *Narragansett* and *Stonington*. In 1875 the Stonington firm and the Providence & New York Steamship Company merged to form the Providence and Stonington Steamship Corporation. The Stonington Line enjoyed its greatest prosperity after this amalgamation, and for decades patrons loved to travel "Old Reliable."**

Track and equipment never ceased to be upgraded on both the Stonington Railroad and the Shore Line Railway. The "Groton Extension" was entirely rebuilt, and much of the early wood piling at coves and inlets of the Shore Line Railway was replaced with fill. A second track was installed on both roads. In 1873 a grand new steamer, *Rhode Island*, joined the Stonington fleet, followed by a new, electrically lighted *Massachusetts*. After the Providence & Stonington Steamship Company formation in 1875, the handsome wooden side-wheeler *Connecticut* appeared, though engine failures plagued her operation. Three years later the firm broke its tradition and ordered the steel steamers *New Hampshire* and *Maine*. Each boasted a triple expansion engine driving a single propellor. They cost $449,000 each. Twenty-four tons of coal were consumed on the average trip from Stonington to New York City, far fewer than previous vessels required. A $68,000 ferry boat measuring 264 feet was put into service for the Thames River crossing in 1877; it could shuttle eight railway passenger cars.

*The vessel was rebuilt but was later wrecked for good off Orient Point, Long Island.

**Blemishing their safety record, *Narragansett* and *Stonington* collided on a calm but foggy night off Cornfield Point, Saybrook, in 1880. Thirty lives were lost.

13

Unquestionably the major railroad engineering project in Connecticut during the nineteenth century was the construction of the Thames River Drawbridge at New London. As early as 1881 the Stonington Railroad made preliminary surveys for such a span. The bridge's final location had to be approved by the Connecticut railroad commissioners, the secretary of war, and the secretary of the navy. The navy, with its shipyard upriver, was deeply opposed to the project, as the bridge could easily block the strategic waterway. However, after serious negotiations the directors of the Stonington Railroad finally reported that the "incipient U.S. Navy Yard situated some miles above . . . will consider a drawbridge with an opening of 200 feet or more, sufficient to allow the passage of the largest vessel ever likely to use it."[15] The structure was built by the Union Bridge Company of Buffalo, New York, and was opened on October 10, 1889. The draw had a clearance of 225 feet on each side, with approach spans of 310 feet. Stone and masonry supplies came from Connecticut's own Leetes Island quarries. As the largest double track steel drawbridge in the world, it measured 1,423 feet in length and had cost $1,600,000. To reach the new structure the Stonington Railroad laid new tracks from Poquonnock Switch (later called Midway) in Groton to the eastern approach span via Long Hill. The Shore Line Railway extended its track from "The Parade" at New London to meet the western approach via Winthrop Cove.

To inaugurate the new structure, the Stonington Railroad sent invitations "to 500 to 600 gentlemen representing the four states of Connecticut, Massachusetts, Rhode Island, and New York."[16] Special trains from New York City and Boston were sold out. One newspaper reported:

> These trains were made up of new and elegant Wagner Palace Cars and were future consists of the first famous shoreline train, the *Gilt Edge Limited*. The Boston train ran to within 30 or 40 feet of the draw where it stopped and passengers alighted. The draw was then opened and a good idea was obtained of its immense proportions. The Woonsocket, Rhode Island, Cornet Band was upon the center of the draw, while on the further span stood the New York City counterpart of the *Gilt Edge Limited*. The big transfer ferry *Shore Line* was loaded with people and passed by through the draw while the band played Auld Lang Syne. Amid the blowing of whistles on tugs, steamers, and locomotives the magnificent steel draw slowly swung into position and a new steel highway between the Hub of the Universe and the Metropolis was opened to public travel.[17]

The ferries Thames River *and* Groton *shuttled railway cars before the drawbridge at New London took their place in 1889.*

Thames River Drawbridge, opened in 1889.

Col. J. Albert Monroe built the new bridge.

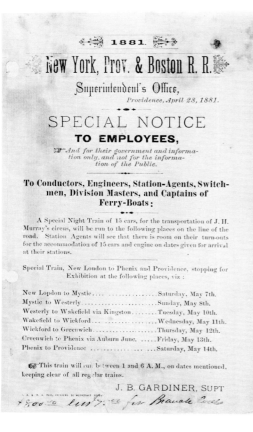

The New York, New Haven & Hartford Railroad Company was formed in 1872 when the Hartford & New Haven and the New York & New Haven railroads merged. The New York & New Haven automatically carried with it the lease of the Shore Line Railway. The new larger company slyly waited for the Stonington Railroad to finish the costly bridge, whereupon it took control of the Stonington road and its steamboat line in 1892. J. Pierpont Morgan had previously made his way into the Stonington boardroom, which eased the delicate negotiations. Morgan's growing empire very much wanted a route of its own to Boston. Shortly thereafter the stocks of the Stonington and Shore Line roads were retired, and their lives as separate enterprises came to an end, consolidated into the growing New York, New Haven, & Hartford system.

Interestingly enough, the name "Shore Line" resurfaced in a dramatic new way in Connecticut around 1910, when the Shore Line Electric Railway was built through woods and marshes of the shore towns between Saybrook and New Haven. It was a special high-speed trolley line. With the acquisition by stock control of such additional lines as the Norwich & Westerly, it was more of a true interurban in the Midwestern American style than the city and rural trolley systems with which it connected. It attained a maximum of 250 miles of routes, connecting with other electric trolley lines to Boston—one set via Providence, the other via Worcester. You *could* travel the whole distance from New York City right up to the State House on Beacon Street, a journey once performed by a party of executives in the parlor trolley *Huguenot*, of the Worcester Street Railways, in an exhausting twenty hours. An ordinary citizen might match the trip only by endless stopping, waiting, and changing—like a butterfly in a field of flowers—for an outlay (someone once figured) of $2.40 in fares. This apparently majestic system enjoyed only a short, butterfly-like life. Bedevilled by a ghastly front-end accident of two cars in North Branford (taking nineteen lives and injuring thirty-five) in 1917, a long power-house failure, a second bad crash, and a strike, the Shore Line Electric Railway closed down, bankrupt, in 1919. It was partially revived in 1923 but closed for good in 1929. Every route of its big green cars was paralleled by New York, New Haven & Hartford Railroad trains, or by highways, or by both. The interurban was a splendid invention which suffered from having been conceived at the very same time as the automobile, and in the vigorous manhood of the steam cars.

Two views of the railway yards, docks, and steamers in the busy heyday of Stonington.

COLLECTION OF HENRY R. PALMER, JR.

Chapter One Footnotes

1. *The Official Guide of the Railways of the United States, August 1946* (New York: National Railway Publication Company, 1946), 104-125.

2. Connecticut General Assembly, An Act to Incorporate the New York & Stonington Railroad, May session, 1832, Public Records, Connecticut State Capitol Building.

3. *New York Journal of Commerce*, 6 April 1833.

4. "Breaking Ground for the Stonington Railroad," *Narragansett Historical Register* III (1884-85): 6.

5. Quoted in Gregg M. Turner, "A Nutmeg First," *The New England States Limited* (Fall, 1978): 8.

6. Ibid.

7. *Providence Daily Journal*, 11 November 1837.

8. Ibid.

9. Ibid.

10. *Annual Report of the New York, Providence & Boston Railroad*, 1844 (Westerly, RI: G.B. & J.H. Utter, 1874), 4.

11. Ibid.

12. *Dictionary of American Biography*, s.v. "Twining, Alexander Catlin."

13. Sidney Withington, *The First Twenty Years of Railroads in Connecticut* (New Haven: Yale University Press, 1935), 29.

14. *Annual Reports of the New York, Providence & Boston Railroad*, 1865-1875, passim.

15. *Annual Report of the New York, Providence & Boston Railroad, 1887* (Westerly, RI: J.B. & J.H. Utter, 1887), 5.

16. *Boston Herald*, 11 October 1889.

17. Ibid.

A wooden interurban of the Shore Line Electric Railway in Madison in 1911.   COLLECTION OF CHARLES F. MUNGER, JR.

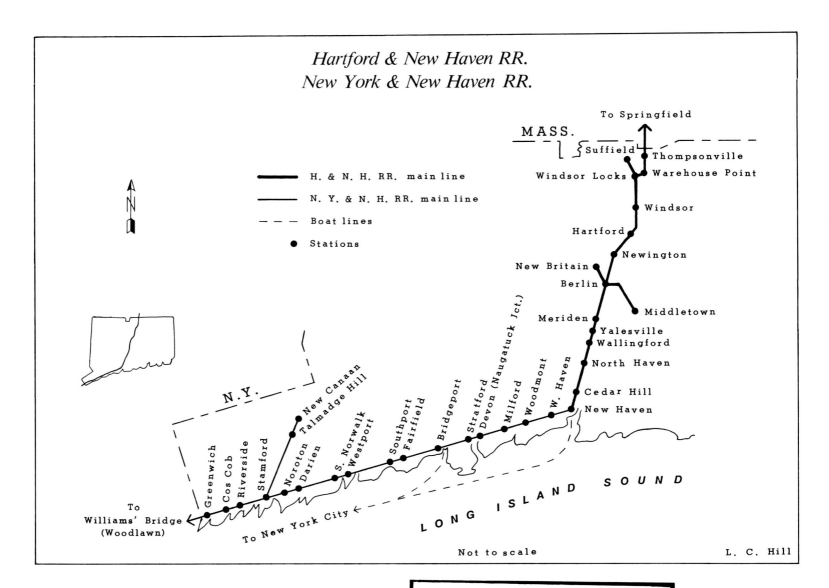

Hartford & New Haven RR.
New York & New Haven RR.

H. & N. H. RR. main line
N. Y. & N. H. RR. main line
Boat lines
● Stations

To Springfield
MASS.
Suffield
Thompsonville
Windsor Locks
Warehouse Point
Windsor
Hartford
Newington
New Britain
Berlin
Middletown
Meriden
Yalesville
Wallingford
North Haven
Cedar Hill
New Haven
Stratford
Devon (Naugatuck Jct.)
Milford
Woodmont
W. Haven
New Canaan
Talmadge Hill
S. Norwalk
Westport
Southport
Fairfield
Bridgeport
Greenwich
Cos Cob
Riverside
Stamford
Noroton
Darien

N.Y.

LONG ISLAND SOUND

To
Williams' Bridge
(Woodlawn)

To New York City

Not to scale

L. C. Hill

•FIG. 15.—ROGERS' PASSENGER ENGINE, 1845—HARTFORD AND NEW HAVEN RAILROAD

Early Hartford & New Haven engines lacked any shelter for the drivers, and even a headlight. There was no night running, for that excellent reason.

HARTFORD And NEW HAVEN

RAIL ROAD.

ON and after MONDAY next, the 6th inst., a train of Cars will leave HARTFORD for NEW HAVEN at 10¾ A. M., and arrive in time for passengers to take the Day Boat FOR NEW YORK, at 1 P. M.

HARTFORD June 4th, 1842.

17

Chapter Two

Uniting Four Cities

The cars of the Hartford & New Haven Railroad are some of the best in the country, and before long we shall be able to leave New Haven after breakfast, reach Hartford and spend some time there, and return in season for an early dinner.

—*comment in the New Haven Palladium, 1838*

The New York & New Haven Railroad was poorly built. The contractors did their own engineering . . . and often to their interests. It has been stated that the curve in the road at South Norwalk was a change from the original location to save expense . . . and undoubtedly the cause of the fearful drawbridge disaster.

—*American Railroad Journal, May 19, 1855*

Of all the dates and events comprising Connecticut railroad history in the nineteenth century, few moments shine so significantly as August 6, 1872—the historic hour when the New York, New Haven & Hartford Railroad Company was created. It was this firm that would ultimately shape the railway affairs of Connecticut for nearly a century, yet it commenced operations without having driven one spike, laid one tie, or built even a single inch of track. Indeed, it was born from the merging of two established lines, the Hartford & New Haven and the New York & New Haven railroads. Both roads made contributions to the state's railway heritage, and together they united the four cities of New York, New Haven, Hartford, and Springfield.

The Hartford & New Haven

From colonial days until 1875 Connecticut had two alternating capital cities, Hartford and New Haven, the government moving back and forth every two years. Between these points the traveller and the shipper relied upon stage lines, wagons, private carriages, or the circuitous Connecticut River boat line. A plan to build a railway between the twin capitals was spoken of in the earliest years of Connecticut railroading; it was deeply opposed by the owners of the Hartford and New Haven Turnpike. By 1832 the state legislature finally granted a charter to the Hartford & New Haven Railroad and empowered it to build a line "by the most direct and feasible route."[1] Two years would pass, however, before the road was officially organized.

James Brewster

Unlike the many railroad companies that launched construction plans right away, the directors of the Hartford & New Haven found wisdom in first organizing "a railroad committee" to investigate all matters pertaining to the best means of financing, construction, and operation. James Brewster, the wealthy carriage manufacturer of New Haven and one of the railroad's guiding prophets,[2] led educational visits to New York, Philadelphia, Baltimore, and Washington. His delegation called on "the enterprising proprietor of the Camden & Amboy," visited the president of the Baltimore & Ohio Railroad, peered into Matthias Baldwin's locomotive shops in Philadelphia, and established a number of other useful contacts. Brewster submitted a report of the committee's findings to the directors in July 1836.

It is a myth that government regulation did not exist in the old days, at any event on the railways, as this document attests. Fares for passengers were high, by standards of 1841, but the freight rates were so low as to be preposterous. Just look at feathers!

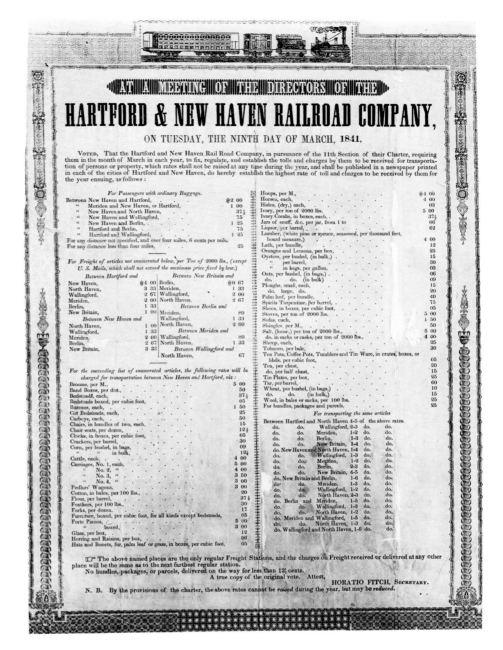

AT A MEETING OF THE DIRECTORS OF THE
HARTFORD & NEW HAVEN RAILROAD COMPANY,
ON TUESDAY, THE NINTH DAY OF MARCH, 1841,

VOTED, That the Hartford and New Haven Rail Road Company, in pursuance of the 11th Section of their Charter, requiring them in the month of March in each year, to fix, regulate, and establish the tolls and charges by them to be received for transportation of persons or property, which rates shall not be raised at any time during the year, and shall be published in a newspaper printed in each of the cities of Hartford and New Haven, do hereby establish the highest rate of toll and charges to be received by them for the year ensuing, as follows :

For Passengers with ordinary Baggage.

Between New Haven and Hartford,	$2 00
" Meriden and New Haven, or Hartford,	1 00
" New Haven and North Haven,	37½
" New Haven and Wallingford,	75
" New Haven and Berlin,	1 25
" Hartford and Berlin,	75
" Hartford and Wallingford,	1 25
For any distance not specified, and over four miles, 6 cents per mile.	
For any distance less than four miles,	25

For Freight of articles not enumerated below, per Ton of 2000 lbs., (except U. S. Mails, which shall not exceed the maximum price fixed by law.)

Between Hartford and		Between New Britain and	
New Haven,	$4 00	Berlin,	$0 67
North Haven,	3 33	Meriden,	1 33
Wallingford,	2 67	Wallingford,	2 00
Meriden,	2 00	North Haven,	2 67
Berlin,	1 33	Between Berlin and	
New Britain,	1 00	Meriden,	80
Between New Haven and		Wallingford,	1 33
North Haven,	1 00	North Haven,	2 00
Wallingford,	1 33	Between Meriden and	
Meriden,	2 00	Wallingford,	80
Berlin,	2 67	North Haven,	1 33
New Britain,	3 33	Between Wallingford and	
		North Haven,	67

For the succeeding list of enumerated articles, the following rates will be charged for transportation between New Haven and Hartford, viz :

Brooms, per M.,	5 00
Band Boxes, per doz.,	50
Bedsteads, each,	37½
Bedsteads boxed, per cubic foot,	05
Bureaus, each,	1 50
Cot Bedsteads, each,	25
Carboys, each,	50
Chairs, in bundles of two, each,	15
Chair seats, per dozen,	12½
Clocks, in boxes, per cubic foot,	05
Crackers, per barrel,	30
Corn, per bushel, in bags,	09
" in bulk,	12½
Cattle, each,	4 00
Carriages, No. 1, each,	5 00
No. 2, "	4 00
No. 3, "	3 50
No. 4, "	3 00
Pedlars' Wagons,	3 00
Cotton, in bales, per 100 lbs.,	20
Flour, per barrel,	37½
Feathers, per 100 lbs.,	30
Forks, per dozen,	17
Furniture, boxed, per cubic foot, for all kinds except bedsteads,	05
Forte Pianos,	5 00
" boxed,	3 00
Glass, per box,	12
Herring and Raisins, per box,	06
Hats and Bonnets, fur, palm leaf or grass, in boxes, per cubic foot,	05

Hoops, per M.,	$4 00
Horses, each,	4 00
Hides, (dry,) each,	03
Ivory, per ton of 2000 lbs.	5 00
Ivory Combs, in boxes, each,	37½
Jars of snuff, &c. per jar, from 1 to	06
Liquor, per barrel,	62
Lumber, (white pine or spruce, seasoned, per thousand feet, board measure,)	4 00
Lath, per bundle,	12
Oranges and Lemons, per box,	25
Oysters, per bushel, (in bulk,)	15
" per barrel,	30
" in kegs, per gallon,	03
Oats, per bushel, (in bags,)	06
do. do. (in bulk)	09
Ploughs, small, each,	15
do. large, do.	20
Palm leaf, per bundle,	40
Spirits Turpentine, per barrel,	75
Shoes, in boxes, per cubic foot,	05
Stoves, per ton of 2000 lbs.	5 00
Sofas, each,	1 50
Shingles, per M.,	50
Salt, (loose,) per ton of 2000 lbs.,	5 00
do. in sacks or casks, per ton of 2000 lbs.,	4 00
Sheep, each,	25
Tobacco, per bale,	30
Tea Pots, Coffee Pots, Tumblers and Tin Ware, in crates, boxes, or hhds. per cubic foot,	05
Tea, per chest,	20
do. per half chest,	15
Tin Plates, per box,	25
Tar, per barrel,	60
Wheat, per bushel, (in bags,)	10
do. do. (in bulk),	15
Wool, in bales or sacks, per 100 lbs.	25
For bundles, packages and parcels,	25

For transporting the same articles

Between Hartford and North Haven, 4-5 of the above rates.				
do.	do.	Wallingford, 2-3	do.	do.
do.	do.	Meriden, 1-2	do.	do.
do.	do.	Berlin, 1-3	do.	do.
do.	do.	New Britain, 1-4	do.	do.
do. New Haven and North Haven, 1-4			do.	do.
do.	do.	Wallingford, 1-3	do.	do.
do.	do.	Meriden, 1-2	do.	do.
do.	do.	Berlin, 2-3	do.	do.
do.	do.	New Britain, 4-5	do.	do.
do. New Britain and Berlin, 1-6			do.	do.
do.	do.	Meriden, 1-3	do.	do.
do.	do.	Wallingford, 1-2	do.	do.
do.	do.	North Haven, 2-3	do.	do.
do. Berlin and Meriden, 1-5			do.	do.
do.	do.	Wallingford, 1-3	do.	do.
do.	do.	North Haven, 1-2	do.	do.
do. Meriden and Wallingford, 1-5			do.	do.
do.	do.	North Haven, 1-3	do.	do.
do. Wallingford and North Haven, 1-6			do.	do.

☞ The above named places are the only regular Freight Stations, and the charges on Freight received or delivered at any other place will be the same as to the next farthest regular station.

No bundles, packages, or parcels, delivered on the way for less than 12½ cents.

A true copy of the original vote. Attest,   HORATIO FITCH, SECRETARY.

N. B. By the provisions of the charter, the above rates cannot be *raised* during the year, but may be *reduced*.

Members of a train crew pose stiffly with station employees at the Berlin depot, 1870.

From these missions a plan of action was prepared for the Hartford & New Haven:
(1) contract at once to purchase timber for ties and stringers; (2) purchase three
locomotives of proven design and known performance; (3) make arrangements to
build its own cars; (4) acquire several acres of land near each terminus for station
facilities and the storage of cars; (5) employ an agent "to go to England to superin-
tend the manufacture of iron"; and (6) secure a competent person to ascertain if the
new road might one day build its own locomotives.[3]

*The first station in Hartford, since replaced
on the same site, was an imposing place.
Some trains stopped outside, others went
through. Nearby Asylum Street was crossed
at grade instead of by today's bridge.*

In the autumn of 1835 the railroad's directors hired Professor Alexander Twining of
Yale to locate a route and prepare an estimate of its cost. Twining, whom railroads
would call upon time after time, organized the project, dispatched survey crews,
and ultimately located three possible routes between Hartford and New Haven. The
easternmost route intersected Middletown, the intermediate passed through Meriden, while the westernmost tapped New Britain and Plainville. Towns along all
three routes competed for the railroad's attention. Town meetings were staged and
Twining "patiently and publicly heard"[4] from all the interested parties. One town
alone disliked the whole idea: Newington on the intermediate route politely
informed the railroad directors that its citizens were "a peaceable orderly people"
and wanted no truck "with Steam Cars and an influx of strangers."[5] But the intermediate route was ultimately chosen because it was an established business and
industrial corridor linking Hartford to New Haven by way of Newington, Berlin,
Meriden, Yalesville, Wallingford, and North Haven. In addition, the route was also
reasonably direct and had few grades to overcome.

Professor Twining's report indicated the thirty-six-mile road would cost
$830,000.[6] He forecast a "local" freight and passenger business, particularly when
the Connecticut River froze over. There was also "through" traffic to be capitalized
upon, which flowed from the upper Connecticut River valley near Springfield, but
this would ultimately require an extension of the line north of Hartford if it was to

Engine Comet *of the Hartford & New Haven was painted in vivid colors and lined with script. She burned wood and belonged to the then-prevalent "American" type because of her 4-4-0 wheel arrangement. This coding system indicates four small wheels in the pilot truck, four large ones as drivers, and no small trailing wheels.*

The Comet *was insured by the Hartford Steam Boiler Inspection and Insurance Company, which still loyally clings to her likeness on its corporate seal.*

be fully realized. At the southern terminus of New Haven, Long Island Sound steamboats would handle the movement of traffic to New York City.

As in the case of many early Connecticut railroads, construction of the Hartford & New Haven unfortunately coincided with the national financial panic of 1837. Stock subscriptions became acutely delinquent, business slumped, most banks withdrew support, the state lent only a deaf ear, and financial solvency largely rested upon such wealthy private investors as President Brewster. By managing its affairs prudently and taking out short-term notes, he and others undertook construction of the line. A contract for the first eighteen miles between New Haven and Meriden was let in 1836. This segment opened in December 1838, a year later than anticipated, owing to the panic. Interestingly, formal service was not unveiled until the Connecticut River was completely frozen over and the boat service curtailed for the season. Thus the railroad opened with "a press of business."

Initially tracks of the Hartford & New Haven were composed of yellow pine timber rails from Georgia topped with iron straps nearly an inch thick that had been produced in England. The strap-iron timber rails were then affixed to ties made of native white chestnut. In December 1839 service to Hartford was inaugurated. Three wood-burning locomotives were on the company's first roster: *Charter Oak, Quinnipiac,* and *Hartford,* all built by the Rogers works in New Jersey. Each had one pair of driving wheels. There were no cabs for the engine drivers, and each engine had an unusually large and flaring smokestack equipped with a spark arrester at the top. A typical train consisted of the engine, tender, and two passenger cars. The latter held about twenty-four passengers each and were divided into three compartments accommodating eight people across (four facing four). A brakeman rode each car, and his hand was always close to the brake lever. Candles provided illumination, and a sheet-iron stove warmed the cars in winter as of 1840. Only primitive chains connected these early coaches.

At the tidewater terminal of New Haven the road obtained control of the so-called

Tomlinson Bridge, which linked New Haven to Fair Haven. Near it the railroad constructed a steamboat dock and dredged a channel enabling steamboats to reach the bridge area so that train passengers could board boats of the New Haven Steamboat Company. The popular Long Island steamer *Belle* used this new facility, from which came the name of Belle Dock.[7] At the northern terminus of Hartford, the Hartford & New Haven track crossed the Park River north of the capitol, then swung east across Bushnell Park. Plans called for the line to reach busy Main Street and the waterfront, but the city fathers felt the trains too great a disturbance and halted the road at Mulberry Street, near what became the Jeremy Hoadley Memorial Bridge.

Most people in 1840 found the sight of an early Hartford & New Haven train to be exciting or frightening—exciting because this was Progress and Enterprise at work, frightening because it belched a fiery and smoky breath. Trains were not much faster than a good stagecoach; in winter, a sprinkling of snow perhaps gave a stagecoach the advantage, as an early account told:

> The conductor and baggageman used to sit in the front of the locomotive one on each side, and brush off the snow from the rails with brooms as the train slowly crawled along. Each had a pail of sand and sprinkled a handful on the rail when necessary. The driving wheels used to slip round and round. On one occasion, a train got stuck on the Yalesville grade by one inch of snow, and the wood and water gave out before the locomotive could overcome it. At last the crew got out the neighbors, yoked four pair of oxen to the train and drew it—passengers, baggage and all—into Meriden with flying colors.[8]

Like Taurus, *many early locomotives carried decorative paintings. The owners were proud of their motive power, and aspiring carriage painters were eager to oblige.*

This single share of stock in the Hartford & New Haven cost $100. After a rough start, this investment would pay high dividends.

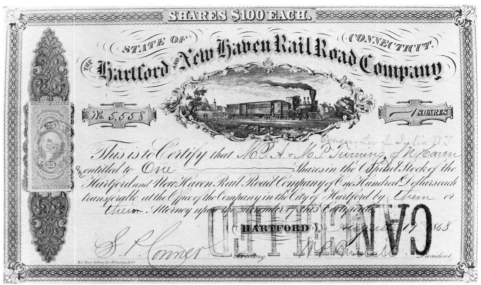

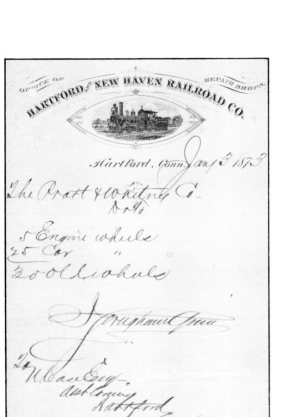

Wheels for engines and cars were often sent outside for repairs. Pratt & Whitney was a small enterprise, glad to have the work.

Extending the railroad for twenty-six miles north of Hartford to Springfield, Massachusetts, was a goal of the directors from the road's opening. Twining knew the project was inevitable if the line was to tap the "through" traffic of the Connecticut River valley. By 1842 the Hartford & Springfield Railroad was incorporated for this purpose with the goal of uniting, at Springfield, with the Western Railroad that ran between Worcester and Albany, New York. A number of route locations were surveyed, with the 1844 extension eventually passing through Windsor, Windsor Locks, then crossing the Connecticut River to Warehouse Point, Thompsonville, and Longmeadow, Massachusetts. Now patrons and freight from the valley could go directly down to New Haven, along with any traffic that came over from Worcester and points east.

Business on the Hartford & New Haven substantially increased with the opening of its Springfield extension. This was not pleasing to the operators of the Connecticut River Line of steamboats, who at one time enjoyed a monopoly of Springfield-Hartford-New York City traffic. In retaliation they announced that their boats would now stop at Belle Dock and directly compete with any services that the little New Haven Steamboat Company was providing to the Hartford & New Haven Railroad. The New Haven concern shuddered at the competitive threat and quickly sold out to the Connecticut River Line. The latter then assumed the contracts, purposely placed on the line its worst possible Long Island Sound steamer, and instituted a judicious campaign of rate cutting.[9] The situation grew intolerable, and the railroad obtained permission from the legislature to own and operate its own boat line. By 1847 the Hartford & New Haven's annual report boasted the purchase of a new steamboat.

During the 1840s the early strap-iron rail of the line was replaced with rails made of solid iron in the "T" design. The roster of rolling stock was enlarged, and improvements were made in the physical condition of the entire route. Cattle guards were erected at various points to keep off livestock that grazed near the right of way. The company began manufacturing its own passenger, baggage, and freight cars. Payroll ledgers in November 1841 revealed that an engineer on the Hartford & New Haven was paid two dollars a day; a first-class machinist in the company's shops made a dollar more. The rate of speed for passenger trains ranged from twelve to eighteen miles per hour.

In 1848 the strategic, long-awaited New York & New Haven Railroad was finally opened from New Haven west to Bridgeport, Stamford, Greenwich, and New York State. From its inception it hoped to attract all the traffic from the Hartford & New Haven that was going to New York City by boat. But the line could not convince the Hartford road to enter into a contract, thus forcing the New York road to obtain something of an advantage by leasing the New Haven & Northampton Railroad. If fully extended, the New Haven & Northampton had the potential of capturing Connecticut River valley traffic currently going down the Hartford & New Haven. Pressed to action, the Hartford & New Haven reluctantly entered into a contract with the New York road for sharing traffic at New Haven. Eventually the Hartford road ran all but its night boat train into the New Haven's Chapel Street depot and interchanged traffic, though the two roads fought for years over terms and revenue splits.

The huge and ornate union depot at Chapel Street in New Haven, designed by architect Henry Austin, was opened in 1849. It embraced Italian architectural features. A year later a huge castlelike edifice was also inaugurated at Asylum Street in Hartford, serving the railroads of the day and dispensing with the Hartford & New Haven's tiny Mulberry Street facility. Trains could actually pass through or stop inside the structure. A mile-long freight branch was put down from the main line at Hartford to reach the busy Connecticut River waterfront area at the South Meadows near Colt's Armory.

Still eager to get its own railroad was Middletown, Connecticut, which the Hartford road by-passed when the "intermediate route" was selected. The Middletown Railroad was subsequently organized by Charles Alsop and other Middletown men in 1848.[10] In the spring of the following year it built a nine-mile line from Middletown to the Hartford & New Haven main track at Berlin. The latter company operated and eventually owned it. By 1860 the Hartford & New Haven had extended the track for one mile further at Middletown to reach the busy Connecticut River wharves. The Berlin station of the Hartford & New Haven came into further use in 1865 when the three-mile New Britain & Middletown Railroad opened for business between Berlin and New Britain. The Hartford & New Haven also operated this line, and it was eventually merged into the Hartford road as well.

Distance from New Haven.	Time Table 49 In Effect June 15, 1908 STATIONS.
0.00	Belle Dock Stati'n
0.00	New Haven_____N
1.65	Cedar Hill _____D
4.00	Quinnipiack _____
6.88	North Haven____D
12.50	Wallingford ____N
15.50	Yalesville _____
18.50	Meriden _____N
25.88	Berlin _____N
31.50	Newington _____N
36.50	Hartford _____N
37.00	Branch Switch__N
39.49	Wilson's _____
42.88	Windsor ____ D
45.50	Hayden's_____
48.50	Windsor Locks__N
50.00	Warehouse Point_
52.25	Enfield Bridge____
53.88	Thompsonville __N
58.50	Longmeadow _____
60.75	Pecowsic _____
62.50	Springfield _____N

---

73   **NEW YORK AND NEW HAVEN RAILWAY.**

William B. Bishop, President, Bridgeport, Ct.
James H. Hoyt, Gen. Supt., New York.

J. T. Shelton, Treasurer, Bridgeport, Ct.
J. Mendel, Gen. Ticket Agent, New York.
J. S. Moodie, Asst. Supt., Bridgeport, Ct.

Henry White, Auditor, New Haven, Ct.
Chas. Rockwell, Gen. Freight Agent, New York.

New York to New Haven.   Nov. 22, 1869.   **New Haven to New York.**

Mail	Pas.	Pas.	Exs.	Acc.	Exs.	Exs.	Acc.	Pas.	Exs.	Acc.	Mls	STATIONS.	Mail	Acc.	Acc.	Exs.	Acc.	Exs.	Exs.	Exs.	Pas.	Exs.	Acc.	Exs.
P. M.	P. M.	P. M.	P. M.	P. M.	P. M.	P. M.	A. M.	A. M.	A. M.	A. M.	0	**N. Y. City Hall** ...	A. M.	A. M.	A. M.	A. M.	P. M.	P. M.	P. M.	P. M.	P. M.	P. M.	P. M.	P. M.
8 00	6 30	5 30	4 30	3 45				8 00	7 00	2	..27th St. and 4th Av.[1]	5 30	8 00	8 50	9 30	11 25	12 50	3 20	5 05	5 40	7 20	8 10	11 20
8 08	6 38	5 39	4 38	3 54	3 08	12 23	11 38	9 08	8 08	7 08	3	........42d street......	5 24	7 52	8 41	9 22	11 18	12 43	3 12	4 58	5 34	7 14	8 04	11 12
....	7 09	6 10	....	4 25	....	....	12 09	9 39	..	7 39	14	...Williams' Bridge[2]..	....	7 22	8 10	....	10 50	....	2 41	....	5 04	....	7 34	...
....	7 17	6 17	....	4 32			12 16	9 46		7 46	17	...Mount Vernon......	....	7 14	8 03	....	10 43	....	2 33	....	4 56	....	7 28	
....	7 26	6 28	....	4 42			12 24	9 54		7 55	20	...New Rochelle......	....	7 06	7 53	....	10 34	....	2 24	....	4 47	....	7 20	
....	7 36	6 38	....	4 52			12 34	10 02		8 04	24	...Mamaroneck	....	6 57	7 45	....	10 25	....	2 14	....	4 39	....	7 11	
....	7 45	6 48	....	5 02			12 44	10 11		8 13	27	......Rye..........	....	6 48	7 35	....	10 15	....	2 04	....	4 31	....	7 02	
....	7 50	6 53	....	5 07			12 49	10 16		8 17	29	...Port Chester......	....	6 43	7 30	....	10 10	....	1 59	....	4 26	....	6 57	
....	7 57	7 01	....	5 15			12 56	10 23		8 24	32	...Greenwich	....	6 36	7 22	....	10 02	....	1 51	....	4 19	....	6 50	
....	8 02	7 07	....	5 21			1 01	10 29	..	8 29	33	...Cos Cob Bridge...	....	6 31	7 16	....	9 56	....	....	....	4 15	....	6 45	....
9 30	8 10	7 17	5 52	5 32	4 22	1 41	1 11	10 39	9 26	8 39	37	...Stamford	4 08	6 21	7 07	8 06	9 47	11 26	1 38	3 42	4 06	6 00	6 37	9 56
....	8 19	7 26	6 01	....			1 20	10 47	..			...Noroton	....	6 12	6 56	....	9 36	....	....	....	3 57	....		
....	8 22	7 29	6 04	5 44			1 23	10 51	..	8 50	41	...Darien	....	6 06	6 53	7 54	9 33	....	1 26	....	3 54	....	6 25	....
9 49	8 30	7 37	6 12	5 52	4 40	1 59	1 31	11 00	9 44	8 58	45	...Norwalk[3]........	3 47	6 00	6 45	7 46	9 22	11 05	1 18	3 22	3 45	5 39	6 17	9 37
....		7 46	6 21	6 01	....		1 40			9 08	48	...Westport	....		6 37	7 37	9 17	....	1 09	....			6 08	....
....		7 56	6 31	6 11	....		1 50			9 18	52	...Southport........	....		6 27	7 26	9 07	....	12 59	....			5 58	....
....		8 01	6 36	6 16	....		1 55			9 23	54	......Fairfield......	....		6 22	7 21	9 03	....	12 54	....			5 53	....
10 33		8 15	6 49	6 30	5 13	2 32	2 09		10 15	9 37	59	...Bridgeport[4]......	3 16		6 08	7 08	8 49	10 27	12 40	2 50		5 05	5 40	9 05
....		8 23	6 58	6 40	....		2 17			9 45	62	...Stratford	....		6 00	7 00	8 41	....	12 31	....			5 32	....
....			7 03	....						9 52	64	...Naugatuck Junc'n[5]..	....				8 35	10 11	....	....			5 27	....
....		8 35		6 52			2 29			10 00	67	...Milford	....		5 49	6 49	8 29	....	12 19	....			5 19	....
11 10		8 55	7 30	7 12	5 50	3 10	2 50		10 50	10 20	76	...**New Haven**[6].....	2 40		5 30	6 30	8 10	9 45	12 00	2 15		4 30	5 00	8 30
P. M.	P. M.	P. M.	P. M.	P. M.	P. M.	P. M.	P. M.	A. M.	A. M.	A. M.		[ARRIVE] [LEAVE	A. M.	A. M.	A. M.	A. M.	A. M.	A. M.	N'ON	P. M.	P. M.	P. M.	P. M.	P. M.

Sunday Mail train leaves New York at 7 00 p.m.   Mail train arrives on Monday 5 20 a.m.

For Montreal.—The 12 15 p.m. train makes direct connection at Springfield for Montreal, &c., arriving there at 9 30 a.m.

Stamford Special Trains leaves New York for Stamford, other than above given, at 2 15, 4 45 and 7 15 p.m. Returning, leave Stamford at 5 00 and 8 15 a.m.

A Special Train leaves Stamford for New Haven and intermediate stations at 6 20 a.m., arriving at New Haven at 7 55 a.m.

[1] Connects with Railways diverging from New York for all parts of the country.
[1] Connects with the various lines of steamers running out of New York.
[2] New York and New Haven Railway diverges from New York and Harlem Railway.
[3] Junction of Danbury and Norwalk Railway.
[4] Junction of Housatonic Railway.
[5] Junction of Naugatuck Railway.
[6] Connects with New Haven, New London and Stonington Railway.
[6] Connects with New Haven, Hartford and Springfield Railway.
[6] Connects with New Haven and Northampton Railway.

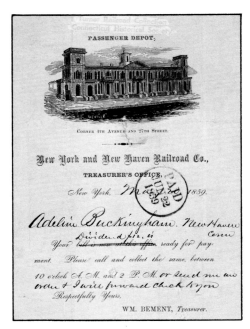

Business ways have changed since creditors — and stockholders — could be told, like Miss Buckingham, to "come and get it."

An attractive 14 percent dividend was declared by the Hartford & New Haven Railroad in 1867. Twenty freight cars and one baggage car were constructed at the company's shops in 1869. An elaborate bridge of seven arches, costing $60,000, was erected in 1867 over the Farmington River at Windsor. Fifty-eight-pound iron rail was being used on the main-line track, more than seven hundred employees were on the payroll, and the engine roster consisted of twenty-nine locomotives. The Hartford & New Haven was a thriving concern.

In the remaining years before its 1872 consolidation, the Hartford & New Haven began laying steel rails and a second main track connecting Springfield, Hartford, and New Haven. It also purchased a quarry in Meriden to supply requirements for ballast. Top speed for passenger trains was then raised to thirty-three miles an hour. More than one thousand people were now employed by the rail line. The last acquisition was the five-mile Windsor Locks & Suffield Railroad, which opened in 1870. It too was operated and soon bought by the Hartford road. The people of Suffield had put up $20,000 for construction; a good part of the balance was absorbed by the Hartford & New Haven.

On April 20, 1870, the Hartford & New Haven received a letter from William Bishop, president of the New York & New Haven Railroad, suggesting a committee be formed to run the affairs of both roads. This led to an agreement that ended hostilities and paved the way for the historic consolidation of 1872.

The New York & New Haven

Running west from New Haven to New York along the scenic, saw-toothed coast of Long Island Sound, the New York & New Haven Railroad was one of the last lines needed to form a chain of rail communications from Boston to New York City. From its inception it was controlled by New Yorkers, yet Connecticut men were involved with its operations. Because of its strategic location and its highly prized connection to New York City via the New York & Harlem Railroad, the New York

& New Haven had to be reckoned with if neighboring lines in Connecticut wanted a New York City entrance.

The New York & New Haven was incorporated in 1844 with authorization to build from the Mill River area in New Haven west to the New York state line via the cities of Milford, Bridgeport, Norwalk, Stamford, and Greenwich.[11] Stock subscription books were promptly opened, and in the following year application was made to the New York legislature for permission to reach Manhattan. Initially the petition was turned down because the Westchester Turnpike Road Company and the New York & Harlem Railroad opposed it. Both knew the encroaching enterprise would take away a substantial slice of their business.

To silence the toll-road operators, the New York & New Haven merely paid $5,500 to settle forever any and all claims. As for the New York & Harlem, the Connecticut road decided to connect directly with that line at Williams' Bridge, New York (near Woodlawn) and avoid building a parallel track to the Harlem River.[12] For that arrangement the New York & New Haven agreed to pay a fixed fee to the New York & Harlem for every passenger coming from Connecticut using the connection to reach New York City. The New York & New Haven dug down even further. It loaned the New York & Harlem money to complete the double track sought at Williams' Bridge, bought large amounts of New York and Harlem stock, then ironed out compensation for any freight traffic to be brought through the junction. In January 1846 an agreement was drawn up covering these points.

With these obstacles removed, the Connecticut road reapplied and received permission from New York State to build to Williams' Bridge from the state line. Alexander Twining was again hired as surveyor and proposed a single-track line along the Connecticut coast; it would be easy to build, even though it faced numerous marshes and river crossings. The sixty-nine-mile line was projected to cost $2,250,000.[13] That huge sum, of course, did not exist in the corporate checkbook. The Bridgeport contractors Alfred Bishop and Sidney Miller helped by taking as partial compensation $900,000 worth of railroad stock. The final cost of the road exceeded the estimate, forcing the owners of the railroad to issue bonds and short-term notes to finish construction. It is interesting that the New York & New Haven was initially conceived as a passenger-hauling railroad with virtually no facilities to accommodate a freight business. Later it sought that traffic as well.

One of the more unpleasant moments of state railway history involved speculator Robert Schuyler. He greatly overissued New York & New Haven stock, using the millions thus received to pay private debts.

R & LHS

N. YORK & NEW-HAVEN RAILROAD CO.

A TRAIN for NEW-HAVEN, BRIDGEPORT, and HOUSATONIC RAILROAD and Intermediate Places, will leave the Station House of the *Harlem Railroad Company* at 32d Street, on FRIDAY MORNING, 29th December inst., at 8 o'clock precisely.

R. B. MASON, Eng'r & Supt'd.
December 28th, 1848.

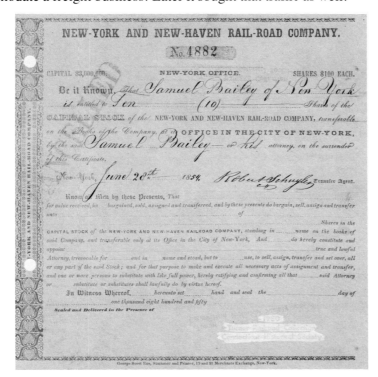

NEW-YORK AND NEW-HAVEN RAIL-ROAD COMPANY.

No. 4882

CAPITAL $3,000,000. NEW-YORK OFFICE. SHARES $100 EACH.

Be it known, That *Samuel Bailey of New York* is entitled to *Ten (10)* Shares of the CAPITAL STOCK of the NEW-YORK AND NEW-HAVEN RAIL-ROAD COMPANY, transferable on the Books of the Company, at the OFFICE IN THE CITY OF NEW-YORK, by the said *Samuel Bailey* or his attorney, on the surrender of this Certificate.

New-York, *June 28th* 1854. *Robert Schuyler* Transfer Agent.

The stock specimen at left is significant for two reasons: it bears the signature of Robert Schuyler, and perhaps it was among the many shares he fraudulently issued.

By using a magnifying glass, the careful reader will observe a host of design details in this New York & New Haven coach, and see some rather interesting passengers.

Some of the early figures associated with this road included Samuel Hitchcock, president of the Hartford & New Haven; Joseph Sheffield, president of the New Haven & Northampton Railroad; and the New York brothers Robert and George Schuyler—railroad speculators, builders, and promoters *extraordinaire*. Sheffield was a heavy investor and alone took twelve thousand shares of stock.[14] Robert Schuyler attained the road's presidency but would later cast a dark and ominous shadow upon the road and himself. When bonds and notes had to be issued to get the line completed, the Schuyler brothers offered their financial services in this department.

Sheffield was consulted when the question arose as to where the New York & New Haven's depot, shops, and yards would be situated in New Haven. The answer conveniently lay at his fingertips: he would merely lease his New Haven & Northampton to the New York road. This provided the New York & New Haven with valuable canal-basin properties in New Haven and a route for tracks in the drained-off canal bed below many of New Haven's busy streets. In addition the lease put the New York road in charge of the Canal Railroad and in control of a line that one day might encircle the Hartford & New Haven. Thus the Sheffield addition was a valuable "bargaining chip."

On Christmas Day 1848 the New York & New Haven ran its first train from New Haven to New York, or at least it thought it would. Upon discovering that the New York track had not been completed to Williams' Bridge as scheduled, the flag-draped inaugural train was forced to return up the single track to New Haven. Since there was no way of turning the engine or train, the disappointed celebrants found themselves in the rather ignominious position of backing into the station! Early the following year the matter was remedied. Trains arriving at Williams' Bridge proceeded fourteen miles down the New York & Harlem to its Canal Street depot in Manhattan. Thanks to city ordinances, horses hauled the trains from Forty-second Street to Canal Street, until the latter terminus was moved uptown to Twenty-seventh Street and Fourth Avenue in 1857. In 1872 it was finally fixed at Forty-second Street, the present site of Grand Central Station. Directors of the railroad were quite taken with the public response to the new line. The *Derby Journal* reported in January 1848 that "passengers are said to be averaging nearly a thousand a day and passenger receipts one day last week were $1,600."[15]

One week before the inaugural run was made, a trial trip through Stamford was observed by a reporter of the *Stamford Advocate* newspaper: "The citizens of the

THE LATE RAILWAY CALAMITY AT NORWALK, CONN.

THE CATASTROPHE.

THE NORWALK RAILROAD CALAMITY.

ANOTHER of those railroad "accidents," or, rather, accidental massacres which have of late become so fearfully frequent, occurred on the morning of the 6th inst., on the New Haven Railroad, at Norwalk, Conn. The morning express train was advancing at full speed the drawbridge where the catastrophe occurred, was opened to admit the passage of the steamboat Pacific, and the signal was accordingly lowered. Of this the engineer took no notice, and consequently the engine, the baggage car, and two of the passenger cars dashed headlong into the river, which was there twelve feet deep. So great was their speed, that the engine struck against the abutment on the opposite side, literally making a leap of about sixty feet!

The scene which ensued was one of incredible horror. Upwards of fifty lives were almost immediately destroyed, by violent concussion or by drowning. But six or seven escaped of those who were in the cars; among these several contrived to beat their way out after they were submerged. The bottom of the third car (there were five in all) broke in two, its fragments hanging over the edge, and several of its passengers were thrown into the stream.

The blame appears to have attached to the engineer, since it is difficult to imagine any palliation for impelling a train of cars rapidly at any time over a drawbridge, while the engineer is said to have been unqualified by experience for the post which he occupied. Among the dead is Mrs. Fluent—a lady who had been married only the day before. She died in her bridal robes. Her husband escaped with slight injures. Miss EMILY GRISWOLD, a daughter of the Rev. RUFUS W. GRISWOLD, is reported injured. Credit is due the citizens of Norwalk for their prompt and energetic efforts to rescue the sufferers. Through their exertions many lives were saved. Many of those rescued were dangerously wounded, among whom was JONATHAN TROTTER, Esq., of this city.

Several of the killed were physicians returning from the medical convention. The history of the hairbreadth escapes effected by different persons on this occasion, would form a volume. A gentleman who happened to be looking out foresaw the accident in time to throw his wife and two children from the window of the car, and to escape with them, suffering only slight bruises. The express agent was sitting in the baggage car, but succeeded in breaking his way through the roof. Dr. Ives and Dr. Carter also went down *under water* in

the baggage car, but escaped in the same manner. A newsboy in the broken car escaped unhurt. Comstock, the conductor, was in the second passenger car, his foot caught in the rubbish, and he was three times submerged in the water, but finally extricated himself, and he was able to crawl out of a window overhead. It was noticed as a singular fact, that many of the killed were wounded in the left temple, as if the shock had cast them all in the same direction. The wounded were at once distributed through the town, and every possible care taken of them. The ladies of Norwalk on this occasion rendered most efficient service, doing all in their power to alleviate the terrible sufferings of the wounded and the anguish of the bereaved.

When our artist reached the spot, the excitement which prevailed was intense. The news spread like wildfire, and the town was speedily filled by the relatives and friends of those who had been in the cars. While the coroner's jury were, at a later hour, viewing the dead bodies, many assembled round the house where the bodies were, and in a state of fearful excitement. They had arrived from neighboring cities, and were desirous of terminating the terrible suspense in which they were placed. The opening of the door was the intro-

(Continued on page 308.)

The press reveled in the gory details of the Norwalk disaster: this comes from the Illustrated News, *a weekly, for May 14, 1853.*

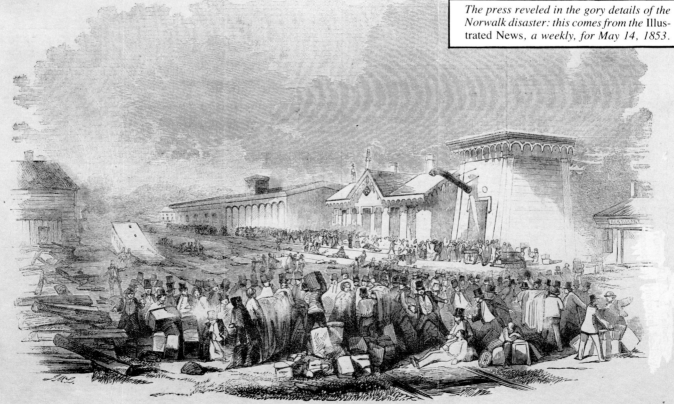

SCENE AT THE DEPOT AFTER THE ACCIDENT—BRINGING IN THE BODIES.

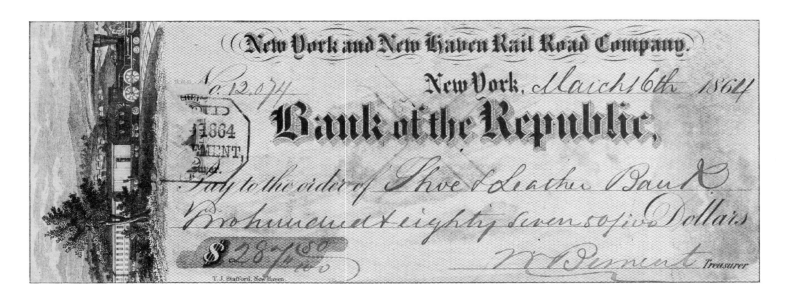

village, as well as horses and cattle, were nearly frightened out of their propriety by such a horrible scream as was never heard to issue from other than a metallic throat. Animals of every description went careening around the fields, snuffing at the air in their terror. In a few moments, the cause of the commotion appeared in the shape of a locomotive, puffing off its steam and screaming with its so-called whistle at a terrible rate."[16] So insistent was the railroad in getting the trial runs started, that this same train was later halted for three hours at the Cos Cob bridge while the last of the iron rails were spiked. The passenger train fare back then, New Haven to New York City, was fixed at $1.50.

From the grand opening the new company connected with several other important Connecticut lines on the way to New York. At Bridgeport it intersected the Housatonic Railroad. When the Naugatuck Railroad was built in 1849, the New York road gratuitously built a track from Bridgeport to Devon (in the town of Milford), where the Naugatuck's main line actually began. In return it got the Naugatuck's traffic to New York City. The steamboat line from Bridgeport, serving the Housatonic and Naugatuck lines, was owned by George Schuyler. By 1852 the Danbury & Norwalk Railroad would tap into the New York road at South Norwalk, while in 1868 the little Stamford & New Canaan Railroad would depend upon the line for its outlet at Stamford.

Henry Austin designed New Haven's first, short-lived station (left) in pagoda style. The second one was photographed after the Blizzard of 1888. Presumably the athletes in Yale sweaters had been helping clean up.

NEW HAVEN COLONY HISTORICAL SOCIETY

NEW YORK AND NEW HAVEN RAILROAD STATION, NEW HAVEN.

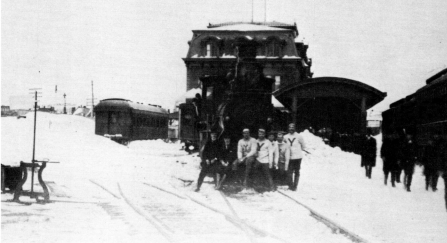

N. Y. AND N. H. R. R.
LIST OF UNCLAIMED BAGGAGE ON HAND
APRIL 1st, 1853.

REMAINING AT CANAL STREET STATION.
NEW YORK AND NEW HAVEN R. R. CHECKS.

9556	Black Trunk.	11918	Large Russet colored Trunk.
10915	Russet Trunk.	9984	Small Russet colored Trunk, marked F. C.
9648	Black Trunk, marked H. M. B.	10446	Bandbox.
11617	Russet Trunk, marked R. F. O., N. Y.	9472	Bandbox, marked Disbo.
10508	Small Brown Tool Chest, no mark.	9275	Black Valise, no mark.
10777	Small Black Trunk, no mark.	6080	An old Bandbox, no mark.
9370	Large Hair Covered Trunk, no mark.		

BOSTON LINE CHECKS.

1711	Large Russet Trunk, marked T. R. Rogers.	195	Black Trunk.
1348	Black Trunk, no mark.		

NORWALK AND DANBURY R. R. CHECKS.

407	Small Black Trunk, marked Mrs. E. Ford.	265	Small Black Trunk, same mark.

CONNECTICUT RIVER R. R. CHECKS.

1497	Russet colored Trunk.	1629	Green Wood Trunk.
1762	Russet colored Trunk.	15	Small Hair Trunk.
529	Black Leather Trunk.		

HOUSATONIC R. R. CHECKS.

1886	Tool Chest, marked Anon Buck.	3948	Bundle, marked Schenick.
3997	Carpet Bag.		

NAUGATUCK R. R. CHECK. - - - 686 Russet Trunk.

1 Bale of Bags, marked Hecker & Bro's.	1 Broken Iron Sled, (Boy's.)
2 Bandboxes tied in White Bag.	1 Bandbox marked E. Field, containing an old hat.

This evidence of heedless travellers scattering baggage everywhere clashes a bit with the image of the careful Yankee.

These comfortable links contributed immensely to the road's overall financial success. In the 1850s a second track was started along the entire route to handle more traffic. By 1855 twenty-six engines were being utilized, along with eighty passenger coaches and more than three hundred freight cars. Total income in 1859 approached the $1,000,000 mark.

But the 1850s were not without spectacular setbacks. On May 6, 1853, a speeding passenger express en route from New York City to New Haven careened through an open drawbridge over the Norwalk River at South Norwalk, Connecticut, taking forty-five lives. The cause was negligence and recklessness by the engineer, who apparently ignored a red stop signal indicating the draw span was open. Many of the casualties were physicians returning from a New York City convention. While there were (for once) plenty of unhurt doctors on hand to care for casualties, nevertheless more than $300,000 was spent by the railroad to settle claims. The South Norwalk disaster was one of the nation's deadliest train wrecks at that time.

In his superbly researched book, *A History of Railroad Accidents, Safety Precautions and Operating Practices*, author Robert Shaw brings to light the lesser known details of the South Norwalk disaster, as demonstrated by this excerpt:

> The Norwalk Bridge was a wooden span which pivoted on a central pier to create two 60-foot openings for the passage of ships. Rail level was about 25 feet above water level at high tide. at which time the water was from eight to ten feet deep. The bridge, which lay about 300 yards east of the South Norwalk station, around a rather sharp curve, was ordinarily closed to ships, and the tender would open it upon their signal only when certain that no trains were approaching. Before opening it he would lower a red, two-foot diameter ball ordinarily suspended from the top of a 40-foot pole. Subsequent investigation showed that the ball could first be seen by eastbound trains at a distance of 3,312 feet from the draw.

One of the great buildings of New York City last century was the first Grand Central Terminal. It was mainly occupied by Vanderbilt's New York & Harlem and Connecticut's New York & New Haven railroads as the right tower lettering announces. Trains of the latter used tracks of the former from the terminal to reach Woodlawn where the New York & New Haven tracks took off to the east. The Commodore's line became part of the New York Central system. Today's commuters use the second Grand Central, completed in 1913.

COLLECTION OF OLIVER JENSEN

At 10.15 on the morning of May 6, 1853, Captain Byxbie of the steamboat *Pacific* whistled for passage through the draw at South Norwalk. Harford, the bridge tender, listened to make sure he heard no train coming from either direction, lowered the ball, waited several minutes more as a safety factor, and then opened the bridge to admit the *Pacific*. That vessel had passed through and Harford was just preparing to close the span when, at 10.30, he was horrified to see a Boston-bound passenger train sweep around the curve at high speed and, with no more than a last-minute effort to check its momentum, plunge into the stream.

This train was the eight o'clock express from New York—the only train on the line not scheduled to stop at Norwalk. Eight minutes late at Norwalk it ran off the bridge at an estimated speed of 25 mph, sufficient to carry the engine clear across the western channel and leave it with its pilot resting against the central pier. A baggage car, two mail cars and two passenger cars followed the engine into the river, while a third passenger car halted suspended over the brink of the draw and broke in half. The two passenger cars to fall in the river were not severely crushed, and most of the 40 victims perished by drowning. The casualty list would have been even higher except that witnesses of the accident, including the crew of the *Pacific*, quickly organized a rescue effort, and pulled a number of dazed passengers from the water. The express messenger, Fuller, riding in the first baggage car, miraculously climbed out almost unhurt. Among the passengers were a large number of doctors returning to New England from the Sixth Annual Meeting of the American Medical Association in New York, and seven of these were included among the dead. Another one of these medical gentlemen, Dr. John C. Warren, was responsible for the resuscitation of a Miss Griswold, of the prominent Connecticut family, by continuing efforts for her recovery long after she had been pronounced dead.

The crew of the train, Engineer Edward Tucker, Fireman Ellman and Conductor Charles H. Comstock, saved themselves by jumping, the engineer suffering only a broken leg, the conductor numerous bruises, and the fireman escaping entirely uninjured. Feeling against the crew ran high in the hastily gathered, excited crowd, and many urged that the engineer be immediately lynched, opinion differing only as to whether he should be hanged or shot. One witness wrote to the *New York Herald* that "it would have a good effect if the engineers, switch tenders and some of the directors of our railroads were occasionally made to feel the force of Lynch law." (The *Herald* had no reason to take exception to this view, as it frequently urged the infliction of summary execution upon malefactors caught in the act.)

The subsequent inquest left no doubt that Tucker, through an act of gross negligence, was primarily responsible for the tragedy. He insisted that he had seen the red ball aloft before he approached the bridge, but too many other witnesses, including bridge tender, master and engineer of the *Pacific*, and passers-by, testified that it had been lowered well in advance of the arrival of the train to leave any doubt that Tucker was mistaken. Eventually, in fact, the unfortunate engineer conceded that the weight of contrary evidence by so many witnesses proved that the ball must have been down, although he had *thought* he had seen it. [17]

A year after the drawbridge disaster, President Robert Schuyler, a supposed paragon of financial stability and integrity, reluctantly announced the failure of his New York City brokerage house, which was intimately tied with the New York & New Haven. Investigations revealed that he had fraudulently overissued nearly twenty thousand shares of New York & New Haven stock worth several million dollars. [18] Schuyler fled to Italy, leaving behind a number of law suits against the railroad. Eventually the company made good on the spurious stock, but the affair shook the commercial and financial world for some time to come.

The 1860s saw an improving picture. A financial recovery was under way, 10 per cent dividends were paid, and New York & New Haven stock sold above par value. Steel rails replaced iron, new stations appeared, and train and yard facilities at various points were enlarged. Interestingly, the greater part of revenues was still being generated by the passenger service. In 1870 a lease was taken out on the Shore Line Railway, and correspondence began with directors of the Hartford & New Haven

Controversy surrounds the new railroad station at Stamford in 1985. Patrons today might prefer using the brick structure of last century. No less than eleven chimneys can be counted. At the far right was a water spout allowing the fireman to fill the tender while passengers headed for seats. A branch line leaves here for New Canaan.

This is another view of the second station at New Haven, an echo of the General Grant era with its Mansard towers and make shift entrance covers. (See also page 29.) The present station, on the same site, looks a little like a high school outside but has a handsome great hall within. It has recently been restored to its original elegance. The neighborhood, alas, remains a shabby one.

Distance from New Canaan	Time Table 49 In Effect June 15, 1908 STATIONS.
0.00	New Canaan ......
2.19	Talmadge Hill ....
---- --	Springdale Ceme'y
4.34	Springdale -------
5.66	Glenbrook -------
7.65	Stamford --------

No doubt the woman at right is exercising extreme caution in crossing the tracks at South Norwalk. The train closest to her is on the main line of the New York & New Haven, the other is from Danbury.

about a possible merger. In 1872 the New York & New Haven and the Hartford & New Haven merged, forming the largest railroad concern in the state.

During its final years as a separate enterprise, the New York & New Haven maintained a close association with the little eight-mile New Canaan Railroad, which had opened on Independence Day 1868. The road cost $242,348 to build, and it linked New Canaan with the main line of the New York & New Haven at Stamford via Glenbrook, Springdale, and Talmadge Hill. United States mail was contracted over the route, and farm produce harvested locally found its way to New York City thanks to the little railroad. The town of New Canaan had invested in the line, but its financial story was disappointing. Bonds had to be issued, and eventually trustees foreclosed and reorganized in 1883 as the Stamford & New Canaan Railroad. [19] Later that year the company was leased to the New York, New Haven & Hartford Railroad, to be known thereafter as its "New Canaan Branch." It serves that wealthy suburb to this day, although commuting brokers and bankers have replaced the farm produce of old. The depot at New Canaan is still often referred to as "the next station to Heaven."

Chapter Two Footnotes

1. Connecticut General Assembly, Resolves and Private Laws of the State of Connecticut, from the Year 1789 to the Year 1836, II: 1002-1005, Public Records, Connecticut State Capitol Building.

2. Edward E. Atwater, ed., *History of the City of New Haven to the Present Time* (New York: Munsell & Co., 1887), 360-362; 558-560.

3. Directors' minute book, 1836, Hartford & New Haven Railroad, Baker Library, Harvard Business School.

4. Withington, *First Twenty Years*, 15, 16.

5. Ibid.

6. *Report of the Engineer, Upon the Preliminary Surveys for the Hartford & New Haven Railroad* (New Haven: J. Peck, 1835), passim.

7. Withington, *First Twenty Years*, 16.

8. Unidentified newspaper extract, Hartford & New Haven Railroad envelopes, Turner Railroad Collection, The Connecticut Historical Society.

9. George Pierce Baker, *The Formation of the New England Railroad Systems* (Cambridge: Harvard University Press, 1949), 74.

10. Corporate and Operating History of the Lines Owned by the New York, New Haven & Hartford Railroad Company, 30 June 1915, 18-21, Turner Railroad Collection, The Connecticut Historical Society.

11. Connecticut General Assembly, Resolves and Private Laws of the State of Connecticut, From the Year 1836 to the Year 1857, IV: 1020-1025, Public Records, Connecticut State Capitol Building.

12. *Report of the Board of Directors to the Stockholders of the New York & New Haven Railroad Company for 1849* (New Haven: T. J. Stafford, 1849), passim.

13. *Engineer's Report of the Survey and Primary Location of the New York & New Haven Railroad* (New Haven: Hitchcock & Stafford, 1845), passim.

14. *American Railroad Journal*, 19 May 1855.

15. Undated clipping, *Derby Journal*, January 1848, Turner Railroad Collection, The Connecticut Historical Society.

16. Quoted in E. B. Huntington, *History of Stamford, Connecticut From Its Settlement in 1641 to the Present Time* (Stamford: published by the author, 1868), 442-443.

17. Robert B. Shaw, *A History of Railroad Accidents, Safety Precautions, and Operating Practices* (Vail-Ballou Press, 1978), 189-191.

18. *Hunt's Merchants' Magazine & Commercial Review*, 31 (1854): 208-209. (For an excellent overview of the Schuyler defalcation, the reader may wish to consult Bulletin No. 141 (Autumn 1979) of the Railway & Locomotive Historical Society wherein author Robert Shaw describes the fraud at length.)

19. Corporate and Operating History of Lines Owned by the New York, New Haven & Hartford Railroad Company, 27.

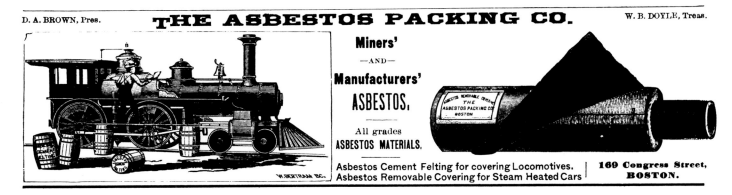

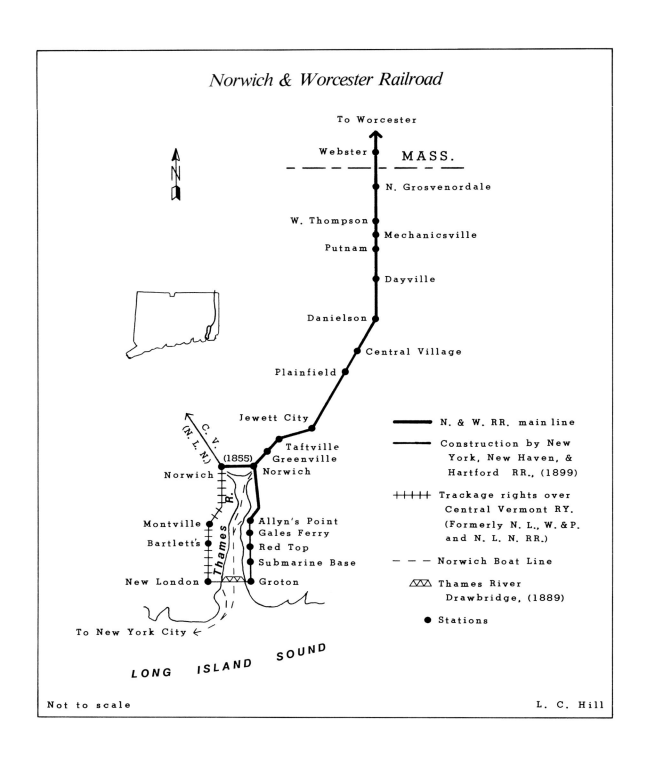

Norwich & Worcester Railroad

To Worcester

Webster   **MASS.**

N. Grosvenordale

W. Thompson

Mechanicsville

Putnam

Dayville

Danielson

Central Village

Plainfield

Jewett City

C. V.
(N. L. N.)

Taftville
(1855)
Greenville
Norwich

Norwich

Montville   Allyn's Point
                 Gales Ferry
Bartlett's   Red Top
                 Submarine Base
New London   Groton

Thames R.

To New York City ←

LONG ISLAND SOUND

————— N. & W. RR. main line

————— Construction by New York, New Haven, & Hartford RR., (1899)

+++++ Trackage rights over Central Vermont RY. (Formerly N. L., W. & P. and N. L. N. RR.)

— — — Norwich Boat Line

◿◺◿ Thames River Drawbridge, (1889)

● Stations

Not to scale   L. C. Hill

Chapter Three

The Norwich Line

The business relations of Eastern Connecticut with Boston will be greatly increased by opening this channel of communication. As a continuation of the Boston & Worcester R.R., the Norwich road and boat line will form one of the most pleasant lines of communication between Boston and New York City.

—*Norwich and Worcester Railroad directors before the Massachusetts Senate, 1837*

William Gibbs McNeill
R & LHS

There was no more beautiful setting for a city than that of Norwich, Connecticut, where two rivers meet some thirteen miles up the deep, navigable Thames from its outlet at New London. On its hills stood a town that was already prosperous, its residential streets lined with fine houses and its harbor full of ships. It was, in those days, a faintly self-conscious center of Yankee culture and called itself proudly "The Rose of New England." Much of this charm lingers to this day, and—if one searches for them—ruined traces can be found of the era when Norwich was something of a great railroad port. For at one time, like so many cities of Connecticut, Norwich with its railroad and steamboat line was a strong contender among the many rival routes between Boston and New York.

The Norwich & Worcester Railroad, which opened in 1840, was patterned after the Stonington arrangement. With the Norwich Line of steamboats it provided a new route for the escalating traffic of freight and passengers between the great cities. At its Worcester terminal it made a valuable connection with the Boston & Worcester Railroad for points east. Whenever the crack and highly patronized Norwich Steamboat Express rolled into Boston from Norwich, a signal was hoisted atop the station's flagpole while another flew at the old Boston State House.

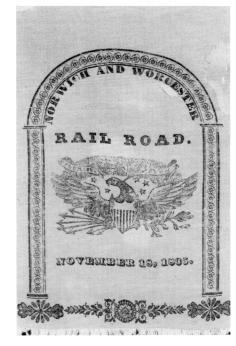

This breast-pocket badge was distributed to those attending groundbreaking ceremonies of the Norwich & Worcester in 1835.

At its southern terminal steamboats of the Norwich Line took patrons for the overnight journey to New York City down the Thames River and thence west along Long Island Sound. In all it was a 233-mile trip from Boston to New York City. The competitive Stonington Line nearby was slightly shorter, but the Norwich promoters were quick to point out that "if one route or the other were to be selected it would not be on account of the difference of one or two miles in a distance of more than two hundred miles, but other considerations such as the pleasantness of the country, scenery, etc."[1] In 1840 that rationale still had its appeal. Americans were not yet infatuated by speed alone.

Before the railroad, some prophets of internal improvements had championed a canal between Norwich and Worcester. A survey by the state of Connecticut in 1824 revealed "that the county was in every aspect favorable for the construction of a canal, and that there was an amount of water power on the Shetucket and Quinebaug Rivers sufficient to drive at least 500,000 cotton spindles."[2] Canal backers

Norwich harbor in 1870 fourteen miles from the Sound. At the Norwich & Worcester big dock is City of Lawrence, *and to her right* Ella *and the* City of Norwich.

actually secured a charter for such a project, but no one ever raised the money to build it. Railroad fever intervened. And the *Windham County Advertiser* spoke up:

> Are the citizens of Connecticut to sit idle while stupendous operations are going forward? Must passengers pass through the *land of steady habits* at the rate of 2 miles an hour? Is there no enterprise here? The people of New England have a work to perform, or lose their glory! Suppose a railroad were constructed from Norwich to Worcester? The expense will be but little compared with that of a canal, and the means are adequate. We now have a canal charter, why not convert this canal into a railroad?[3]

They did! In May 1832 a number of Norwich citizens were granted a charter for the Boston, Norwich & New London Railroad "to locate, construct, and finally complete a railroad in the City of Norwich, thence through the State, on such route towards the City of Boston, and from said City of Norwich to Long Island Sound."[4] Massachusetts chartered the Worcester & Norwich Railroad to bring the road into Worcester.[5] The Connecticut firm was capitalized at $1,000,000 (ten thousand shares of stock at $100 each). At Norwich forty-six hundred shares were subscribed, while the remaining fifty-four hundred shares were sold in New York City by the Board of Brokers—forerunners of the New York Stock Exchange. When the Worcester & Norwich Railroad books were opened, Norwich men subscribed to three-quarters of its $400,000 capital. Legislative approval allowed the consolidation of the two roads in June 1836 as the Norwich & Worcester Railroad.

The railroad's directors were confident of heavy traffic, since there were many manufacturers in the Quinebaug River valley, including more than one hundred textile mills within five miles of the proposed railroad. Another potential source of revenue was "through" traffic. One optimistic report noted: "It is quite apparent that everything now tends in the most direct line to New York City as the great commercial mart. The desire is increasing continually to facilitate the communication of Boston with that emporium of commerce. The manufacturer there purchases his raw material and there sends his goods, and the merchant would there obtain his supplies."[6]

Fresh from the Stonington Railroad survey, and having previously surveyed the Boston & Providence, Captain William Gibbs McNeill was engaged by the directors to locate the Norwich road. His survey of 1832 indicated an average right of way gradient between Norwich and Worcester of a modest eleven feet per mile. He divided the fifty-nine-mile route into four sections of construction: Norwich to Jewett City; Jewett City to Danielson; Danielson to the state line; and from the state line to Worcester. Cost of a fully equipped single-track railroad was estimated by McNeill to be $1,073,119. The United States Congress later helped the Norwich project in ordering a "liberal appropriation" to deepen the Thames River ship channel and to pay for a lightship at the river's mouth in New London.

Governor Henry Edwards of Connecticut was one of many who attended the gala Norwich & Worcester groundbreaking. The huge procession of a thousand or more which marched from Franklin Square, Norwich, to Greenville included such groups as the Norwich Rifle Company and the Norwich Light Infantry. Marching eight abreast were officers and directors of numerous railroad companies and, of course, many children. The scheduled speaker, Daniel Webster, was not there, however, for he had taken ill in Boston the night before. A special breast-pocket badge was passed out as a commemorative souvenir. After an invocation by the Reverend Mr. Nott of Franklin, the Cox Company of Norwich rolled out three decorated wheelbarrows with shovels. The earth flew. Afterward almost everyone marched back to Norwich for a lavish meal at the Franklin House.[7]

The line's first section of construction was the most expensive, owing to a tunnel—one of the nation's first—which had to be blasted under Bundy Hill in Taftville. By 1836 the railroad reached Danielsonville. In the next year work jumped ahead for the eighteen miles between the state line and the Boston & Worcester Railroad depot in Worcester. The final piece, between Danielsonville and the state line, commenced in 1838. A Norwich civil engineer, James Laurie, oversaw construction details and travelled to England to purchase iron rails. The rails were of the "T" design, weighing fifty-seven pounds to the yard, and measured eighteen feet in length. They arrived in 1839 and were laid on crossties which had been installed along the entire route the winter before.[8] Steel rails did not arrive until 1881.

The panic of 1837 managed to dry up most Norwich & Worcester construction funds, forcing the railroad's directors to solicit loans. The always-thrifty state of Connecticut balked, but Massachusetts was more sympathetic and loaned

COURTESY OF MELANCTHON W. JACOBUS

The rock tunnel at Taftville. Below is the Norwich Line dock at Pier 40 in New York.
COLLECTION OF ALICE A. RAMSDELL

The graceful steamer Atlantic *of the Norwich Line is preserved in this sketch by the noted artist Samuel Ward Stanton. Her life was short and tragic, ending when she was dashed to pieces off Fisher's Island.*

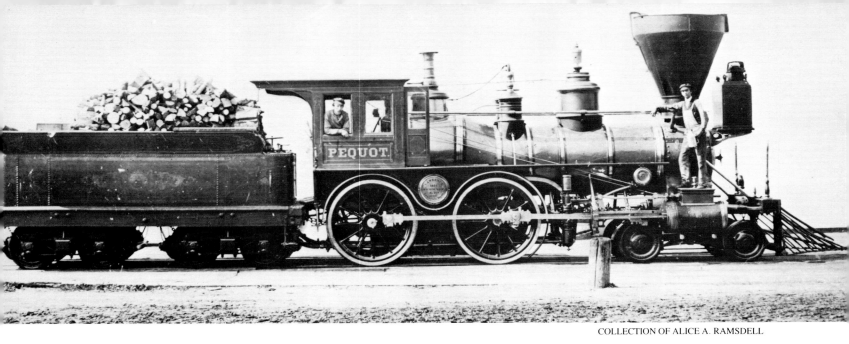

An elegant product of the Lawrence Machine Works of Massachusetts, Pequot *came to the Norwich & Worcester in 1857. The balloon-type smokestack had a large metal screen at the top to trap sparks and live embers. A few always managed to escape; trackside fires arose in dry weather.*

$400,000 for "the purpose of enabling the company to complete that part of their railroad which lies in the Commonwealth."[9] This accounted for the finishing of the fourth section of construction ahead of the third. The Norwich Court of Common Council also responded and lent the railroad $100,000 at 6 percent, taking fifteen hundred shares of railroad stock as collateral. Later the council loaned another $100,000. Without these loans further construction would have been impossible.

Eight years after its charter was granted, the Norwich & Worcester commenced operations, in 1840. However, construction costs were almost $500,000 more than the McNeill estimate; the decade of the 1840s was not a happy one financially. In time the road would be in debt more than $1,000,000, "have a payroll three months in arrears, and machinery and property much dilapidated."[10] Directors had underestimated expenses and the cost of borrowing, and had overcalculated the railroad's revenues. The big $60,000 steamboat dock at Norwich, for instance, was not even finished when the Norwich & Worcester opened, obliging the railroad to transfer traffic by stage some distance to the commercial wharf. Although the Norwich & Worcester was authorized to own steamboats, lack of money forced it initially to contract for such services. Its first contract steamer, *Norwich*, left Monday, Wednesday, and Friday evenings, and arrived in New York City the following mornings. It returned to Norwich every Tuesday, Thursday, and Saturday. Within a

When President Ulysses S. Grant visited Windham County last century, he utilized the Norwich & Worcester. Engine Wauregan, *built in company shops at Norwich, hauled the train and was gaily decorated with bunting and flags. The tender quoted popular Civil War statements by Grant on each side. One said: "Keep quiet! I'll take you through safely," and on the other he told a Confederate general, "I propose to move immediately on your works."*

GREAT NORTHERN AND EASTERN ROUTE,

Via Norwich and Worcester,

For New London, Norwich, Worcester, Providence, Boston,
Nashua, Lowell, Concord, White Mountains, Fitchburg,
Palmer, and all way Stations on the

| Norwich and Worcester, | Worcester and Nashua, | New London, Willimantie and Palmer, | Fitchburg and Worcester, |
| Hartford, Providence & Fishkill, | Stoney Brook & Lowell, | Boston and New York Central, | Boston and Worcester, |

And all Railroads in Massachusetts and Northern New Hampshire and Vermont.

Steamers Commonwealth and Connecticut leave daily, (Sundays excepted,) from Pier 18, N. R.
at 5 o'clock P. M.   Winter months 4 P. M.

Connecting at Allyn's Point with New and Splendid sixteen wheel Cars over the Norwich and Worcester Railroad.
State Rooms can be engaged by applying at the office on the Wharf, or on board the Boats.
An Express Freight Train leaves Allyn's Point immediately on arrival of the Boats.

The flux of human traffic at New York bound for distant New England was immense. Ads like this were common, the Norwich & Worcester always hoping to win patrons away from the rival Stonington Railroad.

SHSA

SHSA

Judging from the weather, substituting an iron snow plow in place of a cowcatcher improved the efficiency of Nathan Hale.

COLLECTION OF ALICE A. RAMSDELL

One of the busiest railroad junctions in northeastern Connecticut was Putnam, where the Norwich & Worcester main track crossed the Boston-Hartford route. In the left foreground a Norwich & Worcester freight train eases up to the first union station, while in the left background a consist steams out for Hartford via Willimantic.

few years daily departures were made possible by using additional steamboats such as *Charter Oak, Thames, Worcester,* and *New York.*

Four of the Norwich & Worcester's earliest engines were built by Rogers, Ketchum, and Grosvenor of New Jersey at $7,000 apiece. Other builders providing locomotives over the years included William Norris of Philadelphia; Hinckley and Drury of Taunton, Massachusetts; and George Griggs of Providence. Then in 1868 the Norwich & Worcester began manufacturing its own engines in the company shops at Norwich. Early Norwich & Worcester coaches were well constructed and differed from the early stagecoach-body designs of the Stonington Railroad. In 1847 the railroad founded the Norwich Car Manufactory, which eventually supplied rolling stock for many other railroads. The firm in the 1860s fabricated luxury cars that were considered "superior to those of any other railroad in the country."[11] They were divided to provide separate accommodations for gentlemen and ladies, according to the sales literature, and "were carpeted and in every respect beautifully finished with wide convenient sofas, dressing tables, washstands, and other arrangements for the comfort of passengers."[12]

The railroad's steamboat dock at Norwich—once completed—was accessible for most of the year, but long and hard winters usually found the Thames River frozen at its headwaters. "In consequence of this state of things, multitudes of travellers

RIDING ON ENGINE OR TENDER
STRICTLY PROHIBITED.

NOTICE TO ENGINEMEN.

No person will be permitted to ride on the Engine or Tender, without special permission from the Superintendent.

P. H. M. Andrews Sup't.

Businesses along a railroad often took ads when it came time for the company to produce a "guidebook," but usually with less cynicism than this hotel proprietor.

The Only Second-Class Hotel in New England.

The Olive Branch Hotel,

DANIELSONVILLE, CONN.

NOTED FAR AND WIDE FOR ITS

Hard Beds, Tough Steaks and Poor Cooking.

Under the Mismanagement of STEPHEN H. COLE,

Notorious as the Stingiest Man in Windham County.

A trio of Shetucket River scenes at Norwich. . .

[TOP] Brick buildings encase works of the Norwich Car Manufactory owned by the Norwich & Worcester.

[RIGHT] The Ferry Street yards with a three-car passenger train at the depot ready to go north.

[BOTTOM] Multiple engines rigorously test the new iron bridge reaching over to Laurel Hill.

With paddle wheels madly churning, City of Worcester *turns in New York's East River and heads for Long Island Sound. Her deck plan and room rates appear underneath.*

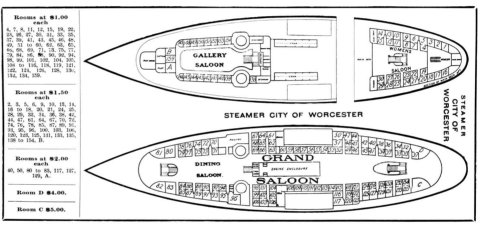

Rooms at $1.00
each

4, 7, 8, 11, 12, 15, 19, 22,
23, 26, 27, 30, 31, 33, 35,
37, 39, 41, 43, 45, 46, 48,
49, 51 to 60, 62, 63, 65,
66, 68, 69, 71, 73, 75, 77,
79, 84, 86, 88, 90, 92, 94,
98, 99, 101, 102, 104, 105,
108 to 116, 118, 119, 121,
122, 124, 126, 128, 130,
132, 134, 159.

Rooms at $1.50
each

2, 3, 5, 6, 9, 10, 13, 14,
16 to 18, 20, 21, 24, 25,
28, 29, 32, 34, 36, 38, 42,
44, 47, 61, 64, 67, 70, 72,
74, 76, 78, 85, 87, 89, 91,
93, 95, 96, 100, 103, 106,
120, 123, 125, 131, 133, 135,
138 to 154, B.

Rooms at $2.00
each

40, 50, 80 to 83, 117, 127,
129, A.

Room D $4.00.

Room C $5.00.

STEAMER CITY OF WORCESTER

[RIGHT AND BELOW] The first boat to serve the Norwich & Worcester was named Norwich. *She terminated her long career on the Hudson River as a tug. In contrast,* City of Lowell *was the last vessel the rail-road bought — seen here at New London.*

shunned the Norwich route in winter, taking the Stonington Line, or the circuitous inland railway route via New Haven, Hartford, Springfield, and Worcester instead," admitted the *Norwich Courier.*[13] This led the railroad to construct a new dock downstream at Allyn's Point in Gales Ferry, where the river was usually free of ice. To reach it, a six-mile single track from Norwich was built across the Shetucket River, tunnelled under Laurel Hill, and continued down the east bank of the Thames to Allyn's Point. It opened in 1843. Today this marine terminal is owned by the Dow Chemical Company.

After the Civil War the Norwich & Worcester became a leased enterprise for the remainder of the nineteenth century, though an actual sellout of the road never occurred. The first lessor was the Boston, Hartford, & Erie Railroad, followed by the New York & New England, its successor the New England Railroad, and finally

Perhaps the glory years of the Norwich & Worcester and its Norwich Line of boats were enjoyed when the entire property was skillfully run by the New York & New England Railroad. The leased line was kept in fine order, and the steamboat express trains were well patronized by the public.

R & LHS

44

These stations, Danielsonville at left and Dayville, were intact in the 1930s when photographed by an inveterate station hobbyist named Irving Drake, more of whose product appears in Chapter Five. But the boat trains were then gone, and the main remaining ornament was the State of Maine Express, *a night sleeper from New York to Portland, Maine, along the main line of the old Norwich & Worcester road. But that train was later rerouted via Providence, then abandoned. You can't get to Maine in a train anymore.*

Distance from New London	Time Table 49 In Effect June 15, 1908 STATIONS.
.....	New London_____N
1.39	Groton _____D
3.57	Navy Yard_____D
6.27	Gales Ferry__ ___D
7.36	Allyns Point_____
.....	Stoddard's Wharf_
9.39	Sand Pit_____
.....	Fort Point_____
12.39	Crown Hill_____
13.53	Norwich _____N
14.82	Greenville _____
15.08	Canal Siding__ ___
16.43	Tafts _____N
18.47	Lisbon Siding_____
.....	Reades _____
22.94	Jewett City_____N
.....	Bishops _____
29.42	Plainfield _____N
32.51	Central Village__N
33.80	Wauregan _____
38.39	Danielson _____D
41.20	Dayville _____D
46.83	Putnam _____N
48.38	Mechanicsville____
48.80	West Thompson D
50.41	Grosvenordale ____
51.92	N.Grosvenord'le_D
.....	Wilsons _____
.....	Perrys _____
56.37	Webster _____N
57.46	North Webster____
61.14	Oxford _____D
63.53	North Oxford_____
64.39	Maywood _____
.....	Stone's Crossing__
68.00	Auburn _____D
70.65	Cambridge Street_
71.45	So. Worcester___N
72.39	Worcester _____N

the New York, New Haven & Hartford. Attractive rentals were negotiated, and the lessor was responsible for keeping the property in good condition. Stockholders collected their dividends and in the last century never resented the arrangements.

Although it longed to own and operate its own steamboats, the Norwich & Worcester failed in its first nautical venture as a result of poor advice and bad luck. The first reversal was the catastrophic sinking of *Atlantic,** then the most luxurious steamboat on Long Island Sound and the first to have gas illumination. Then the *Mohegan* was wrecked shortly thereafter. Because of these losses the railroad sold its remaining boats (*Worcester, Cleopatra,* and *Knickerbocker*) to the Norwich & New London Steamboat Company, which provided the services until 1860, whereupon renewal terms could not be arranged. This forced the Norwich & Worcester (in 1860) back into the steamboat business, setting up the Norwich and New York Transportation Company. The firm took over boats of the Norwich & New London Steamboat Company and also purchased new steamers—known as the "City" series—including *City of Norwich, City of New London, City of Boston,*** and *City of New York.* It became a moneymaker. Its most palatial, iron-hulled vessels were *City of Worcester*—costing $408,000—and *City of Lowell* ("The Greyhound of the Sound"), which arrived in 1881 and 1894 respectively. *Lowell,* regularly clocked at 22.2 miles per hour, was often regarded as one of the finest vessels on the Atlantic seaboard.

In 1852 the New London, Willimantic & Palmer Railroad—the second railroad to enter the "Rose City"—built a connecting track at Norwich across a branch of the Yantic River to connect with the Norwich & Worcester. Land settlements were made in 1853, and by the following March certain steamboat express trains of the Norwich & Worcester could run directly to New London's railroad steamboat dock via the new connection and down the track of the New London, Willimantic & Palmer past Montville and Waterford. Depending upon ice conditions, vessels of the Norwich Line could then put in at either New London, Allyn's Point, or Norwich. In addition to passengers, a large freight business was done in cotton and fruit.

When first leased in 1868 the Norwich & Worcester Railroad had a net income of more than $200,000. Steady growth and success warranted a stock recapitalization to nearly $3,000,000 in 1874. Its Norwich & New York Transportation Company was, in the late 1870s, returning more than $27,000 a year in dividends, owing to the Norwich Line's immense popularity. Through and local freight traffic also

*Built by Bishop & Simonson, New York City. Fourteen hundred tons, 350 feet in length, 1,573-horsepower steam engine. Its run from New York City to Norwich took six hours and 57 minutes. Wrecked in bad weather off New London — Thanksgiving Day, November 26, 1846, crashing to pieces on Fisher Island's rocky shore. Forty-two perished and the ship's bell clanged throughout the calamity.

**Fully equipped purchase cost amounted to $202,000. *City of Boston* and *City of New York* were passenger vessels; *Norwich* and *New London* were freighters. The latter cost $150,000 each. The sumptuous passenger vessel *City of Lawrence* arrived in 1867, delayed by the Civil War.

increased. When the Norwich & Worcester lease was transferred to the New Haven Railroad in 1898, it had an attractive cash surplus of nearly $1,000,000. Its roadbed was substantially built and well maintained, and the company ran a first-class fleet of steamboats. For the next seventy years, though, the Norwich and Worcester would rise and fall with the New Haven Railroad's adventures and disasters.

Thanks to highway competition, to which the state was uncharacteristically generous, Norwich & Worcester steam passenger trains gave way in the late 1920s to a "gas buggy." Not long after even that was discontinued. To the joy of some, self-propelled passenger car service reappeared in 1952, with equipment manufactured this time by the Budd Company, for the route fom New London to Worcester. But that was ended on April 30, 1971, by Penn Central, then bankrupt like the New Haven Railroad it had swallowed. More recently the old Norwich & Worcester was bought by the aggressive Providence & Worcester, which runs its freight service. Once in a while the Providence & Worcester trots out an excursion passenger train along the iron route down which, a century ago, rode the farmers, drummers, and gentry to take the great palace steamers at Norwich for the sinful city of New York.

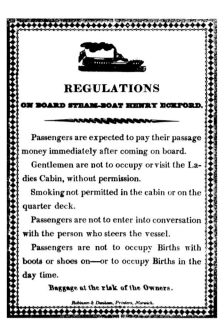

Chapter Three Footnotes

1. *Worcester & Norwich Rail-Road Company, 1835* [annual report] (N. p., n.d.), 28-30.

2. *Norwich & Worcester Railroad, 1835* [annual report] (N.p., n.d.).

3. *Windham County Advertiser,* 25 January 1832.

4. Connecticut General Assembly, An Act to Incorporate the Boston,Norwich and New London Railroad, May session, 1832, Public Records, Connecticut State Capitol Building.

5. Massachusetts General Assembly, An Act to Incorporate the Worcester & Norwich Railroad, 1833 session, Massachusetts State Capitol Building.

6. *Worcester & Norwich Railroad Company, 1835* [annual report] (N.p., n.d.), 35-36.

7. *Norwich Courier,* 25 November 1835.

8. Ibid., 21 November 1838.

9. *Memorial of the Norwich & Worcester Railroad Company before the Senate and House of Representatives of the Commonwealth of Massachusetts in General Court,* January 1838, Document No. 41.

10. *Norwich & Worcester Railroad Annual Report for the Year Ending 1849* (Norwich: John Stedman, 1849), 3-6.

11. Withington, *First Twenty Years,* 11.

12. Ibid., 11-12.

13. *Norwich Courier,* 15 January 1841.

NOTICE.

In consequence of injury to the Norwich Railroad caused by the late storm, no Steamboat Train, via Norwich, will leave Boston to-day.

WM. PARKER, *Sup't B. & W. R. R.*

Boston, March 30, 1843.

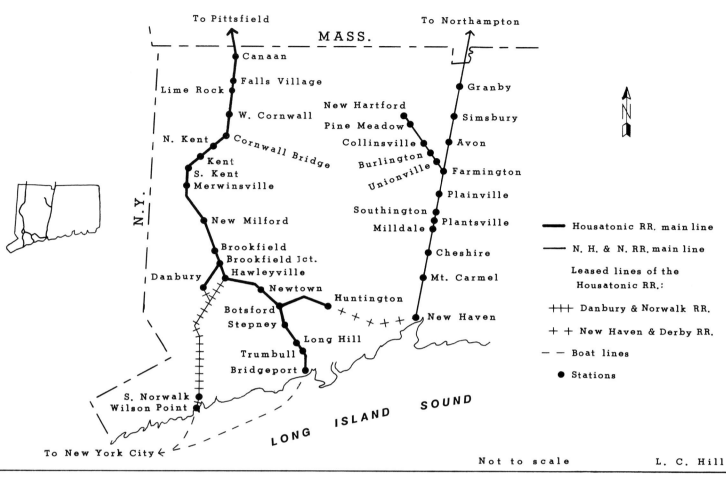

Housatonic Railroad
New Haven & Northampton — The Canal RR.

To Pittsfield

To Northampton

MASS.

Canaan

Falls Village

Lime Rock

Granby

W. Cornwall

New Hartford

Simsbury

N. Kent

Pine Meadow

Cornwall Bridge

Collinsville

Avon

Kent

Burlington

S. Kent

Unionville

Farmington

Merwinsville

Plainville

New Milford

Southington

Plantsville

Brookfield

Milldale

Brookfield Jct.

Danbury

Hawleyville

Cheshire

Newtown

Mt. Carmel

Botsford

Huntington

Stepney

New Haven

Long Hill

Trumbull

Bridgeport

S. Norwalk
Wilson Point

LONG ISLAND SOUND

To New York City

N

—— Housatonic RR. main line

— N. H. & N. RR. main line

Leased lines of the
Housatonic RR.:

+++ Danbury & Norwalk RR.

+ + New Haven & Derby RR.

– – Boat lines

● Stations

N.Y.

Not to scale   L. C. Hill

HOUSATONIC RAILROAD TRAIN PASSING PARLOR ROCK STATION.

Chapter Four

Two Interior Routes

In reviewing the causes which have led to the failure of this road so far to pay dividends, we cannot help feeling that the Housatonic Railroad has deserved better.

—*American Railroad Journal, October 20, 1855*

This is a crisis in the history of New Haven! By prompt action, we can secure a prosperity such as we have never had, and open resources of trade such as we never possessed: by supineness, we lose the whole.

—*Flyer issued by "Friends of the New Haven & Northampton Railroad," 1845*

Two more Connecticut railroad companies aspired to reach Massachusetts from Long Island Sound: the Housatonic and New Haven & Northampton railroads. Their individual histories were quite similar. Canal history had preceded their formative stages; both also suffered through initial years of financial disappointment. The shared dream of uniting with railroads at or near the Berkshires meant communication with Albany on the west and Boston to the east. Some visionaries thought even remote Vermont might be reached as well. In later years both roads built or acquired branches and leased lines. To maintain its monopolistic hold on southern New England, the imperial New York, New Haven & Hartford Railroad Company acquired both these interior routes before the nineteenth century closed, to thwart invading competitors.

The Housatonic Railroad

A movement to make a canal of the Housatonic River from Stratford, Connecticut, north to Great Barrington, Massachusetts, was actively pursued in the early 1820s. A charter was secured for the Housatonic Canal Company, and stock subscription books were opened "at various taverns" along the river at New Milford, Kent, Cornwall, and Canaan. But not even the persuasive powers of strong waters could pry open enough Yankee pocketbooks. The dream and the project were abandoned. Fourteen years later promoters again invaded much the same Housatonic River terrain with a fresh pitch: the new wave of the future was the railroad. At the May 1836 session of the Connecticut legislature a charter petition was favorably acted upon, creating "The Ousatonic Railroad Company."[1] (Though the charter name reflected an early attempt by white men to spell an Indian word meaning "place beyond the mountains," the engrossed act filed with the secretary of state used the more familiar orthography.) The act empowered the incorporators to build a railroad from the Massachusetts state line at Ashley Falls down the Housatonic River valley to Brookfield, beyond which village they could elect to terminate "at the City of Bridgeport, the northern terminus of the Fairfield County Railroad at Danbury, or through Danbury to Ridgefield to the western line of the State as to meet the New York & Harlem Railroad"[2] which was then contemplated. Former Governor Gideon Tomlinson was one of the line's biggest promoters.

NO CHANGE OF CARS BETWEEN NEW YORK CITY AND THE BERKSHIRE HILLS.

HOUSATONIC RAILROAD.

THE ONLY ROUTE TO LENOX.

OFFICE OF THE GENERAL PASSENGER AGENT.

BRIDGEPORT, CONN., JUNE 5TH, 1889.

To THE TOURIST :—

ON Monday, June 10th, 1889, the Housatonic Railroad will commence running THE FAMOUS LIMITED EXPRESS TRAINS between New York City, GREAT BARRINGTON, STOCKBRIDGE, LENOX and PITTSFIELD, making connection to and from North Adams and Williamstown, leaving New York (Grand Central Depot), 3.00 P. M., arriving in Pittsfield 7.45 P. M. Returning, leave Pittsfield 4.20 P. M., arriving in New York 9.00 P. M.

The equipment of the LIMITED EXPRESS TRAINS is unexcelled, the Drawing-Room cars and coaches are of the latest pattern, and built expressly for the Lenox and "Berkshire Hills" travel.

An ancient baggage car of the Housatonic Railroad can be observed here; the occasion that has gathered so many people around it is not known. The engine, No. 11, was an early product of the prosperous Rogers Locomotive Works in New Jersey, and their name is visible on the steam chest.

No active measures were taken to sell Housatonic Railroad stock until the winter of 1836. Through the intervening months an engineer named Roswell B. Mason* located the line and prepared an estimate of construction costs. The corporation was organized in the spring of 1837, with early meetings held at the old Sterling Hotel in Bridgeport. Mason's report was duly accepted, and the city of Bridgeport was selected as the southern terminal. Why Bridgeport?

The answer was purely economic. The city would subscribe to $100,000 of Housatonic stock, and it possessed steamboat connections. Later it took another $50,000 in railroad paper. Interestingly, Bridgeport was not yet a municipality, but it was so eager to get the railroad that it secured a city charter with a provision enabling it to issue bonds for the stock purchase.[3] Mason's construction estimate of the seventy-three-mile road, from Bridgeport to the Massachusetts state line, was slightly over the $1,000,000 mark, or about $14,000 per mile. The railroad would run near the Housatonic to Brookfield, where it would then diverge through the countryside to Hawleyville, Newtown, Botsford, Stepney, and Trumbull, before entering metropolitan Bridgeport.

Promoters of the Housatonic Railroad envisioned their new line as serving two needs. First, it would tap the upstate marble and granite belt, the iron-mine industry around Salisbury, the famous lime business of Canaan, the porcelain clay operations of New Milford, and the iron industry of Litchfield County. These freight manifests would be routed south to the steamboat dock at Bridgeport for transshipment to Atlantic ports. The second goal was to form a water-rail route between New York City and Albany when the Hudson River froze over. At that time no railroad existed along the Hudson's banks. If the Housatonic dream were realized, thousands of New York City patrons could board a year-round Long Island Sound steamboat for Bridgeport, take a connecting Housatonic train to the Berkshires, then travel over the Western Railroad of Massachusetts to reach Albany—somewhat roundabout routing, but nevertheless believable in that day.

*Of New Hartford, New York, later a Housatonic Railroad superintendent. Trained on Schuylkill and Morris canals and later headed construction on the Illinois Central Railroad. Mayor of Chicago when the Great Fire of that city occurred. Succeeded on the Housatonic by George William Whistler, son of Major George Washington Whistler, surveyor of the Stonington Railroad.

49

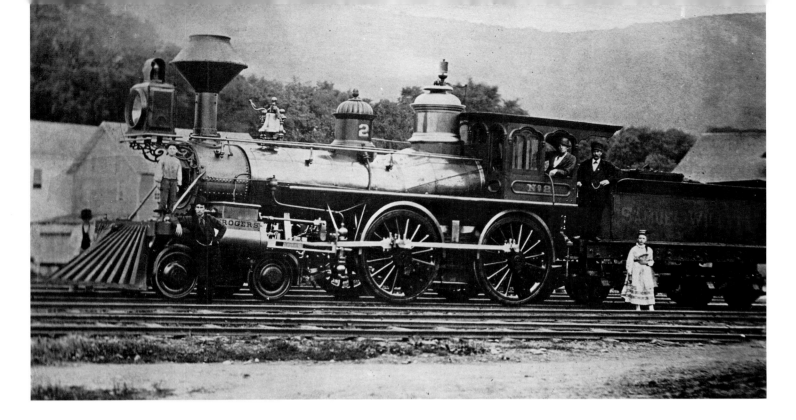

The Bridgeport firm of Bishop & Sykes won the Housatonic construction contract. Alfred Bishop* headed the firm; his own company would later build the Naugatuck and the New York & New Haven railroads. Bishop & Sykes took $636,000 in cash, in addition to nearly $300,000 of Housatonic stock[4] as partial compensation, and thereby became a principal stockholder. By 1840 Bishop could report that the first thirty-five miles of line were completed from Bridgeport to New Milford, including an extensive rock tunnel at Hawleyville. Forty more miles of track opened to the state line two years later. A reporter for the *Bridgeport Sentinel* rode that first train to New Milford: "The black ponies going tandem [referring to two engines] left Bridgeport at 9 o'clock in the morning taking with them some forty rods of cars. The train was decorated with flags and accompanied by the Bridgeport Band."[5] The first timetable noted that cars would leave New Milford every morning, except Sunday, at 6, and arrive in Bridgeport in time for passengers to take the steamboat to New York City. A return trip from Bridgeport was scheduled to leave at 2 p.m. after another steamboat returned.

Sometimes family members appear in old railroad photos. The daughter of one crew member here is bedecked in lace, and the boy, standing under the headlight, is in Sunday best. So also are the crew members.

To extend the Housatonic north of Canaan into the Berkshires and ultimately have trains reach Albany, the state of Massachusetts chartered the Berkshire Railroad from Ashley Falls to Sheffield, Great Barrington, and West Stockbridge. The twenty-one-mile line opened the same month as the Housatonic Railroad, whereupon the latter perpetually leased the former. Then the Housatonic also leased the little West Stockbridge Railroad, which supplied the requisite connection from West Stockbridge to "State Line" station on the Western Railroad of Massachusetts. (The Western Railroad stretched from Worcester to Albany.) The West Stockbridge line was coleased with the Hudson & Berkshire, a firm which was part of the Western Railroad syndicate. To prevent a lopsided alliance, the syndicate permitted the Connecticut road to run as many trains to Albany as it wanted whenever the Hudson River froze over but restricted traffic to only one train a day each way when the river was navigable.[6] The final addition in the Berkshires occurred in 1850 when the Housatonic Railroad leased the twenty-three-mile Stockbridge & Pittsfield. It ran from Van Deusenville (on the Housatonic road) to Pittsfield via Lenox and Lee. Pittsfield was another point also served by the Western Railroad.

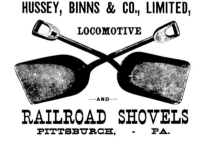
*Born Stamford, Connecticut, 1798. Removed to New Jersey. Active in farming; formulated his own construction data techniques using pickaxe, shovel, and wheelbarrow. Built Morris (New Jersey) Canal, and bridge over Raritan River at New Brunswick. Died at Saratoga, New York, at age fifty-one.

50

Company shops of the Housatonic were situated in the Amesville section of Falls Village. In this close-up view the reader can spot the turntable (with Engine No. 3 upon it), coach and freight cars, wheels, and the engine stalls. The track in the far left foreground has an inspection pit. If all the workers seem to be loafing, be not cynical and remember that for 19th century photographers one had to hold restfully still.

[OPPOSITE PAGE, TOP] An overall view of the Falls Village complex. The Housatonic River was tapped as a water power source. Where once the rich and famous were transported over this route by the New Haven, a tourist rail line now operates.

Financial embarrassment characterized most of the Housatonic's early years, the chief culprit being the panic of 1837. Bridgeport ultimately defaulted on her bonds issued to buy Housatonic stock. The railroad engaged sheriffs, who got judgments and executions against the city for nonpayment. Papers were served on the mayor, clerk, common council, and freemen of the municipality, but no money could be obtained. Amazingly, sheriffs broke into grocery and dry goods stores and sold their stock for cash. They claimed the stores were on the grand tax list and were the last resort. Delinquent stock payments skyrocketed, and obstacles to bank borrowing were common. The railroad's directors eventually went to Hartford to plead with the hardhearted legislature for aid "in any form," but the requests were sharply turned down.[7] Demand notes were ultimately executed, and a preferred stock issue was sold. Only after a return of traffic in later years did finances improve.

Track first installed on the Housatonic Railroad, as on many new railways of the time, consisted of iron straps which were attached to the tops of timber rails. Often the straps would curl up dangerously at broken ends of joints, causing "snakeheads." Occasionally a snake-head would even shoot up through the wooden floor of a passing coach. At least one such incident precipitated a public notice in 1844:

TO THE PUBLIC!

The undersigned passengers in the cars of the Housatonic Railroad this morning feel ourselves bound to caution the Public against said Rail-Road. When within about three hundred paces of the depot at Newtown the car in which we were seated was thrown off the track with great violence, and it was only through the interposition of a merciful Providence that we escaped without the loss of life. The railroad is in a most dangerous condition and we counted in a distance of sixty rods over fifty "snake-heads." Nothing but an imperative sense of duty to the travelling public has induced us to caution them against patronizing said railroad.[8]

The Housatonic's earliest wood-burning locomotives were built by Matthias Baldwin's firm in Philadelphia and the Rogers shops in New Jersey. They were of the 4-2-0 and 4-4-0 wheel designs. An assortment of four- and eight-wheel passenger and baggage coaches was acquired, plus a variety of freight cars. General offices controlled the company from Bridgeport, and company repair shops were situated in the Amesville section of Falls Village, the Housatonic River providing

waterpower for machinery. Like all early nineteenth-century trains, the Housatonic's stopped frequently en route to replenish their supply of firewood, a process called simply "woodin' up." The Pittsfield firm of Rockwell & Pomeroy supplied the locomotive firewood requirements in 1856, delivering 145 cords at Kent, 189 at Lee, and a whopping 350—probably in staggered deliveries—at New Milford. The charge was 15¢ a cord.[9] For the uninitiated, a cord in 1985 sells for $100 or more, a rise which should be taken into account when thinking about financial statistics in the early days of railroading.

From the late 1840s onward the railroad enjoyed a more attractive business climate. The New York & New Haven Railroad opened in 1848, bringing with it a traffic exchange at Bridgeport. A year later the Naugatuck Railroad came to the same

A huge, wedge-type snow plow momentarily pauses at New Milford, Connecticut, while cleaning up after the big Blizzard of 1888. A number of engines are linked together to push the plow car. Often a snow plow train would become stalled in a drift.

This marvelous scene was taken at Bridge-port after the Housatonic Railroad erected facilities there. Engine Lee, *named for that Berkshire hamlet, pokes forth. All those employed at this depot seem to have posed.*

town, at first using the Housatonic's depot and facilities for a rental fee. Gross receipts in 1853 reached $325,000. A typical passenger train during this period left Canaan at 6 a.m. and arrived in Bridgeport four hours later. The Civil War brought a modest increase in traffic earnings with the movement of troops and supplies. A special milk train was now put on to serve Housatonic River valley dairy farmers whose products went to New York City. Stations along the route, however, needed attention, a fact frequently noted during this era by the Connecticut railroad commissioners. A dilapidated freight car, for example, was serving as the public depot at Merwinsville, Connecticut, as late as 1867. Another handicap was the fact that the railroad right of way had very little fencing; cattle frequently strayed onto the tracks and, when struck, caused occasional derailments.

A harplike stub switch stand leads cars into an old quarry at Lee, Massachusetts; at right is a bucolic scene at North Kent.

Much of the railroad was reconstructed or improved in the 1870s. The company installed steel rails, rebuilt nearly every bridge, applied new ballast to tracks, and fitted safety switches. Eighteen new station houses were constructed from 1869 on,

and in 1875 nine "frost-proof" water tanks were fabricated at strategic points along the route. Freight revenues that year alone stood at $460,000.[10] But it was during the 1880s that the Housatonic Railroad took on something of "system" dimensions in Connecticut. The additions included the 1882 purchase of the little New York, Housatonic & Northern; the 1886 lease of the Danbury & Norwalk; the 1889 lease of the New Haven & Derby; and new track construction from Botsford to Huntington in order for the Housatonic to link up with the Derby road.

Chartered in 1864, the New York, Housatonic & Northern was a New York corporation authorized in Connecticut to build from Brookfield (on the Housatonic Railroad) to Danbury and the state line, with the aim of reaching White Plains and the New York & Harlem Railroad. The line was to carry passengers off the Housatonic to New York City by way of the Harlem road and haul milk products produced in

One of the most picturesque of all Connecticut railway depots was located on the Housatonic's main line at Cornwall Bridge. The station platform is enormously long.

A small number of tunnels were engineered in the state in the last century. This one was blasted at Hawleyville. The tools of the trade in the 1840s consisted of black powder, horses and carts, much back-breaking labor, and considerable quantities of liquor.

Wreck at Iron Ledge, Trumbull, about 1900: Two trains came together here, on single track, because train orders were mis-read. Crowning the debris at right is a load of wood boards. The engines are heaped up at left. Several crew members were killed.

the Housatonic River valley. In 1868 the line was opened, but for only five miles, from Brookfield to Danbury. The project then sank, creditors attached the property, and in 1872 it was leased to the Housatonic, which finally bought it ten years later. A single engine, a single passenger coach, and three freight cars made up the rolling stock roster. But the addition of the New York, Housatonic & Northern conveniently connected the Housatonic to the Danbury & Norwalk Railroad at busy Danbury, and that itself was a valuable interchange point, since the New York & New England Railroad also passed through town.

A baggage car and coach make up this Housatonic Railroad train. Engine No. 3 does the honors. The majestic Pittsfield depot towers above this scene in the 1870s.

The leasing of the Danbury & Norwalk and New Haven & Derby roads gave the Housatonic Railroad a new dock on Long Island Sound at Wilson Point (in South Norwalk) and a formal entrance into New Haven proper. These additions rein-

GRAND
EXCURSIONS

ON THE

HOUSATONIC RAIL ROAD,

JULY FOURTH, 1851.

For the accommodation of persons desiring to attend the GRAND CELEBRATIONS of American Independence, to take place at

BRIDGEPORT AND PITTSFIELD,

Trains will run over the Housatonic Rail Road on that day as follows:

TRAINS INTO BRIDGEPORT.

A Special Train will leave Newtown at 7 A. M., arriving at 8.00 A. M.   A Train will leave Barrington at 6.00 A. M. and arrive at 10.15 A. M.
A Train will also leave New Milford at 7 A. M. and arrive at 9.15 A. M.   A Train will also leave Pittsfield at 8.30 A. M. and arrive at 1.45 P. M.

Returning, Trains will leave Bridgeport at 5.30 P. M. for Pittsfield and all intermediate Stations.

TICKETS WILL BE SOLD AT THE FOLLOWING RATES:

From Pittsfield, Lenox Furnace, and Lee, to Bridgeport and back, $1 50 ; South Lee and Stockbridge, $1 25 ; State Line, West Stockbridge, Glendale, Gaylord's Bridge, and all intermediate Stations, to Bridgeport and back, $1 ; New Milford, 75 cts. ; Brookfield and Hawleyville, 62½ cts. ; Newtown, 50 cts. ; Botsford, 37½ cts. ; Stepney, Beers' Mills, and Trumbull, 25 cts.

All Excursion Tickets will be good to return on the 5th.

STEAMERS WILL MAKE EXCURSIONS UPON LONG ISLAND SOUND,

Giving to persons an opportunity of enjoying a sail of two or three hours, and will return in season for the Afternoon Trains going North.

TRAINS INTO PITTSFIELD.

A Special Train will leave Canaan at 7 A. M., arriving at 9.15 A. M.   A Train will also leave Barrington at 10 A. M., and arrive at 11.30 A. M.

Returning, a Train will leave Pittsfield at 3.15 P. M. for Bridgeport, stopping at all Stations.

And in order to afford the people upon the line of the Road an opportunity to witness the display of

FIRE WORKS IN THE EVENING,

A Train will also leave Pittsfield for Canaan and West Stockbridge, at 10 o'clock P. M., stopping at all intermediate Stations.

To enable all who may wish to be present, and participate in the Ceremonies of the Day,

THE FARE TO PITTSFIELD WILL BE REDUCED TO THE FOLLOWING LOW RATES:

From Canaan to Pittsfield and back, $1 ; Sheffield, 87½ cts. ; Barrington, 75 cts. ; Van Deusenville, 70 cts. ; West Stockbridge, 75 cts. ; Housatonic, 65 cts. ; Algers, 60 cts. ; Glendale, 55 cts. ; Stockbridge, 50 cts. ; South Lee, 45 cts. ; Lee, 35 cts. ; Lenox Furnace, 30 cts. ; Lenox Station and New Lenox, 25 cents.

Excursion Tickets will be good to return by either Train on the 5th.

TIME TABLE.

TRAINS GOING SOUTH.

Pittsfield, leave	- 8,30 A. M.	West Cornwall,	- 10,50 A. M.	7,00 A. M.
Lenox Furnace,	- 8,50 "	Cornwall Bridge,	- 11,02 "	7,10 "
Lee, - -	- 8,55 "	Kent, - -	- 11,23 "	7,32 "
South Lee,	- 9,02 "	Gaylord's Bridge,	11,37 "	7,50 "
Stockbridge, -	- 9,10 "	New Milford, -	12,00 M.	8,15 " 7,00 A. M.
Algers, -	- 9,27 "	Brookfield, -	12,30 P. M.	8,35 " 7,20 "
West Stockbridge,	- 9,20 "	Hawleyville, -	12,43 "	8,55 " 7,40 "
Van Deusenville,	- 9,40 "	Newtown, -	12,56 "	9,10 " 8,00 " 7,00 A. M.
Barrington, -	- 9,52 " 6,00 A. M.	Botsford, -	1,07 "	9,30 " 8,20 " 7,15 "
Sheffield, -	- ,10,06 " 6,13 "	Stepney, -	1,20 "	9,50 " 8,45 " 7,35 "
Canaan, -	- 10,21 " 6,30 "	Bridgeport, arrive,	1,45 "	10,15 " 9,15 " 8,00 "
Falls Village, -	- 10,35 " 6,43 "			

TRAINS GOING NORTH.

Canaan, leave	- 7,00 A. M.		2,00 P. M.
Sheffield, -	- 7,15 "		2,15 "
Barrington, -	- 7,30 " 10,00 A. M.	2,32 "
Van Deusenville, -	- 7,40 " 10,10 "	2,42 "
West Stockbridge, -	- 9,20 "	
Housatonic, -	- 7,45 " 10,15 "	2,47 "
Algers, -	- 7,50 " 10,20 "	2,50 "
Stockbridge, -	- 8,10 " 10,34 "	3,07 "
South Lee, -	- 8,17 " 10,40 "	3,12 "
Lee, -	- 8,30 " 10,55 "	3,23 "
Lenox Furnace, -	- 8,50 " 11,00 "	3,35 "
Pittsfield, arrive,	- 9,15 " 11,30 "	3,55 "

No Freight Trains will run upon the 4th. The Regular Passenger Trains will run as usual.

FOR NEW HAVEN.—Trains will leave Bridgeport at 9.35, 9.50, 10.25 and 11.45 A. M., and at 2 00 and 5.25 P. M

BRIDGEPORT, June 25, 1851.   C. A. KIRTLAND, Superintendent.

THE

❖ Connecticut Detective Agency, ❖

Established 1871.

COMPETENT OPERATIVES FURNISHED FOR ANY LEGITIMATE DETECTIVE BUSINESS IN ANY PORTION OF THE UNITED STATES.

FRANK B. TAYLOR, Superintendent.

P. O. BOX 1745.

Bridgeport, Conn. *January 3rd 188 2*

The Housatonic Rail Road Co

To Frank B. Taylor Dr for services rendered and money paid out in capturing Geo E. Botsford who obstructed the Company's track on the night of Dec 26th 1881.

Dec 28.	Dinner at Grand Central Hotel	.50
" "	Paid Patrick Girand for trouble in coming to see me	.25
" "	Team to go to Palestine	2.00
" "	Drinks &c while obtaining evidence in Bar rooms	2.60
" 29	Dinner at Dicks Hotel	.50
" "	Paid for refreshments &c in Bar rooms	1.80
" " " "	Geo E. Botsford supper	.50
" " " "	Stockings for Botsford	.25
" 30	Breakfast for Botsford	.50
" "	Paid for team at Newtown to go to trial	1.25
" "	Dinners for Seymour, Botsford and self	150
		$11.65
Three days services for myself @ 5.00		15.00
		$26.65

Correct

L. B. Gillison
Supt

Received Payment

Frank B. Taylor

57

forced the Housatonic's strength in the western half of the state, and that power attracted overtures from the New York & New England Railroad.

In 1891 "The New England" opened its long-awaited Western Division from Waterbury to the Hudson River at Fishkill (by way of Hawleyville and Danbury). There ferry boats shuttled cars across the Hudson to the important Erie Railroad connection at Newburgh. The New England rivaled certain routes of the New York, New Haven & Hartford, and frequently the former devised plans to break into the latter's monopoly. It also wanted its own entrance into New York City, just as the New Haven Railroad had one. Wall Street speculators got control of the New England about the time the Housatonic underwent expansion, and before long they conveniently obtained a stock control of the Housatonic as well. The dock facilities at Wilson Point were enlarged, and traffic normally interchanged with the New Haven Railroad was now diverted by the speculators and sent directly to South Norwalk. Thence it was ferried across Long Island Sound to Oyster Bay, Long Island, for the trip into New York City via the Long Island Railroad.

This somewhat eccentric route, like nearly every stretch of rails in nineteenth-century Connecticut, naturally offered local and through passenger trains; the oddest to modern eyes was the short-lived, deluxe Long Island & Eastern States Express, a backcountry wanderer until it chuffed up to the dock at Wilson Point for a refresh-

M. C. PECK'S HOTEL AND CANAAN DEPOT

One of America's finest railroad photographers, David Plowden, composed this scene in the 1960s of the historic depot at Canaan, Connecticut. The Housatonic main line crossed the Central New England route here. This view looks towards Hartford on the Central, but the track is just a stub. In 1985, the station is home base for a new Housatonic tourist railroad company.

COLLECTION OF OLIVER JENSEN

ing breath of fresh air on the Sound. This amphibious affair took much longer than the conventional Shore Line Route of trains of its powerful rival, the New Haven. During the Oyster Bay era, the line continued to run barges, tugs, and car floats to other points in New York City and New Jersey. One must remember that back then there were no railroad bridges or tunnels to carry trains through Manhattan; the first railroad bridge across the Hudson north of the city was at Poughkeepsie, and that, it now seems in 1985, is to be dismantled.

The New York, New Haven & Hartford Railroad did not tolerate these menacing activities very long. When the New York financiers (see Chapter 11) abandoned "The New England," the New Haven took stock control and in 1892 formally leased the 190-mile Housatonic Railroad system. A majority of trackage on the old Housatonic Railroad main line eventually formed the scenic Berkshire Division of the New Haven Railroad. It was this artery that carried the wealthy to their sprawling summer homes in the Litchfield and Berkshire hills and transported in huge volume the dairy products of the same region. Today much of the Housatonic Rail-

The map below, issued in 1891, will repay study: The Housatonic had briefly become a "system," with connections to all manner of lines in adjoining New York State, most of them utterly vanished. The tracks are gone to State Line, Litchfield, Ridgefield, Bridgeport, and Derby—New Haven. Except for the commuter line from Danbury to South Norwalk, the rest is either in freight service, or rusting, or used in season by excursion trains from Canaan.

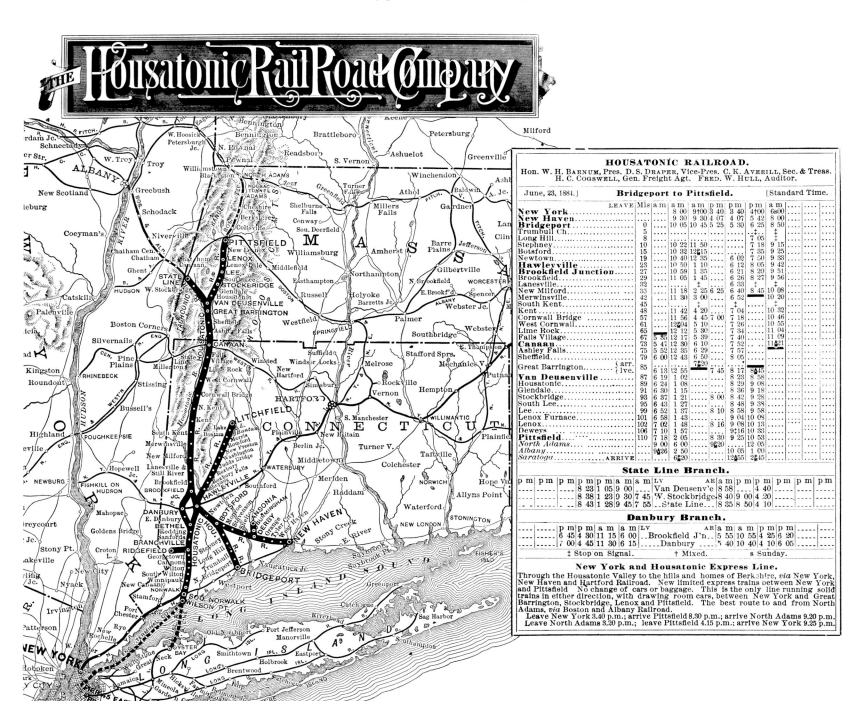

THE Housatonic RailRoad Company

HOUSATONIC RAILROAD.

Hon. W. H. Barnum, Pres. D. S. Draper, Vice-Pres. C. K. Averill, Sec. & Treas.
H. C. Cogswell, Gen. Freight Agt. Fred. W. Hull, Auditor.

June 23, 1884.] **Bridgeport to Pittsfield.** [Standard Time.

LEAVE	Mls	am	am	am	pm	pm	pm	am
New York		8 00	9†00	3 40	4†00	6800		
New Haven		9 30	9 30	4 07	4 07	5 42	8 00	
Bridgeport	0	10 05	10 45	5 25	5 30	6 25	8 50	
Trumbull Ch.	5							
Long Hill	8					7 05	‡	
Stephney	10	10 22	11 50			7 18	9 15	
Botsford	13	10 32	12†15			7 35	9 25	
Newtown	19	10 40	12 35	6 02		7 50	9 33	
Hawleyville	23	10 50	1 10	6 12		8 05	9 42	
Brookfield Junction	27	10 59	1 35	6 21		8 20	9 51	
Brookfield	29	11 05	1 45	6 26		8 27	9 56	
Lanesville	32			6 33		‡		
New Milford	35	11 18	2 25	6 25	6 40	8 45	10 08	
Merwinsville	42	11 30	3 00		6 52		10 20	
South Kent	45				‡			
Kent	48	11 42	4 20		7 04		10 32	
Cornwall Bridge	57	11 56	4 45	7 00	7 18		10 46	
West Cornwall	61	12†04	5 10		7 26		10 55	
Lime Rock	65	12 12	5 30		7 34		11 04	
Falls Village	67	12 17	5 39		7 40		11 09	
Canaan	73	5 47	12 30	6 10	7 52		11†21	
Ashley Falls	75	5 52	12 35	6 29	7 57			
Sheffield	79	6 00	12 43	6 50	8 05			
Great Barrington arr.	85	6 13	12 55		7 45	8†45		
Great Barrington lve.				7†20				
Van Deusenville	87	6 19	1 02		8 23	5 48		
Housatonic	89	6 24	1 08		8 29	9 08		
Glendale	91	6 30	1 15		8 36	9 18		
Stockbridge	93	6 37	1 21	8 00	8 42	9 28		
South Lee	95	6 43	1 27		8 48	9 38		
Lee	99	6 52	1 37	8 10	8 58	9 58		
Lenox Furnace	101	6 58	1 43		9 04	10 08		
Lenox	102	7 02	1 48	8 16	9 08	10 13		
Deweys	104	7 10	1 53		9†16	10 33		
Pittsfield	106	7 18	2 05	8 30	9 25	10 53		
North Adams	110	9 00	6 00	9†20	12 05			
Albany		9†26		10 05	1 00			
Saratoga ARRIVE		6†20		12†55	2†45			

State Line Branch.

pm	pm	pm	pm	am	am	LV	AR	am	pm	pm	pm	pm	pm	pm
		8 23	1 05	9 00		Van Deusenv'e		8 58		4 40				
		8 38	1 23	9 30	7 45	W. Stockbridge		8 40	9 00	4 20				
		8 43	1 28	9 45	7 55	State Line		8 35	8 50	4 10				

Danbury Branch.

pm	pm	am	am	LV	AR	am	am	pm	pm
6 45	4 30	11 15	6 00	Brookfield J'n		5 55	10 55	4 25	6 20
7 00	4 45	11 30	6 15	Danbury		5 40	10 40	4 10	6 05

‡ Stop on Signal. † Mixed. s Sunday.

New York and Housatonic Express Line.

Through the Housatonic Valley to the hills and homes of Berkshire, *via* New York, New Haven and Hartford Railroad. New limited express trains between New York and Pittsfield No change of cars or baggage. This is the only line running solid trains in either direction, with drawing room cars, between New York and Great Barrington, Stockbridge, Lenox and Pittsfield. The best route to and from North Adams, *via* Boston and Albany Railroad.
Leave New York 3.40 p.m.; arrive Pittsfield 8.30 p.m.; arrive North Adams 9.20 p.m.
Leave North Adams 3.20 p.m.; leave Pittsfield 4.15 p.m.; arrive New York 9.25 p.m.

road is decaying or abandoned. Freight service continues in the Canaan, Connecticut, area and on a few other fragments. A tourist rail line works seasonally out of the historic and still-intact Canaan station. Metro-North commuter trains still run from Norwalk to Danbury, although its electrification was stripped away a few years ago. The New Haven & Derby has vanished. At the South Norwalk station of Amtrak, a rusty disconnected spur still curves off to the south, overgrown with sumac and underbrush, but its old destination of Wilson Point is now full of expensive houses and commuters who very likely have never heard of the vanished docks and train yard and wooden glories of the Eastern States Express.

The Canal Railroad

Like the Housatonic, the New Haven & Northampton could point to a waterway in its family tree—namely, the seventy-eight-mile Farmington Canal. Unlike the projected Housatonic Canal, this one was actually built from New Haven to the Massachusetts state line, where it connected with the Hampshire & Hampden Canal to reach the Connecticut River at Northampton. Unfortunately, it was a financial and traffic disappointment to investors, who in 1836 reorganized themselves as the New Haven & Northampton Company.[11] At this moment there appeared on the scene Joseph Sheffield, a Southport man fresh from making a cotton fortune in the South, who became the company's largest stockholder. And it was he who first felt that a railroad ought to replace the canal.

The ever-present Professor Alexander Twining of Yale was hired by Sheffield to survey the rail line.[12] Twining found that the bed of the canal in New Haven, if drained, and its towpath going north, could be utilized in building a rail line from New Haven to Plainville, and thence could reach some northerly destination in Massachusetts. In this regard no definitive northern terminal was named, but it could be Westfield, Northampton, or possibly Pittsfield, he reported. Where the railroad would ultimately go did not hinder Sheffield. He merely secured an 1846 modification to his canal charter and poured his fortune into the newly created railroad's coffers.

A twenty-seven-mile section of track opened from Grand Avenue in New Haven to Plainville in January 1848 by way of Mt. Carmel, Cheshire, Plantsville, and Southington.* Sheffield had organized the construction company that built the line. Before it was even completed, he shrewdly leased the road to the New York & New

*The single track from New Haven to Hamden was largely installed on or along the Cheshire Turnpike, frequently giving rise to accidents involving carriages, wagons, and trains. In 1880 the railroad right of way was relocated in this area for 6-1/2 miles, eliminating at once fifty grade crossings.

Where the Canal Railroad was built, there once ran the Farmington Canal, feeble as it was in its final years. This ad appeared one year before the railroad took over. Travel on the canal had two features: cheap rates and slow going. Parts of the canal bed (in New Haven) and the towpath were naturals for a railroad track. The New Haven & Northampton was the successor to the Canal. Its charter, in 1846, was simply converted to that of a railroad company.

NEW HAVEN COLONY HISTORICAL SOCIETY

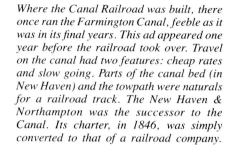
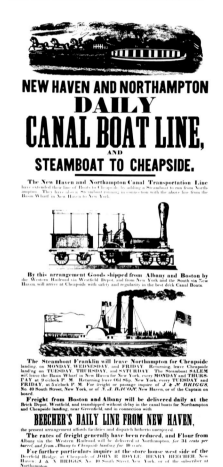

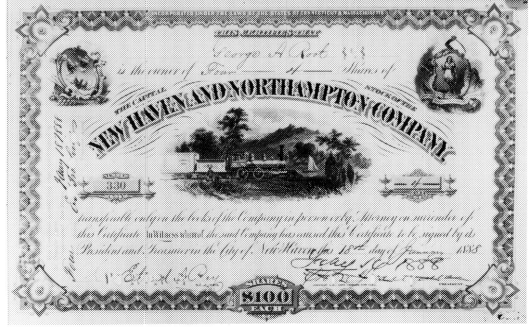

[LEFT] A stock certificate of the New Haven & Northampton Railroad Company. In its heyday, the road was something to reckon with, but today most of it is in ruins.

COLLECTION OF PATRICK GOEDERT

60

Haven Railroad, which was under construction itself west of New Haven to Greenwich. Sheffield invested in that road, too, and was one of its directors. The New York road found three convenient advantages to leasing the Canal Railroad. First, it would give rights to valuable land and canal-basin property in downtown New Haven, allowing for the erection of shops and terminals. Second, it meant control of a small feeder line of traffic to Plainville, or possibly further if extended. And third, it offered a competitive check against the prosperous Hartford & New Haven, which currently monopolized rail operations between its namesake cities. The lease was written for twenty-six years,[13] but business on the Canal Railroad proved far less than anticipated, and the New York road took a $32,000 loss on the Sheffield property as late as 1855.

The well-crafted lease permitted the sagacious Sheffield to build the line on north of Plainville; such extensions could also be leased to the New York & New Haven. And so he pressed on through Avon and Simsbury. In April 1850 the Canal Railroad

The New Haven studio of Daniel T. Cowell made this contemplative portrait of Joseph Earl Sheffield in 1877. He was the financial patron of the canal in its final years but was the first to promulgate a railroad between the same points. His fortune founded Yale's Sheffield Scientific School.

NEW HAVEN COLONY HISTORICAL SOCIETY

For Branches, see p. 31.] **NEW HAVEN & NORTHAMPTON RAILROAD.** [Standard Time.
Edw. A. Ray, *Gen. Ticket Agent.* Offices, New Haven. S. B. Opdyke, Jr., *Superintendent.*

New Haven to North Adams. [June 30, 1884.] **North Adams to New Haven.**

p m	p m	a m	a m	FRS	MLS.	LEAVE — ARRIVE	a m	p m	p m	p m
4 30	2 00	8 00				**New York**	11 45	2 20	7 20	10 30
6 25	4 10	10 25	7 15		73	**New Haven**	9 17	11 52	4 40	8 28
6 35			7 26	20	5½	Centerville f	9 07			
6 40		10 40	7 31	25	8½	Mount Carmel	9 01	11 38	4 23	8 12
6 52	4 34	10 53	7 44	40	15½	Cheshire	8 46	11 27	4 10	7 59
7 00			7 52	50	19½	Hitchcock's	8 37			
7 04	4 45	11 04	7 56	55	21¼	Plantsville	8 32	11 14	3 59	7 47
7 07	4 48	11 09	8 00	55	22	Southington	8 29	11 09	3 56	7 44
7 18	4 58	11 20	8 15	70	27½	**Plainville**	8 15	10 59	3 45	7 33
7 25	5 05	11 30	8 22	75	30¾	**Farmington**	8 07	10 49	3 35	7 25
7 39			8 34	95	37¼	Avon	7 55			7 09
7 43					40	Weatogue f	7 49			
7 50	5 24	11 50	8 44	1 05	41¾	Simsbury	7 43	10 30	3 12	7 00
8 00		12 00	8 54	1 20	46½	Granby	7 34	10 20		6 51
5 57	8 16		9 09	1 50	54¾	Southwick	7 19		6 36	5 15
7 25 8 27	5 56	12 26	9 24	1 70	60½	**Westfield**	7 09	9 55	2 38	6 26 5 00
7 45 8 40		12 39	9 37	1 80	67½	Southampton	6 53	9 37		6 09 1125
8 00 8 49	6 16	12 47	9 45	1 90	71½	Easthampton	6 44	9 28	2 16	5 58 1114
8 20 8 58	6 25	12 58	9 55	2 20	76½	**Northampton**	6 34	9 20	2 06	5 49 1054
6 45	1 19	10 16	2 35		87¾	**South Deerfield**	9 00	1 41	5 25	
6f55	1f29	10 26	2 50		92¾	**Conway**	8 48	1 29	5 13	
7 11	1 45	10 42			99¾	Shelburne Falls	8 35	1 14	5 00	
		10 49			102¾	Buckland f				
7f26	2f02	10 59	2 70		108¼	Charlemont	8-17	12f56	4 41	
		11 06			111½	Zoar			4f34	
7f42	‖2 18	11 15			115¾	Hoosac Tunnel	8 01	12‡41	4 26	
7 59	2 33	11 30	3 00	123		**North Adams**	7 45	12 25	4 10	
8 25	2 59	11 45				**Williamstown**		11 40	3 45	
9 58	6 45	2 15				**Troy**		7 45	1 28	
10 30	4 55	3 20				**Saratoga**		9 45		
a m p m	p m	p m	p m			ARRIVE — LEAVE	a m	a m	a m	p m a m

‖ Stops to leave passengers. ‡ Stops to take passengers. +Mixed. f Flag stations.

NEW HAVEN & NORTHAMPTON RAILROAD—Continued.

June 30, 1884.] **Collinsville Branch.** [Standard Time.

p m	p m	a m	a m	FRS	MLS.	LEAVE — ARRIVE	a m	a m	p m	p m
7 30	5 10	11 35	8 24	75		**Farmington**	8 05	10 40	3 32	7 17
7 37	5 17	12 05	8 32	85	2¾	Unionville	7 58	10 30	3 24	7 09
7 44	5 24	12 15	8 39		5¾	Burlington	7 51	10 05	3 17	7 02
7 50	5 31	12 40	8 44	95	8	Collinsville	7 45	9 55	3 11	6 55
8 02	5 44	1 00	8 57	1 10	13¼	Pine Meadow	7 33	9 25	2 58	6 43
8 08	5 47	1 10	9 03	1 10	14	**New Hartford**	7 30	9 15	2 55	6 40

+ Mixed Train.

Holyoke Branch.

p m	p m	p m	a m	a m	FRS	MLS.	LEAVE — ARRIVE	a m	a m	p m	p m	p m
6 27	2 50	12 27	9 56	7 30	1 50		**Westfield**	7 05	9 18	11 52	2 33	5 52
6 45		12 43				8	Ingleside f			11 35		5 35
6 50	3 20	12 49	10 18	7 52	1 75	10½	**Holyoke**	6 45	8 56	11 30	2 10	5 30

Williamsburg Branch.

p m	p m	p m	a m	a m	FRS	MLS.	LEAVE — ARRIVE	a m	a m	a m	p m
9 00	7 02	1 00	9 56	1 90			**Northampton**	6 33	8 52	11 02	5 42
9 07	7 10	1 08	10 02	1 95	2½		Florence	6 26	8 44	10 55	5 35
9 12	7 15	1 13	10 07	2 00	4½		Leeds	6 22	8 39	10 50	5 28
9 17	7 20	1 18	10 12	2 05	6¾		Haydenville	6 18	8 34	10 44	5 23
9 20	7 24	1 22	10 16	2 10	7½		**Williamsburg**	6 15	8 30	10 40	5 20

Turner's Falls Branch.

p m	p m	a m	FRS	MLS.	LEAVE — ARRIVE	a m	a m	p m
6 46	1 41	10 17	2 20		**So. Deerfield**	8 55	1 17	5 15
6 54	1 49	10 27	2 30		Deerfield	8 47	1 08	5 00
7 06	2 01	10 45	2 45		**Turner's Falls**	8 35	12 55	4 40

Connections.—At New Haven, with New York, New Haven & Hartford R. R., Shore Line Div., Boston & New York Air Line R. R., and New Haven & Derby R. R.; Farmington, with Collinsville Branch; Plainville, with New York & New England R. R.; Westfield, with Boston & Albany R. R. and Holyoke Branch; Simsbury and Pine Meadow, with Hartford & Connecticut Western R. R.; Northampton, with Connecticut River R. R.; North Adams, with Troy & Boston and Boston, Hoosac Tunnel & Western R. R.

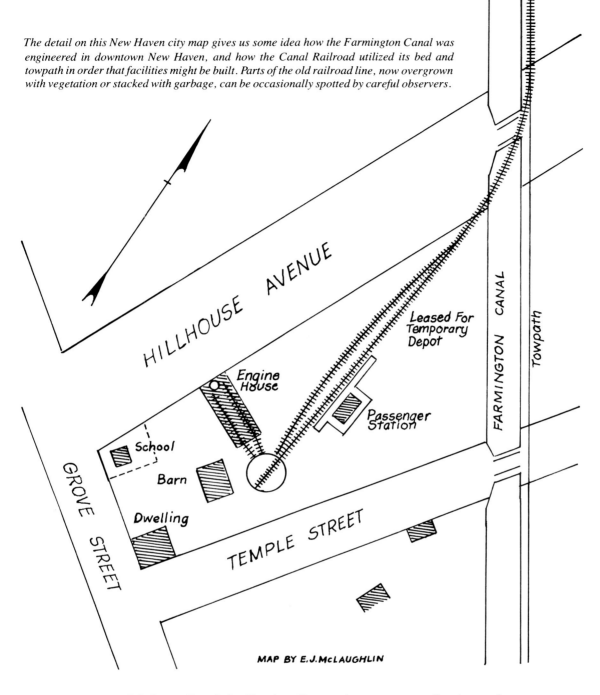

The detail on this New Haven city map gives us some idea how the Farmington Canal was engineered in downtown New Haven, and how the Canal Railroad utilized its bed and towpath in order that facilities might be built. Parts of the old railroad line, now overgrown with vegetation or stacked with garbage, can be occasionally spotted by careful observers.

HILLHOUSE AVENUE

Leased For Temporary Depot

Engine House

FARMINGTON CANAL

Towpath

School

Barn

Passenger Station

Dwelling

GROVE STREET

TEMPLE STREET

MAP BY E.J. McLAUGHLIN

main line reached Salmon Brook in Granby, Connecticut, twenty miles beyond Plainville. By now Sheffield had developed a twofold goal: to get the line up from Plainville to Westfield and Northampton in Massachusetts, and to construct a branch at Farmington to the busy manufacturing town of Collinsville and points beyond. In the summer of 1849 the Sheffield letter book shows him thinking "that the Collinsville Branch could be open by Christmas and I trust it is the stem of a road to Pittsfield, Massachusetts, and Vermont . . . ."[14] The eight-mile Collinsville Branch, serving Unionville, Burlington, and the Collins Axe Company, opened in March 1850. That January Sheffield also built a one-mile branch track from Simsbury to Tariffville to serve that town's burgeoning industrial base. Sheffield had begun grading to the Massachusetts state line north of Granby when the project swiftly ground to a halt: the Hartford & New Haven Railroad had filed a court injunction.

This legal obstacle resulted from a violation of an 1850 traffic agreement drawn up between the New York & New Haven and the not-so-friendly Hartford & New

Agricultural and Horticultural Fair,

CATTLE SHOW,

AND EXHIBITION OF MANUFACTURES,

At New Haven, September 25th and 26th, 1850.

ADDRESS AND PLOWING MATCH ON THE 26th.

EXCURSION

Tickets will be sold at the several Stations upon the line of the

CANAL RAIL ROAD,

To those wishing to attend the above-mentioned Fair and Exhibition, which will be good to return with on the 25th or 26th, at the following

REDUCED RATES:

From Stations North of Plainville,	$1.25
" Plainville,	1.00
" Southington and Hitchcock's,	75
" Cheshire,	62½
" Brooks',	50
" Bradley's,	37½
" Mount Carmel and below,	25

☞ *The trains will run as usual.*

R. B. MASON, Super't.

BENHAM, PRINTER, 55 ORANGE STREET, NEW HAVEN.

Haven. It was a kind of peace treaty between the two lines, and one stipulation was that the New York road must halt Canal Railroad construction at Granby. If it did not, the Canal line could conceivably surround the Hartford road and divert its traffic coming from factories in the busy Massachusetts section of the Connecticut River valley. One authority suggests there were other secret arrangements provided for in this agreement.[15] Buried within it was a $12,000-a-year payoff to keep ties and rails from going down "north of Granby." And Sheffield's activities were in direct violation of this agreement.

Joseph Sheffield quietly eased out of the picture as a result of this litigation and went west to help build the Michigan Southern and the Chicago & Rock Island lines. But he was to return, fueled again with energy, new money, and civic spirit. He financed construction of the Canal Railroad, which opened in 1856, through to Northampton, Massachusetts, after the "treaty" described above was annulled. This extension was accomplished (north of Granby) by chartering the Farmington Valley Railroad to the state line. But Sheffield wasn't finished in Massachusetts. Next came a branch at Northampton to Williamsburg (1868), a northerly extension on the main line from Northampton to Shelburne Falls in 1881 to meet the Hoosac Tunnel Route, and in the same year a branch from the main line at South Deerfield to Turners Falls. Nestled in between was the lease the Canal took in 1870 of the Holyoke & Westfield. The Canal's map in Connecticut did not change in this period, except for the Collinsville Branch, which was extended in 1876 six miles further from Collinsville to New Hartford to serve the Greenwoods Company. The branch never reached Pittsfield as Sheffield once hoped.

Where at the start only a few trains crawled back and forth from New Haven to Plainville, the Canal Railroad at its greatest extent became a property to reckon with. In 1874 the company owned twenty locomotives, twenty-eight passenger and baggage cars, and nearly 450 assorted freight cars. Four hundred persons were regularly employed. During 1874 $440,000 was derived from the movement of freight, $164,000 was tallied from passenger service, with a net income of $73,800. The line's flimsy early construction was radically improved. Steel rails replaced iron, early bridges were totally rebuilt, and many new stations were erected along the various routes.

Just as the Housatonic system of lines fell prey to "outside" parties, the Canal Road also experienced take-over overtures during its final years as a private enterprise in the nineteenth century. They came from the Vanderbilts' Boston & Albany Railroad, which thought the Canal Railroad could help it invade the sacred Connecticut territory of the New York, New Haven and Hartford Railroad. However, a majority of Canal Railroad stock was quietly obtained by the New Haven from Sheffield at a cost far above its selling value.[16] By 1887 the Canal Railroad was formally leased to, and 100 percent owned by, the Connecticut giant, and the struggles, expansions, and dreams of yet another singular railroad slowly left the public memory. Joseph Sheffield retired from railroading, but his civic spirit and commitment to New Haven never flagged. Part of his fortune had founded the Sheffield Scientific School at Yale University, and more went to it later.

An expedition along the old route of the Canal Railroad can be historically interesting. From New Haven, where the line begins in the cut which was the Canal's bed, a rusting, unused track runs through what has become a junkyard and, alas, an informal garbage disposal pit for the adjacent neighborhoods. Some Plainville portions of the line still carry freight, an operation of the B & M. Although very recently repaired by state funds, the line from Avon to the state line at Granby failed to attract freight business; the crossings were paved over and the tracks are (in 1985) being removed. The Massachusetts connections are overgrown with vegetation. One can still find a few preserved sections of the old canal, among them the locks at Cheshire and vestiges of an aqueduct at Avon. The founder's beneficiary, the Sheffield Scientific School, it must also be admitted, has been "consolidated" into Yale University, which no longer gives a distinct "Sheff" degree.

Distance from New Haven	Time Table 49 In Effect June 15, 1908. STATIONS.
0.00	New Haven_____N
3.19	Stock Yard_____D
8.47	Mt. Carmel_____D
11.97	Brooksvale _____
15.47	Cheshire _____N
19.60	Milldale _____D
21.28	Plantsville _____
22.06	Southington ____N
27.40	Plainville _____N
30.69	Farmington _____N
33.56	Unionville _____D
36.48	Burlington _____
38.63	Collinsville _____D
44.03	Pine Meadow____D
44.78	New Hartford___D
37.13	Avon _____D
41.75	Simsbury _____N
46.58	Granby _____D
52.36	Congamond ____D
54.74	Southwick _____D
60.58	Westfield _____N
70.90	Holyoke _____D
67.57	Southampton ___D
71.48	Easthampton ___D
76.36	Northampton ___D
79.05	Florence _____D
81.00	Leeds _____
82.55	Haydenville ____D
83.87	Williamsburgh _D
80.09	Hatfield _____
83.90	Whately _____
87.89	So. Deerfield____D
92.04	Deerfield _____
94.05	Cheapside _____
95.60	Montague City____
96.89	Turner's Falls___D
92.83	Conway _____D
94.66	Shelburne Jct.____N
100.00	Shelburne Falls N

Stations on the old Canal Railroad were substantially built, as the brick structure at Mt. Carmel reveals. Sleeping Giant State Park provides the backdrop. The other station is at Plantsville, Connecticut.

A splendid view of the iron bridge over the Farmington River at New Hartford, on the Collinsville Branch, ca. 1876. By closely examining the cab, it can be determined that the train stopped for the photographer.

NEW HAVEN COLONY HISTORICAL SOCIETY

Readers old enough, in 1985, may recall the busy Burlington, Connecticut, station on the old Collinsville Branch. A homely concession provided rail patrons and the motoring public with soda, hot dogs, and a table outfitted with umbrella and chairs.

Chapter Four Footnotes

1. Connecticut General Assembly, Resolves and Private Laws of the State of Connecticut, 1789-1836, II: 1025-1033, Public Records, Connecticut State Capitol Building.

2. *American Railroad Journal,* 20 October 1855.

3. Samuel Orcutt, *A History of the Old Town of Stratford and the City of Bridgeport, Connecticut* (New Haven: Tuttle, Morehouse & Taylor, 1886) II: 696.

4. *First Annual Report of the Housatonic Railroad Company* (New Haven: Hitchcock & Stafford, 1838), 4-5, 10-12.

5. Undated newspaper clipping, *Bridgeport Sentinel,* 1840, Turner Railroad Collection, The Connecticut Historical Society.

6. Corporate and Operating History of the Lines Owned by the New York, New Haven & Hartford Railroad Company, 47.

7. Withington, *First Twenty Years,* 20.

8. *Danbury Times,* 3 July 1844.

9. Photostatic excerpt, Directors' letter book, 1856, Housatonic Railroad Company, Turner Railroad Collection, The Connecticut Historical Society.

10. *Twenty-second Annual Report of the Railroad Commissioners, of the State of Connecticut for 1875* (Hartford: Case, Lockwood & Brainard, 1875), 123-131.

11. Connecticut General Assembly, Resolves and Private Laws of the State of Connecticut, from the Year 1789 to the Year 1836, I: 308-311, Public Records, Connecticut State Capitol Building.

12. *Engineer's Report on the Survey from New Haven City of the Canal to Plainville, and thence to Collinsville, in the Farmington Valley* (New Haven: Hitchcock & Stafford, 1845), passim.

13. Corporate and Operating History of the Lines Owned by the New York, New Haven & Hartford Railroad Company, 33.

14. Joseph Sheffield to William Imlay, 25 June 1849, Turner Railroad Collection, The Connecticut Historical Society.

15. Baker, *Formation of the New England Railroad Systems,* 78.

16. *Hartford Daily Courant,* 14 April 1881.

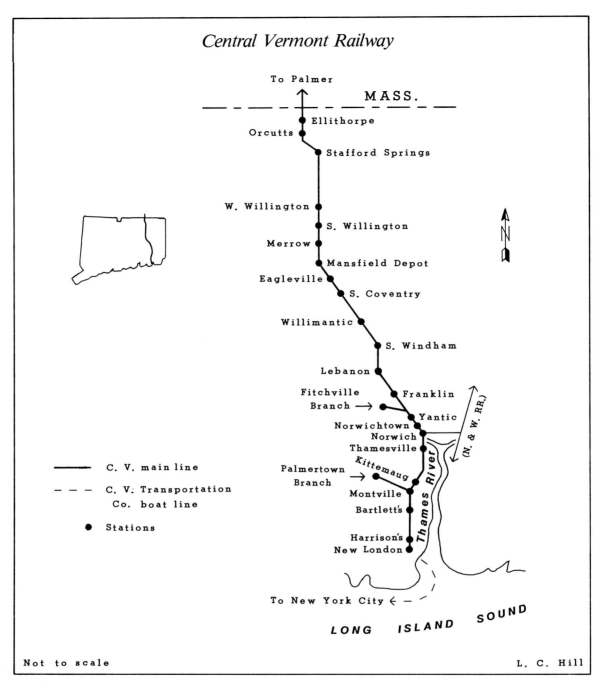

Central Vermont Railway

To Palmer

MASS.

Ellithorpe

Orcutts

Stafford Springs

W. Willington

S. Willington

Merrow

Mansfield Depot

Eagleville

S. Coventry

Willimantic

S. Windham

Lebanon

Fitchville
Branch →

Franklin

Yantic

Norwichtown
Norwich
(N. & W. RR.)

Thamesville

Palmertown
Branch →

Kittemaug

Thames River

Montville

Bartlett's

Harrison's
New London

To New York City ← —

LONG ISLAND SOUND

——— C. V. main line

– – – C. V. Transportation
Co. boat line

● Stations

Not to scale

L. C. Hill

"The Parade" (Foot of State Street) at New London, Connecticut, years before the great Union Station, designed by Richardson, was erected. The building in the right foreground (door facing reader) was the first railroad station. Tracks were in the dirt at street level.

Chapter Five

Fever in New London

In the year 1847, New London seemed to partially awaken from its Rip Van Winkle sleep of 100 years . . . the click of the telegraph was not even an echo from the great cities . . . a popular movement was started . . . to build . . . [a] railroad.

—*James Chew, Records and Papers of The New London County Historical Society,* **1895**

The track of the Central Vermont Railway starts in the old whaling port of New London and extends north towards Montville, Norwich, Willimantic, and Stafford, to Palmer, Massachusetts, and beyond. The line in Connecticut was actually funded in the nineteenth century by New London men, many of whom poured whaling fortunes into the enterprise. Today the Central Vermont is owned by Canadian National Railways of Canada—CN Rail—and overseen by its American property affiliate, the Detroit-based Grand Trunk Corporation. But unlike so many pioneer Connecticut railroads that have vanished, this still runs, and its original main line is very much intact.

The third largest whaling port in the United States, New London found itself facing a serious price drop for whaling products when railroads were first spoken of. In fact, the industry was suffering a serious business depression, not the least cause of which was the scarcity of whales themselves in the old hunting grounds. But when railway fever first spread to New London, many of its citizens wanted the Norwich & Worcester Railroad to build an extension south from Norwich to their own city. They offered the Norwich road use of their big steamboat dock, but unfortunately the Norwich & Worcester did not have the money to build the extension, nor was it convinced that New London was a superior terminal. New Londoners then investigated the idea of building their own railroad up the west bank of the Thames River to Norwich, Willimantic, and all the way to busy Springfield, Massachusetts. There a rail connection could be made with the prosperous Western Railroad, which ran between Worcester and Albany. Yet few Springfield investors felt the New London project to be worthwhile and did not lend enough support. But fifteen miles east of Springfield was the budding town of Palmer, which did show genuine enthusiasm for the New London road. It too was located on the Western Railroad, and Palmer ultimately became the line's destination.

There were costs to stage promotional meetings for their new venture, and these were borne by the city of New London but later repaid from the railroad's treasury. The city fathers agreed that they must have the railroad; otherwise, "the city is done forever . . . her fate is sealed."[1] In May 1847 a charter was secured for the New London, Willimantic & Springfield Railroad. Its incorporators—including whal-

Engine T.W. Williams *of the New London Northern is all shined up and ready to go in this photograph. Note the giant oil head-light and the unusual "inside connection" of the rods from the piston at the forward end to the great main driving wheels.*

Thomas W. Williams was one of the "main driving wheels" of New London's new rail-road. He had made his fortune in whaling.

ing magnate Thomas W. Williams*—were empowered "to locate, construct and finally complete a single, double, or treble railroad in the City of New London—thence on the westerly side of the Thames River to the City of Norwich, and thence to Willimantic and the north line of the State towards Springfield in the State of Massachusetts."[2] Capital stock was set at $500,000 with rights to increase it to $1,500,000. Par value of each stock certificate was $100 in 1847. So far as can be determined, no one in Norwich first subscribed to the line's stock—its citizens were quite content with the Norwich & Worcester Railroad.

In December of that year, the charter was accepted, and the corporation officially formed. General James Palmer was hired as the road's engineer. He prepared a survey booklet of the proposed route showing its location and estimated income. A glowing report it was, but actual costs later incurred told quite a different story. Nevertheless, "having entire confidence in the practical skill and sound judgement of the Engineer, and having also passed over the whole route described and carefully examined the estimates, we [the directors] do not hesitate to declare that the road can be built within the sum named—that business upon the road will be fully realized if not exceeded—and it will be a regular dividend paying stock."[3]

By 1848 stock subscription books were opened in several Connecticut and Massachusetts towns, and advertisements were placed in local newspapers. Direct profits to individuals and indirect benefits to the towns were themes of the promoters. The average person held only a few stock shares. Thirty-four subscribers (mostly the incorporators) accounted for 42 percent of all the railroad's stock. About four thousand shares were taken in New London, tying up $400,000 of local capital. Claims for land damage and business expenses were often paid for by the railroad in stock. In Monson, Massachusetts, twenty-eight stock subscribers paid for their shares by supplying railroad ties. Thomas Williams of New London, the incorporator, had taken two hundred shares and was named the first president. Enthusiasm ran high, according to local historian James Chew:

> Meetings were held at short intervals in Washington or Dart hall, on Bradley Street, [New London] in the furtherance of the enterprise. At these meetings, which were attended with great enthusiasm, the artisan, the humble clerk, the man of business, and the capitalist would register their subscriptions amid the applause of the audience. The town was raked as with a fine comb; public pride and public interest were appealed to.[4]

The railway route was to begin in New London at Fort Trumbull, using its dock, but this was later changed to Winthrop Point near Main and Hallam streets. From there

*Williams bought two hundred shares of stock, liberally subscribed to the railroad's bonds, and was president for all but two and a half years between 1847 and 1861.

Original survey map of the New London, Willimantic & Springfield Railroad. General Palmer projected both Springfield and Palmer as the road's northerly destination. Palmer won out, for Springfield businessmen did not want to support the road. The map was in the Engineer's Report *of 1847.*

the line went over Winthrop Cove in East New London and up the west bank of the Thames River to Montville and Norwich. Many hamlets were passed in this thirteen-mile stretch, and in later years flag-stop stations popped up at Harrison's Landing, Richards Grove, Scotch Cap, Bartlett's, Kittemaug, Thames Grove, and Mohegan. General Palmer had surveyed three possible routes through Norwich but ultimately used the "Shore Route," which hugged the Thames River in Thamesville and skirted a branch of the Yantic River, crossing its falls to reach Yantic further on.

After Yantic the line poked past the rich farmlands of Franklin and Lebanon. In the hilly town of Franklin, two routes were proposed: one through Ayer's Gap and another by way of Peck Hollow.[5] The latter was chosen because it was shorter, but it required a difficult gradient which to this day is known by Central Vermont crews as "Franklin Hill." Tracks then entered industrious Spaffordsville (South Windham) before reaching the great "Thread City" of Willimantic. William Jillson was Willimantic's chief railroad promoter. Willimantic businessmen believed that the railroad must be obtained or the city "would fail in becoming one of the largest and most important inland towns in the country."[6] It was an optimistic time. Beyond Willimantic, General Palmer felt there were no unusual engineering challenges in the towns of South Coventry, Mansfield, South Willington, and Stafford, up to the Massachusetts state line. In 1848 the directors merged their road with the New London, Willimantic & Palmer, which had been chartered in Massachusetts to meet the New London project at the state line. The first joint stockholders' meeting was held

In Sunday best, engineers, firemen, and conductors of the New London Northern pose before the brick engine house at Fourth Street in New London. In center, back row, fully whiskered, is I. W. Dow, the Master Mechanic. [BELOW] Engine Block Island *chugs out of South Windham station.*

the following January, and the name of the Massachusetts road was retained as the new corporate title.[7] The town of Palmer was delighted.

Within nine miles of the sixty-five-mile long railroad there lived nearly seventy thousand inhabitants. Palmer noted that "in no part of Connecticut is there an area more largely engaged in the manufacture of heavy and bulk articles, or which pays more for the transportation of freight and passengers, or possesses in greater abundance the requisites for future wealth and prosperity."[8] An array of products was produced, including textiles, carpeting, leather goods, glass, clocks, wagons, and shingles. These facts had been enumerated in Palmer's engineering report, which was distributed to investors. Many towns along the route did not want to miss "getting the railroad" either. The flourishing manufacturing and health village of Stafford Springs encouraged the line to pass right through the center of town. Its

citizenry's response in buying stock was exceeded only by that of New London. In 1856 the very same townspeople even raised $283 and gave it to the railroad to help pay for snow removal costs around railroad tracks and buildings! In the Mansfield hamlet of Merrow residents gave an outright cash contribution of $118 for a side-track where goods and wares could be unloaded.

A barefoot boy stands near the turntable pit at New London, perhaps hoping for a ride, in about 1870. Maintenance work and cleaning took place in the engine stalls.

A modest groundbreaking occurred in Norwich in 1848, and subsequent contracts divided the work into five sections of construction, of which the most expensive was between Chelsea and Norwich Falls; the least expensive was between Tolland and Willington. The brothers Willis and George Phelps of Springfield, Massachusetts, were the principal contractors. The average cost of one mile of track was calculated as follows:

98$\frac{1}{2}$ tons of iron rails		$6,402
560 chair irons		292
4,250 pounds of spikes		191
1,800 feet of chestnut ties		504
Chair keys (rail joints)		50
Labor		350
Haulage and Contingencies		100
	Total	$7,889[9]

Like many early Connecticut railroads, the New London, Willimantic & Palmer did not require immediate full payment for each stock certificate purchased. Only part would be put down in cash, and assessments made whenever the treasury needed replenishing. A typical assessment occurred when directors purchased fifty-six hundred tons of iron rails in faraway Wales, or when the Troy, New York, Iron and Nail Company produced the first spikes. The Taunton, Massachusetts, Locomotive Works built several early engines for the company, while Dean, Pack-ard & Mills supplied passenger cars. Freight cars were ordered from the Norwich Car Manufactory. A passenger "saloon" car of fifty seats cost $1,775; a baggage

WEEKS HOUSE,

J. W. WEEKS, Proprietor, Palmer, Mass.

The early days of Palmer knew the building, now known as the WEEKS HOUSE, under the name of the Railroad House. A. N. Dewey, upon the completion of the railroad, established it as a Hotel, and for several years did an extensive business for the size of the town. Later on, it passed into different hands and different titles, up to the time of Mr. Shaw's administration, when it was known as the Antique House, and acquired a large and wide-spread reputation. Mr. Shaw being a very popular man and landlord. Mr. Weeks purchased Mr. Shaw's interest, and with keen appreciation of the wants of the case, as well as the public necessities, commenced in 1873 to enlarge, repair remodel, spending a large amount in this manner. He refurnished its thirty rooms, and added many improvements in his efforts to make it the best hotel in this section. Mr. Weeks owns a farm out on the Brimfield road, and supplies his table from its products. With characteristic enterprise, he has established Telephonic connection between both places, and the demands of the house can be immediately supplied. His *Stable* is equipped with good teams, nine in number, and kept in first-class shape.

A Delightful Summer Resort among the Green Mountains.

THE BROOKS HOUSE, BRATTLEBORO, VT.
(The Half-way House between New York and the White Mountains.)

If the proof of the Pudding is the eating of it, then the merit and popularity of the

"Boss Lunch Milk Biscuit,"

Is clearly established by the increasing demand each year, as shown below :

In 1879 the gain over 1878 was 132,000 pounds.
In 1880	"	1879	"	88,000	"
In 1881	"	1880	"	247,800	"
In 1882	"	1881	"	154,200	"

Gain in past four years......622,000 pounds.

The sale of this one Biscuit amounts to about 27,000 barrels per year, from the factory of

Messrs. C. D. BOSS & SON.

It is the Infant's strength, the Invalid's hope, the Children's Luncheon, the Staff of Life to the aged, and indispensable to every household.

The Boss Biscuit Works

New London, Conn.

The advertisements found on this page were taken from the 1883 Guide Book *of the New London Northern Railroad, supplied to passengers using the line. It contained a colorful description of the route, points of interest, and places to visit. By seeking the ads, the railroad probably covered the costs.*

A builder's photograph of the engine A. N. Ramsdell just before leaving the Manchester Locomotive Works in New Hampshire in 1867 for the New London Northern. Below is an early timetable and special notice prepared for the public by the earlier firm.

New·London, Willimantic,
AND
Palmer Railroad.

1860-61.   **WINTER ARRANGEMENTS.**   **1860-61.**
Commencing Monday, Dec. 3rd, 1860.

PASSENGER TRAINS LEAVE NEW-LONDON.

7.15 A. M. Accommodation Train for Norwich, Willimantic, Stafford, Palmer, Amherst, &c., connecting with Hartford, P. & F. R. R. at Willimantic, for Hartford ; with Western R. R. at Palmer for Springfield, Worcester, Albany, & Amherst Road.

1.50 P. M. Accommodation Train, in connection with New York, New Haven, Norwich and Worcester, Hartford, Providence and Fishkill and Western R. R. for Springfield.

PASSENGER TRAINS LEAVE PALMER.

7.55 A. M. Accommodation Train, for New London, in connection with Western Train from Springfield, Hartford, P. & Fishkill, Norwich and Worcester, Stonington and Providence New London and New York Trains.

2.10 P. M. Accommodation Train, for New London, in connection with Trains from Springfield, Hartford, Providence & Fishkill, New Haven and New York Trains and by Steamer from New London to New York.

Special Trains between New-London and Norwich & Worcester Depot.
LEAVE NEW-LONDON.

10.00 A. M.   Special Train in connection with Train from Providence, Stonington and Mystic.

3.00 P. M.   Special Train for Norwich, connecting with 3.15 P.M. Train Norwich & Worcester Road, for Providence and Worcester.

8.45 P. M.   Special Train in connection with New York and New Haven Train.

LEAVE NORWICH AND WORCESTER DEPOT.

6.00 A. M.   Special Train connecting with Trains for New Haven, New York, Mystic, Stonington, Westerly and Providence.

1.30 P. M.   Special Train connecting with Express Train for New Haven and New York.

4.10 P. M.   Special Train connecting with Through Express Train for Mystic, Stonington, Westerly, Providence and Boston, arriving at Providence at 7.30 p. m. Boston at 9.00 p. m.

Trains Leave Stations as follows:

Going North from New-London.						Going South from Palmer.		
L've New-London,	7.15 a.m.	10.00 a.m.	1.50 p.m.	3.00 p.m.	8.45 p.m.	L've Palmer,	7.55 a.m.	2.10 p.m.
Montville,	7.31	10.25	2.05	3.15	9.03	Monson,	8.07	2.23
Norwich,	8.00	10.50	2.35	3.45	9.35	Stafford,	8.43	3.00
Yantic,	8.13		2.49			Tolland,	9.01	3.18
So. Windham,	8.40		3.16			Mansfield,	9.20	3.36
Willimantic,	8.55		3.32			So. Coventry,	9.31	3.50
So. Coventry,	9.09		3.50			Willimantic,	9.42	4.05
Mansfield,	9.20		4.01			So. Windham,	10.00	4.19
Tolland,	9.38		4.27			Yantic,	10.29	4.46
Stafford,	9.56		4 45			Norwich,	6.00 a.m. 10.45 a.m. 1.30 p.m. 4.10 p.m.	5.00
Monson,	10.32		5.24			Montville,	6.30 11.18 2.05 4.42	5.28
Arr. Palmer,	10.45 a.m.		5.35 p.m.			Arr. New-London, 6.45	11.30 2.25 5.00	5.45

Through Tickets for New York and New Haven, by Railroad, sold at Stations.

and by Steamer for New York at Stations North of Lebanon.   Tickets sold at Norwich for Mystic, Stonington and Westerly.

Freight Trains leave Palmer, Monday, Wednesday, and Friday.   **Leave New-London, Tuesday, Thursday, and Saturday.**

New-London, Dec. 3rd, 1860.
RICHARD N. DOWD, Superintendent.

STARR & FARNHAM, PRINTERS, CORNER STATE AND MAIN STREETS. NEW LONDON.

New London, W. & Palmer R. R. Office,
NEW LONDON, 2d June, 1853.

Should Thursday, 9th inst., prove stormy, the Excursion to Amherst will be postponed till the next fair day. A special train will leave—

New London   at 7.45 A. M.
Norwich   "   8.15   "   "
Willimantic   "   9.05   "   "
Stafford   "   9.45   "   "
Palmer   "   10.20   "   "

Arriving at Amherst about 11, and returning, leave Amherst at 3.30 P. M.

Invited guests from stations other than those above named, can take the regular morning up or down trains, and change to the special train at Willimantic.

Wm. R. Starr, Superintendent.

Beyond the brick station at South Windham stands a huge wood crib. Trains would stop here to pick up both passengers and fuel.

Thousands of people located along the route of the Central Vermont Railway came to New London each summer to enjoy the attractions of Ocean Beach. If you didn't take some form of horse-drawn vehicle to the waterfront mecca, or the trolley in later years, you had only to board a steamboat across from the New London depot. It arrived at the resort's long, fingerlike trestle pier. Numerous boats "put in" here, both large and small. The careful observer can see a row of people reflected in a vessel's sail. Steamer Ella *of Norwich is at far right.*

car sold for $775; and freight cars ranged in price from $500 to $600 apiece, roughly their scrap value today—if they could be found. Trial conductors on passenger trains were hired at $40 a month, and the first station agent at South Coventry was put on the pay roll at $120 a year.[10] The line opened between New London and Norwich in October 1849; by August of 1850 the tracks reached Palmer.[11] Inaugural train runs were scheduled, and at least one man's memory of the occasion was preserved:

> When in 1849 the New London, Willimantic & Palmer was open to traffic, a grand free excursion was given to Stafford Springs. My grandfather was half-owner of a typical mill village in Eagleville, and of course, being a probable source of revenue, was invited on the excursion. General James N. Palmer, the engineer of the road, was on hand and everything went off in great shape under his direction. General Palmer in some way learned that there was a veteran of the Revolutionary War named Bingham (my grandfather) on the train and was delighted. Sending for him, Palmer talked over those stirring times and then presented him with a pass for life on the cars, together with the privilege of stopping any train at any point to get aboard, and with the instructions to conductors to stop trains opposite Bingham's house (near Mansfield Depot) to let him off if he so desired.[12]

A Little Relaxation.

To build and equip the road came to $1,182,000, or about $19,000 a mile. Stockholder enthusiasm diminished somewhat, however, after the first year's income fell $85,000 short of Palmer's forecast. Directors responded by organizing three plans to generate more income: connecting the southern terminus with the New Haven & New London Railroad; making a physical connection with the Norwich & Worcester Railroad at Norwich; and extending the line north of Palmer.

By spring of 1852 the railroad got permission to extend its line at Winthrop's Point "to some point at or near the Parade at the foot of State Street" in New London. By summer's end the extension to the New Haven & New London Railroad was completed, and the two companies collaborated on schedules, operation of trains, and division of tariffs. At Norwich a connection to the Norwich & Worcester was made in 1853, allowing the latter to run its Steamboat Express trains directly into New London. The directors then investigated the matter of extending the track north of Palmer. They met intermittently with the promoters of the Amherst & Belchertown

Railroad—a twenty-mile line proposed from Palmer to Amherst via Three Rivers and Belchertown. With a modest investment by New Londoners, the Amherst & Belchertown was able to open in 1853. The New London road leased the line but terminated the agreement owing to lack of rental income.

To finance their plans of expansion, the directors looked towards a large bond issue as a means of stimulating the treasury. The bonds were sold, but the road had a great deal of trouble in paying bondholders their interest. In a moment of despair the directors even offered for sale that part of their road between New London and Norwich to the Norwich & Worcester Railroad. The offer was refused. Irate bondholders eventually foreclosed, and trustees took possession of the bankrupt road. The panic of 1857, triggered by the failure of the Ohio Life & Trust Company, only added to the railroad's troubles.

After receiving legislative approval and restructuring its debt, the line was reorganized as the New London Northern Railroad. Operations by the new corporation began in 1861, and solvency was restored. As the state railroad commissioners reported, "Since the trustees took possession its entire earnings have been expended on the road. Fifteen truss bridges have been re-built, nine of which are covered. More than 3,000 feet of pile bridges besides eleven new truss bridges are in process of erection. Over 700 tons of new iron with upwards of 10,000 repaired rails and nearly 100,000 ties have been laid. Two new engines have been added." [13] A new drawbridge was erected over Winthrop Cove, and the steamboat freight wharf at East New London was refurbished and enlarged. During this period the new company acquired the twenty-mile Amherst, Belchertown & Palmer line. Permission also was granted to complete a link between Amherst and Grout's Corner (Millers Falls). It opened in 1866, and a physical connection was immediately made with the Vermont & Massachusetts Railroad. The New London road had now established its own line of steamboats between New London and New York City. The marine operation grew and was eventually succeeded by the Central Vermont Transportation Company.

In 1871 the New London Northern directors leased their road to backers of the Vermont Central Railroad, which later became the Central Vermont. The New London

Northern Railroad built two individual branch lines in Connecticut during this period: the Fitchville Branch from Yantic, which served the Fitchville Cotton Manufacturing Company (now removed), and the Palmertown Branch from Montville to serve the Palmer Brothers' mill in Palmertown, which specialized in the manufacture of bed quilts and made a fortune which enabled George S. Palmer to help build Connecticut College in New London. Also on this branch were other textile mills and the paper mill of C. M. Robertson, which was "operated by steam and water, giving employment to many men and exporting over 600 tons of manila paper each year."[14] Shortly before the publication of this book the Palmertown Branch, too, passed into history.

Railway accidents were of course common to all Connecticut railroads, and one of the most unusual happened on the New London Northern. It was an "act of God" that took place on March 27, 1877. The Staffordville, Connecticut, mill dam had burst, washing away the tracks, about a dozen railroad cars, and the freight house in Stafford Springs. The deluge also took out two large wooden bridges with their abutments, seven smaller bridges, and two miles of roadbed which simply disintegrated. Fortunately no lives were lost.

The financial history of the New London Northern contrasted sharply with that of its predecessor company. Success, consistent growth, and reward to investors characterized its operations. Net earnings exceeded $130,000 in 1872. Inventories of cars, engines, and stations increased. As promised by the Central Vermont, a large roundhouse was built at the foot of Fourth Street in East New London, along with repair shops. A stone wharf was also constructed on the Thames River, which was eleven hundred feet long and 150 feet wide. A fire destroyed the passenger depot at New London, prompting construction of a new Union Station at the foot of State Street. The city sold property to the railroad for $15,000, provided that it make no claim on the waterfront. The architect Henry Hobson Richardson was engaged to design the building, a huge brick affair which recently was restored. It serves Amtrak, and until the Central Vermont gave up its last "mixed" passenger train more than thirty years ago, was in fact a "union station."

In 1882 the New London Northern lease to the Central Vermont was rewritten at an annual rental of $211,000. Gradually "Northern" markings on engines and cars disappeared and were replaced by Central Vermont lettering. As before, the Central Vermont continued to please New London stockholders by properly maintaining their line and improving services. What was the old steamboat line of the New London Northern became, in 1908, the Central Vermont Transportation Company.

The crumpled mass of metal heaped in this farmer's field in Mansfield is the remains of engine No. 155, whose boiler had exploded a few hours before. The date was 1896.

Over time the long, fingerlike pier of the railroad was refurbished—it stood next to today's modern Connecticut State Pier in East New London. An order was even placed for two new boats. The *New York* and the *New London* were built at the Wilmington, Delaware, yards of Harlan & Hollingsworth. Each was 278 feet long and sailed between their namesake cities via Long Island Sound. A wicked hurricane in 1938 pulverized many of the boat line's facilities at New London. The operation lasted until the late 1940s, when it was shut down forever as a result of a workmen's strike.

In the early part of this century the Central Vermont initiated direct passenger train service from New London all the way to Montreal. The electrically lighted *Seashore Express* first proved popular, but was ultimately withdrawn for lack of patronage. Henry Ford's invention also diminished passenger train use. In response the Central Vermont introduced a novel, self-propelled passenger car in 1924—far less expensive to run than a steam-engine-hauled passenger train. It was built by the

Oops! Locomotives Thames *and* Montville *met head-on in 1891 at South Windham. Disregard of train orders and schedules was the cause. Below are French Canadian track workers plying their craft about 1902.*

Brill Company and utilized storage batteries. Twenty or so patrons were accommodated, and later the unit was converted to gas-electric operation. Summer excursion trains were also run over the Central Vermont in order to bolster revenues. Among the favorites were trains that brought inhabitants from the hinterland to enjoy a day's outing on the white sands of Ocean Beach, or to take a connecting boat to Block Island, or perhaps to watch—in progress—the Yale-Harvard Regatta, which was rowed every June on the Thames River. For the latter event, the railroad supplied "regatta" cars, which amounted to rows of rising bleacher seats on flat cars with striped canvas canopies on top. Jammed with alumni, students, and their ladies, the regatta trains followed the whole four-mile course of the races from start to finish, as in ringside seats. Similar long trains also ran on the opposite, east side of the Thames along the waterside line of the New Haven Railroad. Those in the know took the west, or Central Vermont, side when the tide caused the race to proceed upstream from New London, since the view of the finish line at Bartlett's Cove in Quaker Hill is much closer. But when the tide was running out, and the course was downstream, wise spectators chose the New Haven line because that train, in a burst of speed in Groton, would round its way on to the high New London railroad

79

Central Vermont Railroad.

NEW LONDON DIVISION.

CELEBRATION

—OF—

INDEPENDENCE DAY!

—AT—

Willimantic, Conn.,

Tuesday, July 4th,
1893.

PROCESSION

Of Antiques and Horribles, Floats, Trades Representatives, Civic and Secret Organizations and Bicyclists, Etc., at 10 a. m.

PARADE

Of Bicycles, followed by a Dress Parade on Wheels, Band Concert, and other exercises at 1 p. m., and a

BICYCLE TOURNAMENT

At 2 p. m., under the auspices of the Eastern Connecticut Cycling Club on the grounds of the Willimantic Fair Association, to which the small admission fee of 25 cents will be charged.

EXCURSION TICKETS

To Willimantic and return will be on sale at the following low rates:

FROM	Fare for Round Trip	FROM	Fare for Round Trip
Palmer,	$1.40	South Windham,	$ .15
Monson,	1.25	Lebanon,	.25
Stafford,	.80	Franklin,	.40
Tolland,	.60	Yantic,	.55
South Willington,	.55	Norwich Town,	.60
Merrow,	.45	Norwich,	.65
Mansfield,	.40	Montville,	.95
Eagleville,	.35	New London,	1.20
South Coventry,	.20		

D. Mackenzie,	S. W. Cummings,	J. A. Southard,
Superintendent, New London.	Gen'l Pass. Agt. St. Albans, Vt.	Div. Pass. Agt., New London.

Press of The Day, 270 Bank St., New London, Conn.

EXCURSION

TO

NEW LONDON

And Ocean Beach

SUNDAY
JULY 31
1927

VIA CENTRAL VERMONT RAILWAY

Good BATHING and SHORE DINNERS a Specialty

NEW LONDON

There are many beautiful trips, such as to Crescent Beach and Niantic; Oswegatchie, near the head of the beautiful Niantic River; Poquonock, a very pretty village; Noank, snugly located on the Mystic River, and other trips such as to Mystic, Gale's Ferry, Stonington, which can be made from New London.

OCEAN BEACH

The popular pleasure resort of New London, 30 minutes' ride by trolley. At Ocean Beach, one can get the best of shore dinners, the best of bathing and every kind of amusement found at an ocean summer resort.

ELECTRIC CARS LEAVE NEW LONDON EVERY TEN MINUTES FOR OCEAN BEACH.

GOING
Round Trip Tickets will be sold and Special Trains run as follows:

			Round Trip Fares
Brattleboro	Leave 7.00 A. M.		
Vernon	7.08 "		
East Northfield	7.20 "		$1.75
Northfield, Mass	7.23 "		
Northfield Farms	7.31 "		
Millers Falls	7.38 "		
Montague	7.44 "		
Leverett	7.52 "		
Cushmen	7.57 "		
Amherst	8.02 "		
Belchertown	8.20 "		
Barretts Junction	8.32 "		$1.70
Three Rivers	8.36 "		
Palmer	8.41 "		$1.50
Monson	8.51 "		
Stafford	9.21 "		
Due New London	11.10 "		

RETURNING

Special train leaves New London for Stafford, Brattleboro and intermediate stations at 5.00 P. M.

TICKETS will be good on above trains July 31, 1927, and for continuous passage.

Children between the ages of five and twelve years one-half fare.

J. W. HANLEY,
General Freight and Passenger Agent.
(10,000)

ALISON JENSEN

A Station Scrapbook on the C.V.

Railroad history in Connecticut owes a large debt to a young man named Irving Drake. Without him and his hobby of photographing railroad stations, big and small, there would be no record of scores of little places where trains stopped in the days when they ran everywhere. His pictures, composed to give a sense of the surroundings (though rarely including the trains themselves), will turn up frequently as this book progresses; one can tell them not only by his handwriting but by the fairly steady presence of his car. Quite often a friend will appear as well, or possibly Drake himself. Of these twelve stations along the Central Vermont, recorded in the late 1920s or early 30s, all but three have vanished.

Harrison, in the town of Waterford, had little more than a shelter.

Montville, a branch junction, was the youthful hangout of the author.

Norwich's Central Vermont Station straddled the Yantic River, and the track to the right connected with the Norwich & Worcester Railroad, which had its own depot. Little Yantic (below) is just north of Norwich. No station today.

Old-fashioned Norwichtown had a suitably old-fashioned depot, which has given way to a shopping plaza nearby. Lebanon is in farm country and the station had, in true rural fashion, an outhouse in the rear. The site is bulldozed.

Eagleville Depot is gone, and so are the big textile mills in back.

South Coventry's station still stands; there is a passing siding here. On a lucky day you can see trains pass.

Mansfield Station, which Drake notes was new in 1930, has been converted into a fancy restaurant where trains still rumble by. Little South Willington has quite disappeared.

West Willington Station still exists but you do your banking, not your travelling, here. Orcutts, which took its name from a once-prominent local family, is another vanished depot.

bridge and stop, right in the middle, for a perfect view of the oarsmen below as they sprinted to the finish of the great ordeal. No better way of watching a moving sporting event was ever devised, since boats in the river were not—and are not today—allowed to move or follow the shells during the race. One of the maddest follies of modern railroad history was the scrapping of the regatta cars.

There are no available statistics to confirm the assertion that on boat race day the regatta trains on the Central Vermont carried more passengers than its last, sad, "mixed" passenger trains (one old coach at the end of a local freight) transported in a year. But by the late 1940s the "mixed" had chugged into eternity.

Freight trains were the mainstay on the Southern Division, and the Central Vermont has done everything possible to maintain traffic. In the 1930s it pioneered its "Rocket Fast Freight" service that specialized in the movement of small, less-than-carload-lot (L.C.L.) shipments. The service was so co-ordinated as to take advantage of boat line, train, and company-owned motor truck schedules. Today, small and large freight trains still rumble out of East New London—site of Southern Division headquarters—just as they have since 1849 when the New London, Willimantic & Palmer first began operations.

New London's railroad dream ultimately became linked with the government-owned railways of Canada. In the 1890s the Grand Trunk Railroad of Canada had a

[OPPOSITE PAGE] Engine Brattleboro, in 1886, split a switch at Thamesville leading to the Richmond Stove Works, and nosed into the river. Her tender is at far left.

83

cozy financial relationship with the Central Vermont. It lent large sums of money to the firm and bought its stock, so much that a majority stock control was soon achieved. Thus Grand Trunk policies were felt all the way south to New London. In 1922 the federal government of Canada organized many of its rich and ailing roads, both crucial to the Dominion, into a new Crown corporation—Canadian National Railways of Canada. Among its component firms was the Grand Trunk, with its stepchild, the Central Vermont, and its lease of the New London Northern. New Londoners had no reason to fret over the move. The Canadian National system stretched from Cape Breton and Newfoundland west to Vancouver, north to Prince Rupert, and south to Chicago and the New England states. A disastrous flood in 1927 ravaged and destroyed much of the Central Vermont main line in Massachusetts and Vermont. To help it cope with reconstruction costs, a beneficent Canadian National advanced millions of dollars to help. A "friendly" receivership resulted, with Canadian National Railways emerging as the new Central Vermont owner. As it became available, the Central Vermont continued to buy New London stock until it entirely owned the line. In 1951 the New London Northern Railroad Company evaporated as a corporation.

The American-born railway genius, Sir Henry Thornton, was the first president of Canadian National. But the massive transportation complex (including railways, hotels, ships, communications, and natural resources) was to really flower under the late Donald Gordon, the aggressive Canadian-Scots banker-turned-railroader. Under his aegis Canadian National Railways grew and achieved a new level of financial stability. Among his many tasks upon taking office in 1950 was to convert the railroad from steam to diesel power. Though experimental diesel engines appeared on the Central Vermont property much earlier, in 1957 the first "owned" batch arrived from the Electro-Motive Division of General Motors. Many readers can still recall their khaki green and yellow paint scheme, complete with the famed maple leaf company insignia. Prudent maintenance and rebuilding have made them last until today.

During the 1960s and 1970s the Central Vermont was hustled along into the computer and technological age. Data processing equipment was integrated; numerous stations were closed and operations marshalled to only a few key places; telegraph and telephone pole lines were removed and replaced with sophisticated radio communications; and a new logo appeared. Crucial to any successful railroad is good track, and the Central Vermont has made its main line track conditions equal to any other line in the country, thanks to welded rail and highly mechanized track equipment. An industrious marketing department continues to attract new customers and offer better services. In all, hardly a more fitting future could have been afforded those early whaling merchants who invested so heavily in New London's railroad.

J. Gregory Smith was once a Central Vermont kingpin; he obtained control of the New London road when his empire was being formed.

Sir Henry Ward Thornton, first president of Canadian National, owners of the Central Vermont.

CANADIAN NATIONAL RAILWAYS

The late Donald Gordon, who greatly modernized Canadian National Railways.

KARSH, OTTAWA

Crew members of the last mixed passenger train (No. 101) between New London and Palmer pose with station help in the yard at Stafford Springs, September 27, 1947.

A fresh drop of snow blankets Bridge Street in Willimantic. Its famous "windmill" signal which controlled four rail routes entering this busy center is in the foreground.

[RIGHT] Sunlight streams into the engine house of the Central Vermont at New London, and engine No. 472 basks in it in 1956.

Central Vermont engine No. 450 clatters over switch points enroute to New London, 1955.

Chapter Five Footnotes

1. New London *Morning News*, 19 January 1848.

2. Connecticut General Assembly, An Act to Incorporate the New London, Willimantic and Springfield Railroad Company, 1847, Public Records, Connecticut State Capitol Building.

3. *A Public Notice* attached to *Engineer's Report and Charter of the New London, Willimantic and Springfield Railroad Company 1847* (New London: Bolles & Williams, 1847).

4. James Chew, ''Fact and Reminiscence,'' *Records and Papers of the New London County Historical Society*, Part I, Vol. II (1895): 94.

5. *Engineer's Report and Charter of the New London, Willimantic and Springfield Railroad Company 1847* (New London: Bolles & Williams, 1847), passim.

6. *New London Daily Chronicle,* 7 November 1849.

7. Photocopy of excerpt from Directors' minute book, New London, Willimantic and Springfield Railroad Company, 1 November 1849, Turner Railroad Collection, The Connecticut Historical Society.

8. *Engineer's Report and Charter of the New London, Willimantic and Springfield Railroad Company, 1847,* passim.

9. Ibid.

10. Photocopy of excerpt from Directors' minute book, New London, Willimantic and Springfield Railroad Company, 1 November 1849, Turner Railroad Collection, The Connecticut Historical Society.

11. Henry Varnum Poor, *History of Railroads and Canals of the United States* (New York: 1860), 207.

12. Records of the Railway and Locomotive Historical Society, Baker Library, Harvard Business School.

13. *Report of the Railroad Commissioners of the State of Connecticut, For the Year Ending 1861* (Hartford: Case, Lockwood & Brainerd, 1861).

14. *Guide Book to the Line of the New London Northern Railroad 1883* (New London: Telegram Book and Job Office, 1883), 23.

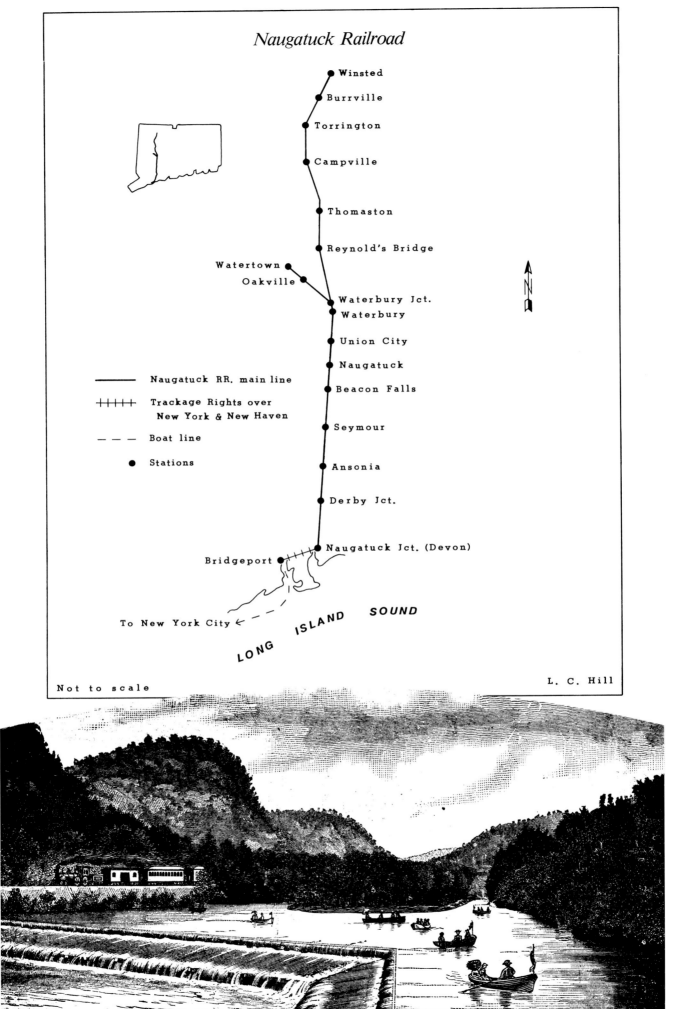

Naugatuck Railroad

- Winsted
- Burrville
- Torrington
- Campville
- Thomaston
- Reynold's Bridge
- Watertown
- Oakville
- Waterbury Jct.
- Waterbury
- Union City
- Naugatuck
- Beacon Falls
- Seymour
- Ansonia
- Derby Jct.
- Naugatuck Jct. (Devon)
- Bridgeport

———— Naugatuck RR. main line

+++++ Trackage Rights over New York & New Haven

– – – Boat line

● Stations

To New York City ←

LONG ISLAND SOUND

Not to scale

L. C. Hill

Chapter Six

Naugatuck's Pride

We question whether any track in Connecticut is better or more permanently laid. The locomotives, passenger cars, and any other appointments of the Naugatuck Railroad are all new, built to order, and of the first class.

—*Waterbury American, 1849*

In the early days of the iron horse many New England promoters hastily thrust impractical railroads into thin and dubious markets. But the line that still serves most of Connecticut's Naugatuck River valley stood in stark contrast to such enterprises. It was intelligently conceived, substantially built, and consistently rewarding to investors. To this day the line remains intact south of Torrington, still serving the regional requirements of industry and the traveller.

A railroad tapping the Naugatuck River valley was first promoted by Alfred Bishop, a Bridgeport businessman who was of "clear perception, strong judgement, never-failing energy, great experience and unstained integrity."[1] Born in Connecticut, a one-time New Jersey farmer with an uncanny interest in construction, he made his first contribution to Connecticut railroading by building, as we have seen, the Housatonic Railroad. Early on he believed that the prosperous metal and other heavy manufacturing companies of the Naugatuck River region—including makers of everything from pins and rubber boots to scythes and coffin fittings—would together amply sustain a rail enterprise.[2] By 1845 Bishop had aroused so much interest in the proposition that a group of enthusiasts successfully secured a charter from the legislature creating the Naugatuck Railroad Company. The charter authorized construction "from some suitable point at or near the Village of Winsted, or from the Town of Waterbury, to Derby and thence to the City of New Haven, or to the Town of Milford, or the Town of Bridgeport, adopting such termination and such routes as should be deemed most convenient."[3] Six thousand shares of stock could be issued (at $100 a share) with the privilege of increasing the total to fifteen thousand. The road had to spend some $50,000 on the line within a three-year span and had to be in operation within five years.

When construction began, the planned terminals were to be Bridgeport and Waterbury. But there was such a strong manufacturing and population base in the region north of Waterbury that the directors changed the northern terminus to Winsted. A typical "above Waterbury" promoter was the brilliant clockmaker Seth Thomas of Thomaston. (The village had changed its name from Plymouth Hollow in his honor.) He led the way by taking $15,000 of Naugatuck stock. The old construction contract which was in effect was nullified, and a new one was drafted reflecting the Winsted destination. Bridgeport had won out as the southern terminal for several

An early scene along the line near Derby shows the multitude of telegraphic lines then in use on the American railroad system. On the facing page is an early engraving of High Rock Grove on the Naugatuck, a summer stopping point for outdoors lovers.

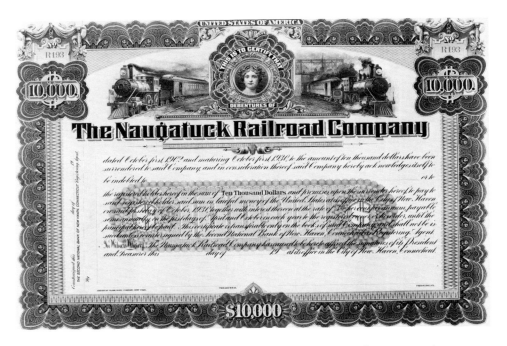

This beautifully detailed and unissued debenture of the Naugatuck Railroad, dated 1903 and carrying the then standard interest rate of 3¹/₂ percent, exemplifies many railroad securities of the era. No longer valid, they have acquired a new standing as "collectibles," often worth many hundreds of dollars. Sometimes the scenes are standardized, good for any railroad company, sometimes specific places and equipment on big-spending lines like the New Haven road. This is one of several certificates kindly loaned to this book by devotee Patrick Goedert of North Haven.

Distance from Bridgeport	Time Table 49 In Effect June 15, 1908 STATIONS.
0.00	Bridgeport _____N
1.59	E.BridgeportY'd N
3.22	Stratford _____D
4.92	Naugatuck Jct.__N
5.92	Junction Gravel Pt
7.41	Baldwin's _____
13.26	Derby Junction__N
13.77	Derby _____
15.42	Ansonia _____N
19.27	Seymour _____D
21.17	Rimmon _____
22.75	Beacon Falls_____
26.61	Naugatuck _____D
27.52	Union City_____D
28.99	Platt's Mills_____
31.19	Bank St Jct. ____N
31.77	Freight St Jct.__N
32.09	Waterbury_____
32.83	Watertown Jct.____
33.67	Brown's _____
35.21	Oakville _____D
36.17	Welton's _____
37.44	Watertown_____D
34.50	Waterville _____D
37.79	Jericho _____
39.02	Reynolds Bridge__
41.08	Thomaston _____D
43.94	Fluteville _____
46.40	Campville _____
48.84	East Litchfield __D
51.70	Torrington _____D
56.88	Burrville _____
61.04	Winsted _____N

reasons. First, the Housatonic Railroad had its headquarters there; second, a steamboat wharf was available; and third, connection could be made with the New York & New Haven Railroad. Moreover, it was the home of Alfred Bishop, who exerted no small influence in the decision. Of particular significance was the plan proffered by the New York & New Haven Railroad. The Naugatuck Railroad track was to halt at Naugatuck Junction in Devon (Milford), where the new road met the New York & New Haven. Eager for additional traffic, the New York & New Haven built a special track from Naugatuck Junction over the Housatonic River bridge, past Stratford, and into Bridgeport—all without cost to the new company. The Housatonic Railroad then offered use of its passenger depot and facilities to the Naugatuck road for a small rental fee.

The newly chartered company organized itself on February 11, 1848, with Timothy Dwight of New Haven as president.[4] In the same month a contract for constructing the line was signed by Alfred Bishop. The total cost of building and equipping the road was set at $1,580,723, or just under $28,000 per mile. Bishop's bill was paid by the railroad with $800,000 in cash and the remaining amount in Naugatuck Railroad bonds. By March 1848 the fifty-seven-mile engineering survey was fully approved by the board, and work commenced the following month. Bishop had great faith in this undertaking, or he would not have accepted bonds as partial payment. He also believed firmly that every manufacturing interest along the route should be forced to help finance it. The business community, unsure whether the line would become a dividend-paying road, decided to make cash contributions instead of subscribing to stock, and in this manner Bishop cleverly raised $75,000 of equity.

Organizing subcontractors, arranging for supplies, and co-ordinating the largest construction project ever undertaken in the Naugatuck River valley were assignments skillfully managed by Bishop. He was particularly concerned in getting the railroad safely engineered along the banks of the Naugatuck River from Derby north to Winsted (via Seymour, Beacon Falls, Naugatuck, Union City, Waterbury, and Thomaston) and in a manner that could withstand the frequent river flooding. The line crossed the river at many points, and bridge construction also came under Bishop's scrutiny. High ridges surrounded the track at various points, and there was a real threat of rock slides. A large amount of cut-and-fill work had to be undertaken, and substantial embankments were constructed to support tracks where required. Directors stipulated that Bishop's work be completed by September 1, 1849, and "in a most substantial manner." Heavy "H"-type iron rail was installed throughout; Erastus Corning, the ironmaster of Albany, produced the requisite spikes.

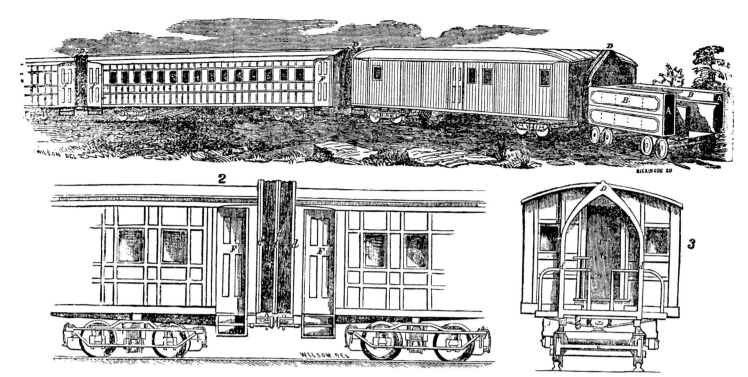

The protective vestibule between railway cars, a great improvement over dangerous open platforms, was first tried out in this country on the Naugatuck Railroad in 1853. The line's superintendent, Charles Waterbury, received a patent on his device the year before. How it provided a safe, warm, dry passage is illustrated in the drawings above for a second patent, in 1854, in which Waterbury was joined in his invention by Charles Atwood, another railroad employee. The tattered contemporary photograph below shows a vestibule-equipped Naugatuck baggage car, behind engine Jericho. The two properly attired gentlemen standing by the vestibule may be the proud inventors themselves. Until improved in later years, the idea caught on very slowly.

A northbound freight train of the "Naugy" at Derby. The first car contains just milk. The Derby Post Office and Drug Store lay just ahead, and a crossing tender's shack.

The use of many craftsmen and construction laborers, coming as they did from varying ethnic and educational backgrounds, often led to strife. The newspapers of the time were relatively blunt when reporting incidents that occurred during the railroad's construction. The *Derby Journal* described some of the details as construction proceeded:

> John A Woodbury & Co., contractors for Section 15 of the railroad, have failed! Our streets are swarming with Irish who have lost every cent of nearly a quarter's wages.

> There seems to be a report of guerrilla warfare being carried on by some of the subcontractors—one party capturing the horses and carts of another, the former re-taking them with the assistance of the law.

> One of the sub-contractors on the Naugatuck Railroad eloped last week, carrying off a large amount of cash which had been advanced for the payment of his hands. He is now in jail in Worcester.

This interesting document is dated 1873. Shipped via the S.S. Italia from Europe have come 1,888 steel rails for the Naugatuck. They have been unloaded at New York and will arrive at Bridgeport by barge.

> More shooting at Wolcotville! For some days a riotous spirit has been exhibited between the Irish and the Germans—on Sunday evening an Irishman named McMahon was shot in the head with a pistol ball. Henry Bauer, a German, was examined and charged with the shooting.[5]

NAUGATUCK RAILROAD

GRAND EXCURSION

JULY 4th, 1849.

For the accommodation of persons wishing to spend the approaching Anniversary in Bridgeport, Excursion Trains will leave the several Stations as follows :

Inchliff's Bridge, 7 A.M., Waterville, 7 08 A.M., Waterbury, 7 15 A.M., Naugatuck, 7 and 7 35 A.M., Humphreysville, 7 28 and 8 03 A.M., Ansonia, 7 50 and 8 15 A.M., Derby, 8 and 8 25, A.M., Baldwin's Platform 8 25 and 8 50 A.M., arriving at Bridgeport at 9 and 9 25 A.M.

Returning, leave Bridgeport at 5 30 P. M., for Inchliff's Bridge, and 6 P. M. for Naugatuck.

ALL EXCURSION TICKETS GOOD TO RETURN ON THE 4TH OR 5TH.

Fare from Inchliff's Bridge and Waterville to Bridgeport and back, 85 cts., Waterbury 75 cts., Naugatuck 65 cts., Humphreysville 50 cts., Ansonia 45 cts., Derby 40 cts., Baldwin's Platform, 37½ cts.

STEAMBOAT EXCURSION !

There will be an Excursion from Bridgeport on the 4th, giving persons an opportunity of enjoying

A SAIL OF TWO HOURS ON LONG ISLAND SOUND,

RETURNING IN SEASON FOR THE CARS.

FOR NEW YORK AND NEW HAVEN.

Trains leave Bridgeport at almost every hour of the day, giving to passengers an opportunity of visiting almost every part of the surrounding country and returning the same day.

FOR THE ACCOMMODATION OF PASSENGERS FROM

PLYMOUTH AND THE TOWNS IN THAT VICINITY,

The Cars will start from the Bridge opposite the House of J. Inchliff, two miles above Waterville, at 7 A. M., and return to the same place in the afternoon.

THE REGULAR PASSENGER TRAINS WILL RUN AS USUAL.

As many of the most prominent citizens have been appointed a Committee of Arrangements, it is expected that the approaching Anniversary will be

CELEBRATED IN BRIDGEPORT

In a manner becoming the occasion. Eminent Speakers are expected from abroad, and a brilliant display of

FIRE WORKS

WILL BE MADE IN THE EVENING.

PHILO HURD, Superintendent.

Bridgeport, June 20, 1849.

Pomeroy's Cheap Job Press, Bridgeport, Conn.

WORKS OF THE FARRELL FOUNDRY AND MACHINE COMPANY, ANSONIA, CONN.

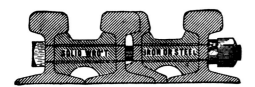

Despite these problems, in May 1849 Bishop had unofficial trains operating between Bridgeport and Derby, and to Naugatuck by month's end. Stagecoach service was set up between the upper points and Waterbury, bringing passengers to meet the trains. Though Waterbury became fully supportive of the Naugatuck project, its initial commitment to the enterprise was hesitant. Before the Naugatuck Railroad plan was known it was rumored that a special Canal Railroad branch would be built from that company's main line at Cheshire to Waterbury, which prompted much Waterbury interest in the rival undertaking. When the Naugatuck proposal reached the Brass City, consternation ensued. Which project to support? But it soon became apparent that the Naugatuck line would most directly serve the city's interests, as well as those of its sister cities along the river.

On June 11, 1849, the first Naugatuck railroad train steamed into Waterbury with "an unearthly yell of the whistle and hissing breath of the locomotive."[6] On September 24 trains rolled into the northern terminus of Winsted, even though stations were not quite finished when that first train ran the entire route. Certain construction details had not been attended to since the man in charge, Alfred Bishop, died a day before the first train ran into Waterbury. His son William Bishop would one day be called to the Naugatuck's presidency, and he in later years would become the first president of the mighty New York, New Haven & Hartford Railroad Company.

The "Naugy's" first trains were hauled by wood-burning locomotives. They were ordered—all five of them—from the Rogers firm in Patterson, New Jersey. They cost $7,600 apiece and were named *Naugatuck, Winsted, Plymouth, Waterbury,* and *Alfred Bishop.* The rolling stock also included a small assortment of passenger, baggage, and freight cars. Business receipts for the time operated in that first year, 1849, netted just under $30,000. At Bridgeport the Naugatuck road had to place New York-bound passengers and freight temporarily on steamers until the New York & New Haven Railroad finished its road into New York State. The pioneer years which followed on the Naugatuck provided a typical chronicle of accidents, cash shortages, natural calamities (caused by the flooding Naugatuck River), and the usual struggle of any railroad to gain financial independence. In 1851, however, more than 150,000 passengers were carried and a 7 percent dividend was declared. The physical plant was improved and expanded, and the company strove to keep its line in prime operating condition.[7] But a report by the *Derby Journal* in 1849 bears witness to the fact that there is always the unexpected event: "On Friday, the freight train 'down' was turning a curve about a mile and a half this side of Naugatuck. The Locomotive suddenly came upon a large cow, which threw the engine off the track

down an embankment about thirty feet into the river killing the Fireman and severely bruising the Engineer. The Locomotive and the baggage car were so much injured that they probably will be of no further use."[8]

New engine and yard facilities were erected in 1863 on the Naugatuck's recently purchased property in Bridgeport. A few years later the company installed a track turn-out at Naugatuck Junction, allowing trains to be run directly into New Haven over the New York & New Haven Railroad. Financial success was being achieved, and dividends moved up to 10 percent. New cars and engines were added to the rosters, and most of the wooden truss bridges were gradually converted to safer ones of masonry or iron. Maximum speed for passenger trains was twenty miles per hour. Steel rails were installed in the 1870s.[9]

The people and the businesses of Watertown looked longingly at the Naugatuck's success story. A railroad from their own town to Waterbury would be a welcome addition and would eliminate the need for townsfolk to use stages to reach Waterbury for train connections. And so in 1869 the Watertown & Waterbury Railroad was chartered to connect the two points via Oakville. Construction began the following year. Local figures ran the line, and the town of Watertown subscribed to thirteen hundred shares of stock. The Naugatuck Railroad also bought its stock and

This is Derby Junction in 1902. Here, the main line of the Naugatuck crossed that of the New Haven & Derby, the latter in the immediate right foreground. The exact spot where they crossed was called a "diamond," and was protected by signals.

Another scene at Derby Junction: the bridge complex over the Naugatuck River. The old Naugatuck main line went right: today left, crossing to the other bank.

provided building expertise to the little five-mile road, which opened November 1, 1870. A five-year lease to the Naugatuck Railroad was written upon opening, though the short line was in bankruptcy before the lease expired. The financial panic of 1873 had proved too much, and the line was eventually purchased by the Naugatuck.

The Naugatuck Railroad was a "local" road, originally built with no connections at its northern end at Winsted. Later in the nineteenth century, however, the road made connections with other companies north of Bridgeport. The Hartford, Providence & Fishkill came to Waterbury as well as the Watertown & Waterbury; the Connecticut Western Railroad eventually intersected the Naugatuck road at Winsted; the New Haven & Derby met the line at Derby; and finally at the Brass City there arrived the Meriden, Waterbury & Cromwell.

On April 1, 1887, the splendidly maintained property of the Naugatuck Railroad, including its Watertown Branch, was leased to the New York, New Haven & Hartford Railroad Company for ninety-nine years at an annual rental of $200,000. By 1906 financial control of the line had enabled the New York, New Haven & Hartford Railroad to retire its corporate stock and have it officially brought within the empire. The Naugatuck Railroad became the "Naugatuck Division," and its short line the "Watertown Branch."[10]

Engine Thomaston *stands at the ready. Main Street of its namesake town is at left, and the quaint old Thomaston House inn.*

All too familiar to residents of Waterbury is the famed railroad depot in that town. This is the one which preceded it, built in 1876.

Seymour's railroad station boasted an enormous roof. Some rather slick characters can be studied among the waiting crowd.

96

This train is bound from Waterbury up the little branch to Watertown. The scene dates from 1903. As is the case with many little-used lines, this one too has vanished.

The year after these leases were signed, Connecticut took the brunt of the still-remembered Blizzard of 1888. It paralyzed the railroad network of the state, and the Naugatuck Division was hit hard. The *Waterbury American* reported some of the scenes:

SNOWBOUND IN THE CARS

There were many pleasant incidents connected with the first night's sleep in the Derby car. When the passengers realized they would have to stay there for the night, they made the best beds possible among the seats. They were all tired out and were just falling asleep when the "meows" of a feline intruder fell upon the tired ear. The dozers rubbed their eyes when the calls were repeated, and one man started out to find the feline. When he quieted everything down and was dozing off to sleep again, the meowing was worse than before, and the whole carload became anxious to find the cat. At last it was discovered in the person of a drummer (a salesman!) who was somewhat of a ventriloquist.

———————

Stewart, the yeast man, was tired out and fell asleep too. A joker stuck toothpicks into his whiskers, lit them, and then yelled 'FIRE' The scene that ensued was enjoyed by the whole party.

———————

The dead engines (with no water) were eventually towed back to Beacon Falls and in order to procure water a path was dug to the bank of the river and a line of men, among whom were many passengers, was formed and water was passed along the line until 2,700 pails full had been emptied into the tanks, after which the fires were started and the work resumed.[11]

Alfred Bishop—the railroad genius of Bridgeport—never saw his Naugatuck dream officially opened to Winsted, but he had proposed an enterprise that served people and industry, and one that made money for its investors. And for that, the Naugatuck Valley can point to a transportation heritage that has endured for nearly 140 years. Today, new faces share and operate the line—from Conrail and Boston & Maine freights to modern one-car passenger commuter trains.

A quiet day and youthful train watchers at the terminus of the Watertown Branch.

Chapter Six Footnotes

1. Quoted in Edward Chase Kirkland, *Men, Cities, and Transportation* (Cambridge: Harvard University Press, 1948), II: 241.

2. *Second Annual Report of the Board of Directors to the Stockholders of the Naugatuck Railroad, February 18, 1850* (New Haven: J.H. Benham, 1850), 4-10

3. *American Railroad Journal,* August 1855, 40.

4. *Derby Journal,* 17 February 1848.

5. Mattatuck Historical Society, *The Naugatuck Railroad, 1849-1949* (Waterbury: 1949), passim.

6. Ibid., passim.

7. Photocopy, Naugatuck Railroad Corporate Journal "A", 1849, 45, Turner Railroad Collection, The Connecticut Historical Society.

8. Undated newspaper excerpt, *Derby Journal*, 1849, Turner Railroad Collection, The Connecticut Historical Society.

9. Railroad Commissioners of Connecticut, *Annual Report for 1854*.

10. Corporate and Operating History of the Lines Owned by the New York, New Haven & Hartford Railroad Company, 30 June 1915, Turner Railroad Collection, The Connecticut Historical Society.

11. Undated newspaper excerpts, *Waterbury American*, 1888, Turner Railroad Collection, The Connecticut Historical Society.

These two rather interesting chums stand in front of the new Oakville station on the Watertown Branch. Who are they?

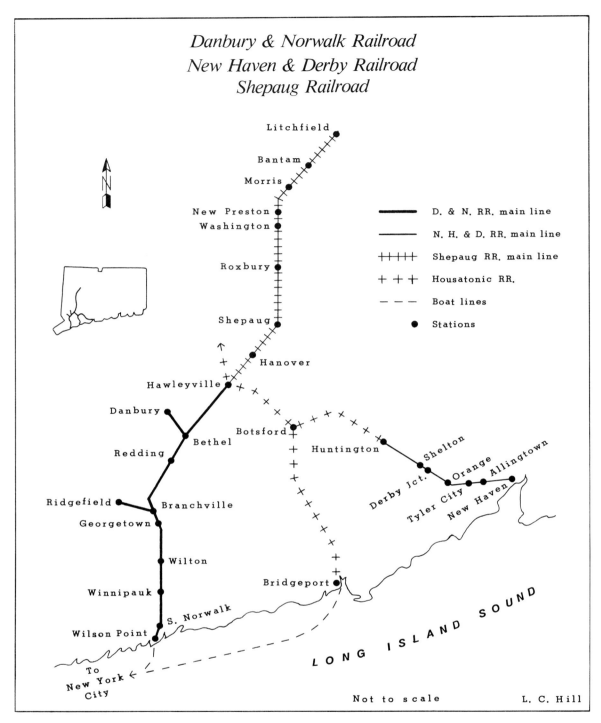

Danbury & Norwalk Railroad
New Haven & Derby Railroad
Shepaug Railroad

Litchfield

Bantam

Morris

New Preston
Washington

Roxbury

Shepaug

Hanover

Hawleyville

Danbury

Bethel

Redding

Botsford

Huntington

Shelton

Ridgefield

Branchville

Derby Jct.

Orange

Allingtown

Tyler City

New Haven

Georgetown

Wilton

Winnipauk

Bridgeport

S. Norwalk

Wilson Point

LONG ISLAND SOUND

To
New York
City

━━━━━	D. & N. RR. main line
─────	N. H. & D. RR. main line
++++	Shepaug RR. main line
+ + +	Housatonic RR.
- - -	Boat lines
●	Stations

Not to scale   L. C. Hill

Chapter Seven

A Trio of Short Lines

From about 1832 to the end of the century epidemics of a disease that came to be known as Railroad Fever broke out sporadically in the United States. A really violent outbreak in any particular region was almost sure to be followed by a relapse; and the relapse, in turn, was followed by a condition approaching sanity in which railroads were looked at realistically.

—Stewart H. Holbrook, The Story of American Railroads, 1947.

In railway parlance a "short line" merely denotes a small railroad company. Its route might be a connector to larger railroads, a feeder to other short lines, or simply a local road with a metropolitan center at one end and a provincial outpost on the other, "from somewhere to nowhere," as it has been unfeelingly described. Many short lines were built in Connecticut during the nineteenth century, particularly when railroad fever ran high. Some of these ventures proved to be sensible undertakings. Three typical short lines grouped in the western half of Connecticut included the Danbury & Norwalk, the New Haven & Derby, and the Shepaug railroads.

The Danbury & Norwalk

Danbury was still recovering from a raid by British troops when, in 1780, Zadoc Benedict set up the town's first hat factory, using local beaver fur. In the years that followed the little settlement grew to be the "hat capital" of the United States, with fifty-one factories turning out headgear and related items. Far away in Australia rabbits perished by the millions to furnish fur to keep America capped in felt fashioned in Fairfield County. One firm, founded in 1833 by proud and powerful Ezra Mallory, would not receive any salesman who came to the plant bareheaded. Labor poured in, hats poured out, and Danbury soon acquired other distinctions as a home for trotting horses and the setting for a great country fair.

[OPPOSITE PAGE] Pausing at an unknown street in Danbury is engine Bethel. *In the scene above, another early woodburner enters Sanford's Cut. The line is still being used by Fairfield County commuters.*

A growing town needs transportation, and in 1825, during the brief period of enthusiasm for canals, promoters eyed nearby Neversink Pond, rising 395 feet above tidewater, as a natural feeder for a canal to harbors at Westport or Fairfield to the south. Some rough surveys soon revealed, alas, that there would be too much "heavy locking" over a relatively short distance. No spade touched earth. By 1835, when transportation thinking had all turned to railways, a new group of promoters and prophets secured a charter for the Fairfield County Railroad.

It would, after the free and easy language of such early documents, run "from Danbury to some suitable point on tide-water in the Town of Fairfield or the Town of Norwalk."[1] Capitalization was set at $200,000. The popular Connecticut railroad surveyor Alexander C. Twining was hired by the promoters to locate the new line. Twining found two river routes—one along the Saugatuck River to Compo Point

Residents of elite Ridgefield may not recognize their station of yesteryear at Prospect Avenue. The children likely belong to a railroad man. Engine Norwalk *is at the rear.*

Alexander Catlin Twining
(1801-1884)

below Westport, and the other beside the Norwalk River to Wilson Point in South Norwalk. Backers of the Fairfield County had grander visions than that, however. They proclaimed that the line should not only be extended to Danbury, but all the way north to the Berkshires. From that point, they speculated it would connect with the Western Railroad and form a substitute route to Albany, New York. Connecting steamboats would run along the Sound to New York City. But the Berkshire part of the dream was far beyond the powers of the Fairfield County Railroad, and the task was left to the up-and-coming Housatonic road.

Twining estimated the Fairfield County Railroad would cost approximately $203,339,[2] and, amazingly, the entire project was conceived of as a "horse railroad" with nearly $24,000 alone allotted for horses, harnesses, carriages, wagons, stables, and depots with appropriate carriage houses. Two horses could pull a single car, said Twining, and the trip from Danbury to Norwalk would take three hours of travel time. The concept of a horse railroad soon faded when iron horses were proven to be longer winded. For the next fifteen years the Fairfield County Railroad project slumbered.

Once the Housatonic Railroad was completed, local interest was revived in a rail line between Danbury and Norwalk. Municipal aid helped finance the successor project of 1850—the Danbury & Norwalk Railroad—with Norwalk itself pledging to buy $100,000 of its stock. The cost of the line was now estimated at $370,828. Construction went forward, even through a rather intense winter. Iron rails were actually laid directly on the ground near Redding; the earth was so frozen that chestnut ties could not be inserted underneath until warmer weather. The twenty-four-mile short line, which opened on February 22, 1852, also served Bethel, Georgetown, and Wilton. At South Norwalk the road met the New York & New Haven Railroad, which allowed use of its station and provided the Danbury & Norwalk with an outlet to New York City.

In 1870 the Danbury & Norwalk constructed its four-mile Ridgefield Branch from Branchville and the following year commenced the Bethel Branch from Bethel to Hawleyville, in order that the Shepaug Valley Railroad might connect with its main line. The Danbury & Norwalk's last construction project occurred in 1882, when the railroad, tired of its congested steamboat connection on the Norwalk River at South Norwalk proper, laid down a track extension to Wilson Point on Long Island Sound. Here it built a commodious dock and terminal facility and stepped up its steamboat connections. The earnings history of the Danbury & Norwalk was enviable as short lines go. Gross revenues, for instance, amounted to $165,245 in 1877,

DANBURY & NORWALK RAILROAD. [Standard Time.

H. WILLIAMS, *Treas. & G. T. & P. A.*, Danbury. CHAS. M. CRAWFORD, *Superintendent*, So. Norwalk.

Danbury to So. Norwalk. [June 9, 1884.] **South Norwalk to Danbury.**

p m	p m	p m	p m	a m	a m	a m	LEAVE ARRIVE	p m	p m	p m	p m	p m	p m	p m	MLS	FRS
------	s3 30	2†05	1 55	------	6 20	------	*Litchfield*	12 50	------	8 00	------	1 10	s1 20	------		
------	6 12	5 45	3 40	------	8 00	------	*Hawleyville*	10 53	------	6 15	------	8 45	11 15	------		
------	6 37	6 37	3 55	------	8 18	------	*Bethel*	10 25	------	5 40	------	7 30	10 55	------		
------	6 20	6 15	3 50	12 05	8 15	6 40	**Danbury**	10 30	3 13	5 45	7 16	1 45	11 00	------	23½	80
------	6 37	6 37	3 56	12 10	8 20	6 46	**Bethel**	10 23	3 05	5 39	7 11	1 30	10 52	------	20½	75
------	6 47	6 51	4 04	12 17	A	6 52	Reading	10 13	2 57	B	7 05	1 10	10 44	------	17¼	70
------	6 57	6 59	f	f	------	6 57	Sanford's	f	f	------	6 59	12 55	10 38	------	15¼	65
------	7 07	7 12	4 15	12 30	8 35	7 06	Branchville	9 58	2 45	5 23	6 51	12 40	10 30	------	12¾	55
------	7 14	7 27	4 18	12 33	------	7 09	Georgetown	9 52	2 42	------	6 46	12 24	10 25	------	11⅛	50
------	7 25	......	f	f	------	7 15	Cannon's	9 47	f	------	6 39	12 04	10 18	------	9	40
------	7 32	......	4 27	12 42	8 46	7 19	Wilton	9 43	2 32	5 12	6 35	11 54	10 13	------	7½	35
------	7 39	......	f	f	------	7 25	South Wilton	f	f	------	6 29	-----	10 05	------	5	25
------	7 44	......	4 35	12 51	------	7 29	Winnipauk	9 31	f	------	6 26	-----	9 58	------	3¼	15
------	7 51	8 10	4 39	12 55	8 58	7 34	Norwalk	9 25	2 18	4 59	6 20	-----	9 52	------	1⅛	10
------	8 01	8 25	4 45	1 00	9 03	7 40	**So. Norwalk**	9 20	2 13	4 55	6 15	11 30	9 45	------		
------	------	------	5 05	1 20	9 20	7 55	Wilson Point	8 30	2 40	4 25	5 40	-----	------	------	2½	
------	10 53	10 53	6 00	2 20	10 33	9 13	*New York*	8 00	1 00	3 40	4 45	10 00	8 00	------		
------	11 57	10 16	5 19	2 21	9 48	9 20	*Bridgeport*	8 40	1 35	4 21	5 36	9 36	8 40	------		
------	12 30	10 50	5 51	3 00	10 20	10 00	*New Haven*	8 10	1 00	3 50	5 07	9†03	8 00	------		
p m	a m	p m	p m	p m	a m	a m	ARRIVE LEAVE	a m	p m	p m	p m	p m	a m	p m	MLS	FRS

† Mixed. f Flag Stations. s Sunday milk and accommodation. * Mondays only.
A—To take on passengers. B—To leave passengers.

Ridgefield Branch.

	p m	p m	p m	a m	a m	LEAVE ARRIVE	a m	p m	p m	p m	a m		
------	6 00	3 55	12 10	8 15	6 45	**Ridgefield**	10 17	3 03	5 43	7 08	7 48	16¾	80
------	6 20	4 13	12 30	8 33	7 05	Branchville	9 58	2 45	5 23	6 51	7 30	12¾	55
------	8 25	4 45	1 00	9 03	7 40	So. Norwalk	9 20	2 13	4 55	6 15	------		
	p m	p m	p m	a m	a m	AR. LV.	a m	p m	p m	p m	a m		

Connects at So. Norwalk with New York, New Haven & Hartford R. R. At Bethel with Shepaug R. R. At Danbury with Housatonic R. R. and N. Y. & N. E. R. R.

and after expenses were deducted a net profit of $50,275 was realized.[3] Fifty-six-pound iron rail was installed throughout the somewhat serpentine route. Six locomotives as well as eight passenger coaches were on the roster.

It was the Wilson Point facility and the fact the Danbury & Norwalk was not leased to some larger road that attracted a take-over. The interested party was the Housatonic Railroad, which was undergoing a systemwide expansion. (Even the Housatonic itself was being courted, by New York City speculators associated with the big New York & New England Railroad, which went across central Connecticut). In 1886 the Danbury & Norwalk was leased to the Housatonic, forming its "Danbury & Norwalk Division," and soon afterward the Wall Street men gobbled up the gobbler. The "New England" promoters desperately wanted an entrance of their own into New York City and a way to divert traffic that the New York, New Haven & Hartford Railroad was monopolizing. Invasion was the key word, and Wilson Point the strategic place.

A splendid view of the railroad's dock at Wilson Point, Norwalk, in 1882. From here the famed Long Island & Eastern States Express *was ferried across the Sound to Oyster Bay, Long Island, to the tracks of the Long Island Railroad and New York.*

A builder's photograph of Danbury & Norwalk No. 3, for some reason shorn of its headlight. It was named for a director.

What the "New England" and its ally the Housatonic thought up was the Long Island & Eastern States Express route, mentioned in Chapter Four. Trains soon sped between Boston, Putnam, Willimantic, Hartford, and Waterbury, over to Hawleyville, whereupon they went south over the Danbury & Norwalk Division to Wilson Point. Here cars were floated across Long Island Sound to Oyster Bay, Long Island, there to be reassembled and run into Brooklyn via the Long Island Railroad. The "New England" went so far as to provide a first-class Pullman train over the whole route.

For a brief period the amphibious operation did catch the public's fancy. But the project incurred the New Haven Railroad's wrath. War briefly erupted. Internal problems then arose on the New England road, and the speculators were ousted. This gave the New Haven a chance to pick up stock control of the Housatonic system. In 1892 it leased the Housatonic and the Danbury & Norwalk properties, and travel patterns returned to normal. Under the New Haven, the former Danbury & Norwalk main line was electrified and was once part of the route of Berkshire expresses, with parlor and dining service for visitors to Great Barrington, Lenox, and Stockbridge. Today, though, the electrification is but a memory. Passenger service ends once again at Danbury, with mostly single-car commuter trains running out of South Norwalk, a branch of Metro North. It still amazes commuters on this line to learn their branch had its origin as a horse railroad.

A local passenger train glides to a stop at Georgetown, beside the Norwalk River.

Crew members pose at the Norwalk turntable with D & N engine Emma. *Note iron cowcatcher.*

The New Haven & Derby

Set in a pleasant valley where the Naugatuck and Housatonic rivers meet, and still possessed of many fine old nineteenth-century business buildings that ought to be preserved, the little mill town of Derby was "the sticks" to sophisticates in New Haven. It was also the home of the fictional Miss Antoinette Birby, heroine of a raucous and ancient Yale song by Cole Porter about a restless small-town girl whose downfall began when she left home to sample the fast life of the Elm City:

> ...As the train pulled out of the station,
> She gave forth this explanation,
> "I'm off for New Haven, so long, goodbye;
> I'm off for New Haven, I don't know why..."

[OVERLEAF] An inside view of a New Haven & Derby coach, in the 1890s. Most patrons have special ribbons pinned to pockets, suggesting a convention delegation.

Busy Derby was served by the New Haven & Derby and the Naugatuck railroads. East Derby, below, was serviced by the latter.

One must draw the veil not only over Antoinette and her sordid fate but also over the forgotten New Haven & Derby on which she embarked so long ago. Indeed it is curious that the railroad was ever built, since New Haven and the towns of the Naugatuck valley were already indirectly connected by rail. The route of the New Haven & Derby was only thirteen miles long, but the terrain was difficult, intersected by ridges and ravines; the right of way, conforming to natural contours, curved this way and that; cuts were blasted through rocky outcroppings; and spidery timber trestles spanned the deep voids and valleys.

But civic spirit embraced the Derby Road. Its spokesman was Francis Harrison of New Haven, a postal official who thought it would "facilitate public travel and transportation of mails between New Haven and the Naugatuck Valley." Morris Tyler, a future lieutenant governor of Connecticut, was also a key figure. By 1864 a charter for the New Haven & Derby Railroad was obtained.[4] The road was to run via Orange to some suitable point in Derby, where it would connect with the Naugatuck Railroad. Promotional campaigns were staged, but three years would pass with hardly any progress. The financial response was definitely sluggish until

The Rogers Locomotive Works in New Jersey built this steamer. It was named for Morris Tyler, an official. Ansonia eventually became this short line's destination, as the letter "A" on the tender informs us.

Train time at Shelton on the branch to Botsford. It is not known why so many onlookers have gathered. A canal runs close by here.

in 1867 the city of New Haven gave its blessing to the enterprise. It bought $200,000 worth of stock and won a controlling interest. The city fathers could then oversee how the investment was spent. Another $200,000 was raised elsewhere.

Spidery Round Hill trestle was located on the branch extension between Derby and Botsford. Photograph was taken in 1889.

A survey of the New Haven & Derby Railroad was performed in the fall of 1867 by Colonel M.O. Davidson of New York City. Once the railroad commissioners of Connecticut approved its location, the construction contract was let to George Chapman & Company. Though the work began, the railroad still did not have its financial house in order; twice bonds had to be sold to raise cash. When litigation arose in 1869, Chapman abandoned the contract unfinished. Even the railroad's charter had expired. An extension of time was received, and a new contractor was ultimately found in the person of Willis Pratt of Springfield, Massachusetts. But in 1871 Pratt, too, threw in the towel.[5] Among his aggravations: Ansonia got switched in as the destination instead of Derby, the route was changed at certain points, and numerous new construction headaches and unforeseen problems arose. The directors hastily engaged local engineers and labor until the railroad finally opened on August 5, 1871, when the first trainload of proper New Haven visitors poured into little Ansonia. As the tongue-in-cheek Derby newspaper reported:

> Saturday last was a great day for New Haven. These citizens appeared like boys on a frolic, or rather as if just let out of school. The sights of our place, evidently new to their

We are uncertain whether this is Davis Brook trestle or another view of Round Hill. Information will be welcomed by the author.

provincial eyes, almost took their breath away; and when they entered our Ansonia Hall they all at once fell to laughing, handshaking, speech-making, until it required almost a gentle violence to detach them from the wonders on which they were feasting their eyes. We did not know before that New Haven could be so easily and so greatly delighted. We knew not we had such power to impart pleasure. Our beautiful scenery, beautiful women, fine halls, large mills, crowds of people, etc. being a common, everyday matter with us we thought little of it, and this coming forth of these crowds from the rural districts of the Elm City.[6]

Two trains a day each way started service. Trains at New Haven utilized the huge Chapel Street Union Station erected by the New York & New Haven Railroad; the Canal road offered other facilities. At Derby connection was made with the Naugatuck Railroad, and through-ticketing and baggage arrangements were drawn up. Despite the financial hardships and construction dilemmas, the New Haven & Derby began to make some money. In 1877 it grossed nearly $100,000, paid out slightly more than $50,000 in expenses, and ended up with a $46,475 net profit. Forty-eight men were employed full-time that year, and more than 110,000 passengers were carried. All thirteen miles of the route had quality iron rails, the earliest produced by the Abbott Iron Works of Baltimore. In time rolling stock increased, fragile trestles were filled in, and a pooling agreement for freight traffic was drawn up with the Naugatuck Railroad. Stations along the Derby road included New Haven, Orange, Derby, Birmingham, and Ansonia; flag stops were at West Haven, Alling Crossing, and Turkey Hill.

Tyler City was mapped out in Orange as a boom town. Lots were sold; the town prospered. This was taken in later, sadder days.

NEW HAVEN & DERBY RAILROAD.

Connects at New Haven with New York, New Haven & Hartford R.R.; New Haven & Northampton R.R.   At Ansonia, with Naugatuck R.R.

J. H. BARTHOLOMEW, *President*, Ansonia, Conn.   [*Standard Time*
      E. S. QUINTARD, *Superintendent*, New Haven, Conn.

New Haven to Ansonia.

Nov. 19, 1883.] LEAVE	MLS	FRS	a m	a m	p m	p m	p m	p m
New Haven	----	----	7†00	9 50	2†00	5 40	6 20	11t00
West Haven f	10		7 08	9 56	------	5 46	6 27	------
Tyler City	20		7‡20	10‡02	2‡16	5 53	‡6 35	------
Orange	30		7 26	10 05	2 22	5 58	6 41	11 27
Derby	----		7 40	10 16	2 37	6 10	6 54	11 43
Birmingham	45		7 47	10 20	2 43	6 14	6 58	11 50
Ansonia	50		7 55	10 27	2 50	6 20	7 05	11 58
Waterbury ARRIVE	----		8 48	11 15	4 13	7 10	9 00	------

Ansonia to New Haven.

LEAVE	a m	a m	a m	a m	p m	p m		
Waterbury	5 30	8 26	------	10 50	2 44	6 45	------	
Ansonia	6†35	9 05	------	11†40	3 25	7 31	------	
Birmingham	6 43	9 11	------	11 50	3 31	7 40	------	
Derby	6 47	9 17	------	11 55	3 38	7 44	------	
Orange	7 01	9 27	------	12 07	3 48	7 58	------	
Tyler City	7‡05	9 30	------	12‡13	3‡51	8†02	------	
West Haven f	7 18	9 37	------	12 23	3 57	8 14	------	
New Haven ARRIVE	7 25	9 43	a m	12‡32	4 03	8 22	------	

t Saturday only.   f Flag Station.   † Mixed train.   ‡ Stop on signal.

Like the Danbury & Norwalk, the New Haven & Derby had its dreams of being part of a much larger railroad system. Various "paper" railroads thought of connecting with the Derby road—unrealized dreams like the New Haven, Danbury & Erie, and the New England & Erie railroads. The goal was a line stretching from a Hudson River bridge at Bear Mountain to New Haven. Other schemes had the road headed towards Woodbury, Sandy Hook, and Southbury. A more serious proposal was for the Derby road to parallel the New York & New Haven Railroad. The Derby & State Line Railroad was widely spoken of to fulfill that last dream, although it was never built.

A take-over, however, did come. Just as it had acquired the Danbury & Norwalk, the Housatonic thought that the New Haven & Derby would help it invade the empire of the New York, New Haven & Hartford. In 1889 the Housatonic leased its "New Haven & Derby Division." The year before a small amount of new construction had connected the two roads together: the New Haven & Derby extended itself from Derby to Huntington, while the Housatonic threw out an extension from Botsford to Huntington. Trains then ran directly into New Haven from the Housatonic system. When the Housatonic was finally leased to the New York, New Haven & Hartford Railroad in 1892, the little New Haven & Derby short line got passed along to the "Consolidated" by lease as well. All that survives in 1985 is a short length of rail that curves away to the north from the old New Haven main line as it comes out of the deep cut just west of the New Haven station. It disappears into a huge automobile scrap yard, just after the filth of the cut and before the man-made mountain where modern New Haven deposits its trash and garbage. Such, in this enlightened age, is the railway "Gateway" to that former seat of culture, the City of the Elms.

Another view of Round Hill trestle with the Housatonic River in background. In this century, the track from Derby to Botsford was thoroughly upgraded by the New Haven Railroad in an effort to perfect its rail route from the Cedar Hill yards in New Haven to the Poughkeepsie Bridge. Trestles like this were rebuilt, filled in, or replaced.

SHEPAUG RAILROAD. [*Standard Time.*]

Leave or arrive in New York by N. Y., N. H. & H. R. R., at Grand Central Depot, connecting at South Norwalk with Danbury & Norwalk R. R.

Offices, Litchfield.   E. McNEILL, *Supt.*

		From Litchfield.			[July 2, 1884.]		**To Litchfield.**		
FRS	MLS	p m	p m	a m	LEAVE ARRIVE	p m	p m	p m	
....	....	3s30	2 00	6 25	**Litchfield**	12 45	7 55	1 20	....
....	2¼	3 40	2‡06	6‡31	Lake	12‡38	7‡48	1 14	....
....	3	3 50	2 09	6 33	Bantam	12 35	7 45	1 09	....
30	6¼	4 05	2‡19	6‡42	Morris	12‡25	7‡35	12 58	....
....	8¾	4 17	2‡25	6 48	Romford	12 18	7‡29	12 50	....
....	12	4 35	2 36	6 59	New Preston	12 06	7 18	12 35	....
55	13¼	4 50	2 40	7 03	Washington	12 00	7 12	12 26	....
....	17½	5‡08	2‡56	7‡18	Judd's Bridge	11‡41	6‡57	12‡06	....
85	20	5 20	3 04	7 25	Roxbury	11 32	6 50	11 59	....
....	23¾	5‡33	3‡15	7‡36	Roxbury Falls	11‡20	6‡40	11‡47	....
....	27½	5‡45	3‡25	7‡46	Shepaug	11‡09	6‡30	11‡35	....
1 25	32¾	6 12	3 40	8 00	**Hawleyville**	10 53	6 15	11 15	....
1 50	38¼	6 37	3 55	8 18	*Bethel*	10 25	5 40	10 55	....
....	41¾	.....	4 34	9 09	*Danbury*	8 15	3 45	.....	....
2 20	58¾	8 01	4 45	9 03	*South Norwalk*	9 18	4 55	9 45	....
3 05	....	10r30	6 00	10 33	*New York—N.H.R.R...*	8 00	3 40	8 00	....
....	55¼	7 30	5 20	9 48	*Bridgeport*	10 05	5 30	8s50	....
....	72½	12 30	5 51	10 20	*New Haven*	9‡30	4 07	a m	....

‡ Stops on signal.   s Sunday milk train.   r Via Bridgeport.

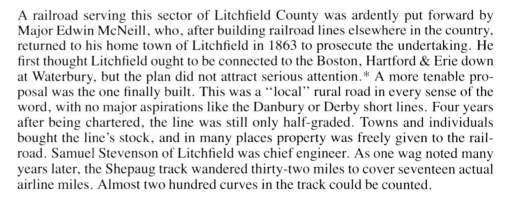

The Shepaug Railroad

The Shepaug Valley Railroad, chartered in July 1866 by the Connecticut legislature,[7] served the passenger and freight requirements of the pretty Shepaug River valley in Litchfield County. Its thirty-two-mile route —first estimated to cost $850,000—opened in January 1872 from beautiful Litchfield to Bantam, Morris, New Preston, Washington, Roxbury, and Shepaug. At Hawleyville the Shepaug road met the Housatonic Railroad. A few months before the grand opening a contract was made with the Danbury & Norwalk for a branch from Bethel towards Hawleyville. This connection opened in the summer of 1872 and allowed patrons of the Shepaug to reach the Danbury & Norwalk, at whose southern terminus connections could be made to New York City. Shepaug engine *Waramaug* hauled the first train.

A Crossing Flagman.

A railroad serving this sector of Litchfield County was ardently put forward by Major Edwin McNeill, who, after building railroad lines elsewhere in the country, returned to his home town of Litchfield in 1863 to prosecute the undertaking. He first thought Litchfield ought to be connected to the Boston, Hartford & Erie down at Waterbury, but the plan did not attract serious attention.* A more tenable proposal was the one finally built. This was a "local" rural road in every sense of the word, with no major aspirations like the Danbury or Derby short lines. Four years after being chartered, the line was still only half-graded. Towns and individuals bought the line's stock, and in many places property was freely given to the railroad. Samuel Stevenson of Litchfield was chief engineer. As one wag noted many years later, the Shepaug track wandered thirty-two miles to cover seventeen actual airline miles. Almost two hundred curves in the track could be counted.

Like many Connecticut short lines—and larger roads too—the Shepaug Valley started construction without the estimated cost fully in hand. Great faith was placed in future stock sales. Inevitably the difference had to be raised by selling bonds, which are higher grade securities. Like the Derby road, the Shepaug floated two issues, but when the time came to pay the bond interest there wasn't enough cash on hand after the costly construction bills had been paid. Two mortgages amounting to $600,000 were written on the little Shepaug property. When the second mortgage holders received no interest in 1873 they foreclosed, only to reorganize under the shortened style of the "Shepaug Railroad." With only three engines, three passenger coaches, a single baggage car, twenty-four merchandise cars, and gross revenues of exactly $13,498, the Shepaug was a pauper.

*McNeill nevertheless ultimately made a full and gratis engineering survey.

The following year, however, business took off, and a gross of $42,750 occurred. In the 1880s revenues were in the area of $60,000, but it was still not enough. In March 1887 owners of the first mortgage bonds foreclosed, for their interest now had also been skipped. The entire property then went through a second reorganization, and the short line emerged as the Shepaug, Litchfield, & Northern. In 1892 the property was leased to the New York, New Haven & Hartford Railroad, forming its Litchfield Branch. The following description drawn from the 1891 *Annual Report of the Railroad Commissioners* illuminates the Shepaug's last independent gasps:

> New York men linked with Housatonic Railroad interests occupied senior positions of management. Gross earnings amounted to $63,336; less expenses of $55,981 this left an income of $7,355. The Adams Express Company pays a flat rental of $2,000 to conduct the freight express business of the Company. The Western Union Telegraph Company owns and operates all telegraphic services. 68 people were in the road's employ and the two largest freight commodities carried included stone and milk products. Of the 32 miles of railroad track, the aggregate length of curves was fourteen miles while straight track amounted to seventeen miles.[8]

And such was the Shepaug's profile. The short line has long since vanished, but its abandoned right of way can still be seen and hiked upon in places. For many, there is regret that it ever was removed, and a few can still recall the little railroad's parlor car of quartered oak with light blue upholstery.

An idyllic summer morning at Litchfield, Connecticut, about 1890. A horse and buggy stand at the ready; milk cans await the "down" freight. The Shepaug Railroad specialized in pastoral settings like this.

Engine No. 3 of the Shepaug line was well cared for; other Connecticut roads boasted far more engines. The sand dome denotes the engine number. A small pipe runs from it to the main driving wheels. The engineer applied sand, using compressed air, if the drivers began to slip or spin. Modern diesel engines of today have the very same feature.

Engine No. 372 slows for yard work ahead at Roxbury.

This was the small switching yard at Litchfield.

A natural rock tunnel was engineered in Washington. The strings, or "tell tales," hanging down from an overhead arm served to alert brakemen to duck for the tunnel; in the bad old days before air brakes they walked along the box of cars to spin the brake handles.

All hands turn engine No. 372 on the Litchfield table.

Chapter Seven Footnotes

1. Connecticut General Assembly, Resolves and Private Laws of the State of Connecticut From the Year 1789 to the Year 1836, II: 1025–1033, Public Records, Connecticut State Capitol Building. The incorporators included Ira Gregory, Russell Hoyt, E. S. Tweedy, Daniel Benedict, George W. Ives, and others.

2. *Report of the Engineer, Upon the Preliminary Surveys for the Fairfield County Railroad* (N.p., n.d.), Turner Railroad Collection, The Connecticut Historical Society.

3. *Twenty-Fifth Annual Report of the Railroad Commissioners, State of Connecticut for the Year Ending 1878* (Hartford: Case, Lockwood & Brainard, 1878), 125.

4. Connecticut General Assembly, An Act to Incorporate the New Haven & Derby Railroad, 1864, 188-191, Public Records, Connecticut State Capitol Building.

5. See Robert Belletekie's excellent and unusually complete "History of the New Haven & Derby Railroad" in *Shoreliner Magazine* 12, no. 4 (1981), a publication of the New Haven Railroad Historical and Technical Association.

6. *Derby Transcript*, 11 August 1871.

7. Corporate and Operating History of the Lines Owned by the New York, New Haven & Hartford Railroad Company, 30 June 1915, Turner Railroad Collection, The Connecticut Historical Society.

8. *Thirty-Ninth Annual Report of the Railroad Commissioners of the State of Connecticut, for 1891* (Hartford: Case, Lockwood & Brainard, 1891), 346.

In 1948, the year it closed amid widespread sorrow, a railroad enthusiast named Carroll O. Bickelhaupt, a senior executive with the American Telephone and Telegraph Company in New York, published a private booklet about the Shepaug Railroad, as a Christmas present to friends. The pictures on both these pages are reprinted from it. We thank the Litchfield Historical Society for locating a copy.

Veteran crew members pose just before branch closed.

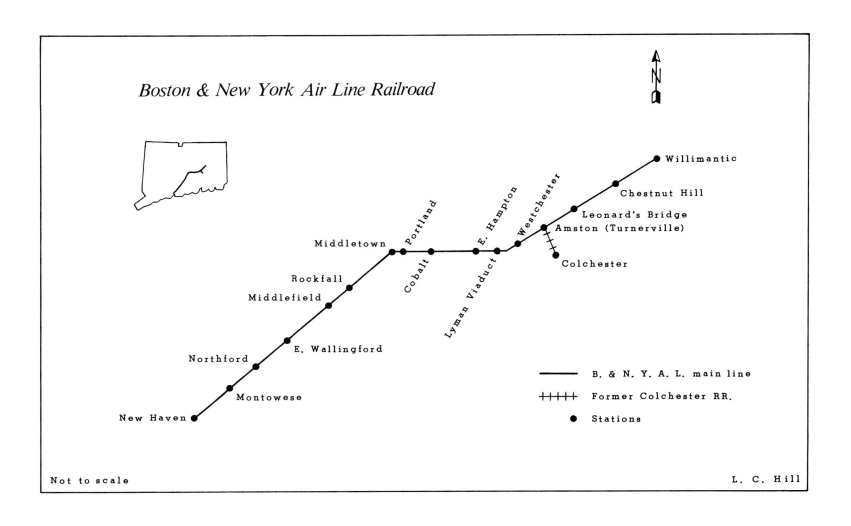

Boston & New York Air Line Railroad

N

Willimantic

Chestnut Hill

Leonard's Bridge

Amston (Turnerville)

Westchester

Colchester

E. Hampton

Portland

Lyman Viaduct

Cobalt

Middletown

Rockfall

Middlefield

E. Wallingford

Northford

Montowese

New Haven

——— B. & N. Y. A. L. main line

+++++ Former Colchester RR.

● Stations

Not to scale

L. C. Hill

Chapter Eight

The Air Line Saga

*Various plans are on foot to defeat the construction of this Rail Road, char-
tered by the State of Connecticut, to construct a road nearly in an air line from
New Haven through Middletown to Boston.*

—*Scientific American, May 13, 1848*

Southern New England is, very roughly, a wide rectangle, with Boston near its
northeast end and New York City just over the line at the southwest corner. The
shortest route between these two great cities, therefore, would be a straight diagonal. Yet as we have seen in earlier chapters, Connecticut's early railways ran
mainly north and south, while the shore line, with its river interruptions, went east
and west. The other east-west route was through southern Massachusetts. Consequently intercity trains and rail-and-steamboat passenger routes took two sides of a
triangle, more or less, to reach their destinations. Why not try the hypotenuse?

So reasoned many a nineteenth-century engineer or financier, dreaming over his
map. The hypotenuse would go as the crow flies—presumably straight through the
air, with no waste of distance. It would be faster and better; Connecticut has no
mountains. That it has ridges—pesky and seemingly endless ridges—weighed
lightly on the dreamers. So did the fact that the hypotenuse ran through the farm
country and few large places. The idea was alluring, and great numbers of normally
shrewd and cautious Yankees, bemused by the logic of geometry and the reputed
wisdom of the crow, fell into the trap.

The "Air Line Route" (one can see whence came the name) was planned to run
diagonally across the state from New Haven, through Middlefield, Middletown,
Cobalt, Amston, Willimantic, Goshen, Dayville, Woonsocket, and on to Boston.
It specialized in hamlets. Remarkable for its engineering originality and desire to
run "fast passenger trains," the Air Line nevertheless suffered reversals without
end, and its independence was always threatened by the fact that it depended on the
New Haven road, absorber of so many companies, for its connection to New York
City.

The promoter, attorney, and first president of the Air Line was Charles Alsop of
Middletown. He was joined by the mercantile brothers Edward and Samuel Russell, and together the three men received a charter in 1846 creating the New York &
Boston Railroad Company.[1] Previously Alsop had pushed for the Middletown Railroad between his home city and the Berlin station on the Hartford & New Haven.

*Bishop's Cut in East Hampton, one of many
ridges between Middletown and Willima-
tic, placed heavy demands on the Air Line's
builders. The post with a "W" warns engineers to use the whistle for next crossing.*

[OPPOSITE PAGE] A trestle at Cobalt.

116

A construction photograph shows an unfinished cut before full ballasting and ditching for drainage. By careful study, one can find a small boy perched on a rock at the side.

Hatred of the so-called Air Line road surfaced early. Hartford speculators and investors were infuriated that a potentially strategic line by-passed their city completely. The powerful Connecticut River maritime lobby was equally indignant, since the railroad had the incredible right to bridge the Connecticut River at Middletown—creating what might be a dangerous obstruction to marine traffic. Opponents of the railroad pleaded with Governor Isaac Toucey, who responded by vetoing the railroad's charter. But his veto was overridden by the General Assembly. Unruffled, the new company pushed on, mindful that only 135 miles of track were needed to connect Boston with New Haven. Fast passenger trains could make the future run in four hours, one and one-half hours faster than trains using the Inland Route, which was twenty-five miles longer. Great promise was also perceived in an imaginary mass of freight that might be transported over its rails.

But disappointments and obstacles kept creeping into the road's history. There was, for example, a locustlike invasion of Boston speculators who appointed fictitious directors. There were construction scandals, with Connecticut stockholder money being spent illegally for work in Massachusetts. In addition, construction delays forced the directors to appear before legislators seven times for charter extensions. In their 1857 report the state's railroad commissioners devoted forty pages of evidence as to why the road was "in a deranged condition."[2] And it remained so, at least in Connecticut, for twenty years.

Back in 1846 Edwin Ferry Johnson conducted a comprehensive engineering survey of the proposed Air Line. A civil engineer who had worked on the Erie and Champlain canals and would later serve the Erie and the Northern Pacific railroads, Johnson released his survey in 1847. His Air Line started at a point where the New York & New Haven Railroad came off the Mill River bridge in New Haven. It then headed over to East Wallingford, via the Quinnipiac River swamplands, to a "land depression" known as Reed's Gap—an area Johnson felt contained much valuable traprock. (It did, and does still.) Another valley was reached, bringing rails near the Coginchaug River for Middlefield and Rockfall. The line then entered Middletown on a southwesterly approach and stopped at the Connecticut River ferry slip.

Engine Middletown *poses on a handsome Air Line bridge, with a space for a road in the near abutment. Room was provided on it for a second span but it was never used.*

To cross the river Johnson's report described plans for a suitable bridge with a draw spanning an opening twice the width of any boat likely to use it. Water and ice would easily flow between the piers, the draw would always be open except when trains were due, and the cost was estimated at $100,000. Once over the river, the Air Line crisscrossed the Colchester Turnpike to Cobalt and East Hampton. It was then projected through the Salmon and Black Ledge river valleys to enter Westchester, Hebron, and Lebanon; then it used the Ten Mile River valley as far as Willimantic. Johnson foresaw that the best route from the "Thread City" to Rhode Island would be to intersect Chaplin, Hampton, and Dayville. His survey then terminated at the Rhode Island state line. Promoters envisaged the Air Line Railroad linking with the (unbuilt) Woonsocket Union line across Rhode Island, then uniting

Two high viaducts had to be built at East Hampton. This is the Rapallo, named for a director; it was 1,380 feet long and sixty high, with unused space for a second track.

[OVERLEAF] The sister to the Rapallo, and the most imposing on the Air Line, was the single-track Lyman Viaduct, named for the road's first president. It was 1,108 feet long and towered 128 feet above Dickinson's Brook. The New Haven road later filled in both the Lyman and Rapallo, and one can still walk them. The rails are gone.

118

Financial disappointment overtook all three companies that created and ran the Air Line before it was absorbed into the New Haven. Ornate securities like these trumpeted each incarnation, with a glimpse of the Connecticut River on every one.

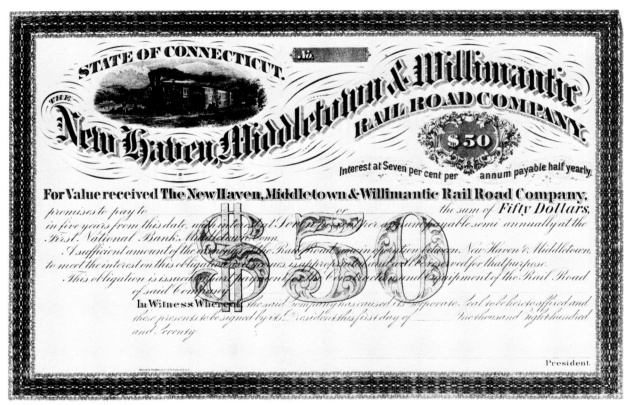

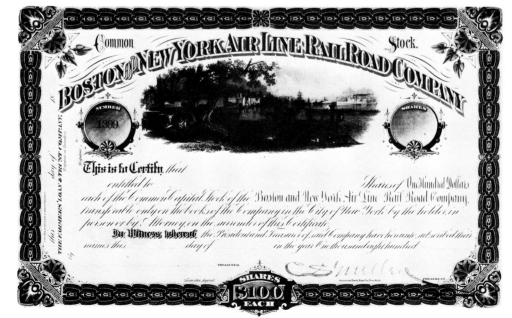

with the Charles River railroad to Brookline, Massachusetts. At Brookline a connection would be made with the Boston & Worcester Railroad, allowing trains access to Boston proper.

Johnson divided the Connecticut portion into ten areas of construction.[3] The least expensive of these was from Mill River in New Haven towards East Wallingford, the most expensive from Cobalt to Black Ledge Brook in East Hampton, where a great deal of cut-and-fill work and high viaducts were required. Between New Haven and Middletown, Johnson planned a nine-mile stretch of straight track, but there would be a great deal of curvature and only three miles of straight track east of Middletown to Willimantic. The challenging terrain and uplands northeast of Willimantic to Dayville were quietly played down in his report. Grades would be no more than forty feet to the mile, he claimed, and iron rails, weighing sixty-eight pounds to the yard, would be installed throughout. And the cost of completion, noted Johnson, would be approximately $2,565,000, or about $31,000 per mile. This did not include construction needed to continue the line into Rhode Island and Massachusetts. The report was widely distributed.

This is an "employees' timetable." Unlike those issued to the public, it contains information vital to safe operations in 1881. See, under Colchester Branch, how accurate time was then transmitted by Yale College.

DISTANCES from NEW HAVEN

TO

Cedar Hill, 2.0
Montowese, 4.0
Northford, 7.7
Wallingford, 12.0
Middlefield, 18.0
Middlefield Center, 19.0
Rockfall, 20.6
Middletown, 24.0
Portland, 25.0
Cobalt, 29.7
East Hampton, 33.0
Lyman Viaduct, 36.2
West Chester, 39.2
Turnerville, 44.0
Colchester, 47.6
Leonard's Bridge, 46.7
Liberty Hill, 49.2
Willimantic, 54.0

TIME TABLE NUMBER 20.

Boston & New York Air Line Railroad Company

TO TAKE EFFECT MONDAY, NOV. 14, 1881.

DISTANCES from WILLIMANTIC

TO

Liberty Hill, 4.8
Leonard's Bridge, 7.3
Turnerville, 10.0
Colchester, 13.6
West Chester, 14.8
Lyman Viaduct, 17.8
East Hampton, 21.0
Cobalt, 24.3
Portland, 29.0
Middletown, 30.0
Rockfall, 33.4
Middlefield Center, 35.0
Middlefield, 36.0
Wallingford, 42.0
Northford, 46.3
Montowese, 50.0
Cedar Hill, 52.0
New Haven, 54.0

RUNNING DIRECTIONS.

I. *In all cases of doubt take the safe side.*

II. The word train as used in these rules includes engines running detached. Regular trains are such as have a representation in the time table. All others are irregular. Extras are irregular trains running under signal. All others are either gravel trains or wild trains.

III. Trains must at all times keep out of the way of trains of a superior grade. They are graded and have right of way over each other as follows:

Regular.
1. Regular passenger.
2. Regular freight or mixed.

Irregular.
3. Extras east bound.
4. Extras west bound.
5. Gravel trains (not under flag).
6. Wild trains.

IV. Regular trains west have right of way for twenty minutes *after their own schedule time* over trains of the same grade east, and must then keep entirely out of the way.

V. Therefore regular trains east must keep twenty-three minutes behind the schedule time of an over-due west bound train of the same grade, the three minutes being allowed under Rule VII.

VI. Regular trains east must be upon the side track three minutes before trains of the same grade west, and all trains five minutes before trains of a superior grade are due to leave the point of meeting or passing.

VII. As a margin of safety for possible variation in watches, three minutes must *always* be allowed without regard to the grade of the expected train, and trains must *never* use any portion of this time.

VIII. The Conductors and Engineers of irregular trains must, before starting, inform themselves of the rights and whereabouts of all other irregular trains, either running or signaled, and when they run as extras must personally attend to having proper signals carried for them. Engineers of all engines carrying signals, when passing irregular trains and engines, must call attention to the fact by giving the proper signal.

IX. When signals are carried for extras running in opposite directions, the extra east has right of way, as provided in Rule III, but it must proceed *slowly and with caution* until it passes the extra west, and the extra west must wait indefinitely for the extra east at the point where the signal is met or passes them.

X. If a white flag is put on, or a red flag taken off at any station other than New Haven or Willimantic, the engineer must notify the station agent and call his attention to this rule, and the agent must thereupon flag all irregular trains passing in the direction opposite to that signaled, cautioning those running east, and holding those running west, until the extra arrives or the flag is ordered in. Between stations, and at stations where no agent can be found, a brakeman must be left to perform this service.

XI. No train other than those timed in the table will be allowed to run on the road except under orders from the Superintendent. Gravel trains may work without flag between the limits assigned them for the day, but must notify all section foremen within those limits, and can only exceed them when protected by flag. Wild trains will be run only in urgent cases, under special orders from the Superintendent. They must run with the greatest care, flagging themselves at all doubtful points, and keeping a sharp lookout for section men and other irregular trains, and at their first opportunity must become extras, running under signal.

XII. After 6.00 A. M. all signals previously carried for extra trains cease to be of effect, and all trains not having arrived at destination become wild and must run accordingly.

XIII. All special orders for the movement of trains by telegraph will be signed by the Superintendent, addressed to the conductor and engineer of the train, and must be written in ink and a copy furnished to both. Both are required to sign their understanding of the order, to be transmitted to the Superintendent, and in no case will an operator accept signature of either by the other and they must not leave the station until they have in their possession a written copy of the order with the Superintendent's reply of "correct" thereto.

XIV. No train will run ahead of its schedule time except under special orders from the Superintendent, and, unless otherwise ordered, trains between stations will run uniformly at the speed indicated, using all their time except what is actually necessary for transacting the business of the station.

XV. All trains running in the same direction must keep ten minutes apart; *this rule is imperative.*

XVI. Whenever a train is stopped or can proceed only at a slow rate, or is obliged to back over the road, or for any other reason is on any portion of the road without right of way, a man with signals to protect it must be sent in each direction at least half a mile or 20 standing telegraph poles, and torpedoes used if necessary, and this must be done without regard to whether other trains are due or not, for *employés have no right to assume that none are approaching.*

XVII. In stormy, thick and foggy weather, or immediately after a storm, trains must be run very cautiously and without any regard to making time table time, run very slowly while approaching all doubtful points and see your way is clear, and if delayed, do not attempt to make up time.

XVIII. At all railroad junctions and crossings engineers will not exceed four miles per hour and before proceeding must carefully observe that all signals and switches are right, and in thick weather if signals can not be seen must make a full stop, and when such stop is made they must not proceed until everything is known to be right.

MAIN LINE.

EAST. 1 Mixed. A. M.	3 Passenger A. M.	5 Passenger A. M.	7 Passenger P. M.	Time Card for Extras.	STATIONS.	Distances.	WEST. 2 Passenger A. M.	4 Passenger P. M.	6 Mixed. P. M.	8 Passenger P. M.
6.00	8.05	10.45	6.05		Lv. NEW HAVEN. Ar.		9.25	1.40	4.40	8.00
6.08	8.10	10.51 †	6.10	6	CEDAR HILL JC.	2.0	9.20	1.35	4.34	7.55
6.17	8.17 †	11.01 †	6.18 †	10	MONTOWESE.	2.0	9.11 †	1.27 †	4.19	7.47 †
6.28	8.24	11.09	6.26	11	NORTHFORD.	3.7	9.04	1.20	4.07	7.39
6.42	8.33 †	11.18	6.35 †	13	WALLINGFORD.	4.3	8.56	1.12	3.48	7.30
7.03	**8.45**	11.31	6.47	18	MIDDLEFIELD.	6.0	**8.45**	1.00	3.25	7.19
	†	†	†	3	MIDDLEFIELD CENTER.	1	†	†		†
7.12 †	8.51 †	11.39 †	6.55 †	5	ROCKFALL.	1.6	8.34 †	12.51 †	3.12 †	7.11 †
7.40	8.58	11.57	**7.04**	10	MIDDLETOWN.	3.4	8.25	12.43	3.00	**7.04**
7.50	9.03	12.02	7.09	5	PORTLAND.	1.0	8.19	12.37	2.26	6.52
8.09	9.12	**12.27**	7.18	14	COBALT.	4.7	**8.09**	**12.27**	1.58	6.37
8.38	9.18	12.35	7.25	10	EAST HAMPTON.	3.3	8.01	12.20	1.37	6.28
8.55 †	9.29 †	12.47 †	7.35 †	13	LYMAN VIADUCT.	3.2	7.51 †	12.08 †	1.07 †	6.16 †
9.11	9.36	**12.55**	7.41 †	10	WEST CHESTER.	3.0	7.44	12.02	**12.55**	6.08
9.45	**9.45**	1.06	7.50	14	TURNERVILLE.	4.8	7.33	11.51	12.20	5.56
†	†	†	†	8	LEONARD'S BRIDGE.	2.7	†	†	†	†
10.35 †	9.54 †	1.18 †	8.00 †	8	LIBERTY HILL.	2.5	7.22 †	11.41 †	11.57 †	5.43 †
10.48	10.02	1.28	8.08	13	N. Y. & N. E. R. R. JC.	4.2	7.12	11.32	11.43	5.32
10.50	10.05	1.30	8.10	2	Ar. WILLIMANTIC. Lv.	0.6	7.10	11.30	11.40	5.30
A. M.	A. M.	P. M.	P. M.				A. M.	A. M.	A. M.	P. M.

COLCHESTER BRANCH.

SOUTH. 9 A. M.	11 P. M.	13 P. M.	15 P. M.	Time Card for Extras.	STATIONS.	Distances.	NORTH. 10 A. M.	12 A. M.	14 P. M.	16 P. M.
9.47	1.08	5.58	7.52		Lv. TURNERVILLE. Ar.		9.40	11.46	5.51	7.45
10.02	1.23	6.13	8.07	15	Ar. COLCHESTER. Lv.	3.6	9.25	11.31	5.36	7.30
A. M.	P. M.	P. M.	P. M.				A. M.	A. M.	P. M.	P. M.

The standard of time of the New York City Hall, as transmitted daily by the Winchester Observatory of Yale College, to all telegraph stations along the line, shall be the standard time, and all Conductors, Engineers, and other employés are required to regulate their time by that standard daily, and compare time with each other at Stations on the road.

The figures of this table denote the leaving time for trains.

Full Face Figures (**12.31**) denote the regular Meeting and Passing Places and time for trains. Large Figures (10.25) indicate that train will stop. Small Figures (1. 2. 3) indicate in general that train will not stop at the station against which they are placed, but when followed by a dagger (†) indicate that the train will stop when signaled, or to leave passengers or freight.

☞ Train No. 8 will take side track for train No. 7.

SPECIAL INSTRUCTIONS.

I. While running on the tracks of the New York, New Haven & Hartford and New York and New England Railroad Companies, employés will observe the time table and other rules and regulations of those companies. Boston time, which is the standard of the New York and New England Railroad, is 12 minutes faster than New York time.

II. *At New Haven* trains will arrive and leave subject to the orders of the depot master and yard master.

III. *At the New Haven and Northampton Co's crossing* trains have right of road only when the signal shows white. When it shows red they must come to a full stop before reaching it, and it must always be approached slowly and with caution.

IV. *At Cedar Hill Junction* trains have right of road only when the signal shows white. West bound trains (and, when the signal shows red, all trains) must come to a full stop before reaching it.

V. *At Shore Line Junction* trains have right of road only when the semaphore arm is vertical, or white lights are displayed. If the semaphore arm is horizontal, or either red discs or red or green lights are displayed, all trains must come to a full stop before reaching the Junction.

VI. *At Connecticut River drawbridge* and *Hartford and Connecticut Valley Railroad Crossing*, trains must be brought to a full stop by hand brakes between the 800 foot post and the stop post. The safety signal given from the draw of the bridge is a white flag waved by day, or a white light swung by night. Red lights, red flags, or red balls displayed either on the bridge or at the junction are danger signals.

If no danger signals are displayed the train after stopping and receiving the safety signal may cross, occupying at least two minutes in crossing, and keeping the furnace door open at night until over the Junction, but at all times, especially in stormy and foggy weather the engineer must know that the signals are right before starting to cross.

VII. *At Turnerville* trains will approach the "Y" with great care, keeping a sharp lookout for trains of the Colchester branch.

VIII. *At Willimantic* trains will arrive and leave as scheduled in the time table of the New York & New England Railroad. They must come to a full stop before entering the track of the New York & New England Railroad, or crossing that of the New London Northern Railroad, and all delayed and irregular trains not having orders from the General train Despatcher at Boston, must be flagged between the station and the junction.

IX. Except under special orders from the Superintendent no train will be allowed to run between New Haven and Willimantic in less than one hour and forty minutes, nor between East Hampton and Westchester faster than schedule time. Cross all bridges and piling slowly and with care, brakes off, and damper to ash pan closed. Cedar Hill piling, Lyman, Cobalt, and Rapallo Viaducts, not to exceed 15 miles per hour.

J. H. FRANKLIN, Supt.

☞ *READ THE OTHER SIDE.*

Drawn by Joseph D. Kuecker, Architect.

Lith. of P.S. Duval, Phila

PLAN FOR A RAIL WAY SUSPENSION BRIDGE.
ACROSS THE CONNECTICUT BELOW MIDDLETOWN BY CHARLES ELLET JNR.

Above is the stupendous suspension bridge with which Charles Ellet, Jr., quieted opponents of the Air Line in 1848 (see adjoining text). It absurdly diminishes "The Narrows" of the Connecticut River just south of Middletown (background). It never left the drawing board; what was actually built was the drawbridge in the foreground of the photograph at the top of the opposite page. (Behind it is the first highway bridge). As opponents of a drawbridge had predicted, there was an accident, in 1876, when steamer City of Hartford *rammed it. The westerly approach span lies crumpled on her bow (opposite, bottom). A second drawbridge, built since in the same spot, is shown at the very end of Chapter Thirteen.*

As noted, Connecticut River maritime interests were enraged over the railroad's right to bridge the river at Middletown. Captains of vessels, sloop owners, and steamboat company operators felt the bridge would be a grave hazard, particularly at night and in foul weather. They also believed that ice would pile up around its piers in winter, and that its draw opening would not accommodate larger vessels— even though Johnson had designed one of ample width. Neighboring farmers also expressed their opposition; if the river backed up at the bridge, it would flood their fields, and crops would be ruined. Thus the stage was readied for war between the "Bridgers" and the "Anti-Bridgers." So well organized was the opposition that it forced the General Assembly to put the whole bridge question on trial in 1847. A "Joint Select Committee on Railroads" was appointed to adjudicate the affair, and the committee persuaded the General Assembly to pass a bill requiring the railroad to raise at least $2,000,000 in stock subscriptions before it could undertake bridge construction. This would allow more time to evaluate the matter and to determine if there was genuine investor support for the road. Then in the following year, a highly controversial bill was passed forbidding the Air Line Railroad to erect a drawbridge at all! Based on the committee's report, the General Assembly did grant the railroad permission to build a high "suspension" bridge farther down the Connecticut River in Middletown at "The Narrows." [4]

Charles Ellet, Jr., who was hired to ascertain if such a structure was feasible, had erected similar bridges at Philadelphia and at Wheeling, West Virginia. [5] As a leading authority in the field, Ellet appeared before the committee in 1848 only to have his initial testimony rejected, apparently for lack of sufficient documentation. The following year he reappeared with the requisite material, including an affidavit signed by fellow engineers who agreed with his Middletown proposals. One of them was Benjamin Latrobe, the distinguished chief engineer of the Baltimore & Ohio Railroad. [6] Impressed with the new evidence, the committee recommended that a suspension bridge be constructed, but how the Air Line's directors actually took this decision is not fully known. On paper it was one thing; to finance and build such a structure was another. No doubt the city of Hartford and the Connecticut River maritime interests rejoiced over the new stumbling block they had put in

HIGHWAY AND AIR LINE RAILROAD BRIDGES OVER THE CONNECTICUT RIVER - MIDDLETOWN, CONN.

J.A.BROATCH

the railroad's path. The Middletown *Constitution* remarked, "Hartford may exult over her victory, but she may blush at the means by which she secured it."[7] The suspension bridge was never built.

Equally distressing was the Air Line's futile effort to get the line completely opened in Connecticut, Rhode Island, and Massachusetts. After fifteen years constituent companies could only point to a track between Brookline and Woonsocket. Virtually nothing was completed in Rhode Island, and only a scant amount of construc-

Turnerville, later called Amston, was named for Phineas Turner, an industrialist. From the box-like depot departed daily trains along the tiny branch to Colchester.

Another attractive station went up at Colchester, terminus of the 3.6-mile branch, serving passengers and the Hayward Rubber complex. It is still standing.

tion had taken place in Connecticut—though Connecticut money still poured into the project because investors believed it was being used within the state alone. The railroad commissioners of Connecticut thought this all very odd. The corporate books of the railroad were called for, including stockholder lists, but when a sheriff opened the company safe in Middletown it was conveniently empty. Payoffs were secretly used to switch construction contracts in Connecticut, insinuations and fights erupted with the contractor, work halted, and after twelve years all that existed in Connecticut were a few culverts, bridge abutments, and some cut-and-fill work. The project faltered until 1865, when the Air Line franchise was absorbed by the speculative Boston, Hartford & Erie Railroad.[8] The latter's ambition was to control a railroad route from Boston to Willimantic, Hartford, Waterbury, Danbury, and the Hudson River. However, the Boston, Hartford, & Erie dropped the idea of finishing the Air Line. The franchise expired in 1867, which gave rise to a revival of the dream.

Leading the new movement was a Middlefield man, David Lyman, who helped obtain a charter for the New Haven, Middletown & Willimantic Railroad.[9] Lyman invested generously with profits from his washing machine business and his large farming interests. The new company had the right to build the suspension bridge, but through Lyman's persuasive testimony the clause was rescinded, and the right to build a 1,250-foot drawbridge was reinstated. Public spirit got the new railroad open despite the fact that the large earlier investments had been wiped out. Aided by one thousand construction workers, management opened the line in 1870 from New Haven as far as Middletown, and to Willimantic in 1873. The cost had greatly exceeded the original estimate of 1847. Towns bought the railroad's stock and bonds, and three mortgages totaling $7,000,000 were secured by the assets of the line. Middletown would eventually ante up $887,000. When interest on bonds could not be met, bond owners and trustees of the third mortgage foreclosed, and the company was reorganized as the Boston & New York Air Line Railroad in 1875. A new name, new stock, and still a vestige of the original name.

125

2130 Railroad Station, Cobalt & Middle Haddam, Conn.

This depot, and freight house at left, served rural Cobalt and Middle Haddam. Advertising was often nailed to the walls.

This shedlike structure served Rockfall, on the Air Line segment west of Middletown.

2839 Rockfall, Conn.

New Haven engine 3022 is "on the point" of one of the last steam-hauled freights on the Colchester branch, in the winter of 1948.

Strategically the fifty-mile New Haven, Middletown & Willimantic Railroad was a natural link between the New York & New England Railroad at Willimantic and the New York, New Haven & Hartford Railroad at New Haven. The three lines formed the shortest route to Boston. A great deal of freight traffic eventually flowed between the systems during the nineteenth century. In summer, solid trainloads of strawberries, peaches, and fish were common. Joint passenger trains also were run, including the fabled deluxe "White Train," started in 1891 (see Chapter Eleven). The line's major drawbacks were its numerous grades and curves, along with several high and weight-restricting viaducts between Middletown and Willimantic, the most noted being that at East Hampton named for enterprising David Lyman, which was eleven hundred feet long and 137 feet above the ground.

In 1876 the Colchester Railroad was chartered and built from Colchester to Turnerville (Amston) on the Air Line. The town of Colchester paid for half of its $50,000 cost. It was three miles long, was laid with fifty-six-pound iron rail, and opened in 1877. The Air Line Railroad supplied engines and cars, and operated the trains.

As might have been predicted, the Connecticut River bridge had its accident in due course. It occurred in 1876 when the steamboat *City of Hartford* misjudged clear-

127

ance lights and crashed into it, a misadventure long rumored to have been intentional because maritime interests were still opposed to the drawbridge. In 1882 the New York, New Haven & Hartford Railroad Company stepped in and leased the Boston & New York Air Line, and this route became designated as its "Air Line Division". A "pooling" arrangement of earnings between the two lines had been previously drawn up. Great volumes of freight went over Air Line routing, but its history in the twentieth century was one of steady decline. Today its tracks between New Haven and Portland see only the occasional appearance of engines and freight cars. The rest of the Air Line dream has vanished. The long drawbridge at Middletown—the second—still stands as a memorial, and with luck a traveller may see a Conrail diesel locomotive haul a car or two across it.

Chapter Eight Footnotes

1. Connecticut General Assembly, Resolves and Private Laws of the State of Connecticut, Incorporating the New York and Boston Railroad Company, 1846, IV: 999, Public Records, Connecticut State Capitol Building.

2. *Fourth Annual Report, General Railroad Commissioners of the State of Connecticut* (New Haven: Carrington & Hotchkiss, 1857), 23.

3. Edwin Ferry Johnson, *Engineer's Report, New York and Boston Railroad* (Middletown: Chas. Pelton, 1847), 7. (Johnson was later the chief engineer of the Northern Pacific Railroad.)

4. Connecticut General Assembly, Resolves and Private Laws of the State of Connecticut, Repealing the 17th Section of the Charter of the New York and Boston Railroad Company, 1848, IV: 1005, Public Records, Connecticut State Capitol Building.

5. Gene D. Lewis, *Charles Ellet, Jr.* (Urbana: University of Illinois Press, 1968), passim.

6. *Opinions of Civil Engineers on a Suspension Bridge for the Air Line Railroad* (Hartford: Case, Tiffany & Company, 1849).

7. Quoted in Marguerite Allis, *The Bridge* (New York: G.P. Putnam & Sons, 1949).

8. *Memorial of the Directors New York and Boston Railroad Company to the General Assembly;* (New Haven: Thomas Stafford, 1864), p. 5.

9. Connecticut General Assembly, Resolves and Private Laws of the State of Connecticut, Incorporating the New Haven, Middletown and Willimantic Railroad Company, VI: 286. Public Records, Connecticut State Capitol Building.

Passengers crowd the East Hampton platform around 1900.

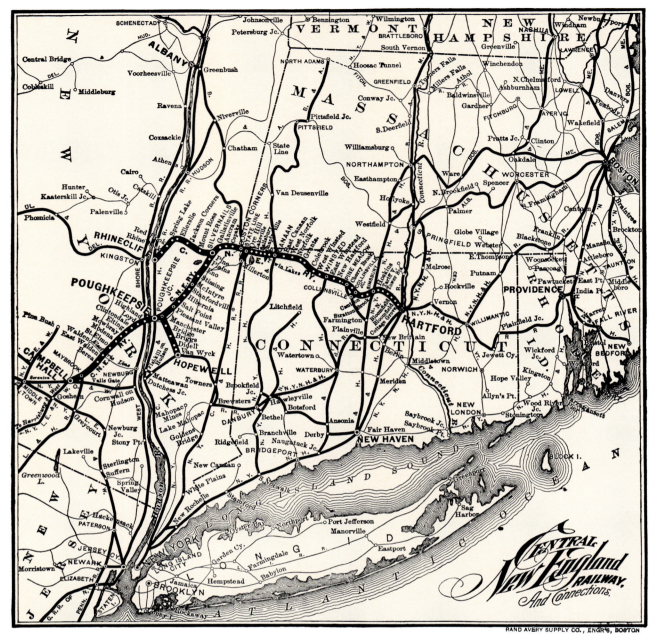

Train time at Collinsville, Connecticut, on the Central New England Railway. Because the main-line track was on the outskirts of town, trains actually backed into the station.

Chapter Nine

Remembering
the Central New England

Build a railroad through Norfolk? Why, when I was a boy and lived there it was with difficulty that even the crows could fly over the Norfolk Hills.

—comment of a wealthy New Yorker in Theron Crissey's History of Norfolk, 1900

What is remembered by many as the old Central New England Railway—a rather grandiose name for a single pair of steel rails linking Hartford with the Berkshire foothills in Litchfield County and the highlands of New York—was really the creation of one man, Egbert Butler of Norfolk, Connecticut. His crusade for a railroad, often reaching fever pitch, started in the 1860s and eventually was fulfilled in 1871.

The father of the Connecticut Western Railroad[1] was born at Plymouth, Connecticut, in 1813. Butler later moved to Norfolk, where his self-made business career began in earnest. He helped secure a charter for the Norfolk Bank, served as secretary to the Norfolk Leather Company and president of the Lawrence Machine Works, and represented his district in the state legislature. He was convinced that a railroad could awaken the provincial towns dotting the Norfolk Hills.

As late as the Civil War, railroads had hardly pierced the region Butler loved. The closest rail was west of Norfolk at Canaan, where trains of the Housatonic Railroad arrived. East of the Norfolk Hills at Winsted was the northern terminus of the Naugatuck Railroad. And still further east, at Collinsville, was the stub track of the Canal Railroad's "Collinsville Branch," which stemmed from its main line at Farmington. Butler first promoted the idea of a new company extending the Collinsville Branch to busy New Hartford, having it arc left to Winsted to connect with the Naugatuck line, then continue west for Norfolk, eventually meeting the Housatonic road at Canaan.[2] A $500 survey was paid for by Butler, and in 1866 a charter was obtained for the Connecticut Western Railroad. However, public and investor support was not forthcoming.

Butler did not falter, and the temporary disappointment only increased his determination. He obtained the aid of William H. Barnum of Lime Rock, Connecticut, a wealthy investor and future president of both the "Western" and the Housatonic, and also of ex-Connecticut Governor Alexander Hamilton Holley* of Salisbury.

Egbert T. Butler for years fought for a railroad between Hartford and upstate New York and lived to see its last spike driven.

*Governor in 1857, from a family concerned with manufacturing iron. Helped found the Iron Bank at Falls Village. His son, Alexander Lyman Holley, attended Brown University and introduced the theory of Bessemer steelmaking into the United States.

130

CONNECTICUT WESTERN RAILROAD.

TIME TABLE No. 5. FOR EMPLOYES ONLY.

DESTROY ALL PREVIOUS TABLES.

Commencing Wednesday, April 3d, 1872.

In all cases of doubt, take the side of safety.

No Train will leave a station before time named in the Time Table. No Train will follow another within ten minutes.

Agents at Telegraph Stations on the line of this road, must report to Hartford by Telegraph when Trains are delayed, and keep the Superintendent informed as to delays and their causes,—also the leaving time of Extra Trains.

All Telegraph messages and other special orders directing the movement of Trains, whether received by Agents, Conductors, or Engineers, must be replied to (by repeating) in full before acting on such messages or orders.

Going West, Read Down. | **Going East, Read Up.**

FREIGHT.		PASSENGER.					Miles.		Name and Number of Station.		Miles.		PASSENGER.					FREIGHT.	
No. 1.		No. 3.	No. 4.	No. 5.	No. 6.	No. 7.							No. 8.	No. 9.	No. 10.	No. 11.	No. 12.		No. 14.
A. .M			P. M.	P. M.	A. M.	A. M.							A. M.	P. M.	P. M.	P. M.	P. M.		P. M.
6.00	*Runs Monday, Wednesday, and Friday.*		This Train runs daily.	3.40	9.50				HARTFORD,	1	2	68¾	10.17		6.53		This Train runs Sundays only.	*Runs Tuesday, Thursday, and Saturday.*	2.00
...				....	....		2	2	Blue Hills,		3½	66¾	....		....				....
6.25				3.53	**10.03**		5½	3½	Bloomfield,	3	4	63¼	**10.03**		6.38				1.35
....				....	....		9½	4	Scotland,		2	59¼	....		....				....
6.55				4.13	10.23		11½	2	Tariffville,	5	2	57¼	9.42		6.17				1.10
....				*	*		13½	2	Hoskins,	7	1½	55¼	*		*				....
7.15				4.28	10.38		15	1½	SIMSBURY,	9	2½	53¾	9.32		6.07				12.50
* 7.25				* 4.37	*10.47		17½	2½	Stratton Brook,	11	4	51¼	* 9.22		* 5.58				*12.35
* ..				*	*		21½	4	Canton,	13	2½	47¼	*		* ...				* ....
8.00				4.55	11.06		24	2½	Collinsville,	15	4	44¾	9.00		5.36				12.00
*				* ...	*		28	4	Pine Meadow,	17	1	40¾	*		* ...				* ...
8.40				**5.18**	**11.26**		29	1	New Hartford,	19	6½	39¾	**8.40**		**5.18**				**11.26**
9.25			3.00	5.38	11.53	8.00	35½	6½	WINSTED,	21	0¾	33¼	8.15	1.40	4.48	10.10	8.43		10.30
9.40			3.10	5.43	12.00	**8.07**	36¼	0¾	WEST WINSTED,	23	5	32½	**8.07**	1.35	4.43	10.05	8.38		**9.40**
....			*	....	....	*			Brook's,	24			...	*	....	*	*		...
....			*	*	*	*	41¼	5	Grant's,	25	4	27½	*	*	*	*	*		....
....			*	....	....	*			Summit,	26			....	*	....	*	*		....
10.25			3.50	6.13	12.30	**8.37**	45¼	4	Norfolk,	27	2¾	23½	7.35	12.50	4.13	9.34	8.07		**8.37**
* ...			**4.00**	*	**12.38**	*	48	2¾	West Norfolk,	29	3¼	20¾	*	**12.38**	**4.00**	*	* ...		* ...
*			*	*	*	*	51¼	3¼	Canaan Valley,	30	1	17½	*	*	*	*	*		* ....
*			*	*	* ...	*	52¼	1	East Canaan,	31	2½	16½	*	*	*	*	* ...		* ...
12.10			4.25	6.44	1.00	9.07	54¾	2½	CANAAN,	33	2¾	14	6.55	**12.10**	3.35	8.55	7.28		7.40
....			....	....	....	....			Foley's,	34			....	....	....	....	....		....
....			....	....	....	....	57½	2¾	Twin Lakes,	35	2	11¼	....	...	....	....	....		....
*			*	*	*	* ...	59½	2	Chapinville,	37	2¾	9¼	* ...	*	*	*	*		* ....
12.55			4.50	7.07	1.25	9.30	62¼	2¾	Salisbury,	39	1¾	6½	6.30	11.30	3.10	8.30	7.03		6.55
1.10			4.57	7.14	1.32	9.37	64	1¾	Lakeville,	41	2	4¾	6.20	11.15	3.00	8.20	6.53		6.40
1.23			5.05	7.22	1.40	9.45	66	2	Ore Hill,	43	1¼	2¾	6.13	11.00	2.52	8.12	6.45		6.27
....			....	....	....	....	67¼	1¼	State Line,	45	1½	1½	....	....	....	....	....		....
1.37			5.13	7.30	1.47	9.52	68¾	1½	D. & C. R. Road,	46			6.05	10.47	2.45	8.03	6.37		6.15
....			5.20	7.35	1.53	9.58			MILLERTON,	47			6.00	10.40	2.40	7.55	6.30		....
P. M.			P. M.	P. M.	P. M.	A. M.							A. M.	A. M.	P. M.	P. M.	P. M.		A. M.

Stars (*) show where Trains stop to leave or take passengers on signal, or when Conductor is notified.
Large figures (1, 2, 3, 4,) show regular Passing Stations.

Trackmen and Gravel Train Conductors, and Engineers will take the most extreme care to guard against any delay or accident, and study the Rules thoroughly. Use signals in all cases when raising or repairing track. To warn Trains, signals should be displayed in each direction, as a Train may approach unexpectedly.

All Trains must approach the Naugatuck track and station very carefully, and not incommode the Naugatuck Trains. Naugatuck Railroad Agent will direct as to use of tracks and grounds.

Trains will not leave Millerton till their opposite Train has arrived. Opposite Trains are those run by same Engine and men.

Trains **7** and **4** will wait at Winsted till Trains **11, 12** and **9** arrive.

Special Rules for Conductors and Engineers.

1. The standard time is that of HARTFORD, PROVIDENCE, AND FISHKILL RAILROAD CLOCK at Hartford Station, and the Conductors are required to regulate their time by it, and see that the clocks at all the way-stations conform to it. Conductors should allow ten minutes for variation of watches.

2. Trains going West will have the right of road till they are forty minutes late, then they will keep clear of Trains going East.

3. If Trains going East cannot reach the Passing Station on time, they must keep clear of Trains going West till Trains going West are forty minutes late, then proceed at Table rate of speed till the delayed train is passed.

4. Freight Trains will wait for each other at Passing Stations, unless ordered differently from Superintendent's Office. They will in all cases keep ten minutes clear of Passenger Trains. They must not obstruct highway crossings more than five minutes. If delayed, or obliged to occupy the main track contrary to this rule, they must place signals at least eighty rods distant in both directions, and in plain sight of any approaching Train.

5. Freight and Working Trains must not run at greater speed than 15 miles per hour.

6. Extra Trains will keep ten minutes clear of all regular Trains unless otherwise ordered in writing from Superintendent's Office. Extra Trains are all Trains which are not timed on the Table,—either Passenger, Freight, or Working Trains of any description.

7. Regular Trains are those whic*l* are timed on the Time Table.

8. Delayed Trains must not run or the time of regular Trains.

9. All Bridges must be run over with ash pan closed, and if possible at a speed of not over eight miles per hour. The brakes are to be used on the bridges as little as possible. Extra care is required on the part of the Engineers on account of track raising, and other work. And no point, where work is going on near the track, is to be passed unless the Signal of Safety is seen by the Engineer. (The Signal of Safety is a WHITE Flag held over the rails by the man in charge on the spot.)

Signals.

10. One sharp whistle is a signal to apply the brakes; two to let off brakes; three, to back the train; four, a call for the switchman. A long whistle signifies that the Train is approaching a highway crossing or a Station.

11. A Red Light must be exhibited at night at the rear of all Trains, or Engines detached, while on the road. All Trains, or Engines detached, must be supplied with signal flags and lanterns, and must have, when running at night, at least two red lights burning ready for use as signals; and all Freight or Working Trains must carry a Red Flag by day, and the Red Light by night, on the rear car, where it can be seen by the Engineer.

12. A Red Flag by day, and at night a Red Light exhibited on the front of an Engine, shows that an Extra Train is to follow. A White Flag by day, and at night a Green Light exhibited on the front of an Engine, shows that a Train may be expected to return. But Conductors and Engineers of Extra Trains must recollect that these signals may not have been seen, when carried, and run with care accordingly. Conductors of Extra Engines or Trains must report to the Conductor of Trains which they follow, and see that a Red Signal is carried for them by the Train followed; and all Conductors must also know that their Engine or Train is properly supplied with signal lanterns, flags, and white lanterns.

The trio met with George H. Brown, head of New York's little Dutchess & Columbia Railroad, which ran from the Hudson River at Beacon to Pine Plains—not far from Lakeville, in Connecticut. Brown was seeking a rail outlet that would enable his road to move Pennsylvania coal to Connecticut and tap his area's rich agricultural and timber trade. If the Dutchess & Columbia extended its road a bit more to the east, and the Connecticut Western to the west, and if the latter also made Hartford its eastern terminus, the linkup would result in a number of economic benefits for both lines. Butler agreed; his dream had crystallized.

Advocates of the ambitious project subsequently appeared before the Connecticut legislature to ask for a revised Connecticut Western Railroad charter, which was duly granted in 1868 with a stock authorization of $3,000,000.[3] The line would begin in Hartford and link the towns of Bloomfield, Tariffville, Simsbury, Collinsville, New Hartford, Winsted, Butler's beloved Norfolk, and then proceed to Canaan, where it would continue west to Salisbury and Lakeville. New York State cooperated by approving construction to a place the company named "State Line." There the Connecticut Western would meet the Dutchess & Columbia. The Dutchess & Columbia granted trackage rights to the new line; at Millerton, just before Pine Plains, the Connecticut Western also intersected the New York & Harlem Railroad, resulting in a direct connection to New York City.

Most of Butler's 1866 survey was used in creating the line between Collinsville and Canaan. The remaining areas were located by Chief Engineer Oliver W. Barnes,

Toll roads in Connecticut were common, like this one at a wildly unsafe curved railway crossing near Winsted. The stern woman at right might be the collector.

132

Crossing hilly terrain challenged Connecticut Western Railroad builders. An enormous amount of fill work was required at the Whiting Viaduct in East Canaan, allowing the track to span both river and a local road. Blasting through cuts was also needed, as evidenced above at Stony Lonesome in West Norfolk. Below, a local train with only a baggage car and coach leaves the Norfolk Hills.

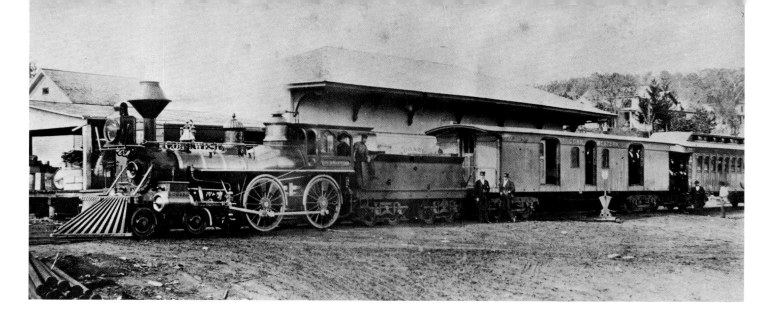

who was brought over from the Dutchess & Columbia. Barnes claimed that the sixty-seven-mile road from Hartford to State Line, New York, could be built for under $3,000,000, or about $40,000 a mile. Forced to overcome very hilly terrain, the road's physical profile resembled a roller coaster route as its right of way tackled the Connecticut highlands. Steep grades and sharp curves were unavoidable. The highest elevation was plotted at Norfolk Summit, where tracks would be 1,333 feet above sea level—a state record. Iron rails of "T" design were spiked to ties hewn from native oak and chestnut. Local governments and individuals along the route subscribed to the line's stock, and in Hartford alone nearly $800,000 was pledged. Construction loans were obtained, and work was fully under way by 1870.

Because the Connecticut Western went across half of Connecticut, it immediately obtained connections with other rail lines. The busy Hartford & New Haven road was met at Hartford, as well as the Hartford, Providence & Fishkill—then the longest line in the state, and one also vying for the Hudson River market place. At Simsbury the New Haven & Northampton ("The Canal") Railroad was encountered. The Naugatuck Railroad was met at Winsted, while at Canaan the Western's main line crossed the Housatonic. In order to preserve capital, Connecticut Western directors did not erect passenger depots at these junction points, but opted instead to pay rent and jointly occupy their neighbors' facilities. At Winsted the Western even used the Naugatuck's track through town until it built its own years later. By and large the new route embraced some of Connecticut's finest scenery: fertile farmlands, idyllic pine forests, roaring river settings (such as Satan's Kingdom in New Hartford), the rolling Norfolk Hills, craggy mountain cuts like Stoney Lonesome, and natural wonders such as beautiful Twin Lakes, where the railroad would eventually erect a park and dancing pavilion.

Egbert Butler helped break ground for the railroad at Winsted in October 1869 and was on hand to help drive the last spike at Canton in September 1871. The first train made its way over the lines on December 21 amid acclamation and ten-below-zero weather. The typical run from Hartford to Millerton took four hours. The five original wood-burning locomotives were all built by the Rogers Locomotive Works in Patterson, New Jersey.[4] Rolling stock also included a small number of wooden passenger, baggage, mail, freight, coal, and gravel cars.

Although promoters had forecast a prosperous Connecticut Western, the 1870s were not as lucrative as anticipated. In 1873 the line achieved its highest gross earnings ($442,734); thereafter, with the financial panic of that year, revenues declined steadily. A meager $50,714 profit remained after the 1879 business year. Interest on short-term and construction loans had mounted, a bond issue had to be floated to shore up the cash position, and dividends were passed. The worst event to occur during this period in the Western's history, one that aroused a tidal wave of public indignation and struck hard at the company's conscience, was the Tariffville Bridge Wreck.

Standing proud with her cars at West Winsted is engine City of Hartford. *Train staff pose by a fine wooden baggage car.*

[OVERLEAF] This superb scene was composed by the noted photographer of Norfolk, Mrs. J. C. Kendall. The Day Express *of the Central New England is passing full speed through West Norfolk and by Haystack Mountain. The picture later won a national photographic prize.*

THE NORFOLK HISTORICAL SOCIETY

134

Because an alert Hartford photographer, D. S. Camp, rushed to Tariffville the morning after the railroad bridge collapse, his stereopticon slides have preserved the horrors of that tragedy. Here a dangling coach rests against the remains of the broken truss.

This is a better view of the same half-submerged coach. Even though the bridge was not high over the Farmington River, many of the passengers perished in the icy water.

Engine Salisbury *flipped upside down after breaking through the defective bridge.*

137

The disaster occurred on the twin (Howe) wooden truss bridges over the Farmington River at Tariffville, Connecticut. The structure, so common on many American railroads, was built of massive wood timbers and iron suspension rods. The Tariffville spans were low-slung; the floor of each was only about ten feet above the Farmington River. On Tuesday, January 15, 1878, the Connecticut Western collected excursionists along its line to attend an evening revival in Hartford conducted by the famous evangelist Dwight L. Moody. The evening proved a grand success, and when the program was over many of his spiritually refreshed listeners headed for Union Station on Asylum Street for the return trip home. There a ten-car special, drawn by the engines *Salisbury* and *Tariffville*, waited to take them to Bloomfield, Tariffville, and points in Litchfield County. The special left around 9:20 p.m., briefly stopped at Bloomfield, and then made a station stop at Tariffville around 10 p.m.; all the while its riders sang gospel revival songs.

Engineer George Hatch, in the cab of *Salisbury*, slowly pulled out of the Tariffville station and within moments eased the train onto the bridge. He passed through the

Spectators gather as the grim search for bodies is renewed the morning after. Workmen balance themselves on huge trusses at left; a man braces himself in the coach doorway in foreground. Inadequate suspension rods may have caused the collapse.

Snow gently falls on the old hand-pushed "armstrong" turntable at West Winsted. The long wooden arm jutting out to the right of the turntable is where you applied the muscle. In the picture below, the first train enters Norfolk after the Blizzard of 1888. The road overhead later became Route 44.

first span, but as he was nearing the end of the second something went terribly wrong. With a sickening groan the bridge collapsed and hurled *Salisbury* and its crew upside down onto the river bank. Engineer Thomas Franey, at the controls of *Tariffville*, immediately felt his own engine lurch, whereupon it rolled to its side and also came crashing down. A baggage car and three passenger coaches quickly followed the engines into the gap. Cracking timbers and cries of agony filled the crisp night air.

Almost immediately after the collapse the vital task of getting help was miraculously underway. Prying himself out of the wrecked baggage car, Jonathan Jones, the Western's superintendent, made his way back to the Tariffville depot. His first telegraphic dispatch went to company offices at West Winsted: "Send extra train with surgeons and Mr. Greer. Three cars through bridge at Tariffville."[5] Mr. Greer was the railroad's roadmaster. Within an hour an emergency train was leaving with doctors, medical supplies, and railroad workers. Following this, Jones telegraphed the Hartford office of the Hartford, Providence & Fishkill Railroad and asked for a similar train of mercy, having remembered that the Western's Hartford office

closed after the revival train departed. The Fishkill road responded; by 1 a.m. a Fishkill train left for Tariffville with twenty more doctors on board.*

While Superintendent Jones handled railroad details, Connecticut Western President Caleb Camp, who happened to be a passenger in one of the last, unwrecked, coaches, enlisted help from Tariffville residents. Church bells rang; homes of individuals and businesses were flung open. Crowds of rescuers and spectators dashed for the scene, and many helped in the grisly task of extricating people from the wrecked train. Just after midnight the West Winsted special arrived, and by 1:30 a.m. the Fishkill train appeared. At 3 a.m. the Fishkill special went back to Hartford with many of the dead, as well as those who had survived the wreck. In tow were the cars that had remained intact. President Camp accompanied the train and

*Dr. D. P. Pelletier was the first Hartford surgeon notified. He rushed to the Capitol Avenue Drug Store and used the store's telephone to summon other doctors. It has often been asserted that this was the world's first emergency telephone call (*Hartford Courant,* January 15, 1978, p.12).

The great Blizzard of '88 brought out all the photographers. One caught the engine of a westbound train near Norfolk bucking a huge drift. Surely it must have stalled.

Tracks were cleared enough to let this freight through West Winsted. Note the brakeman riding atop a car, a dangerous practice long since outlawed on railroads.

consoled many of the survivors. Early Wednesday morning the rescue search was continued, and the bodies of five New Hartford teenagers were recovered. In Hartford that day, the Reverend Mr. Moody conducted a prayer service attended by two thousand people. His topic was the shortness and uncertainty of life.

A jury of inquest was subsequently formed to ascertain the wreck's cause, and, to avoid double interrogation, Connecticut's railroad commissioners sat in on the hearings. More than fifty witnesses appeared, bridge experts were called in, and further investigations were held. The jury was split in its final verdict. Some felt the bridge was in perfectly safe condition; others believed the natural elements had taken their toll, and the huge weight of the special train had brought it down. The commissioners assigned no guilt but were convinced that "shock" had precipitated the collapse. As to what caused the shock no one was certain, though many felt *Salisbury's* tender had derailed and struck exposed trusses, thereupon collapsing the span. The commissioners quickly ordered all railroads in the state to verify if adequate planking protected their bridges' critical trusses and chords, and commended the adoption of larger suspension rods. Rods broken at Tariffville were ultimately sent for scientific testing at Colt's Patent Firearms Manufactory in Hartford. The railroad's other large Howe truss bridge, also crossing the Farmington River but at Satan's Kingdom in New Hartford, was replaced, in 1879, with a 206-foot wrought iron structure built by the Niagara Bridge Company of Buffalo.

The Connecticut Western paid $200 to $600 for each life lost and absorbed the monetary damages to engines, cars, and the bridge itself. Both engines were raised, repaired, and returned to service, and the bridge was rebuilt on the same design. Early in the inquest one of the railroad's directors, ex-Governor Holley, remarked

Hartford & Connecticut Western engine No. 6 prepares to leave the depot at Norfolk. Haystack Mountain looms up at left.

that many of the road's bridges were overdue for reinforcement, and that he was about to introduce a measure for corrective action.[6] Years slowly passed before the great tragedy left the public's memory. Thirteen people died at Tariffville; seventy had sustained injuries.

Shaken by the accident, the railroad's management again turned to the road's sagging financial condition. Bond interest could not be paid, and debts were mounting; now the Tariffville horror further drained the road's finances. On April 28, 1880, the company's mortgage, created under the bond issue, was foreclosed by disgruntled bondholders and by the treasurer of the state in his capacity as trustee for the instrument. The company was bankrupt. In March of the following year a reorganization created the "Hartford & Connecticut Western Railroad Company" with a capital structure of $2,200,000.[7] The bonds of the old company were converted into preferred stock of the new one at 50 percent of their face value. The old stockholders were completely wiped out. On August 1, 1881, the new company finally got title to its property from the state treasurer. Almost immediately after the corporate failure President Camp had attempted to sell the line to the New York & New England Railroad. The latter, based in Boston, had its main line across central Connecticut and was striving for a Hudson River destination. The "New England" had

Greenwoods Road, today Route 44, went over the track at Norfolk. When the railroad was taken up in this century, the semitunnel underneath this overpass was filled in. But the beautiful guard posts were kept and today are restored. The station seen in both pictures is the second serving this picturesque spot. The one below was taken by Mrs. J. C. Kendall. The town was a mecca in summertime. The summer home of the Yale School of Music is situated on a local estate.

Photograph 5375 C. N. E. Ry. Bridge, Satan's Kingdom, New Hartford, Conn.

These two views show famous Satan's Kingdom at New Hartford, with the Central New England's bridge across the Farmington River, a 206-foot iron lattice span built in 1878 by the Niagara Bridge Company of Buffalo. In the photograph at top, the rails at right were the Collinsville branch of the old Canal Railroad. Both lines are gone, and today no whistle breaks the quiet.

The stock certificate at left and the travel guide below (with a glimpse of the Poughkeepsie Bridge) help trace the ever-changing names of a charming old railway.

dispatched a representative to evaluate the Western,[8] but the amount of work needed on the line and the poor earnings record discouraged a serious offer, and the matter was dropped.

The Western's history following the 1881 rebirth is heavily involved with upstate New York railroads in and around rural Dutchess and Columbia counties. Many lightly patronized lines were struggling in this area, and the Connecticut road struck alliances with some of them. It even bought the little thirty-five-mile Rhinebeck & Connecticut Railroad. These endeavors, however, made only a modest contribution to the company coffers.

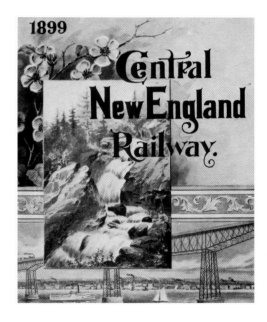

One event did have great consequences. That was the opening in 1888 of the immense, high, Poughkeepsie Railroad Bridge over the Hudson river. It provided New England with a direct link to the Pennsylvania coal fields, Lake Erie ports, and western markets. Numerous companies were founded to construct the bridge and bring in the necessary approach routes. Backed by Philadelphia money interests, a group of these railroads consolidated as the Central New England & Western, and this firm in 1889 went so far as to lease the Hartford & Connecticut Western to get its freight manifests into New England. When the bridge opened, a Hartford & Connecticut Western Railroad engine pulled the first train over the huge span. *Tariffville* did the honors, the same engine involved in the Tariffville bridge collapse of 1878.[9] The Central New England & Western rebuilt the Connecticut road in response to traffic requirements and installed seventy-pound steel rail to handle the heavy freight trains. Joint passenger trains were also run via the "Poughkeepsie Bridge Route," including the *Day Express* (between Boston, Hartford, Winsted, and Harrisburg, covering the 464 miles in sixteen hours) and the *Boston-Washington Express*, later called the *Federal*. It must be remembered that there was then no through rail route, without the use of car ferries, in the New York City area. Poughkeepsie's was the first bridge below Albany. It was only in 1911 that the completion of the Pennsylvania Railroad tubes under the Hudson and the East River, together with the building of the Hell Gate Bridge, made it possible to run the *Federal* through Pennsylvania Station in New York City.

Another merger of Poughkeepsie Bridge-area lines occurred in 1892, with the Central New England & Western becoming the Philadelphia, Reading & New England Railroad. Behind virtually all these consolidations was the Philadelphian A. Archibald McLeod, who was creating a syndicate of lines to control the flow of immense amounts of Reading coal into the homes and mills of New England. McLeod even

[OVERLEAF] A dramatic view of the huge Poughkeepsie bridge over the Hudson River, built by the Central New England. It helped link southern New England with the Pennsylvania coal fields and the western markets. Enormous amounts of freight were transported over it by the New Haven Railroad. Today it still stands, unused.

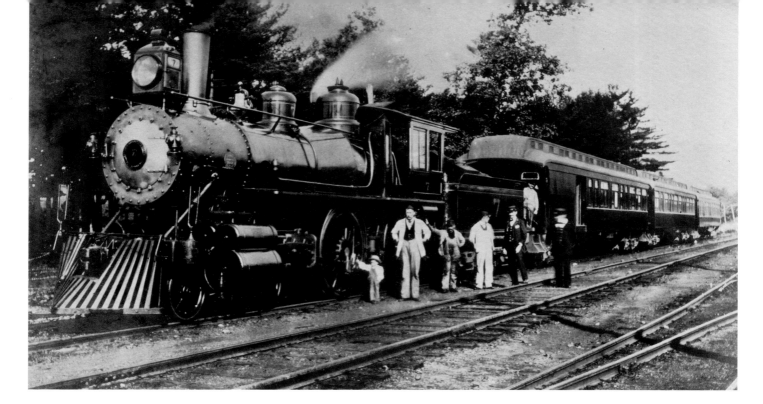

By far the fanciest train of the Central New England was the Mountain Express, *which ran early in this century. No. 7 burned coal.*

secured a stock control of the New York & New England and the Boston & Maine railroads, enabling his products to reach all of New England without utilizing the New York, New Haven & Hartford Railroad system, then falling increasingly under the power of J. Pierpont Morgan. McLeod despised Morgan and once remarked that "I would rather run a peanut stand than be dictated to by J.P. Morgan."[10] When the New York & New England and Boston & Maine take-overs were announced by McLeod, the earth shook at Drexel, Morgan, & Company in New York City. The sacrosanct empire of "The Consolidated" had been invaded! Morgan retaliated and began to manipulate Philadelphia & Reading securities, ultimately forcing it into receivership. The Philadelphia & Reading was then forced to dispose of its Boston & Maine holdings. By 1893 the New York & New England was bankrupt, and the daring Mr. McLeod was forced out of New England.[11] J.P. Morgan would have been happy to supply him with peanuts.

While the captains of industry (or pirates, if one prefers) carried out their railroad manipulations, an atmosphere of mistrust continued to prevail on the Hartford &

Here we have the sad case of one Webster, first name unknown, who drunkenly drove this rig onto the railroad trestle at New Hartford. One horse was shot, one survived, and Webster was taken off to the pokey.

Connecticut Western property, particularly during its brief role in the Philadelphia, Reading & New England era. Morale was low, wages were slashed, and maintenance was relaxed. One typical incident involved the compensation of Connecticut section men who had diligently cared for the track. In August 1892 everyone on the line quit when wages were dropped to $1.25 a day. The railroad responded by recruiting and bringing in as replacements what it described as "eager Hungarians" from the Poughkeepsie area. The new immigrant workers were quickly disillusioned; upon arriving they discovered that the wage was actually 25¢ a day. They returned on the evening train.[12] Wrecks, too, were a frequent occurrence. A month after the Hungarian incident a twelve-car freight train suddenly blew up while rumbling between Winsted and New Hartford because of a carelessly loaded car of dynamite. A brakeman was hurled two hundred feet from the scene, and the explosion was so great that "four cars were blown into atoms."[13] Local newspapers recorded the troubles and the frequent accidents. Finally, in 1898, the game was up for the Philadelphia, Reading & New England. It went into receivership, to emerge later as the Central New England Railway.

The story now returns to Connecticut with construction of a fifteen-mile branch from Tariffville to Agawam and West Springfield, Massachusetts, another bold attempt to get coal deep into New England without using the New York, New Haven & Hartford Railroad Company. From the Central New England's point of view, it meant a connection at West Springfield with the powerful and friendly Boston & Albany Railroad, controlled by the Vanderbilts. Running rights would be obtained over the Boston & Albany to Springfield's Union Station, where the Central would also meet the Boston & Maine network. Connecticut Valley tobacco growers thought the branch line a good idea, since the railroad could cheaply haul fertilizer. Work on the Tariffville Extension began in 1899, but the road faced protracted problems over title to a 313-foot parcel of farmland in East Granby, Connecticut. The railroad had originally given the owner $500 for the strip; soon, however, one Charles C. Montague appeared and offered the farmer $4,000 for the same parcel. The farmer played dumb and quickly took the money. Track workers then appeared and tore up the Central New England's new rails and ties on the piece of property. Some of the workers' tools were left behind, and they were found to be marked as property of the New York, New Haven & Hartford Railroad.[14] Thus began the "Montague Farm incident."

Investigations revealed that the New York, New Haven & Hartford Railroad had bought the land in Charles Montague's name for the purpose of blocking construc-

According to information on the back of this picture, this was "Mr. Welch's train," so-called for its highly respected conductor. It was taken in the summer of 1924 outside Norfolk, pulled by No. 45. Trains like this ran to Hartford in reasonably quick fashion. One wonders if the modern-day Route 44 commuter would leave his auto and take to the rails, if such trains still ran there.

(Text Continued on Page 153)

These two pictures illustrate the bizarre "Montague Farm" incident described in the text on the preceding page, when newly-laid Central New England track and roadbed were torn out on 313 feet of land illegally (it turned out) acquired by a front man for the New Haven Road named Montague. This briefly halted the Central's 1899 extension from Tariffville to Springfield, Massachusetts, via East Granby, although the Central quickly built a loop (not shown here) around the disputed area and used it until the court ruled against the New Haven's sly maneuver. The original route, in the large photograph, ran straight from the handcar in the foreground to the locomotive at rear. The removed track sections, going up to the right over a rise, have apparently been set up as a "shoo-fly" for handcar use by Central crews moving materials around the break. The inset above records the day when legislators, officials, and the railroad commissioners came to East Granby by rail to inspect the scene of this well-publicized imbroglio, so typical of that age.

BOTH: COLLECTION OF JAMES M.S. ULLMAN

Distance from Tariffville	Time Table 34 In Effect Oct. 3, 1909. STATIONS.		
0.0	BD	Tariffville	D
3.0	AG	East Granby	D
5.6		Sheldon Street	
6.7	SU	West Suffield	D
8.6		Freemans	
12.2	OD	Feeding Hills	D
14.2	GW	Agawam Jct.	N
17.7	FH	Springfield	N

This large edifice was the main depot of the Central New England at Hartford, across the tracks from the New Haven station.

This is Bloomfield, where old Central rails still carry occasional freight from Hartford.

Collinsville, the axe town, was served by the Central New England and a branch of the old Canal Line. Neither goes there now.

Norfolk Summit, at the highest rail altitude in the state, had a log cabin for a station.

COLLECTION OF LEROY ROBERTS

This is relatively busy Twin Lakes Station, near Salisbury. When first built, the Central New England used trestle piling over the lake's edge, but in 1881 some 200 feet of it sank in 30 feet of water. Later it was filled in.

The Salisbury Station boasted a huge water tank, but every trace of railroad is now gone. The old depot at Lakeville remains.

Engine No. 32 stands ready to leave New Hartford with a long freight for the West.

Central New England
RAILWAY.

tion of the Central New England's new line. The case was tried in state and federal courts, and, owing to a technicality in statute language, the New Haven road temporarily won. Montague, the front man, was conveniently represented by the New Haven's senior corporate attorney. But the resourceful Central was not to be outdone. It secured a charter for the "East Granby & Suffield Railroad" in 1901, which was simply a means of building around the Montague property. In 1902 the extension opened. Ownership of the strip was later obtained, the loop around it eliminated, and the original line through the Montague property finally utilized. Such were the financial games of that era, smaller in scale but not unlike others in our times.

The Tariffville Extension was one of the last acts the Central undertook. About the time it opened the extension, the New York, New Haven, & Hartford Railroad began buying up Central stock. One of the first things the president of the former, Charles Mellen, did was to obtain a dominant interest in the line and thereby take control of its valuable Poughkeepsie Bridge. Unfortunately, the importance of the Central New England's northern route diminished as Mellen developed another more southerly one, from New Haven via Danbury to the same bridge, as the better freight gateway to western markets. Gross earnings of the Central New England in 1906 stood at $1,670,000, and the line could only boast a net profit of around $7,500. No dividends on the stock were paid. In 1927 the Central was officially incorporated into the New York, New Haven, & Hartford empire. Where once the luxurious *Mountain Express* glided over the Central New England, service reductions soon took place. Significant abandonment of track occurred between Bloomfield and Salisbury during and after the 1930s. The dream so ardently fought for by Egbert Butler of Norfolk was shattered.

Part of the old Central New England track is still in service from Hartford to the Griffin's Industrial Park in Bloomfield, and around the Canaan station. Abandoned vestiges of the line can still be spotted while motoring west of Canton on Route 44. It is difficult, though, to find traces of the old Tariffville bridge over the Farmington River, scene of the disaster. More easily located and standing silent is the huge

Whiting Viaduct in East Canaan, that great earthen and cement structure that carried track over both highway and river. In smart Norfolk, its jewel-like station—largely paid for early this century by private donations—still stands but is commercially occupied. Also in Butler's beloved Norfolk is the Route 44 overpass near the library. Residents in the last century, led by the Congregational minister, actually forced the railroad off the town green and into this modest land depression. Today guard railings on the overpass have been lovingly restored, as if Central New England trains still chugged underneath.

Chapter Nine Footnotes

1. Theron W. Crissey, *History of Norfolk* (Everett, MA: Massachusetts Publishing Co., 1900), 341-350.

2. Ibid.

3. Connecticut General Assembly, Resolves and Private Laws of the State of Connecticut, An Act to Incorporate the Connecticut Western Railroad Company, IV: 339, Public Records, Connecticut State Capitol Building.

4. W. Robinson, *Locomotives of the Central New England Railway,* Railway and Locomotive Historical Society Bulletin no. 50.

5. Robert B. Adams, "A Centennial Look Back at a Rail Wreck,"*Lakeville Journal*, 5 January 1978, Supplement. (This article is probably the most accurate and complete summary prepared about the Tariffville Wreck.)

6. Robert B. Shaw, *A History of Railroad Accidents, Safety Precautions and Operating Practices* (Vail-Ballou Press, 1978), 57.

7. Connecticut General Assembly, Resolves and Private Laws of the State of Connecticut, IX: 169, Public Records, Connecticut State Capitol building.

8. J.C. Raun, Report upon Condition, Cost of Maintenance, Grades, etc., Upon the Connecticut Western Railroad, June 1880, Turner Railroad Collection, The Connecticut Historical Society.

9. D.W. McLaughlin, *Poughkeepsie Gateway*, Railway & Locomotive Historical Society Bulletin no. 119, 6-32.

10. Lewis Corey, *The House of Morgan* (New York: G. Howard Watt, 1930), 202.

11. *Commercial and Financial Chronicle*, LVIII (1894): 513.

12. *Winsted Evening Citizen*, 9 August 1892.

13. [Winsted] *Litchfield County Leader*, 23 August 1892.

14. [New York] *Tribune*, 7 April 1901.

In 1938 a rail gang dismantles the Central New England main line. Good scrap for Japan.

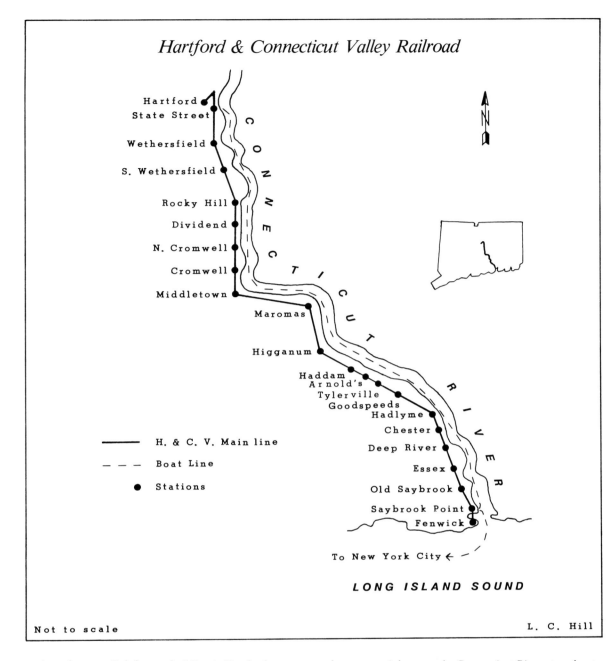

Hartford & Connecticut Valley Railroad

N

Hartford
State Street
Wethersfield
S. Wethersfield
Rocky Hill
Dividend
N. Cromwell
Cromwell
Middletown
Maromas
Higganum
Haddam
Arnold's
Tylerville
Goodspeeds
Hadlyme
Chester
Deep River
Essex
Old Saybrook
Saybrook Point
Fenwick

CONNECTICUT RIVER

———— H. & C. V. Main line
- - - - Boat Line
● Stations

To New York City ←

LONG ISLAND SOUND

Not to scale

L. C. Hill

Atop the great Colt factory building in Hartford one can see the commercial center, the Connecticut River steamboat dock at foot of State Street, and shipbuilding activity. A Valley Railroad train crosses the Park River drawbridge.

HARTFORD, FROM COLT'S FACTORY.

Chapter Ten

Down the Valley!

The line of the Valley Railroad is on the west bank of the Connecticut River, is 44 miles in length, extending from Hartford to Saybrook on the Sound— touching all the important towns and villages on the route.

—*Connecticut Valley Railroad bond publicity, 1871*

If scenic beauty ever surrounded a Connecticut railroad route, it was what a passenger could view from the coach windows of the Connecticut Valley Railroad between Hartford and the Long Island Sound shore town of Old Saybrook. Few railroads in the country followed a waterway so scenic as the Connecticut River, which was dotted with white sails, steamboats, and quaint villages. In the last century it carried vacationers to beach resorts and specialized also in coal, lumber, grain, and feed. The line enjoyed particular significance when the Connecticut River froze over and ships were immobilized at their piers.

Interest in a railroad line between Hartford and Saybrook first arose in 1853 when a charter was secured for the Hartford & Middlesex County Railroad.[1] General James Palmer, surveyor of the New London, Willimantic & Palmer Railroad, was engaged to run a survey from the capital city to Long Island Sound. About $1,000 in expenses were incurred in getting the charter and paying for the survey, which was raised through voluntary donations. Unfortunately the substantial sums necessary for actual construction were lacking. Enthusiasm waned, and the project slumbered for fifteen years.

In the late 1860s civic spirit embraced the idea again; its champion was James Walkeley of Hartford. A graduate of Yale College and Harvard Law School, Walkeley was clerk of Hartford's superior court, a state representative, and president of the Charter Oak Life Insurance Company. He was also a free and easy financier who speculated in mining and western railroad stocks. On July 17, 1868, Walkeley and his colleagues received a charter creating the Connecticut Valley Railroad Company. Construction of a railroad from Hartford, along the Connecticut River, to some point in "either Clinton, Westbrook or Saybrook,"[2] was authorized. The privilege of erecting and maintaining docks on the Sound was also granted. Capitalization of the line was set at $1,500,000, with the option of issuing another $1,000,000 of stock if required. Towns along the line were allowed to invest in the line, and the directors were given until 1876 to open the railroad.

James C. Walkeley was first president of the Connecticut Valley Railroad. Groundbreaking for the line occurred at his home at Walkeley Hill in Haddam. [BELOW] Fenwick Hall. New Saybrook later became known as Fenwick Borough.

FENWICK HALL. New Saybrook, Conn.

This new and elegant hotel is situated at the mouth of the Connecticut River; commanding a fine view of the Sound on the south, and Connecticut River and Bay on the east and north. It was built expressly for the comfort and convenience of families seeking a sea-side resort, and has all the modern improvements. It contains upward of one hundred and fifty rooms, single or en suite, all of which are large, well ventilated and nicely furnished. There are four large parlors on the office floor. The halls are spacious and nearly two hundred feet in length and the veranda covers two stories, is sixteen feet wide and nearly four hundred feet long. It has good accommodations for horses and carriages, and there are many pleasant drives about the Town of Saybrook. Good bathing, fishing and sailing, add greatly to the attractions of this popular resort. It has superior advantages of access by rail and steam-boats. The proprietor, Mr. D. A. Rood, will give further information to those who desire it.

HARTFORD & CONN. VALLEY R. R.

On and after Monday, Sept. 13th, 1880,

TRAINS WILL RUN AS FOLLOWS.

HARTFORD TO Middletown & Saybrook Point.

LEAVE.	PASS. A. M.	PASS. A. M.	PASS. A. M.	FREIGHT. P. M.	PASS. P. M.	PASS. P. M.
Hartford, State street,	6 40	7 30	10 10	12 05	4 05	6 20
Wethersfield,	6 47	7 42	10·19	12 20	4 14	6 29
South Wethersfield,	6 51	7 47		12 31	4 19	6 34
Rocky Hill,	6 56	7 52	10 28	12 45	4 25	6 40
North Cromwell,	7 03	8 00		1 00		
Cromwell,	7 06	8 05	10 37	1 12	4 37	6 56
Middletown Junction,	7 13	8 13	10 46			
Middletown,	7 15	8 15	10 49	1 45	4 48	7 13
Maromas,		8 26		2 05		7 28
Higganum,		8 37	11 04	2 30	5 03	7 39
Walkley Hill,		8 41	11 10			
Haddam,		8 44	11 14	2 45	5 10	7 47
Arnold's,		8 47	11 17	2 50		
Goodspeed's,		8 53	11 23	3 00	5 20	7 59
Chester,		9 02	11 33	3 15	5 30	8 11
Deep River,		9 05	11 36	3 25	5 34	8 16
Essex,		9 14	11 46	3 40	5 45	8 28
Saybrook Junction,		9 26	12 19	4 30	6 08	8 40
Saybrook Point,		9 36	12 27	4 40	6 15	8 50
New Haven,			1 38		7 46	
New London,		10 10	12 46		7 49	
Stonington,		10 52	1 51			
Newport,			4 15			
Providence,		12 35	3.45			

SAYBROOK POINT TO Middletown & Hartford.

LEAVE.	FREIGHT. A. M.	PASS. A. M.	PASS. A. M.	Ft. & Pass. A. M.	PASS. A. M.	PASS. P. M.
Providence,					9 40	2 03
Newport,					8 00	1 00
Stonington,			5 53		11 05	3 22
New London,			7 03		11 35	3 52
New Haven,				8 08	10 40	3 18
Saybrook Point,	3 00		7 35	9 00	11 50	4 02
Saybrook Junction,	3 15		7 50	9 26	12 19	4 30
Essex,			7 59	9 41	12 28	4 39
Deep River,			8 07	9 56	12 38	4 47
Chester,			8 10	10 06	12 41	4 50
Goodspeed's,			8 19	10 22	12 50	4 58
Arnold's,				10 33	12 56	
Haddam,			8 28	10 38	12 59	5 10
Walkley Hill,					1 02	
Higganum,			8 37	11 04	1 06	5 16
Maromas,				11 15	1 14	
Middletown,	4 35	7 28	8 53		1 25	5 34
Middletown Junction,		7 30	8 56	11 45	1 28	5 36
Cromwell,		7 38	9 03	11 57	1 37	5 44
North Cromwell,		7 42			1 41	
Rocky Hill,	5 00	7 52	9 12	12 22	1 49	5 54
South Wethersfield,		7 57		12 31	1 54	
Wethersfield,	5 15	8 01	9 21	12 40	1 58	6 04
Ar. Hartford, State st.,	5 30	8 10	9 28	12 50	2 07	6 12

One Stop-over Check given on the trains.   Trains stop only at stations where time is given.

CONNECTIONS.

The **7.30 A. M.** train from Hartford connects at Middletown with trains of the Boston and New York Air Line to New Haven; at Saybrook Junction with trains of the Shore Line for Niantic, New London, Stonington, Providence, Watch Hill, Narragansett Pier, Taunton, New Bedford and Martha's Vineyard.

The **10.10 A. M.** train, from Hartford, connects at Middletown with trains of the Boston and New York Air Line, for New Haven, New York, Willimantic, Boston and intermediate stations, and at Saybrook Junction with the Shore Line R. R. trains going East to New London, for Norwich, Stonington, Watch Hill, Narragansett Pier, Newport, Providence, Boston, Taunton and New Bedford; and West to New Haven, New York and intermediate stations.

The **4.05 P. M.** train from Hartford, connects with N. Y. & N. E. train from Springfield, and at Middletown with trains of the Boston and New York Air Line for New Haven, New York, Willimantic, Boston and intermediate stations; and at Saybrook Junction with the Shore Line Railroad trains for New Haven, New York, New London, Norwich, Stonington, Providence, Boston and all intermediate stations.

The **6.20** P. M. train, from Hartford, connects with steamer for New York.

The **3.00 A. M.** train from Saybrook Point connects with steamers from New York.

The **7.35 A. M.** train from Saybrook Point makes close connection with the Boston and New York Air Line at Middletown, for Willimantic, Norwich, New London, Putnam, Boston, Worcester, Blackstone and Providence, and at Hartford with N. Y. & N. E. R. R. for Springfield.

The **7.35** and **9.00** A. M., and **4.02** P. M. trains from Saybrook Point connect at Saybrook Junction with trains of the Shore Line R. R., to and from New Haven, New York, New London, Norwich, Stonington, Watch Hill, Providence, Newport, Boston and intermediate stations; at Middletown with trains of the Boston and New York Air Line R. R., to and from New Haven, New York, Willimantic, Providence and intermediate stations; and with trains of the Conn. Western, New York and New England, and New York, New Haven and Hartford Railroads.

The **11.50 A. M.** train from Saybrook Point connects at Saybrook Junction with trains of the Shore Line from Providence, Stonington, Newport, Watch Hill, New London and New Haven; at Middletown with trains of the Boston and New York Air Line from Willimantic and New Haven.

HARTFORD, Sept. 10, 1880.

LEVI WOODHOUSE, Ass't Sup't and Gen. Pass. Ag't.

PRESS OF WILEY, WATERMAN & EATON, HARTFORD, CONN.

After receiving the charter, the directors ordered their civil engineer, Seth Marsh, to make a new survey and submit estimates of construction costs.[3] His survey recommended that the railroad begin in downtown Hartford at the intersection of State and Commerce streets—close to modern-day Constitution Plaza. The line was to cross the Park River near its mouth, heading for Wethersfield and Rocky Hill, and after passing Cromwell Neck aim directly for the waterfront of Middletown. South of Middletown the projected right-of-way ran along the river bank to Maromas, Higganum Village, and to a point opposite Goodspeed Landing in East Haddam. Further south, Marsh again chose a right-of-way close to the river, crossing Chester Creek and Deep River Cove, an area of flowering marshes and wild birds, to reach Pratt Cove in Deep River. There the tracks would angle towards Salt Island in Westbrook harbor, although he also indicated other possible destinations in Old Saybrook and Clinton. All this added up to forty-four miles of railroad. Marsh indicated that grades were quite modest, that land damages would be affordable, that stone quarries were conveniently at hand, and that an ample supply of timber existed along the route for bridges, ties, and piling. He also noted that "a very friendly feeling prevails among the inhabitants along the route towards the road, and the completion of the same."

Valley main line opposite Goodspeed's Opera House, decades before the modern drawbridge was built. Note the picnic.

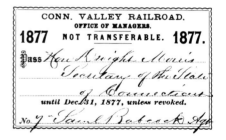

Providing passes for free travel was good public relations. The one above was issued to the Honorable Dwight Morris, who at the time was secretary of the state. Such benevolence helped pave the way when favors might be needed. The railroad's checking account was with President Walkeley's Charter Oak National Bank, as the check at left reveals. When Walkeley's Charter Oak Insurance Company collapsed, his bank ultimately foundered, and because it held mortgage bonds on the railroad, the Valley line went bankrupt. The latter got reorganized as the Hartford & Connecticut Valley.

Marsh's survey divided the work into three divisions of construction: the "North Division," which ran from Hartford to Middletown; the "Middle Division," which took the road south to a point opposite Goodspeed Landing; and the "South Division," which would have brought the line to Salt Island in Westbrook. Marsh's calculations showed that construction costs would come to $1,482,903, or about $34,000 per mile. The engineering report, along with publicity pamphlets, made its way into the hands of potential investors. Ultimately Saybrook Point at the river mouth, not Westbrook, was selected as the southern terminus.

Money to build the Connecticut Valley Railroad was raised through the traditional sale of stocks and bonds. Individuals and towns subscribed, and the state even went so far as to abate taxes on bonds in support of the project. The first bond issue amounted to $1,000,000 and was placed with the help of the Connecticut River Banking Company in Hartford. All the assets of the railroad were pledged for the bond issue, and the treasurer of the state was named as trustee. The city of Hartford responded and subscribed to nearly $500,000 of stock. The single-track line—it never had but one—was built and opened with a suitable celebration on July 29, 1871. The speed limit for passenger trains was set initially at twenty-two miles per hour. The main line crossed fifty-two public roads at grade. There were seventy-five men on the payroll. In its first year of operations the Connecticut Valley grossed $34,000; but, as was the case with many early Connecticut railroads, no dividends were paid. At Old Saybrook a junction was made with the Shore Line Railway, while at Middletown the road crossed the track of the New Haven, Middletown & Willimantic—the Air Line Railroad.

A Valley engine intrudes on this pastoral advertisement for the Maplewood Music Seminary. River boats competed with the railroad; none could match the railroad in hauling vast quantities of coal.

MAPLEWOOD MUSIC SEMINARY FOR LADIES, EAST HADDAM, CONN.
[ESTABLISHED 1863.]
Prof. D. S. Babcock, Principal and Proprietor.

Hartford and New York Boats,

Formerly Connecticut River Steamboat Company,

AND NOW OWNED BY THE

Hartford & New York Transportation Co.,

OFFICE AND WHARF:

FOOT OF STATE STREET (No. 285), HARTFORD.

New York Office, **PECK SLIP, PIER 24, EAST RIVER.**

CAPITOL CITY,
CAPT. JAS. RUSSELL.

CITY OF LAWRENCE,
CAPT. RICHARD K. MINER.

CITY OF SPRINGFIELD

Leave Hartford DAILY (SUNDAYS EXCEPTED) at 4 o'clock P. M. For New York

AND INTERMEDIATE LANDINGS ON THE RIVER.

FARES—First Class Cabin passage to New York, (no charge for berths,) $1.50
Second " on Deck, ... 1.00
First " Excursion Tickets, New York and return, good on
either Boat and for the Season, (no charge for berths), . 2.50

BOATS STOP AT ALL RIVER LANDINGS,

And IF NOTIFIED IN ADVANCE, at those that are *

WETHERSFIELD,	MIDDLETOWN,	DEEP RIVER,
GLASTONBURY,	*MIDDLE HADDAM,	*BROCKWAY'S
SOUTH GLASTONBURY,	*ROCK LANDING,	*ELY'S,
ROCKY HILL,	EAST HADDAM,	ESSEX,
*GILDERSLEEVE'S,	GOODSPEED'S	LYME,
PORTLAND,	*HADLYME,	SAYBROOK.

For Distances of and between these Landings, see Page 485.

E. H. WILLIAMS, President.

C. C. GOODRICH, General Agent.

⁕OFFICE OF THE⁕

Hartford & Connecticut Valley R. R. Co.

Hartford, Conn July 24 1880

Gen J H Wilson
    Vice Prest
        Boston Mass

Dear Sir

Your favor of 28ᵗʰ inst relating to leasing Locomotive came duly. The Locomotive came into our service yesterday morning (July 23) for which please accept thanks.

Very truly yours
Saml Babcock
Prest

Chg.
$12 per day
JHW

Correspondence plays a role with any business, as do purchases. The document at right, dated 1880, is from Valley president Samuel Babcock. In it, he advises General James Wilson, vice president of the New York & New England, that the engine they leased the Valley had arrived. But what is unique is the penciled figure at bottom left; Wilson approved a $12 a day rate! The document below the letter is a bill from the Copeland Manufacturing Company, which made railway crossing gates. The Valley had just bought a set for its Wethersfield Avenue crossing in that town. The cost? $250. A set built to modern-day standards costs about $37,500, before the great expense of installing it and wiring it up.

. BEARD, *President,*	JOHN L. BICKFORD, *Sec. and Treas.*	W. C. BAIRD. *V. Pres.*	COPELAND MANUFACTURING CO.

MANUFACTURERS OF

→ **RAILROAD SAFETY GATES,** ←

No. ~~19 Park Place,~~ 2314 Broadway

New York, Dec 27ᵗʰ 1886

FACTORY,
Syracuse. N. Y.

TERMS, NET CASH,

Sold to Hartford & Conn. Valley R.R. Co
    Hartford Conn.

1886 Dec.	8	One Crossing Gate Weathersfield Ave. Span 50 feet	250	00

Correct
C L Davidson
    Supt
Approved
Saml Babcock V.P.

161

COLLECTION OF DOUGLAS K. PATTERSON

The Connecticut Valley in the next year extended its track from Saybrook Point, via a half-mile trestle over a wide cove, to the growing summer colony of Fenwick, bringing crowds to listen to revivalists, "bathe," enjoy clambakes, and to stay at a huge new wooden summer hotel, Fenwick Hall, whose mortgage was held by Walkeley's Charter Oak Company. By 1873 directors ordered a track extension in Hartford to reach the Asylum Street depot of the Hartford, Providence & Fishkill Railroad.[4] The line steadily grew in public acceptance, and its gross revenues approached $250,000 a year. Six steam locomotives were on the engine roster, and 142 people were on the payroll. Vacuum brakes were used on passenger cars, and the engines burned coal. By 1874 another $1,000,000 bond issue was floated to handle expenses, improvements, and the cost of prior debts. But still no dividends were forthcoming, for construction debt still plagued the directors.

A railway between two large cities has a chance of survival and success. But a line between a city and a string of villages is unlikely to succeed, however beautiful the scenery. Because a bar at the mouth of the Connecticut River kept all but shallow-draft steamers and sloops from navigating northward, the valley never went industrial to any extent, and the villages remained villages. While this is a source of joy and thanksgiving to the present inhabitants, it condemned the Connecticut Valley Railroad to branch-line rank. Whether the directors took this view or not a century ago we do not know, but they did thrash about for more business. Why not expand? Why not get the line up to Springfield, an important distribution point for the coal which the Valley Railroad was hauling in increasing quantities?

Consequently, in January 1876 they leased the little Connecticut Central Railroad, which ran from East Hartford to Springfield by way of Melrose, Hazardville, and East Longmeadow. To reach East Hartford, across the Connecticut River from the Asylum Street depot, the Valley obtained running rights over the track of the Hartford, Providence & Fishkill. Geographically this made sense, but the Valley could not afford the rent, or much of anything. Its original angel, President Walkeley, was in financial difficulties owing to the collapse of his Charter Oak Insurance Company. The Valley defaulted on its second-mortgage bonds, of which $1,000,000 worth turned out to be held by the floundering Charter Oak Insurance Company, and in June 1876 the company went into receivership. It could not pay its first-mortgage interest, either. Even Fenwick Hall failed, to add to Walkeley's troubles. The state treasurer stepped in as trustee and cancelled the Connecticut Central lease. The company was reorganized in 1879, emerging as the Hartford & Connecticut Valley. The following year the stockholders took title to the property once more; the new president was Samuel Babcock of Middletown, a wealthy politician who had made money in locks and eyeglasses.

This is Deep River which, until 1947, was still known as Saybrook. Amidst trees, its Valley Railroad station stands sentinel to a pastoral Connecticut River. Statia Island is in the mid-foreground; Selden Island beyond. An early timetable is below, showing many connections, including (under the 3:25 from Saybrook Point) a prize misprint.

COLLECTION OF OLIVER JENSEN

162

(Continued on Page 169)

More details are desired about this strange Valley train wreck. It happened in Deep River in 1908, according to what little information is on the back of the photograph. The picture was taken fifteen minutes after the occurrence. Apparently, two freight trains were in town one day—perhaps one heading south, another going north—and were to pass safely using the passing siding. But something went wrong. One (or both!) backed up, and they crashed, demolishing both cabooses and a few cars. The wreck took place when the Valley was a branch line of the New Haven.

The reorganization was a thorough one, and Babcock's administration set about making overdue improvements to the road and capping runaway expenses. Steel rails and more than twenty-five thousand new ties were eventually installed. There were seven engines on the locomotive roster, and more than 175 cars. About 200,000 passengers a year were being carried, and revenues hovered around $200,000. Little by little, Babcock spent money to fill in the long stretches of wood piling and trestles along the route.[5] About $725,000 of stock was issued, and bond-holders from the old company had the privilege of redeeming their foreclosed bonds for stock of the new one. The railroad operated daily freight and passenger service and offered special summer excursions from Hartford to Saybrook and Fenwick.

While the little railroad was being put in better physical shape, the management was looking for a way to sell out, but at a good price. To succeed at this game requires art. The word "leaked out" that the Valley line, having lost out with its lease on the Connecticut Central (which the New York & New England had now leased), was now contemplating building its own line from Hartford, via Granby, to West Springfield and Holyoke. One must look prosperous. One must also stir up competition between possible buyers, and for that wily purpose the time was most opportune, since three other railroads were interested and making overtures. One applicant was the Connecticut River Railroad, whose southern terminal was Springfield. The Valley would be a valuable southward extension to that line, and the two roads could quote favorable rates on the movement of coal. The expanding Boston and Albany Railroad—Vanderbilt's jewel—also saw the Valley acquisition as a means of entering the Connecticut marketplace. And third, there was the New York, New Haven & Hartford Railroad, which was on a buying spree to protect its Connecticut empire.

The Hartford & Connecticut Valley Railroad played its hand shrewdly. The directors simultaneously announced that the line definitely was for sale, and that it would build the West Springfield Extension.[6] With a touch of Madison Avenue, it even released the construction contract. The New Haven Railroad, which had been stalling, grew fearful and came forward with the best offer, obtained a stock control

This is Middletown's Union Station as it looked in 1886, with a passenger car at right and a horse drawn omnibus across the platform. It served the Valley road, the Air Line Route, and patrons of the Middletown to Berlin line. The Valley track is at far right; the view looks north. The track at left connected the Valley to the Air Line. In the picture below, engine No. 2 of the Hartford & Connecticut Valley simmers in the Hartford yard, in full view of tenement homes. This type of engine got approximately 78 miles out every ton of coal.

STATION SCRAPBOOK
of the
VALLEY RAILROAD

Some of the station pictures illustrated here were built by the Valley Railroad itself; others were rebuilt or built anew by the New Haven Railroad. Usually a depot was a busy spot, especially at train time.

HARTFORD: State Street depot, steamer Hartford *is under way.*

WETHERSFIELD: Photographer Irving Drake's car in foreground

SOUTH WETHERSFIELD: Note automatic crossing gates at right.

ROCKY HILL: Freight and passengers were served in one building. At MIDDLETOWN, *below, the Air Line's* White Train *is about to cross the Connecticut River. In the distance, crossing in front of it, is a southbound Valley local train.*

CROMWELL: A Valley line train is approaching in the distance. The depot has the characteristic "Flat W" roof of many stations on this road, with a standard freight house behind it. Below is HIGGANUM *on an early morning.*

HADDAM: *Ubiquitous Drake, like Kilroy of later days, was also here.*

EAST HADDAM & MOODUS: *A bigger depot, also known as Goodspeed's*

HADLYME: *Ferry to Hadlyme at left, at rear, the then-visible river*

CHESTER: *This carpenter-gothic structure is now a private house.*

ESSEX: *The Flat W depot is gone, but the present Valley Railroad has restored the old freight house instead. At SAY-BROOK POINT, below, stood, from left, roundhouse, car storage and steamboat dock. All this is gone today.*

SAYBROOK: *The same angled station serves Amtrak today. About 1910, here, it is busy with a northbound Valley train (right), a main-line train ahead of it, and one at left from New Haven. FENWICK is below, boarded up for winter.*

THE STRANGE CASE OF THE MAROMAS TRAIN WRECK

There are dozens of causes of train wrecks. The Maromas affair involved an act of sabotage. An engineer has few maneuvers left him when he discovers that someone has taken out rails in the track ahead. He can close the throttle, throw the brakes into emergency, and possibly reverse the driving wheels. He can also choose, along with his fireman, to jump from the cab or stay at his post. At Maromas, the fireman escaped; the engineer perished. The scene at the upper left shows railway officials standing in the remains of the engine's tender. The first car has been dashed into a gully. The other photograph graphically illustrates what happened to the engine upon hitting the open rails. No. 1211 went over on her side and skidded to her resting spot. An accordion-like progression of cars followed. The set of pilot wheels on the hill actually belong under the crippled engine.

The author of this memoir, Ernest Alexander Inglis, Sr. (1887-1973), was State's Attorney for the County of Middlesex, at Middletown, and prosecuted the case described below. He later became Chief Justice of the Supreme Court of Errors of Connecticut, and at the age of 85 in 1972, delighted by the revival of the Valley Railroad, composed this account of a bizarre wreck on the Connecticut River bank at Maromas, a mile or two south of Middletown. We are obliged to his daughter, Marion (Mrs. Deryck) Waring, of Westbrook, for the right to include it here. We also thank Douglas K. Patterson of Old Saybrook for furnishing these photographic images of the wreck from his extensive collection of Connecticut postcards.

The only wreck on the Valley Road in recent years came in August of 1911. It was the practice in those days during July and August to run Sunday excursions by train down the Valley Road, going down to Saybrook in the morning, then along the shore, and coming back on Sunday evenings. On the occasion of one of these, on August 27, 1911, the train was derailed in Maromas, the engineer was killed, and some of the passengers were more or less injured. Sabotage was suspected.

The New Haven Road had in its employ a detective by the name of Alessi. The population of Middletown was made up of a relatively large number of residents of Italian descent; and in the search for clues among them, the railroad sent Alessi to Middletown. He came out with the story that during his stay here he had become well acquainted with a group of four men of Italian extraction, and they boasted to him that they were the people who caused the wreck on the Valley Road. They told him in detail of just what they did, and that was to take a rowboat across the river from Middletown to a toolhouse operated in Portland as accessory to the Airline Road. They had broken into this toolhouse and extracted whatever tools they thought would be necessary, and then rowed the boat down the Connecticut River from Portland to Maromas.

At a certain point in Maromas, the single track was laid out along the side of a low hill stretching from the highway on the west down to the water's edge. These four had intended, in the confusion which would result from the wreck, to circulate among the passengers and steal some of their money and valuables. However, when they saw the great damage which had been done by the train being derailed, they ran up the hill and walked back to Middletown.

When Alessi reported that story to the Middletown police, warrants were issued for the four men whom he had named, and they were brought in and tried in the city court. It developed, however, that each of the four men had a valid alibi, so the case was dismissed.

About four years later, in 1915, a man of Italian descent was arrested in Bridgeport, charged with arson. He was released on bail and "jumped" his bail. Very soon he was located in Ohio, and the state police arrested him and brought him back. On the way back he told them that the only crime he had ever participated in was the wreck of the train in Maromas in August of 1911. He described in detail what he had done. His story was that a group of four men had crossed the river from Middletown, broken into a toolhouse in Portland, and taken whatever tools they thought would be necessary to accomplish the wreck and then rowed down to Maromas. When they got to this wooded point where the train ran close to the river, they had unscrewed the angle irons which connected one rail with the next rail and pulled the spikes from this one rail and had used an angle iron to elevate the south end of that rail above the level of the rail next south. When the train came along, it was derailed and landed down next to the Connecticut River, but was stopped from falling into the river by a line of trees along the river bank.

He named the three men who were his accomplices; they were picked up and later tried and found guilty and sentenced to state prison. In fact the story of what had happened was exactly the same as the story which had been reported by Alessi except that it involved four altogether different men. It was curious that the story told to Alessi in a sort of boastful fashion by his four acquaintances in Middletown was the same in detail as the story finally revealed by the Bridgeport man, except, of course, that the two stories involved four different men.

It seems very likely that the story which Alessi reported might have been current among the Italian colony and had evidently been adopted by the four men whom he mentioned. In fact, the story reported by Detective Alessi was generally supposed, by the people in Middletown, to have been a frame-up on the part of the railroad seeking to escape liability for negligence in not having patrolled the track of the railroad itself as it should have done, but this apparently was not true.

Railway men and sight-seers survey No. 1211, noting how she burrowed herself into the earthen bank. A New Haven Railroad wreck train pulls abreast of the scene; the door of the tool car is open. After such a disaster, and after the passengers and employees are safely and quickly extricated, the business begins of righting the cars and engine, and of clearing the line as soon as possible. The wooden passenger coach at bottom right had its toll of window breakage and sill damage. Steel cars began to appear on the railways about this time, but the branch lines got them last.

of the Valley, silenced the extension project, and destroyed any possibility that the huge Vanderbilt system or the Connecticut River Railroad would ever get into Connecticut. A ninety-nine-year lease of the property was later drawn up in 1887. Another piece of the New Haven empire was now in place.

This dilapidated old house, boasting four Ionic columns, served as the Valley Railroad's first depot at Middletown. It stood at the foot of Washington Street. Patrons using the Middletown to Berlin line used the facilities of the brick structure next door. Both were dispensed with when a union station was built to serve all the railway lines.

Like so many "light density" lines, the Valley Division of the New Haven Railroad served a thinly settled region of the state with too few manufacturing points. Around 1905, in an effort to prop up business, the New Haven Railroad began running New London to Hartford trains via the Valley line (Hartford-Old Saybrook-New London), but this proved short-lived. In the heyday of the trolley, the New Haven Railroad strung wires over the short segment between Middletown and Cromwell and ran its Connecticut Company yellow cars under them, but only briefly. In 1916 the Fenwick Branch was taken out of service, and the station at Fenwick was actually seen leaving one day on a railroad flatcar. The long causeway eventually became an automobile road. The little borough, after the burning of Fenwick Hall, was no longer a public resort. In 1922 service halted to Saybrook Point and its boat docks. During the 1930s the railroad concentrated on Valley Division commuter train requirements between Middletown and downtown Hartford, and the last passenger train ran in 1933, just as steamboat service was also ending on the Connecticut River. The automobile had taken its toll. Freight continued but diminished through the 1940s and 50s to a vanishing point in the 1960s, except for separate fragments at Hartford and Middletown. The branch's last great deed was to bring in to Deep River the long heavy steel for the great Baldwin Bridge—serving the Connecticut Turnpike as it crosses the river. It was the only way to get its huge girders to barges at water side. With abandonment in 1967, vegetation began to hide the uneven track; tree saplings sprouted between ties. An unusual fate, however, awaited this abandoned line (see Chapter Fifteen.)

Chapter Ten Footnotes

1. *Fourth Annual Report of the General Railroad Commissioners State of Connecticut,* (New Haven: Carrington & Hotchkiss, 1857), 62.

2. Connecticut General Assembly, Resolves and Private Laws of the State of Connecticut, An Act to Incorporate the Connecticut Valley Railroad Company, 17 July 1868, Public Records, Connecticut State Capitol Building.

3. *Report of the Engineer on Preliminary Survey for the Proposed Connecticut Valley Railroad* (Hartford: Case, Lockwood & Brainard, 1868), 1-12.

4. *Nineteenth Annual Report of the General Railroad Commissioners of the State of Connecticut* (Hartford: Case, Lockwood & Brainard, 1872), 198.

5. *Annual Report, Hartford and Connecticut Valley Railroad Company for the Year Ending 1883* (Hartford: Wiley, Waterman & Eaton, 1883).

6. Connecticut General Assembly, Resolves and Private Laws of the State of Connecticut, Authorizing the Hartford & Connecticut Valley Railroad to Extend Its Road, 6 April 1881, IX: 203, Public Records, Connecticut State Capitol Building.

Certainly one of the most interesting spectacles on the Valley line occurred in 1916, when residents of Fenwick watched as their station departed on flat cars. Where once patrons enjoyed taking the Valley Railroad's half-mile trestle extension over wide South Cove to Fenwick, the passenger market dipped when Fenwick Hall and other pretty attractions disappeared. By 1917 the (filled-in) trestle was converted to a two-lane automobile causeway, still in use. For a few years after 1916 the Valley Railroad ran trains between Saybrook Point and Saybrook Junction; but by 1922 the latter was also officially abandoned.
COURTESY OF MRS. ROCKWELL STANIFORD

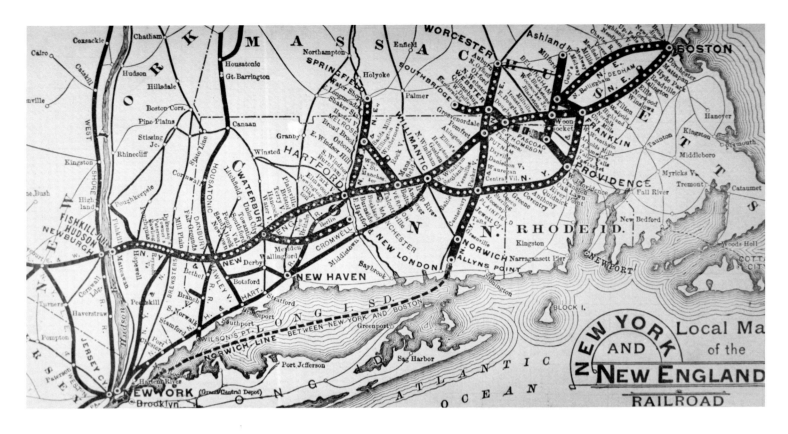

The deceptive map-making common to the age makes the New York & New England of the early 1890s dominant in southern New England. What it actually owned or leased and how the big, rickety combination was put together in Connecticut is made clear below in Mr. Hill's diagram for this book, and explained in the text. Observe how little trackage the company actually built; the rest was financial shuffling.

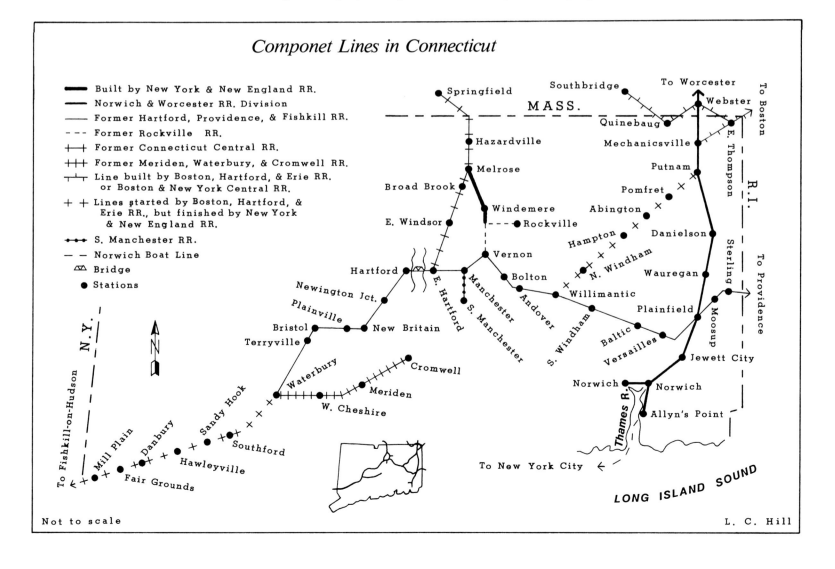

Componet Lines in Connecticut

Built by New York & New England RR.
Norwich & Worcester RR. Division
Former Hartford, Providence, & Fishkill RR.
Former Rockville RR.
Former Connecticut Central RR.
Former Meriden, Waterbury, & Cromwell RR.
Line built by Boston, Hartford, & Erie RR. or Boston & New York Central RR.
Lines started by Boston, Hartford, & Erie RR., but finished by New York & New England RR.
S. Manchester RR.
Norwich Boat Line
Bridge
Stations

Not to scale

L. C. Hill

Chapter Eleven

Forgotten Leviathan

The New York and New England Railroad managed to make a terrific noise and keep competitors around it worried for thirty years by sheer nerve and bluff.

—Alvin F. Harlow, Steelways of New England

Charles Peter Clark brought the New England to its greatest operating hour, then became president of the rival New Haven.

One has to be very long in the tooth to remember the great days of the New Haven Railroad in all its full and foolish glory just before the first world war; most of us knew it only in decline. But if you try to tell even the most excessively senior citizen that there was once another competing monopoly in Connecticut—a combine boasting almost as many route miles, revenues, and assets—you draw a blank stare. "Hardly a man is now alive," saving perhaps a few centenarians and railroad specialists, who can remember the legendary New York & New England Railroad.

Like the New Haven, the New England was mainly a "put-together" system—that is, assembled from smaller railroads it acquired by lease or purchase. In earlier chapters we have seen how small companies lost their independence to one or another of the maneuvering giants. The New England's base was in Massachusetts, where it owned valuable terminals in downtown Boston. Its main line swept down to Blackstone, Putnam, Willimantic, Hartford, Waterbury, and Danbury, ultimately reaching the Hudson River opposite Newburgh, New York. Ferryboats at Fishkill-on-Hudson brought cars to Newburgh for a connection with the Erie Railroad and the western markets. Important branches stemmed from the New England main line in Connecticut, including the strategic arm at Willimantic for Providence, the Norwich & Worcester (Railroad) Division, and the East Hartford to Springfield, Massachusetts, branch. The company's perpetual drawback, though, was that it never owned an entrance into New York City, try as it would to secure one. As New Haven Railroad President Charles P. Clark once remarked, "There is no more chance of the 'New England' getting into New York City than there is of my going to hell, and I am too good to go to hell."[1]

The New Haven Railroad, on the other hand, highly valued its New York City connection via the New York & Harlem Railroad. Various divisions of the New Haven crossed the New England's main line track in Connecticut, providing the latter with ample interchange points to reach Manhattan. Of these, Willimantic was the most important. For decades the New Haven's disadvantage was it owned no entrance into Boston, the reverse of the New England's problem. Thus co-operation between the two firms was mutually profitable, but this relationship was not an entirely harmonious one even in the best of times, and frequently it became hostile.

HARTFORD, PROVIDENCE AND FISHKILL RAILWAY.

Operated by Trustees.

PROVIDENCE TO HARTFORD AND WATERBURY.

Trains Leave.								**May 1870.**		**Trains Arrive.**							**CONNECTIONS.**
Acc	Acc	Acc	Pas	Acc	Acc	Pas	Mls	STATIONS.	Frs.	Acc	Acc	Pas	Acc	Pas	Acc	Acc	
*P.M	P.M	P.M	P.M	A.M	A.M	A.M				A.M	A.M	A.M	P.M	P.M	*P.M	A.M	
10 30	6 40	5 05	2 20	11 45	10 10	7 00	0	....**Providence** ¹....		6 30	8 40	10 17	2 00	6 10	8 40		¹ Connects with R'ways diverging from Providence.
....	6 50	5 17	2 30	12 00	10 25	7 09	4	....Cranston.....		6 17	8 30	10 07	1 48	6 00	8 30		² Connects with Norwich and Worcester Railway.
							7	....Searls' Corner....									³ Connects with New London Northern Railway.
....	7 02	5 30	2 42	12 20	10 37	7 21	9	.....Natick.....		6 05	8 18	9 55	1 36		8 12		⁴ Connects with New Haven, Hartford and Springfield Railway.
11 00	7 10	5 42	2 50	12 35	10 44	7 29	11	....River Point...		5 58	8 10	9 49	1 30	5 42	8 12		⁴ Connects with Steamers for New York, New Haven, and the various points on Long Island Sound.
11 05	7 15	5 49	2 56	12 45	10 49	....	13	....Quidnick.....		5 50	8 02	9 41	1 23	5 36	....		⁵ Connects with Canal Railway Line.
11 12	7 22	5 56	3 02	12 50	10 55	7 40	14	....Washington.....		5 45	7 56	9 36	1 18	5 31	8 00		⁶ Connects with Naugatuck Railway.
P.M.	P.M.	....	3 08	P.M.	11 01	7 47	17	....Nipmuc.....		A.M.	7 47	9 28	....	....	P.M.		
		6 17	3 20				22	....Summit.....			7 35	9 16	12 57	5 12			
		6 27	3 30		11 22	8 06	24	....Greene.....			7 28	9 10	12 50	5 05			
		6 37	4 37		11 29	8 13	27	....Oneco.....									
		6 42	3 41		11 34	8 17	29	....Sterling.....		7 10	8 55	12 34	4 50				
		6 52	3 51		11 43	8 26	32	....Moosup.....		7 00	8 45	12 24	4 40				
		7 02	4 02		11 51	8 33	35	....Plainfield ².....		6 50	8 35	12 15	4 30				
		P.M.			A.M.		40	....Canterbury.....		A.M.		P.M.	4 17				
							42	....Jewett City.....									An Extra train l'ves Hartford for New Britain at 1 20 p.m. Returning, leaves N'w Britain at 2 40 p.m.
							46	....Lovett's.....									
		4 32				9 05	48	....Baltic.....			8 05		3 57				STANDARD OF TIME—Clock at Hartford Depot.
		4 40				9 12	51	....Waldo's.....					3 46				
		4 49	A.M.			9 22	55	....South Windham....		P.M.		7 49		3 35				Connections by Stage are made at Willim'tic for Eastford and Ashford; at Moosup for Brooklyn; at Riverpoint for Hope, Centerville and Crompton.
		5 00	6 20			9 40	58	....Willimantic ³....		8 00		7 41		3 25				
		5 12	6 45			10 02	67	....Andover.....		7 37		7 21		3 01				
		5 34	7 05	A.M.		10 15	73	....Bolton.....			P.M.	7 05	P.M.	P.M.			
6 05	2 40	5 49	7 18	5 58		10 32	74	....Vernon.....		7 07	6 55	5 32	2 35	8 13	10 32		
6 18	2 50	5 58	7 28	6 08		10 42	81	....Manchester.....		6 55	6 42	5 20	2 23	8 00	10 20		
6 35	3 08	6 15	7 45	6 25		11 00	88	....East Hartford.....		6 35		6 25	....				
6 50	3 23	6 30	8 00	6 40		11 15	90	arr { ....Hartford ⁴ .... } lve		6 20	6 10	4 45	1 50	7 25	9 45		
P.M.	4 10	6 30	8 20			11 20		lve { } arr		6 05	8 05	A.M.	3 05	1 45	8 10	9 35	
							95	....Newington.....									
4 35		6 53	8 45			11 45	99	....New Britain.....		5 40	7 42		2 40	1 22	7 45	9 10	
4 50		7 05	8 55			12 08	104	....Plainville ⁵.....		5 25	7 30		P.M.	1 10	7 30	8 55	
4 55		P.M.	9 05			12 20	106	....Forestville.....		5 15	....			12 58	7 10	8 45	
5 05			9 18			12 20	108	....Bristol......		5 05	7 15			12 50		8 37	
5 18			9 33			12 35	112	....Terryville.....		4 47	A.M.			12 35		8 23	
							118	....Hoadley's.....									
5 49			10 07			1 07	123	....**Waterbury** ⁶....		A.M.				12 05		7 50	
*P.M.			A.M.	A.M.	A.M.	P.M.		ARRIVE] [LEAVE		P.M.				P.M.		P.M.	

*Saturdays only.

76½ Rockville Railway.—(A. H. PUTNAM, Superintendent, Rockville, Conn.) Trains leave Rockville for Providence at 5 45 a.m. and 2 20 p.m. for Willimantic at 5 45 a.m., 2 20 and 6 40 p.m.; for Hartford at 5 45, 7 05 and 10 15 a.m., and 2 15 and 5 30 p.m. Trains leave Hartford for Rockville at 6 10 and 9 45 a.m., 1 40, 5 35 and 7 20 p.m. Rockville to Vernon—Distance, 5 miles.

Timetable-making improved considerably in the fifteen years between the one on the preceding page and the one at right. The secret of arrival time is out; stagecoach connections are still being made at Willimantic and Moosup! The bad news is that quiet line at top, "operated by trustees," so frequent on Connecticut timetables of last century.

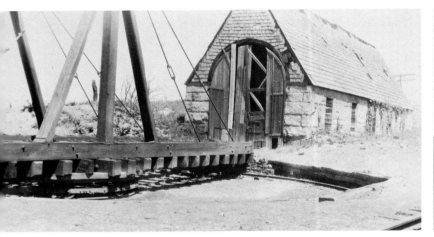

Some stations on this part of the line are, in pairs left to right: the turntable and an abandoned engine house at Plainfield; a big overhanging roofed depot at little Sterling (far-wandering photographer Irving Drake is on the platform); Canterbury, with a station agent and passengers waiting; and Baltic, where the station is in somebody's basement. On the opposite page, South Windham's window to the outside world was in an old house.

The Hartford, Providence & Fishkill consequently operated a 122-mile railway between Providence and Waterbury; with ninety-six of those miles in Connecticut, it was the longest in the state. The cities of Hartford and Providence responded, and each bought $500,000 worth of its bonds. Rhode Island ex-Governor William Sprague was president of the firm in 1855, and he covered the road's losses through his own firm, the A. & W. Sprague Investment & Banking Company. When the financial panic of 1857 swept the country, trustees of the road's three mortgages foreclosed and operated the line for more than twenty years. George Bartholomew became its chief figure. At the end of 1857 the road started to return to normal, carrying nearly 320,000 passengers and earning $340,000 in gross revenues.

The construction of the Rockville and the South Manchester railroads took place at the same time. The four-mile Rockville Railroad, chartered in 1857 and capitalized at $100,000, opened between Vernon and the flourishing textile town of Rockville in 1863.[5] At Vernon connection was made with the Hartford, Providence & Fishkill, which operated the short line from 1868 to 1878, when it was later leased to the New York & New England. Rolling stock in 1866 included but two engines, two passenger cars, and a single baggage car. Revenues that year amounted to $28,000.[6] The Cheney textile family of South Manchester financed the little South Manchester Railroad—one of the smallest railroad firms in America. Its track left the Hartford, Providence & Fishkill main line at North Manchester and went for 2¼ miles to the southern part of town to serve the requirements of the Cheney silk mills and other local patrons. Fifty-six-pound iron rail—heavy for that era—was used in its construction, and the short line, capitalized at $40,000, opened in June 1869.[7] The Jarvis Construction Company of Providence built the road for about $30,000 a mile. From 1869 to 1878 it was managed by the trustees of the Hartford, Providence & Fishkill, whereupon the South Manchester was returned to the Cheneys for private operation. Passenger train service lasted until 1933, and ultimately the short line was acquired by the New Haven Railroad.

The Boston, Hartford & Erie

While trustees of the Hartford, Providence & Fishkill attempted to resolve their road's financial plight, two rail projects connecting Connecticut with Boston temporarily captured public interest: the Boston & New York Central, and the New York & Boston Air Line. Each planned to intersect the main line of the Hartford, Providence & Fishkill at Willimantic, then known as "The Thread City."

What became known as the Boston & New York Central—another composite firm—opened from Boston to Mechanicsville (above Putnam, Connecticut) in 1854 via Norwood, Franklin, and Blackstone, Massachusetts.[8] Originally their line at East Thompson, Connecticut, was to go over to the mill town of Southbridge,

Link-and-pin Coupler.

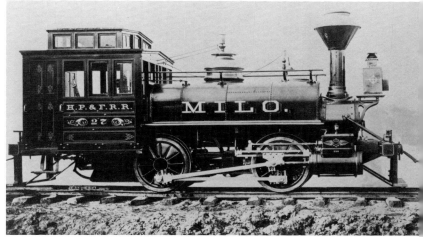

Milo *was a classic four-wheeled switching engine, of the type that is forever panting up and down railroad yards, shunting and making up trains for bigger locomotives to haul out on the main line. But that gothic cab, the scrollwork, that fancy lettering on a work-a-day switcher! Somebody must have loved her. And who we ask was* Milo?

R & LHS

176

June 29, 1884.] SOUTH MANCHESTER RAILROAD. [Standard Time.
R. O. CHENEY, General Manager.
Trains leave South Manchester for Manchester, 6.30, 7.30, 9.08, 9.50 a.m., 12.20, 1.48, 2.25, 4.50, 6.45, 7.33 p.m.
"   Manchester for South Manchester, 6.45, 7.45, 9.20, 10.05 a.m., 12.40, 1.55, 2.40, 5.05, 6.12, 7.00, 8.05 p.m.
Connections.—The 7.30 a. m. train connects at Manchester for Hartford, New York, Vernon and Rockville;
9.35 a. m. for Boston, Providence, Hartford and New York; 12.45 p.m. for Vernon and Rockville: 1.35 p. m. for
Hartford and New York; 2.30 p.m. for Hartford, Boston and Providence; 4.50 p. m. for Hartford, Willimantic
and Putnam; 6.10 p. m. for Hartford; 7.55 p. m. for Hartford and Rockville.

This delightful scene at the Cheneyville Station of the South Manchester Railroad would make the most resolute stay-at-home eager to ride this tiny, 2¹/₄-mile line, at its opening the shortest in America. It was owned by the Cheney silk mills, ran frequent service for employees and residents of South Manchester who wished to go to Manchester, and was briefly operated by the Fishkill road. See the fine book by Thomas R. Lewis, Jr., Silk Along Steel, which is listed in the Bibliography.

COLLECTION OF GEORGE CHENEY

This ticket to a civic flag-raising in 1888 reminds us of how often railroads long ago handled the great crowds for public events; they often staged their own. You only had to board the train, at cut rates: there you were with no parking problem. Once discovered, the excursion business was welcomed.

COLLECTION OF THOMAS R. LEWIS, JR.

Massachusetts. But money was tight, and at the last minute—without any authority—the owners quietly altered their route and laid their track down from East Thompson to Mechanicsville. A turntable and engine house were built there, and a handy connection was made with the Norwich & Worcester Railroad. The state's railroad commissioners frowned at the maneuver, but they later approved the track's location and issued their permit to operate. Financial trouble was regular at the Boston & New York Central, and service was irregular; in short, the line was a feeble enterprise. It never reached its goal of Willimantic, though it owned the franchise of the (unbuilt) Thompson & Willimantic Railroad Company. Feebler still was the life of the New York & Boston Air Line Railroad, already mentioned in Chapter Eight. This road was projected diagonally from New Haven to Middletown, Willimantic, Dayville, Woonsocket, and Brookline, Massachusetts. Despite much fanfare and drum beating, virtually nothing was built in Connecticut, though trains eventually ran between Woonsocket and Brookline.

From a financial and competitive viewpoint, some rail visionaries felt that all these roads should be consolidated. As individual lines they certainly needed help: the bankrupt Hartford, Providence & Fishkill was run by trustees and still fell short of reaching its Hudson River destination. Successor companies to the Boston & New York Central only ran the road periodically because of foreclosures and its poor condition, while the Air Line dream continued to be haunted by unscrupulous contractors, speculators, and reversals. Salvation was at length promised by the formation of the quaint-sounding Boston, Hartford & Erie Railroad, chartered in Connecticut in 1863, with George Bartholomew as president.[10]

This confection of companies purchased or leased the lines described above (or their franchises) for the purposes of completing a trunk line from the Hudson River east to Willimantic, whereupon the line would divide: one route to Boston, the other to Providence. Although the new company had acquired four hundred miles of line, two critical links remained unfinished: the seventy-seven miles from Waterbury to the Hudson River, and the twenty-six miles from Putnam to Willimantic.

177

NEW YORK & NEW ENGLAND RAILROAD—Rockville Branch.
Trains leave Rockville for Vernon, 7.00, 7.20, 9.05 a.m., 12.05, 1.30, 2.10, 4.55, 7.10 p.m.—Running time, 12 min.
" Vernon for Rockville, 7.40, 10.00 a.m., 12.35, 12.50, 3,00, 5.50, 7.30, 8.15 p.m.

Another branch operation, heading north and east from the Fishkill road, was the little Rockville Railroad, about as majestic as the South Manchester. The Rockville Depot appears at left, when the line was part of the New Haven Road and carried commuters to Hartford via Vernon. They might like to ride it again, but government allowed the line to be torn up, like so many others.

The plan to build the Air Line Railroad between Willimantic and New Haven was dropped, although this last decision presently stirred others to construct a railroad on this very route: the New Haven, Middletown & Willimantic Railroad.

At Fishkill-on-Hudson, New York, promoters of the Boston, Hartford & Erie anticipated using ferry boats to move railroad cars across the Hudson River to Newburgh, a branch terminal of the Erie Railroad and something of a gateway to the western markets. Publicity handouts underscored the immense amount of freight that the Erie would bring from the West to New England via the Boston, Hartford & Erie, painting alluring pictures of a heavy Pennsylvania coal traffic and long trains of Hudson River lumber and iron ore, plus the agricultural and cattle trade of Dutchess County, New York. But strategic problems persisted. The Boston, Hartford & Erie went east-west over the succeeding ridge lines of Connecticut, which meant very difficult grades indeed. More perplexing was the fact that the highly-unstandard gauge of track on the Erie Railroad at that moment was six feet wide while the Boston, Hartford & Erie used the common 4′ 8½″ width, complicating

Inspect below, if you will, the newly-arrived iron horse Rockville, with its single main driving wheels, its palatial cab (for those antediluvian times), and its proud, loving staff. All knew her whistle.

Fast financial footwork marked the short, shabby life of the Boston, Hartford & Erie. Promises to link its namesake cities with the Erie Railroad were never quite fulfilled. Money that was raised or borrowed found its way into the pockets of Boston speculators. A few pieces of rolling stock were bought, but most were inherited antiques. Typical of the times was the frail engine above, though an interesting detail is the triple-axle tender. Among the roads that the group took in was the Boston & New York Central. Its track went southwest from Boston to Franklin and Blackstone, then west to Mechanicsville, Connecticut. There, patrons could board trains of the Norwich & Worcester. A typical train left Boston at 3:00 p.m. and arrived at Mechanicsville at 5:45. By seven o'clock the train entered Norwich, and here you could board an overnight Norwich Line steamer for New York City. The Boston, Hartford & Erie prospered from the arrangement and briefly leased the Norwich & Worcester.

an efficient interchange of cargo between the railroads. In addition, the Erie route was considered by many to be inferior to the group of lines which would ultimately form the New York Central line to Chicago, which ably served New England via the (future) Boston & Albany Railroad. Most important of all, no bridge existed at Fishkill, where time-consuming ferries would someday transfer cars.

Undaunted, Boston, Hartford & Erie salesmen continued to dispense persuasive testimony and literature. President Bartholomew was soon replaced by Boston men. Since the Erie Railroad was central to its success, the new regime invited key Erie figures onto the Boston directorate. They whipped up public support for state loans from Massachusetts, which was then eager to aid a rail project of such apparent promise. A $20,000,000 mortgage was arranged, with proceeds supposedly to be used in finishing the missing links in Connecticut and New York, as well as in paying off inherited debts of the component companies. Massachusetts opened its coffers and gave $3,000,000 in grants.[11] Unfortunately, almost all this loot fell into the hands of such Wall Street buccaneers as Jim Fisk, Jay Gould, and Daniel Drew, who were fighting over the Erie with Cornelius Vanderbilt. State Street contestants in Boston also saw a rare opportunity for personal gain. Bribery, corruption, bookkeeping irregularities, and substantial loans to insiders resulted; Massachusetts was bilked for millions. Bankruptcy and general disaster overtook these high flyers in 1870. When receivers confronted the shambles of the Boston, Hartford & Erie they discovered the checking account held the grand sum of $10.[12] An intense investigation by the Massachusetts House of Representatives followed, with one observer later characterizing the road as "a great leprous body."[13]

[OPPOSITE PAGE] A Boston, Hartford & Erie timetable, stock certificate, and a notice to landowners along its proposed route from Putnam to Willimantic, never fully built until the New York & New England stepped in and finally finished it.

ALL PICTURES: R & LHS

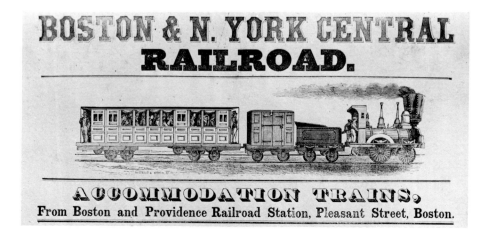

BOSTON & N. YORK CENTRAL RAILROAD.

ACCOMMODATION TRAINS.

From Boston and Providence Railroad Station, Pleasant Street, Boston.

179

BOSTON, HARTFORD AND ERIE RAILROAD.
BLACKSTONE DIVISION.

John S. Eldridge, President, Boston, Mass. | William M. Parker, Supt., Boston, Mass. | A. C. Warren, General Ticket Agent.

Boston to Southbridge.

Pas.	Exs.	Pas.	Pas.	Pas.	Pas.	Pas.	Pas.	Pas.	Mls	STATIONS.	Mls	Exs.	Pas.	Pas.	Pas.	Pas.	Pas.	Pas.	Pas.
P. M.	P. M.	P. M.	P. M.	P. M.	P. M.	A. M.	A. M.	A. M.				A. M.	A. M.	A. M.	A. M.	A. M.	P. M.	P. M.	P. M.
6 25	6 15	5 15	3 30	2 30	12 15	12 40	8 00	7 30	0	lve....Boston[1]....arr	70	5 40	6 47	8 04	9 00	10 30	12 40	2 20	3 55	7 10
6 43	...	5 35	3 47	2 46	12 31	10 56	8 16	7 46	4	......Mt. Bowdoin......	66	...	6 31	7 48	8 44	10 16	12 24	2 04	3 39	6 54
6 51	...	5 45	3 53	2 54	12 39	11 04	8 23	7 54	6	......Mattapan......	64	...	6 23	7 40	8 36	10 10	12 16	1 56	3 31	6 46
6 57	...	5 53	3 59	3 00	12 45	11 10	8 29	8 00	8	......Hyde Park......	62	...	6 17	7 34	8 30	10 10	12 10	1 50	3 25	6 41
7 01	...	5 58	4 03	3 03	12 48	11 13	8 34	8 03	9	......Readville......	61	...	6 13	7 26	8 20	9 58	12 00	1 44	3 15	6 36
7 06	...	6 04	4 08	P. M.	12 52	A. M.	8 38	A. M.	11	......Dedham......	59	...	6 08	7 21	A. M.	9 53	NO'N.	1 36	P. M.	6 31
...	...	...	...	...	...	...	...	...	13	......Ellis's......	57	...	...	...	...	...	...	...	...
7 18	...	6 15	4 17	...	1 03	...	8 49	...	14	......South Dedham......	56	...	5 58	7 10	...	9 44	...	1 28	...	-6 21
P. M.	...	6 21	4 21	...	P. M.	...	8 55	...	16	......Winslow's......	54	...	A. M.	7 01	...	9 37	...	P. M.	...	6 15
...	6 55	6 32	4 32	...	...	...	9 07	...	19	......Walpole......	51	4 52	...	6 51	...	9 20	...	...	...	6 05
...	...	...	4 42	...	...	...	...	...	22	......Campbell's......	48	...	...	...	...	...	...	...	...
...	6 43	4 47	...	...	...	9 18	...	23	......North Wrentham......	47	...	...	6 39	...	9 18	...	...	5 54
...	7 12	6 56	4 55	...	...	...	9 32	...	27	......Franklin......	43	4 30	...	6 26	...	9 05	...	...	5 42
...	...	7 06	5 03	...	...	...	9 40	...	30	......Wadsworth's......	40	...	...	6 18	...	8 57	...	...	5 35
...	7 22	...	...	...	...	...	...	...		......Woonsocket[2]......		...	...	6 00	...	...	...	...	...
...	7 31	P. M.	5 18	...	...	...	9 55	...	36	arr { lve } Blackstone { lve } arr	34	...	...	A. M.	...	8 42	...	...	5 21
...	...	...	5 21	...	...	...	9 56	...				...	4 07	...	...	8 39	...	...	5 15
...	...	...	5 27	...	...	...	10 02	...	38	......Millville......	32	...	...	...	...	8 33	...	...	5 05
...	...	...	...	...	...	...	10 07	...	41	......Iron Stone......	29	...	...	...	...	...	...	...	...
...	...	...	5 47	...	...	...	10 22	...	46	......East Douglas......	24	...	...	...	...	8 13	...	...	4 42
...	...	...	5 52	...	...	...	10 27	...	48	......Douglas......	22	...	...	...	...	8 08	...	...	4 36
...	7 52	...	6 05	...	...	...	10 40	...	52	arr..East Thompson .lve	18	...	...	...	...	7 56	...	...	4 22
...	...	...	6 05	...	...	...	10 40	...	52	lve..East Thompson .arr	9	...	...	...	...	7 56	...	...	4 22
...	...	...	6 18	...	...	...	10 53	...	56	......Thompson......	5	...	...	...	...	7 43	...	...	4 08
...	...	...	6 25	...	...	...	11 00	...	59	......Mechanicsville......	2	...	...	...	...	7 36	...	...	4 01
8 29	...	...	6 30	...	...	...	11 05	...	61	......Putnam[3]......	0	3 00	...	...	...	7 30	...	...	3 55
P. M.			P. M.				A. M.			ARRIVE] [LEAVE		A. M.				A. M.			P. M.
...	...	...	6 05	...	...	...	10 40	...	52	lve..East Thompson .arr	18	...	...	...	...	7 56	...	...	4 22
...	...	...	6 19	...	...	...	10 54	...	58	......East Webster......	12	...	...	...	...	7 28	...	...	4 08
...	...	...	6 38	...	...	...	11 13	...	64	......New Boston......	6	...	...	...	...	7 07	...	...	3 48
...	...	...	6 44	...	...	...	11 19	...	67	......West Dudley......	3	...	...	...	...	7 01	...	...	3 42
...	...	...	6 54	...	...	...	11 29	...	70	......Southbridge......	0	...	...	...	...	6 50	...	...	3 30
			P. M.				A. M.			ARRIVE] [LEAVE						A. M.			P. M.

N. B.—An Extra train leaves Boston for South Dedham, Everett and intermediate stations, at 10 00 p.m., Tuesdays and Fridays 11 00 p. m. Leaves South Dedham for Boston and intermediate stations, 8 45 p.m.; on Tuesdays and Fridays 9 30 p.m.

CONNECTIONS

[1] With Railroads diverging from Boston.
[2] With Providence & Worcester Railroad.
[3] With Norwich and Worcester Division, for Norwich, New London, and Steamboat line to New York.

NORWICH AND WORCESTER DIVISION.

P. St. M. Andrews, Division Superintendent, Norwich, Ct.

Exs.	Pas.	Pas.	Pas.	Pas.	Mls	STATIONS.	Mls	Exs.	Pas.	Pas.	Pas.
P. M.	P. M.	P. M.	A. M.	P. M.				A. M.	A. M.	P. M.	P. M.
7 20	6 35	5 15	9 50	6 35	0	lve..Worcester[1]..arr	73	4 20	9 00	2 30	6 50
...	6 45	...	...	6 40	1	..Worcester Junction..	72	...	8 53	2 25	...
...	6 55	5 31	10 06	6 50	4	....Auburn....	69	...	8 43	2 15	6 37
...	7 05	5 43	10 17	7 00	9	..North Oxford..	64	...	8 39	2 03	6 25
...	7 12	5 50	10 23	7 06	11	....Oxford....	62	...	8 20	1 57	6 18
...	7 22	6 00	10 33	7 16	15	..North Webster....	58	...	8 08	1 45	6 06
7 58	7 27	6 05	10 43	7 26	16	....Webster....	57	...	8 03	1 42	6 02
...	P. M.	6 17	10 50	7 31	20	.North Grosvenor Dale..	53	...	7 50	1 30	5 50
...	...	6 21	10 54	7 34	21	..Grosvenor Dale..	52	...	7 46	1 25	5 46
...	...	6 26	11 00	7 40	24	....Thompson......	49	...	7 40	1 18	5 41
...	...	6 35	11 10	7 49	26	....Putnam[2]......	47	...	7 27	1 09	5 27
...	...	6 50	11 25	8 02	31	....Daysville....	42	...	7 14	12 57	5 12
8 41	...	6 58	11 35	8 10	34	....Danielsonville..	39	...	7 06	12 47	5 02
...	...	7 10	11 50	8 23	39	....Wauregan....	34	...	6 54	12 30	4 48
...	...	7 15	12 00	8 27	40	..Central Village..	33	...	6 50	12 25	4 43
...	...	7 25	12 15	8 37	44	..Plainfield Junction[3]..	29	...	6 41	12 15	4 32
...	...	7 45	12 33	8 58	50	....Jewett City....	23	...	6 26	11 58	4 12
...	...	...	...	...	58	....Greenville....	15	...	...	...	...
9 35	...	8 15	1 00	9 30	60	....Norwich.....	13	1 55	6 00	11 30	3 45
10 12	...	...	...	...	73	..New London[4]..	0	1 15	...	...	...
P. M.		P. M.	P. M.	A. M.		ARRIVE] [LEAVE		A. M.	A. M.	A. M.	P. M.

(Steamb't Exp's, on arrival of boat from N. Y., daily except Monday.)

The Norwich and Worcester Division

RUNS IN DIRECT CONNECTION WITH THE

PASSENGER AND FREIGHT STEAMERS

OF THE

NEW YORK TRANSPORTATION COMPANY.

The NEW YORK STEAMBOAT EXPRESS TRAIN leaves Boston at 6 15 P. M., from Boston, Hartford and Erie Depot, foot of Sumner Street, connecting at New London with the splendid Steamers,

"City of New York" and "City of Boston."

Returning from New York, Steamers leave Pier 40, North River, daily, Sundays excepted, at 5 00 P. M., connecting at New London with trains for Boston, Worcester, &c.

[1] With Boston & Albany Railway for Springfield, Albany and Boston; with Fitchburg and Worcester Railway, and with Worcester and Nashua Railway.
[2] With Boston, Hartford and Erie Railway.
[3] Crossing of the Hartford, Providence and Fishkill Railway.
[4] With New London Northern Railway.

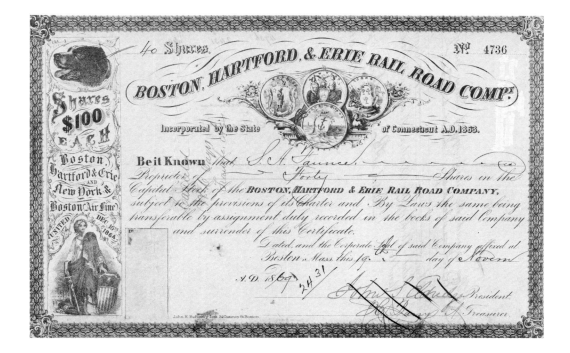

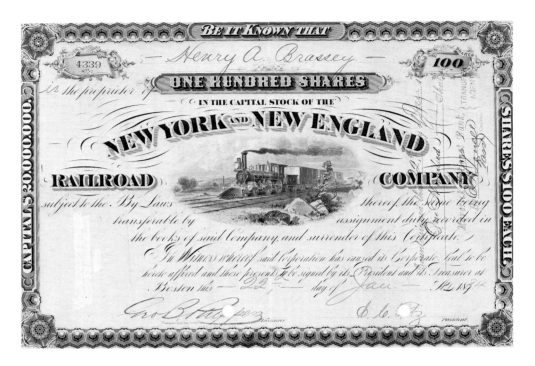

From the Boston, Hartford & Erie scam arose the New York & New England. Its Summer Street terminal and Boston yards are seen below, where old South Station is now being rebuilt. Shops were in Norwood.

TERMINAL FACILITIES OF THE NEW YORK AND NEW ENGLAND RAILROAD, BOSTON.

A raised ball signal ("highball") advances a New York & New England train at Waterbury, over the track of the Naugatuck line. Such "diamond" level crossovers are now rare, but still carefully protected.

Where once optimism prevailed as to what the Boston, Hartford & Erie might accomplish, the looting that took place was viewed in Connecticut with appropriate distaste. The Boston road had actually built the twelve-mile branch from East Thompson, Connecticut, to the mill town of Southbridge, Massachusetts, in 1867. On the other hand, it still had not completed the vital Putnam-Willimantic mainline link.[14] Four hundred thousand dollars worth of work still was needed, according to the contractor, Norman C. Munson. West of Waterbury, construction to the Hudson River was being guided by the one-time Union Pacific Railroad contractor Sidney Dillon, until the axe fell. The only other real Boston, Hartford & Erie accomplishment in Connecticut was to lease, in 1869, the Norwich & Worcester Railroad, with its valuable boat line to New York City.

The New York & New England

Among the receivers whom Massachusetts ultimately appointed to sort out the affairs of the disgraced and bankrupt Boston, Hartford & Erie was Charles Peter Clark, who was destined to become probably the finest New England railroad executive of the nineteenth century. Born in Nashua, New Hampshire, Clark was a graduate of Dartmouth College and could point to considerable experience in the

The westernmost point of the New England was Fishkill-on-Hudson, New York. Trains of cars were then broken up and ferried across the Hudson, where they were taken by the Erie Railroad for points west. Immense car ferries were the workhorses. The transfer steamer William T. Hart, *three hundred feet long and eighty in beam, could accommodate twenty-two freight cars. She cost $175,000. The New England's terminal on the Hudson covered some twenty acres of land, reclaimed from the river and filled in. A bridge was discussed, but the firm could never bridge the "Rhine of America."*

West Indies trade. Within five years the "New York and New England Railroad" emerged from the shambles, thanks to Clark as general manager. While reorganization went forward, he helped obtain enough money to finish construction of the vital Putnam-Willimantic link and opened it in August 1872. This valuable addition, passing through the picturesque towns of Pomfret, Hampton, and North Windham, finally completed the road's Eastern Division main line from Boston to Hartford via Putnam.

Litigation, however, slowed Clark's efforts to get final title to the old Hartford, Providence & Fishkill, since Boston, Hartford & Erie operators had failed to pay interest on the former road's mortgage bonds. The great extension project west of Waterbury to the Erie Railroad was completely halted and left to rust, despite the fact that it was three-quarters completed and had cost so far $3,500,000. Instead, Clark's administration sought friendly connections and traffic from the New Haven Railroad rather than with the Erie. The two roads most handily connected at Willimantic, thanks to the newly opened New Haven, Middletown & Willimantic Railroad. Clark arranged for jointly operated freight and passenger trains over this routing; the three roads conveniently formed the very shortest route from New York City to Boston.

In 1879 Clark resigned from the New York & New England to travel in Europe. The road's new managers, led by a West Pointer named General James Wilson, proceeded to complete the controversial Erie Railroad connection at Fishkill in 1882, much to the chagrin of New Haven Railroad executives. The New England could ill afford the construction cost, but that did not concern the likes of such of her direc-

Putnam was once a busy rail hub, ranking just behind Willimantic. Its first Union Station served the New England's trains working the old Norwich & Worcester (at right) and the main line between Boston and Hartford (train at left). The elegant White Train *and the* Long Island & Eastern States Express *made their appearances there in the early 1890s. The second brick station at Putnam still stands in 1985, beautifully maintained and commercially occupied.*

One could almost walk into this stark, wintry, poignant landscape. It seems so real, but it is Manchester, Connecticut, in 1900. A railway official, a Mr. Bardo, stands between the main tracks in this scene that looks towards Hartford. The morning is cold and damp as the horse blankets attest. The lowly bicycle probably belongs to the Western Union messenger. Diverging at the left is the single track of the little South Manchester road. Its patrons alighted to the curved platform, then strode across the tracks for main line trains. The track to Hartford is today operated by Conrail, but gone from Manchester to Willimantic.

Hartford to Boston.

LEAVE	pm	am	am	am	am	pm	am	pm	pm	pm	pm
New York, N.Y.N.H.	11 35					1100					
Hartford	$3̄50	6 50			9 00	12 05	2̄20		4 40	6 35	7̄40
East Hartford		6 59				12 18			4 49	6 43	7 48
Burnside		7‡02				12 23			4 53	6 47	7 52
Buckland		7‡08				12 33			5 00	6 54	8 00
Manchester		7 12			9 20	12 38	2 38		5 04	6 58	8 04
Talcottville						12‡45					8‡08
Vernon		7 19			9 27	12 50	2 46		5 12		8 15
Bolton		7 28			9‡36				5 26		
Andover		7 38			9‡48				5 40		
Hop River		7 45							5‡48		
Willimantic	5 00	7 55	6 30						6 10		
North Windham			6 40		10 15		3 25		6 20		
Goshen			6 48						6 30		
Hampton			6 56						6 39		
Elliot's			7 05						6 48		
Abington			7 09						6 52		
Pomfret	5r37		7 14		10 47		3 57		6 58		
Putnam	5 55		7 30		11 00		4 10	5 00	7 10		
Thompson			7 40		11‡09			5 10			
E. Thompson			7 50		11 18		4 27	5 20			
Douglas			8‡01					5 31			
East Douglas			8 06		11 30		4‡40	5 36			
Ironstone			8‡16								
Millville			8 20					5 53			
Blackstone		6 40	8 30		11 50		5 00	6 00			
Woonsocket Jc.			8 36		11 53			6 04			
Wadsworths			8 50					6 14			
Milford			7 10		9 00		12 20		5 45		
Franklin	7 00	7 30	9 05		9 25	12 06	12 55		6 20		
City Mills			7 37		9 33		1‡02		6‡26		
Norfolk			7 42		9 36				5 29		
Highland Lake					9 39		1‡09		6‡32		
Walpole	7 15	7 53	9 22		9 45	12 22	1 16		6 38		
Tilton's			7 57		9 48				6 41		
Winslow's			8 02		9 52		1 24		6 46		
Norwood Central			8 04	9 30	9 53	12 31	1 26		6 47		
Norwood			8 06		9 54		1 28				
Ellis			8 10		9 56						
Islington			8 17		9 57		1 32				
Elmwood			8 17		10 01		1 36				
Oakdale			8 19		10 02		1 37				
Readville			8 20		10 03		1 39				
Hyde Park			8 24	9 43	10 06		1 43		7 02		
River street											
Mattapan			8 28		10 12						
Dorchester					10 14						
Harvard street					10 15						
Mt. Bowdoin					10 16						
Bird street					10 18						
Dudley street					10 20						
South Boston											
Boston		7 50	8 40	10 00	10 30	1 00	2 00	6 00	7 20		
ARRIVE		am	am	am	am	pm	pm	pm	pm		

Station Scrapbook
of the
Eastern Division

People remember stations. This group served the Eastern Division of the old New York & New England, which ran from Hartford to Boston. The patient reader can key their locations with the 1884 timetable at left. In 1898, the New England was folded into the New Haven Railroad empire. The latter rebuilt many of the buildings below. The one at Pomfret, still standing, was an entirely new structure early this century.

Thompson (above) had an oddly "Spanish" depot; busy Vernon (below) needed space.

Elegant Pomfret got this fancy big station but Talcottville little more than a shack.

tors as Jay Gould. An entrance into Springfield, Massachusetts, was achieved in this era by leasing, in 1880, the twenty-mile Connecticut Central Railroad.[15] It left the New England main line at East Hartford and served South Windsor, Connecticut, and Melrose, East Longmeadow, and Springfield, Massachusetts. A seven-mile branch existed at Melrose to reach the Rockville Railroad at Rockville, built in 1876.

Clark returned from Europe in 1882 without a job, but was immediately hired as vice president of the rival New Haven. While employed there in the camp of the enemy, so to speak, Clark and his friends bought enough New England stock to oust the old directors. Thereupon he installed himself as president. He remarked, "It seemed to be my duty to return and repay to the property what it had done for me when I was a young man, when it gave me confidence and position as a railroad manager."[16] Thanks in large part to General Wilson's expensive push to finish the Erie Railroad connection, the New York & New England was in rickety condition. An extended receivership had to be arranged. Once again, Clark romanced the New Haven Railroad for traffic, and once again he inaugurated jointly operated trains via the Air Line Railroad connection at Willimantic. Certainly the most famous was the *New England Limited*—later called the *White Train*.

Hardly a New England train of the last century commanded more attention. Beginning in 1885 and speeding between Boston and New York City via the Connecticut uplands, the *Limited*'s original twin trains of "Palace Drawing Room Cars" in Pullman olive green left from both terminals at three each afternoon, making the 213-

Elliott's, like Buckland (below) got, depot-wise, the back of the NY & NE's lordly hand.

A train stops for milk at Hampton; the architect stopped at nothing at East Hartford.

Station Scrapbook of the Western Division

These stations were located west of Hartford. All across America station scenes like these made their way onto postcards and collectors treasure them today. The grandiose building at New Britain contrasts sharply with the little toylike structure at remote South Britain.

NEW YORK & NEW ENGLAND RAILROAD.—Western Division.

Eastern Time.] E. HOLBROOK, *Div. Supt.*, Hartford.

Hartford to Brewsters. [June 29, 1884.] **Brewsters to Hartford.**

FRS	MLS	p m	p m	p m	p m	p m	a m	a m	a m	a m	LEAVE ARRIVE	a m	p m	a m	m	p m	p m	p m	p m	p m
			3 30	2 00			9 00				*Boston*		1 00			6 00				
3 20	117¼		8 20	6 10	4 25		1 00	10 45	8 15	6 35	**Hartford**	6 45	8 47	11 55		2 10	4 25	6 30	9 20	
3 30	119		8 24	6 13	4‡29				8‡19	6 39	Parkville	6 40		11‡51				6 26		
	120¼		8 28	6 18	4‡32			10‡53	8‡23	6 41	Charter Oak	6‡37		11‡48				6 24	9 13	
	121		8 30	6 19	4 34			10 54	8 25	6 43	Elmwood	6 35	8 39	11 46			4 13	6 22	9 11	
3 35	122¼		8 34	6 24	4 37			10 58	8 28	6 46	Newington	6 32	8 36	11 43			4 10	6 18	9 07	
	124		8 38	6 28	4‡42			11 02	8 32	6 49	Clayton	6 28		11 39			4 05	6 14	9 03	
3 40	124¾										Pratt's									
3 45	126½		8 44	6 35	4 48		1 18	11 09	8 39	6 55	New Britain	6 23	8 26	11 33		1 55	3 57	6 08	8 57	
3 60	131		8 55	6 47	4 58		1 26	11 20	8 50	7 07	Plainville	6 14	8 15	11 20		1 44	3 45	5 56	8 45	
3 65	132¾		9 00	6 52	5 03			11 25	8 55	7 12	Forestville	6 10	8 10	11 15			3 39	5 50	8 39	
3 75	135¼		9 05	7 00	5 10		1 35	11 32	9 00	7 19	Bristol	6 05	8 05	11 10		1 35	3 33	5 45	8 33	
3 85	139½			7 12			1 45	11 42		7 30	Terryville		7 56			1 22	3 22		8 23	
3 95	142¼										Tolles'									
4 00	143¼							11‡51		7‡39	Hancock		7‡47				3‡14			
4 05	144¼			7‡23				11‡54		7‡44	Wheaton's		7 44				3‡12		8‡10	
4 05	145			7‡25						7‡45	Hoadley's		7‡40				3‡09		8‡08	
4 10	147¼			7 30				12 00		7 50	Waterville		7 35				3 05		8 02	
4 20	149¾			7 35		2†25	2 15	12 05		8 05	**Waterbury**		7 30		12 00	1 00	3 00		7 55	
4 30	153					2 36				8‡12	Union City				11 44				7‡38	
4 45	158	Sundays only.				3 00				8‡22	Towantic				11 20				7‡28	Sundays only.
4 55	161¼					3 20	2 36			8 29	Southford				10 45	12 28			7 22	
	164¼					3 50	2 42			8 36	Pomperaug Valley				10 15	12 21			7 15	
4 85	168¾					4 25	2 51			8 45	Sandy Hook				9 30	12 12			7 05	
4 85	171½					4 35	2‡56			8‡50	Newtown				9 03	12‡06			6‡59	
4 95	174	p m				5 00	3 01			8 55	Hawleyville				8 55	12 02			6 54	p m
5 10	180¼	3 35				5 55	3 15			9 10	Danbury				8 10	11 49			6 40	12 25
	182¾					6 05					Fair Grounds				7 15					
5 25	185	3 46				6 28	3 24			9 20	Mill Plain				7 07	11 38			6 28	12 14
5 40	190½	4 00				6 45	3 38			9 35	**Brewsters**				6†45	11 28			6 15	12 00
											New York, So. Ferry.									

New Britain's big station is imposing; Southbury's (below) ho-hum. Mr. Drake is there!

Many trains stopped at Forestville, but at South Britain's shed they merely paused.

mile jaunt in six hours flat. In masterful style the Pullman Company six years later manufactured two new rakes of luxury cars in creamy white and gold. Even the coal in the tender was whitewashed for the first run while engine crews wore eye-catching tropical white overalls and hats. The redesigned *White Train* became an instant favorite of business men, wealthy ladies, and swells. "The *New England Limited* in its slip loomed larger and more magnificent in my imagination than ever the *Queen Mary* was to seem in a later factual experience,"[17] observed the connoisseur of luxury on rails, the late Lucius Beebe.

Cars for both the east- and westbound sections of the *New England Limited* were jointly owned by the New York & New England and the New York, New Haven & Hartford. The names of both firms appeared on the letter boards. The New England owned the dining car, which ran only between Boston and Willimantic. When the westbound *Limited* arrived in Willimantic the diner was taken off, cleaned, reprovisioned, and attached to the rear of the eastbound section when it came in forty minutes later. Staffed against custom with white personnel, it was operated on a concession basis. Clark disclosed years later that the train was the most lucrative of all New York & New England passenger operations.

On March 16, 1891, the westbound segment of the *White Train* made its first trip out of the Summer Street depot in Boston, and the *Boston Herald* recorded the event:

Rolling out of the New York & New England Railroad station at 3:00 P.M. yesterday

Terryville had freight but poor passenger service (see timetable). Sandy Hook, below.

Women in white grace Southford's humble depot; behind Newtown is—Drake again!

Station Scrapbook
of the
Springfield Division

The former Connecticut Central formed the New York and New England's Springfield Division. The line ran from East Hartford to Springfield. At Melrose, a branch track headed for Rockville. The Central was built by Springfield contractor George Phelps and guided by chief engineer Samuel Clapp. Promoters wanted to go further south of East Hartford; sleepy Glastonbury and Portland said no. And it didn't.

Drake posed a friend at Shaker Station.

Hazardville was below the Bay State line.

At Melrose, a line went off to Rockville; and at Broad Brook (below) a Brill car pauses.

Ellington, on the branch, looks weed-grown; East Windsor Hill (below) normal.

afternoon, the famous *New England Limited* took on all the glories that could be attached in a complete new train of cars resplendent in white and gold.

For three months past, items have appeared in the daily papers about a new departure in car decoration that the New York & New England Railroad was about to inaugurate, and yesterday saw the fulfillment of those announcements.

The Pullman Palace Car Company has built for the service seven parlor cars, four passenger coaches, and two royal buffet smokers. These cars are divided into two trains, owned respectively by the New England and the New York, New Haven & Hartford Railroads. The New England road has provided a dining car of the same general design to run between Boston and Willimantic, Connecticut. The cars are heated by steam directly from the locomotive and are lighted by the Pintsch system of gas. The parlor cars are furnished with velvet carpets, silk draperies, and white silk curtains. The chairs are upholstered in old gold plush, and large plate glass mirrors set off the car handsomely. Three of them have each a stateroom and twenty six chairs in the main salon, while the other four have thirty chairs each. The royal buffet smokers which will be run in addition to the ordinary smoking cars are decorated in the same manner as the parlor cars and contain twenty handsome upholstered chairs for the passengers.

Two card tables with stationary seats, and writing desks with all needed stationery for letters or telegrams are also provided. The regular passenger coaches seat sixty persons each, and are comfortable and easy riding. The train that left Boston yesterday was seen by crowds and people who were lined enroute to gaze with mingled curiosity and delight at its handsome appearance.

Engine No. 167 momentarily slows with the fabled White Train *at Putnam, Conn. Moments before, the fireman lowered a scoop under the tender to gather water from special track pans. The spray confirms it.*

190

The White Train *at East Thompson, 1891.*

This apparition, passing through eastern Connecticut at twilight, prompted many local residents to nickname it the "Ghost Train," or "White Wings," as it flickered past clumps of trees. Naturally it won national attention, and even President Benjamin Harrison came to ride it. On January 27, 1895, the *White Train* was cited by Putnam, Connecticut, officials for rocketing so fast through town that a local man said it "shook magazine and paper stocks from the shelves of Talbot Chapman's newsroom." Children loved to watch it steam by, and when the *White Train* made its inaugural run school children at Norwood, Massachusetts, were allowed to go home early to view the marvel and hear the first chime whistle on a New York & New England locomotive. Philip Hale, the erudite columnist of the *Boston Herald*, frequently devoted space in that paper as late as the 1920s to the *White Train's* legends. Readers of his column often responded, recalling such days as when the train arrived in Boston splashed with red paint—a prank—or when one of the *White Train's* engines arrived in Boston with a crumpled water scoop—an employee having failed to turn on the steam pipe in the frozen track pans at Putnam one winter day.

The track pans, of course, were another novelty. The *New England Limited* covered 213 miles in the then-remarkable time of just six hours because it did not have to stop for boiler water between Boston and Willimantic—some eighty-six miles. Clark himself made this timesaver possible by having special pans filled with water installed between the rails at Putnam. Locomotive tenders fitted beneath with scoops could collect twenty-five hundred gallons of water in about thirty seconds, while the train glided along at forty-five miles per hour. Track pans were pioneered, like so much else in railroading, by an ingenious Englishman, John Ramsbottom, in 1859, and were first used on the London & North Western Railway. Clark saw them in use while in England, and his pans may have been the first in America; they antedate those on the New York Central, for use by the *Empire State Express*, by about twenty-five years. Each pan measured fifteen hundred feet in length, and was twenty-eight inches wide by seven inches deep. Steam pipes were included in the trough to prevent winter freeze-ups.

A train as famous as the *New England Limited* could not escape some adulation for its crew members, and heading that list was Eugene Everett Potter, engineer of the *Limited* on the Willimantic-Boston run. It was not unusual for Potter's name, or that of his conductor, Michael Crowley, to appear in the social columns of Boston newspapers, for the city was much taken with its celebrity express. According to Francis Donovan, a former officer of the Railway & Locomotive Historical Society, "Gene [Potter] could make headlines at will." On August 21, 1888, the Boston papers even noted that the famed six-foot engineer had shaved off his luxurious moustache! As a boy Donovan personally knew Potter and inherited the engineer's scrapbooks and personal effects. The former were filled with publicity clippings and mementos, including moral verses by Ella Wheeler Wilcox, which he often quoted

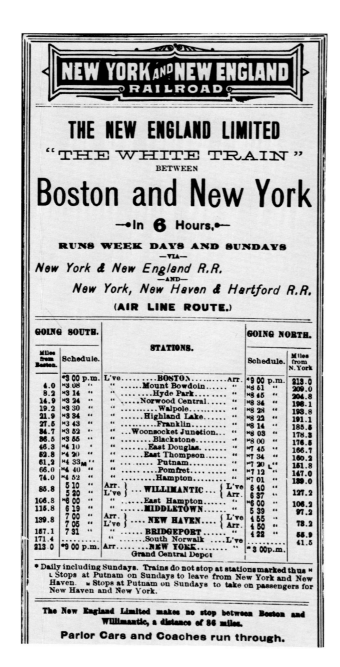

NEW YORK AND NEW ENGLAND RAILROAD

THE NEW ENGLAND LIMITED

"THE WHITE TRAIN"

BETWEEN

Boston and New York

→In **6** Hours.←

RUNS WEEK DAYS AND SUNDAYS

—VIA—

New York & New England R.R.

—AND—

New York, New Haven & Hartford R.R.

(AIR LINE ROUTE.)

GOING SOUTH.			STATIONS.		GOING NORTH.	
Miles from Boston.	Schedule.				Schedule.	Miles from N. York
	*3 00 p.m.	L've	.........BOSTON.........	Arr.	*9 00 p.m.	213.0
4.0	*3 08 "	"	......Mount Bowdoin......	"	м8 51 "	209.0
8.2	*3 14 "	"	..........Hyde Park......	"	м8 45 "	204.8
14.9	*3 24 "	"	....Norwood Central.....	"	м8 34 "	198.1
19.2	*3 30 "	"	.........Walpole.........	"	м8 28 "	193.8
21.9	*3 34 "	"	......Highland Lake......	"	м8 22 "	191.1
27.5	*3 43 "	"	.........Franklin........	"	м8 14 "	185.5
34.7	*3 52 "	"	...Woonsocket Junction...	"	м8 03 "	178.3
36.5	*3 55 "	"	.........Blackstone......	"	*8 00 "	176.5
46.3	*4 10 "	"	......East Douglas.......	"	м7 45 "	166.7
52.8	*4 20 "	"	......East Thompson......	"	м7 34 "	160.2
61.2	*4 33 м "	"	.........Putnam.........	"	м7 20 L "	151.8
66.0	*4 40 "	"	.........Pomfret........	"	м7 12 "	147.0
74.0	*4 52 "	"	.........Hampton........	"	м7 01 "	139.0
85.8	5 10 " Arr. }		...WILLIMANTIC	{ L've	6 40 "	127.2
	5 20 " L've }			{ Arr.	6 37 "	
106.8	*6 00 "	"	.....East Hampton.......	"	м6 00 "	106.2
115.8	6 19 "	"	......MIDDLETOWN.......	"	5 39 "	97.2
139.8	7 00 " Arr. }		....NEW HAVEN	{ L've	4 55 "	73.2
	7 05 " L've }			{ Arr.	4 50 "	
157.1	7 31 "	"	......BRIDGEPORT.......	"	4 22 "	55.9
171.4	....	"	......South Norwalk ....L've		....	41.5
213.0	*9 00 p.m.	Arr.	......NEW YORK.........	"	*3 00p.m.	
			Grand Central Depot			

*Daily including Sundays. Trains do not stop at stations marked thus м
   L Stops at Putnam on Sundays to leave from New York and New
   Haven. м Stops at Putnam on Sundays to take on passengers for
   New Haven and New York.

**The New England Limited makes no stop between Boston and
Willimantic, a distance of 86 miles.**

Parlor Cars and Coaches run through.

Eugene Everett Potter

from memory. Potter frequently wrote articles for newspapers and addressed countless groups.

Potter's reputation was based on the fact that he was a nonpareil, a skillful and safe
engineman who ran fast trains. During his tenure he was not involved in a single
accident. That does not mean that extraordinary events failed to occur, for they did:
on the night of March 10, 1888—during that famed New England blizzard—the
Limited became snow-bound on the grade at Hampton, Connecticut, the steepest
section of the Eastern Division. On that bitter evening all 105 passengers ate well
and slept in the cars. Potter received his usual day's pay of $7.

Gene Potter was not at the throttle when Chauncey Gott was killed by the *White
Train*. Gott, a Hebron, Connecticut, landowner and farmer, sold property to the Air
Line Railroad and loved to watch the passing trains. But he told residents of Turnerville (later Amston, Connecticut) that he'd never ride one. In 1893 he was prepared
to watch the Ghost Train make its passage one evening through Turnerville. Upon
hearing its whistle he remarked to a section hand that it was about time to make the
crossing before the train came. However, two steps away the train caught and
instantly killed him. He got to ride the *White Train* to nearby Westchester—in the
baggage car—whereupon the coroner performed his office.

Michael Crowley

THE NEW ENGLAND LIMITED

— BETWEEN —

Boston and New York

"THE WHITE TRAIN."

The Pullman Palace Car Company have constructed for the NEW YORK & NEW ENGLAND and the NEW YORK, NEW HAVEN & HARTFORD RAILROAD COMPANIES Parlor Cars and Coaches, which are to be run on the

NEW ENGLAND LIMITED TRAIN

leaving New York and Boston daily at 3 p.m. These cars which are painted White externally, are superior in comfort and ornamentation to any cars of like character operated in the United States. A Royal Buffet Smoking Car will be attached to each train to be used exclusively by Parlor Car passengers.

The Royal Buffet Smoking Cars are a unique feature in railroading, the acme of beauty, convenience and comfort. They are handsomely and artistically decorated, and are furnished with easy chairs and sofas. These conveniences will certainly be appreciated by those who have been accustomed to crowd into the smoking apartment heretofore in use.

The Day Coaches are built on entirely new and broad principles, securing to the traveling public all that can be desired.

These cars will now form the two trains widely known as the "New England Limited," running between Boston and New York, via the Air Line, leaving either city at 3 p.m. daily, including Sundays, and arriving at the other at 9 p.m.

A Dining Car runs between Boston and Willimantic, and meals are served Table d'Hôte, or a la Carte. All the delicacies of the season are served.

The cars are lighted by gas and heated by steam.

No Extra Charge for this Unsurpassed Service.

TAKE "THE WHITE TRAIN"

AND SIX HOURS OF HAPPINESS.

Dining car menu of the New England Limited.

R & LHS

Between New Haven and Boston the White Train *ran on a diagonal course, by-passing New London and Providence. But the Shore Line Route proved to be the superior way with the public and the New England's route gradually diminished in importance. The* White Train *was succeeded by the* Air Line Limited. *After the New Haven Railroad take-over, the latter was replaced with the* Knickerbocker Limited *which ran the shore-line course via New London.*

Rudyard Kipling was acquainted with the resplendent train of white and gold, for his wife was from Middletown, Connecticut, one of the train's few stopping points. He once wrote a short story, while summering in Vermont, entitled ".007"—a whimsical account of locomotives talking to each other in a roundhouse. One of those "talking" locomotives hauled cars remarkably like those of the *White Train*.

> Now, in the darkest night, even as *The Purple Emperor* said, if you will stand on the bridge across the freightyard, looking down upon the four-track way, at 2:30 A.M., neither before nor after, *The White Moth* takes the overflow from *The Purple Emperor* and tears south with her seven vestibuled cream-white cars.

The *White Train*, costly to keep white, was retired by Clark's successors in 1895 and superseded by yet another New York & New England flyer, the *Air Line Limited*. It had twin locomotive headlights and was the only train ever to run regularly through New Haven, Connecticut, without stopping for passengers.

By 1886 President Clark had now guided the New York & New England out of its extended, inherited receivership. A lease of the firm to its strongest rival, the New Haven Railroad, was seriously considered. Depressed New York & New England

These prices, read aloud, may fetch a tear from old gentlemen, but they were quite standard in the 1890s. What memories!

Interior of the sole dining car used on the New England Limited. R & LHS

Without a jar or roll or antic,
Without a stop to Willimantic,
The New England Limited *makes its way*
At three o'clock on every day.
Maids and matrons, daintily dimited,
Ride every day on the New England Limited;
Rain nor snow ne'er stops its flight,
It makes New York at nine each night.
One-half the glories have not been told,
Of that wonderful train of white and gold,
Which leaves each day for New York at three,
Over the N.Y. & N.E.
—White Train *advertisement*

stock was now recovering and steadily climbed to $115 a share. But persistent New York speculators—now led by Jabez Bostwick, a former cotton dealer and Standard Oil refiner—returned and proved strong enough to remove Clark from office in 1886. It proved to be a suicidal move, for Clark resurfaced as president of the New York, New Haven & Hartford. Meanwhile the Bostwick gang revived relations with the New York, Lake Erie & Western Railroad (the "Erie" in lengthier guise), itself a lemon in the garden of railway finance. The speculators temporarily got control of Connecticut's Housatonic Railroad system and inaugurated the roundabout *Long Island & Eastern States Express* route described in Chapter Seven.

They also "proposed" lines from the Housatonic main line to reach New York City or New Haven. Years later an Interstate Commerce Commission investigation revealed just how turbulent the times were.

I.C.C. Examiner: "What was the state of competition between the New York & New England and the New Haven?"

Witness: "Any form you can imagine—one man cutting the heart out of another, except they were two railroads. It was the worst form of cut-throat competition I ever had any experience with in forty-four years."[18]

194

Engine No. 5 of the Meriden, Waterbury & Connecticut River, built by the Schenectady Locomotive Works in 1888, with crews.

A wooden trestle of "The Meriden Road" near Cheshire. The "combination" car at the right was built to accommodate passengers, freight, and baggage. The Meriden Road was small and employees could and did know all their comrades personally.

COLLECTION OF JAMES M.S. ULLMAN

The witness was Charles S. Mellen, a future president of the New York, New Haven & Hartford. All the years of conciliation sought by Clark had almost come to nought.

One acquisition occurred in Connecticut during this speculative period, that of the Meriden, Waterbury & Connecticut River Railroad Company. This line was a consolidation of two smaller firms: the Meriden & Cromwell, and the Meriden & Waterbury. The eleven-mile Meriden & Cromwell opened in 1885 between its namesake cities. Irate Meriden manufacturers, distressed with the high rates of the New Haven Railroad, thought a by-pass or crosslots route to some town east on the Connecticut River was the solution. Horace Wilcox, a silver industry pioneer, led the movement. At the road's destination of Cromwell, barge and steamboat connections were made and soon a mere thirty-five-minute railroad run connected the cities. In similar fashion manufacturers in Waterbury seeking to escape the New Haven Railroad's high rates in 1887 got a charter for the Meriden & Waterbury, aiming then to connect with the other new company. The following year they consolidated as the Meriden, Waterbury & Connecticut River. In the summer of 1888 seventeen miles of track were opened between Waterbury and Meriden via West Cheshire. But in 1892, after only four years as an independent, the little railroad leased itself to the New York & New England system. Unfortunately, the acquisition was not that fruitful to the New York & New England; they closed the line. New purchasers appeared when the short line was finally auctioned; it was reincorporated as the Middletown, Meriden & Waterbury Railroad, but eventually, in 1898, fell into the hands of the very railroad its founders had sought to avoid.

Disappointment after disappointment clouded the final chapters of the New York &

New England Railroad Company. Within five years Bostwick had made his exit; the brief administrations of Austin Corbin and Charles Parsons followed. Corbin had prior experience in subway transportation, while Parsons had trained on upstate New York railroads. Plans were still devised to reach New York City without the New Haven Railroad. Bookkeeping accounts of the firm were falsified and at one point three different sets of company books were in use—a state of affairs in which the left hand knew nothing of the deeds or misdeeds of the right. But the most startling episode, and actually the last, was the unexpected appearance in New England of the Pennsylvania rail baron A. Archibald McLeod, as described in Chapter Nine, and his defeat by J. P. Morgan.

To cripple the New York & New England in the McLeod era, Morgan directed Clark to shut off valuable interchange traffic from the New Haven, forcing the New York & New England also into receivership. In 1895 the latter resurfaced as simply "The New England Railroad," and its president now was none other than C. P. Clark. Three years later the New England was leased to the New Haven Railroad.

Thirty and forty trains a day had once passed over the New England's main-line tracks in Connecticut. As Alvin Harlow noted: "The New York and New England Railroad did some of the most spectular railroading; and how it managed to put on so brave a show, to do so much with so little, is still a matter of wonder." [19]

This forgotten leviathan left behind a tragic yet little known footprint in the history of American railroading: a spectacular train wreck which occurred in 1891 at East Thompson, Connecticut, in the extreme northeast corner of the state.

Mls	May 7, 1893.	
	LEAVE]	[ARRIVE
o	....**Waterbury**.....	
2.6	.. Dublin Street	....
6.1	.....East Farms	......
7.9	......Summit	....
9.7	......Prospect	....
10.9	..West Cheshire	.....
12.9	..Southington Road	..
14.9	..Cheshire Street	....
16.3	.......Hanover	....
18.0	......**Meriden**	......
23.9	.....Highland	.....
25.5	.......Smith's	......
27.2	.....**Westfield**	....
28.2	....West Cromwell	....
30.5	arr...**Cromwell**..lve.	

196

Engineer Joe Page of the Southbridge Local had quite a scare the morning of December 4, 1891. His train never got to Southbridge.

COLLECTION OF FRANCIS DONOVAN

Southbridge Extension.

	to Southbridge.				Southbridge to Boston.			
p m	p m	a m	a m	LV AR	a m	p m	p m	p m
3 30	....	9 00	....	....Boston.....	10 00	1 00	....	6 00
5 40		10 40	8 00	**E. Thompson**	7 50	1118		4 27
5 55	1245	10 53	8 12	..East Webster..	7 33	1018	12 40	4 17
6 00	1250	10 58	8 18	....Webster.....	7 30	1015	12 30	4 13
6 15	1 10	11 13	8 33	..Quinnebaug ..	7 15	1000	12 15	3 59
6 21	1 25	11 20	8 40	..West Dudley..	7 09	9 46	12 01	3 52
6 26	1 35	11 25	8 45	...Sandersdale ..	7 04	9 40	11 50	3 49
6 30	1 40	11 40	8 50	**Southbridge.**	7 00	....	11 40	3 45
p m	p m	p m	a m	AR LV	a m	a m	a m	p m

A youthful Harry Taber, engineer of the fast Long Island & Eastern States Express, *met his death in East Thompson, as did his fireman, Fitzgerald. Their demolished engine No. 105 is seen on the opposite page, and disaster, as always, has drawn a large and curious crowd of onlookers, young and old.*

COLLECTION OF FRANCIS DONOVAN

The hamlet of East Thompson is not a familiar town to most people in Connecticut, unlike nearby Thompson with its picture-book town green and jewel-like houses. East Thompson was something of a provincial boomtown, a junction point on the New York & New England Railroad boasting a well-maintained country depot, freight house, signal cabin, and turntable, not to mention an express agency and Western Union facilities. An earthen embankment faced the building complex and in it small, round, whitewashed stones proudly spelled out EAST THOMPSON. A branch track went off to the northwest from East Thompson to Southbridge, Massachusetts, via Lake Webster. Today, the spot boasts only an overgrown right of way.

December 4, 1891, dawned in East Thompson as foggy and wintry. Most villagers except for farm folk were just getting up when the Boston dispatcher's train sheet was coming alive in the Putnam area. Putnam was a New York & New England nerve center situated some ten miles west of East Thompson. Here the twin track Eastern Division main line crossed the company's Norwich & Worcester Division. The signal and telegraphic operation, located in the big Union Depot, hummed away; it was manned around the clock. On this morning three of the four trains that would be involved in the great East Thompson Wreck were in the Putnam vicinity. One was the fast-approaching eastbound *Long Island & Eastern States Express*; the second a ready-to-leave Boston-bound express freight originating at Putnam (on the timetable as No. 212); and the third the *Norwich Steamboat Express*, which was making its way up the Norwich & Worcester Division towards Putnam. The fourth train destined to take part was the *Southbridge Local* freight. It was based over at East Thompson, and its crew was coming on duty and getting ready to make up its train in the yard.

The *Eastern States Express* had left Long Island City in Brooklyn at 11 the night before with its Pullman sleepers. At Oyster Bay the ferryboat *Cape Charles* floated the cars across Long Island Sound to Wilson Point at South Norwalk, Connecticut. Once landed, New York & New England power was attached, and the crack flyer ran to Hawleyville, to Hartford, and then to Putnam, where it was due at 5:53 a.m. Owing to some mechanical problem, first experienced around Hawleyville, the crew out of Hartford relayed word for a new engine at Putnam. Help was made ready in the form of New York & New England engine No. 105. Since this locomotive was the pet and pride of Engineer Harry Taber, the Hartford engine crew would come off at Putnam, and Taber, with his No. 105, would come on. Firing for Taber that morning was Gerry Fitzgerald; the man normally assigned, Mike Flynn, marked off the roster because he had that night a premonition of disaster. The *Eastern States* now was gliding over the long Quinebaug River bridge at Putnam, about ready to make its customary station stop, whereupon the engine swap would begin under the watchful eye of Conductor George Cross.

No. 212, the hotshot freight, was itching to leave the Putnam yard, with Engineer Harry Wildes and Fireman Jacob Boyce. Eleven cars made up the train; some carried loads of apples, bricks, salt, leather, and hardware, and a few were empty. She had just received written train orders as the *Eastern States* came in. In fact, the latter pulled up almost neck-to-neck with No. 212, allowing both engine crews to exchange talk.

Meanwhile the *Norwich Steamboat Express* was rapidly approaching Putnam; it had left New London around 4:30, an hour later than usual because the steamboat had been late from New York City. At Putnam this train would be switched over to Eastern Division Track No. 2 for the fast run to the New York & New England's Summer Street Depot in downtown Boston. Ed Hurley was at the controls that morning, and his fireman was Will Loudon. The veteran conductor George Engles was back in the cars accounting for his seventy-five or so patrons who had come off the boat. Thus the Boston train dispatcher had three trains to think about at Putnam: the *Eastern States*, fast freight No. 212, and the *Norwich Steamboat Express*.

197

Keeping trains rolling is an art, and to alleviate the congestion at Putnam that morning the dispatcher decided on an unusual plan. First, the *Eastern States* would leave whenever it completed the engine swap. It would take the eastbound No. 2 track all the way to Boston. Freight No. 212 was another matter: hesitant to release it ahead of the *Eastern States* lest it slow down or stop the much-touted passenger train, the dispatcher issued train orders allowing it to leave AHEAD of the express, but on the westbound track—Track No. 1. In railway parlance this is called "a move against the current of traffic," or running "left-handed." No. 212 now had the right to run east on the westbound track all the way past East Thompson to East Douglas, Massachusetts, whereupon it would be switched over to No. 2 track, the one normally used for Boston-bound trains. The dispatcher imagined that the *Eastern States* would catch up to the freight and overtake it somewhere after East Thompson. The benefit of the left-handed move was that it got both trains rolling out of Putnam and cleared the way for the *Norwich Steamboat Express*. The latter had only to make its Putnam station stop, then highball to Boston.

But the fact remained that the dispatcher and the crew of No. 212 totally forgot about the Southbridge Freight Local at East Thompson, which was now on duty and exercising its privilege to use westbound Track No. 1 in making up its train.

Over at East Thompson, Engineer Joe Page was running engine No. 31 around the small yard and, for some elbowroom, would soon back his train out on main line Track No. 1. Employee timetable instructions gave him that right. Later his eight-car train would presumably pull back into the yard and head over the Southbridge Branch. A little after 6:30 a.m. Page heard a shrill whistle in the distance. Since Page's crew hadn't seen the *Eastern States Express* go by, they imagined it was "her running late." But as the whistle blew again and the yellowish glow of the

Above is the official publicity pose of the ill-fated Long Island & Eastern States Express. *It was used by "Business Men, Tourists, and Theatricals." Pullman vestibuled cars were used in both east and westbound editions. The train was short-lived.*

COLLECTION OF ALICE A. RAMSDELL

Engineer Taber's fatal engine. The coach sustained only moderate damage, though the Pullman cars behind it were rammed full-tilt by the Norwich Boat Train.

COLLECTION OF ALICE A. RAMSDELL

A few hours after the four-train calamity at East Thompson, workers search the rubble, eager to extinguish the smouldering fires. By studying the scene at far left, one can discern two engines and their smokestacks: that is where fast freight No. 202 met the Southbridge Local head on. At right, crowds gather to inspect the Eastern States Express. *In the right foreground are the mangled engine, tender and cars of the* Norwich Boat Train, *which rear-ended the derailed* Express. *Thus, in sequential order, there occurred: a head-end smash, a derailment, and a rear-end collision.*

headlight came rounding the station curve at East Thompson, Joe Page received the greatest shock of his life: it was attached to an oncoming train on the same track as his. Page yelled to his fireman, "Head for the woods!" and both quickly jumped from the cab. The shock was no doubt equally electrifying for the engine crew of No. 212. The crash splintered the early morning air; ruptured steam shot to the heavens. Steel and wooden parts went sailing onto nearby Track No. 2, and fires broke out. Cars of the *Local* were hit so hard that most of them jackknifed.

Unaware of the carnage ahead, the fifty-mile-an-hour *Eastern States Express* rounded the station curve a few minutes later and dashed into the debris spewed on Track No. 2. Its engine derailed and did a 180-degree turn before burying itself in sand and gravel, snuffing out the lives of Harry Taber and Gerry Fitzgerald. The engine's boiler safety valve snapped off and live steam blasted an enormous hole. Patrons in the Pullman sleepers *Midland* and *Cato* were badly shaken in their compartments, and one by one they stumbled out into the cold dawn. The time was permanently fixed, as the pocket watch of Engineer Taber was found stopped at 6:47 a.m. Pullman conductor Frank Jennison quickly closed the valves on the gas lighting system. Then someone remembered the *Norwich Steamboat Express* was

Judging by this telegraphic message, the company was keen to preserve certain Pullman items, which were charged for if not returned. The wreck was whitewashed.

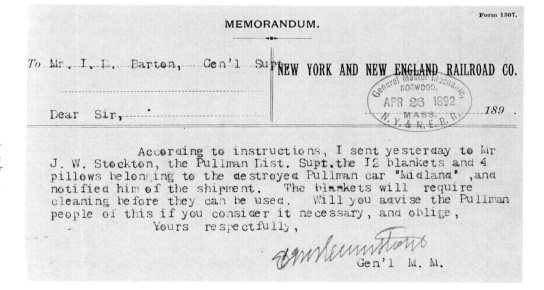

MEMORANDUM.   Form 1307.

To Mr. I. L. Barton, Gen'l Sup't **NEW YORK AND NEW ENGLAND RAILROAD CO.**

Dear Sir,   189 .

According to instructions, I sent yesterday to Mr J. W. Stockton, the Pullman Dist. Supt. the 12 blankets and 4 pillows belonging to the destroyed Pullman car "Midland", and notified him of the shipment. The blankets will require cleaning before they can be used. Will you advise the Pullman people of this if you consider it necessary, and oblige,

Yours respectfully,

Gen'l M. M.

due. A flagman was hastily sent out, but too late. The Norwich boat train came roaring in and rammed the rear of the partly standing *Eastern States Express*, setting the *Midland* on fire was well as its own engine cab. Hurley and Loudon miraculously walked away from the boat train's engine with no more than bad cuts and scrapes.

Engineer Joe Page had jumped from Engine No. 31 in the upper photograph. No. 175 that pulled the fast freight is at right. Both have been separated and jacked up. The scene below shows what happened to the last cars of Joe Page's Local: they jack-knifed and fell down into the Post Road. The Norwood Wreck Train has now arrived.

COLLECTION OF ALICE A. RAMSDELL

Among the seventy-five passengers running around was one Irishman, just over from the mother country, who was seen clutching cages of goldfinches. He stopped Conductor Engles of the boat train and asked, "Is *this* Boston?" In just minutes, four trains had crashed: two as a result of a head-end collision, one that ran into its debris and derailed, and one that rear-ended the latter. The East Thompson milkman, whose name has not come down to us, approached a railroader later in the day and said he saw all four trains "get wrecked." So he tied up his horse and stepped out on the tracks to see if any more trains would crash before he crossed his rig.

By now the village was awake and aware of what had happened. The East Thompson station agent, Otis Clark, made his way to the telegraph key and called for help. At nearby Webster, Massachusetts, Conductor Joslyn of the local passenger train cancelled his run and ordered local firemen to load a pumper and hose cart onto an empty flat car. A lightning trip was then made to East Thompson. Mrs. Clark finally made her way to the station and immediately asked, "Otis, did you make a mistake?" "Mother, my work is clear. They must have done it in Putnam!" he replied. Mrs. Clark then tore off her apron and began making bandages.* The diminutive Reverend Joseph Jackson of the Methodist Church appeared to help, and railroad men later remarked he was seen scrambling in and out of coaches carrying people.

Janney Automatic Coupler applied to a Freight Car.

Three wreck trains arrived by midmorning: one from Hartford, one from Willimantic, and a larger one from the company shops at Norwood, Massachusetts. Supervising the cleanup was the wreckmaster, Hunton Bradley, who said the demolished engines "looked for certain like a row of plucked chickens." Fires were eventually put out, cars and engines righted, and the wreckage cleaned from the rails.

About $36,000 worth of damage had been done to company property at East Thompson. The bodies of the dead crew members of the *Eastern States Express* were extricated and sent to Webster. A search was made in the burned-out Pullman *Midland* for one R. H. Rath, a real estate salesman from New York, but his body was never found. Official Car No. 95 arrived on the back of the Norwood wreck train with several officers. A veteran train dispatcher from another railroad, Delbert Peckham of the New Haven, who visited the wreck that day and saw the car, recalled:

> I got pretty hungry and some fellow directed me up the hill to a store where I bought some crackers and cheese. I walked east from the wreck and Official Car #95 was standing maybe a thousand feet east. As I went for my feed there was a flagman asleep on the track with a flag in his hand. I woke him up and asked if he was flagging Official Car #95. He said yes, but he couldn't keep awake as he had had no sleep in five days. We walked along and I told him he'd better try and stay awake as he was flagging an official car, but before I lost sight of him he was back in the hay.

By late afternoon Track No. 1 had been cleared enough for the westbound edition of the famous *White Train*. December 4, now the day of the Great East Thompson Train Wreck, was coming to a close. The final irony, however, must be a news item about another wreck at East Thompson just two weeks later:

> The passenger train due in Southbridge here at 8:40 A.M. did not arrive this morning until 9:30 having been delayed at East Thompson by another accident at that point on the Eastern Division. A freight train was being switched from a sidetrack when along came a through freight which crashed into it demolishing a caboose, damaging an engine, and blocking the tracks. . . .[20]

That gleaning from the *Southbridge Journal* of December 17th, 1891, confirms again that the New York & New England, in its final years, was highballing trains regardless of the cost.

*The author is indebted to Alice A. Ramsdell, noted rail historian of West Thompson, Connecticut, for supplying many of the lesser-known details about the wreck.

In a quieter moment over at East Thompson, the local section crew prepares for work on Track No. 1. Among the laborers rides a small dog, with blanket. The freight house, depot, and signal cabin can be seen. The branch to Southbridge is behind the complex, today all quite overgrown.

COLLECTION OF ALICE A. RAMSDELL

Chapter Eleven Footnotes

1. Arthur Pound, *More They Told Barron* (New York: Harper & Brothers, 1931), 128.

2. Connecticut General Assembly, Resolves and Private Laws of the State of Connecticut, May 1833, I: 1014, Public Records, Connecticut State Capitol Building.

3. Ibid., IV: 904. Passed 1847.

4. Ibid., IV: 907, 1012. Passed 1845.

5. Ibid., V: 139.

6. *Annual Report, Railroad Commissioners of Connecticut for 1866* (Hartford: Case, Lockwood & Brainard, 1866), 101.

7. *Annual Report, Railroad Commissioners of Connecticut for 1874* (Hartford: Case, Lockwood & Brainard, 1874), 127.

8. Connecticut General Assembly, Resolves and Private Laws of the State of Connecticut, IV: 873. Passed 1854. Public Records, Connecticut State Capitol Building.

9. Ibid., IV: 884. Passed 1853.

10. Ibid., V: 543.

11. Massachusetts General Assembly, Senate, 1870, Senate Doc. 133.

12. *The New York & New England Railroad Company, Final Disposition of the Several Railroad Companies* (Boston: Alfred Mudge & Son, 1874), 552-567.

13. Massachusetts General Assembly, House, 1870, H. Doc. 360, 3.

14. Connecticut General Assembly, Resolves and Private Laws of the State of Connecticut, V: 76, Public Documents, Connecticut State Capitol Building.

15. Ibid., VII: 46.

16. Massachusetts General Assembly, House, 1886, H. Doc. 438, 234.

17. Lucius Beebe, *Two Trains to Remember* (Privately printed, 1965).

18. *New York Times*, 22 October 1915.

19. Harlow, *Steelways*, 196-197.

20. *Southbridge Journal*, 18 December 1891.

William D. Bishop was elected the first president of the New York, New Haven & Hartford in 1872. His portrait is above. The first four presidents of the New Haven—Bishop, George Watrous, Charles Clark, and John Hall—were consistent in their policies of financial stability, conservative investments, improvements, and expansion. All despised any form of competition.

Speculators like those pictured below gambled steadily on railroad stocks during the long Pierpont Morgan period. Some got rich, and some, as usual, did not.

What is unique about this lovely security is that it illustrates the three powerful means of transport that made up the New Haven: the trolley lines, the steam railway operations, and the extensive boat lines. The holdings were immense; few could actually recite the entire portfolio.

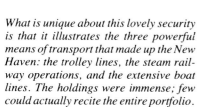

203

$10,000.

№ X 1609

UNITED STAT

THE NEW YORK, NEW

Railroad

Total Authorized Issue $ 39,029,600.

The New York, New Haven and Hartford Rail

Chapter Twelve

A Yankee Empire

The story of the New Haven Railroad should be an object lesson to those . . . . who believe that the business thinking and financial guidance of the great enterprises of all the country can safely be committed to a few men.

—*U.S. Supreme Court Justice Louis D. Brandeis, 1913*

We have traced in the first eleven chapters the many independent companies which formed the once-dense railroad network of Connecticut. In the simpler days before the Civil War they filled our forefathers with pride and even awe, slow and fragile and quaint as they may seem to our own eyes. But they were the engine of progress then, and in the hustling era of big business and frantic finance that followed the war they became pawns in a cutthroat game waged by powerful, ambitious men. At the end of the nineteenth century, as we have seen, all but one of them—the former New London Northern, now Central Vermont Railway—had been gathered into the huge New York, New Haven & Hartford Railroad, well-nicknamed "The Consolidated." At its greatest extent it was composed of no fewer than three hundred former companies, many of them situated outside Connecticut. It was a seemingly invincible empire on the land and on the sea, the mightiest business enterprise in New England. It was like the Roman Empire, and it suffered a similar fate.

A rather contemplative J. Pierpont Morgan reflects over a cigar while on board his palatial yacht Corsair, *June 30, 1910. Morgan came to the New Haven board in the late 1880s, after William Rockefeller, but not until 1903 did his electrifying moves begin. It was on the long black steam yacht that Morgan assembled rival financiers and won settlements. He was a Hartford native.*

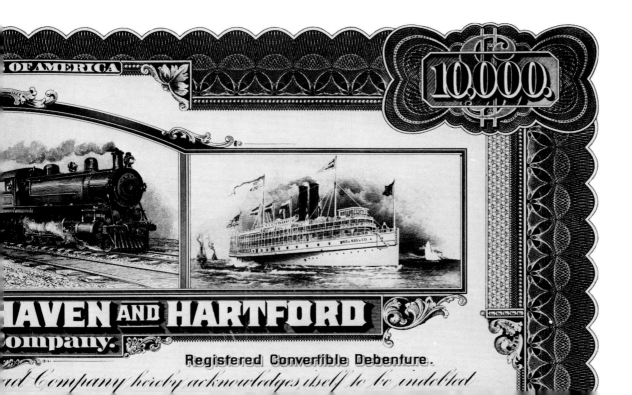

This map presents the New York, New Haven & Hartford Railroad at its greatest extent, shows the many steamboat lines, and includes the New York, Ontario & Western in adjoining New York. For all practical purposes the company controlled the railway affairs of Connecticut, Rhode Island, and a good part of Massachusetts. The map does not show the immense number of trolley lines nor does it include two other great systems the New Haven briefly owned, the Maine Central and the Boston & Maine—both taken captive at the height of the Morgan-Mellen combine. Escaping the behemoth's clutches, in Connecticut, was the little Central Vermont Railway, shown in the eastern half of the state as a thin, black line. Unlike most of the New Haven system, that diminutive road still runs.

From the day it was chartered in 1872, the New York, New Haven & Hartford laid almost no new lines. That was unnecessary, for it lived by take-over, and it would grow steadily for forty years, until its monopoly was complete. It was, under its succession of nineteenth-century presidents, a generally beneficent oligarchy. It got its way if you did not stand in its way. It knit the state—and much of southern New England—into an economic whole, moving goods and people wherever they needed to go, opening new avenues of communication, and contributing enormously to the industrial revolution of our busy, inventive, and prosperous commonwealth. It was then a jewel-like property with little debt, whose stock was as solid as bedrock, selling steadily in the $200's, paying between 8 and 10 percent to the widows, orphans, trustees, and banks who swore by it. In this enviable condition it was almost bound to attract the interest and avarice of an autocrat. And it did.

That autocrat was Connecticut's own J. Pierpont Morgan, the greatest of American financiers, sometimes referred to as a "one-man Federal Reserve." He, of course, antedated that institution, but perhaps helped bring it on by his overweening follies.

THE NEW YORK,
NEW HAVEN & HARTFORD RAILROAD
OPERATED AND CONTROLLED LINES.

As the century turned, he became *de facto* master of the New Haven Railroad and installed his own man, Charles S. Mellen, as president. What everyone else called "The New Haven," however, Morgan called the "The Hartford." He had been born there and may have had a fleeting affection for the capital city, however much he might despise the government that sat there. To this great financial manipulator, and his henchmen, state governments were mere obstacles, to be variously bamboozled, placated, or bribed in order to have one's way. He had been at it a long time, reorganizing industries, setting up and combining railway systems all over America, eliminating wherever he could what he regarded as the untidy evils of competition. But "The Hartford" was to be his last hurrah.

To understand the era of Morgan and the temper of those times when railroads were America's greatest business and railway kings the most powerful and famous (or infamous) men in the land, there is no better source than that great book on the political and social institutions of this country, *The American Commonwealth*, by James Bryce. This astute and sage Englishman knew America better than most

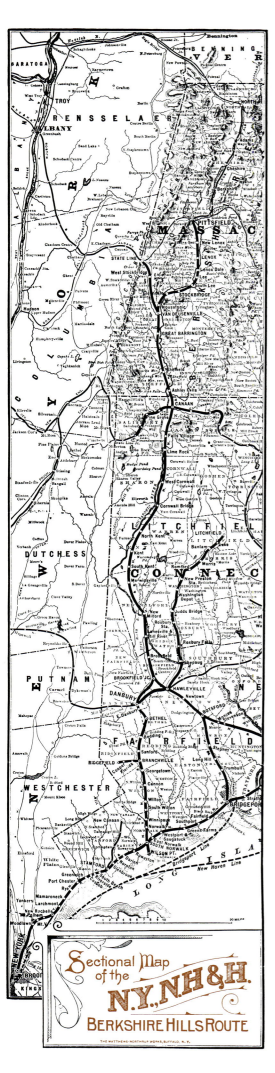

Americans. Listen to this extended passage, which modern-day railroad executives may read with nostalgia:

> War is the natural state of an American railway towards all other authorities and its own fellows. . . . The president of a great railroad needs gifts for strategical combinations scarcely inferior to those of a great general. . . . If his line extends into a new country, he must be quick to seize the best routes,—the best physically, because they will be cheaper to operate, the best in agricultural or mineral resources, because they will offer a greater prospect of traffic. He must so throw out his branches as not only to occupy promising tracts, but keep his competing enemies at a distance; he must annex small lines when he sees a good chance, damaging them first so as to get them cheaper; he must make a close alliance with at least one other great line, which completes his communications with the East or with the farther West, and be prepared to join this ally in a conflict with some threatening competitor. He must know the Governors and watch the legislatures of the States through which his line runs; must have adroit agents at the State capitals, well supplied with the sinews of war, ready to "see" leading legislators and to defeat any legislative attacks that may be made by blackmailers or the tools of rival presidents. And all the while he must not only keep his eye upon

Even in a remote spot like Merwinsville, Connecticut, the traveller could choose from a variety of New Haven trains. In this pre-World

the markets of New York, prepared for the onslaught which may be made upon his own stock by some other railroad or by speculators desiring to make a profit as "bears," and maintaining friendly relations with the capitalists whose help he will need when he brings out a new loan, but must supervise the whole administrative system of the railroad—its stations, permanent way, locomotives, rolling stock, engineering shops, freight and passenger rates. . . .

These railway kings are among the greatest men, perhaps I may say are the greatest men, in America. They have wealth, else they could not hold the position. They have fame, for every one has heard of their achievements; every newspaper chronicles their movements. They have power, more power—that is, more opportunity of making their personal will prevail—than perhaps any one in political life, except the President and the Speaker, who after all hold theirs only for four years and two years, while the railroad monarch may keep his for life. . . . I do not think that the ruling magnates are themselves generally disliked. On the contrary, they receive that tribute of admiration which the American gladly pays to whoever has done best what every one desires to do.[1]

War I scene, a brisk business is being performed. The map on the opposite page locates the town above New Milford; schedules are at right.

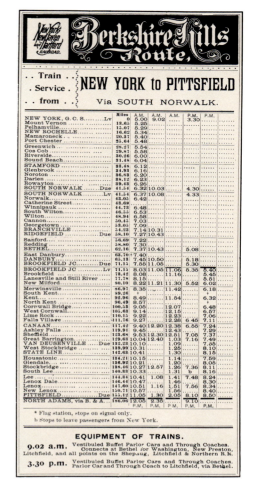

Berkshire Hills Route

Train Service from NEW YORK to PITTSFIELD Via SOUTH NORWALK.

Station	Miles	A.M.	A.M.			P.M.	P.M.
NEW YORK, G.C.S. Lv	0	5.00	9.02			3.30	
Mount Vernon	13.65	5.25					
Pelhamville	15.07	5.29					
NEW ROCHELLE	16.62	5.34					
Mamaroneck	20.37	5.40					
Port Chester	25.64	5.48					
Greenwich	28.27	5.54					
Cos Cob	29.57	5.58					
Riverside	30.26	6.00					
Sound Beach	31.48	6.04					
STAMFORD	33.48	6.12					
Glenbrook	34.93	6.16					
Noroton	36.83	6.20					
Darien	38.12	6.23					
Rowayton	39.43	6.26					
SOUTH NORWALK Due	41.54	6.32	10.03			4.30	
SOUTH NORWALK Lv	41.54	6.37	10.08			4.33	
Norwalk	42.05	6.42					
Catherine Street	43.69						
Winnipauk	45.18	6.48					
South Wilton	46.55	6.53					
Wilton	48.94	6.58					
Cannon	50.61	7.03					
Georgetown	53.05	7.09					
BRANCHVILLE	54.22	7.14	10.31				
RIDGEFIELD D	58.10	7.27	10.43				
Sanford	56.69	7.22					
Redding	58.80	7.30					
BETHEL	62.16	7.37	10.43			5.08	
East Danbury	63.70	7.40					
DANBURY	65.13	7.45	10.50			5.18	
BROOKFIELD JC. Due	71.13	7.55	11.05			5.30	
BROOKFIELD JC. Lv	71.15	8.03	11.05	11.05		5.35	5.40
Brookfield	78.42	8.08		11.16			5.45
Lanesville and Still River	77.78	8.15					5.51
New Milford	80.10	8.22	11.21	11.30		5.52	6.02
Merwinsville	86.97	8.35		11.42			6.18
South Kent	89.26	†					
Kent	92.96	8.49		11.54			6.32
North Kent	96.49	8.57					†
Cornwall Bridge	100.53	9.05		12.07			6.48
West Cornwall	105.62	9.14		12.15			6.57
Lime Rock	110.15	9.22		12.23			7.06
Falls Village	111.74	9.27		12.28		6.45	7.11
CANAAN	117.42	9.40	12.20	12.38		6.55	7.24
Ashley Falls	119.91	9.45		12.43			7.29
Sheffield	123.05	9.53	12.30	12.51		7.05	7.37
Great Barrington	129.63	10.04	12.40	1.03		7.16	7.49
VAN DEUSENVILLE Due	132.23	10.10		1.09			7.55
West Stockbridge	139.99	10.31		1.25			8.10
STATE LINE	142.63	10.41		1.30			8.15
Housatonic	134.25	10.15		1.14			7.59
Glendale	136.92	10.21		1.20			8.05
Stockbridge	138.46	10.27	12.57	1.26		7.36	8.11
South Lee	140.83	10.33		1.31		b	8.16
Lee	144.84	10.41	1.08	1.41		7.48	8.24
Lenox Dale	146.41	10.47		1.46			8.30
Lenox	147.60	10.51	1.16	1.51		7.56	8.34
New Lenox	150.71	10.57		1.56			8.40
PITTSFIELD Due	155.12	11.05	1.30	2.05		8.10	8.50
NORTH ADAMS, via B. & A.	186.06	12.05	2.35			9.10	
		P.M.	P.M.	P.M.		P.M.	

* Flag station, stops on signal only.
b Stops to leave passengers from New York.

EQUIPMENT OF TRAINS.

9.02 a.m. Vestibuled Buffet Parlor Cars and Through Coaches. Connects at Bethel for Washington, New Preston, Litchfield, and all points on the Shepaug, Litchfield & Northern R.R.

3.30 p.m. Vestibuled Buffet Parlor Cars and Through Coaches. Parlor Car and Through Coach to Litchfield, via Bethel.

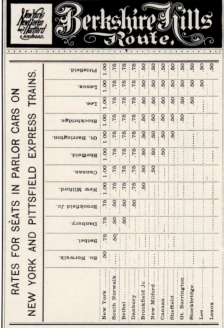

Berkshire Hills Route

RATES FOR SEATS IN PARLOR CARS ON NEW YORK AND PITTSFIELD EXPRESS TRAINS.

	Pittsfield	Lenox	Lee	Stockbridge	Gt. Barrington	Sheffield	Canaan	New Milford	Brookfield Jc.	Danbury	Bethel	So. Norwalk
New York	1.00	1.00	1.00	1.00	1.00	.75	.75	.75	.75	.50	.50	.50
South Norwalk	1.00	1.00	1.00	1.00	.75	.75	.75	.75	.50	.50	.50	
Bethel	1.00	1.00	1.00	.75	.75	.75	.75	.50	.50	.50		
Danbury	1.00	1.00	.75	.75	.75	.75	.50	.50	.50			
Brookfield Jc.	.75	.75	.75	.75	.75	.50	.50	.50				
New Milford	1.00	1.00	.75	.75	.75	.50	.50					
Canaan	.75	.75	.50	.50	.50	.50						
Sheffield	.50	.50	.50	.50	.50							
Gt. Barrington	.50	.50	.50	.50								
Stockbridge	.50	.50	.50									
Lee	.50	.50										
Lenox	.50											

RESERVATIONS IN PARLOR CARS.

For reservations in Parlor Cars address Parlor and Sleeping Car Agent, Grand Central Station, New York, or by Telephone, Call No. 968-38.

Reservations will be booked three days in advance, and reservations the tickets for which have not been purchased ten minutes before leaving time of train will be cancelled.

The time schedules shown in this folder give the time at which trains may be expected to arrive at and depart from the several stations, but their arrival or departure at the times stated is not guaranteed, nor does the Company hold itself responsible for any delay or any consequences arising therefrom.

The time of connecting roads is shown only for the convenience of the public. This Company will not be responsible for errors or changes that may occur.

A.F. Bishop was a pioneer railroad photographer hailing from New Haven, Connecticut. Naturally trains of the New Haven were ideal subjects. Engine No. 5, built by Danforth & Cook in 1865 and having driving wheels 69 inches high, runs a consist by Lenox Street in Fair Haven. The co-subject at right may be his wife, girlfriend, or model. But more important was the fact this was a typical New Haven Railroad train when the company first got going. Compare her size and elegance to one of the last New Haven steam-hauled passenger trains shown on the opposite page, bottom.

The fine sketch below, like those on pages 211 and 212, comes from The Railroad Book, written and illustrated by the painstakingly accurate artist, E. Boyd Smith (1860-1943), a longtime resident of Wilton, Connecticut.

Train ferries like the one above shuttled railway cars and engines across wide rivers and bays until mighty bridges were built.

The early masters of the New Haven Railroad were not, in fact, quite the harsh warriors described by Lord Bryce. Nevertheless, they were aggressive and clever. The first was William D. Bishop of Bridgeport, the persuasive and well-connected president of the busy New York & New Haven Railroad, and son of Alfred Bishop, the railroad contractor. We have seen that as early as 1870 the son sought a consolidation of his line with the rich Hartford & New Haven Railroad. Bishop sat in the legislature, and when the time came he carefully guided the touchy merger bill through a political maze.

In the hot legislative debates over the merger, critics repeatedly claimed that a monopoly was being formed with its own rules of rate setting. So fierce was the battle that the state representative from Enfield, while denigrating parts of the bill in a speech, literally collapsed on the legislative floor at the old State House in Hartford and had to be carried away, clasping his heart and gasping in anguish. Unmoved, proponents of the consolidation merely reassured all that they had no desire to make the company any larger. Their favorite retort: "We do not desire to consolidate with any other competing road." This total untruth rather sets the tone for all that followed.

On August 6, 1872, the New York, New Haven & Hartford Railroad Company was created; Bishop became its first president. At once a double-track railroad route was formed from Springfield, Massachusetts, south to Hartford and New Haven, then west along the lower Connecticut shore line to Bridgeport, Stamford, Greenwich, and Woodlawn, New York. A perpetual easement allowed Connecticut trains then to enter upon tracks of the New York & Harlem to reach New York City. Of no little importance was the transferable lease Bishop's predecessor road conveniently carried on the Shore Line Railway that ran from New Haven to New London. It was quietly advanced funds for a substantial rebuilding—a portent of things to come when the firm would strike out for Boston.

Succeeding Bishop as master was George Watrous, a prominent New Haven attorney, Yale alumnus, railroad director, and the legal brain behind the consolidation bill. Under Watrous the company prospered to such a point that its revenues nearly tripled those of the state. He cultivated widespread support and gladly placed free railroad passes in the hands of those who could advance his endeavors. He once said, "I want those people who have got the power to apply the knife to my throat to feel kindly towards me."[2] The Consolidated earned more money moving passengers than freight. It conveniently set its own rates and schedules, and paid handsome 10 percent dividends. It was in Watrous's time that the New York, New

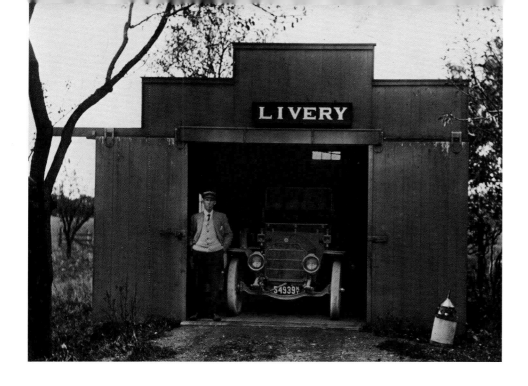

This somewhat comic photograph, place unknown, reveals the future. In 1910, everyone underestimated what the auto would do to the railroads, the cities, and to America, even though the iron horse was improving steadily. It doomed trolleys, too.

New Haven engine No. 1404 resumes her pace to Boston, having just crossed the Thames at New London. The big Gold Star Memorial bridge looms above. Heavyweight Pullmans and classic "American Flyer" coaches are part of this post-war train, representing the railroad's finest hour with steam passenger service. This engine, technically an I-5 Hudson (a 4-6-4), could haul a fifteen-car train along the Shore Line at 80 m.p.h.

Haven & Hartford gathered in its Air Line Route, the Canal Line, and its Valley Division. (Their stories have been told in previous chapters.) Amazingly, only muffled outcries arose as the Consolidated continued to expand.

From its earliest years the New York, New Haven & Hartford either acquired valuable additions on its own initiative or seized them to thwart competitor invasion.

COLLECTION OF THOMAS McNAMARA/KENT COCHRANE PHOTOGRAPH

A BUSY PLACE IN PUTNAM, CONN.

PUBL. BY JEWELER SHAW, PUTNAM, CONN.

Though passenger trains produced enormous revenues for the New Haven, the company also entertained a huge freight business as well. Take for instance all this activity at the mill town of Putnam at the turn of the century. The yards are jammed with freight cars. The manufacturing interests in the area filled the cars; local trains brought them to the yards; switchers zigzagged over the maze of tracks and made up trains; through trains dropped off or picked up cars; and, finally, trains were dispatched. Thirty trains a day were common.

COLLECTION OF ALICE A. RAMSDELL

Inside the busy mail car men sort and bag . .

Under the invader category were many proposed parallel roads that the Consolidated began addressing in the 1870s. At best they were "paper" projects, conceived to compete with lines of the Consolidated and break up the growing monopoly (See map in Appendix). Extensive press coverage and propaganda surrounded each one of these dreams. Some were surveyed, graded, even partially built, but none were completed in Connecticut, thanks either to political blockades or public nonsupport. Forgotten now are such schemes as the New York & Connecticut Air Line, the Hartford & Harlem, and the New York & Boston Inland railroads. But in their day each made the Consolidated shudder.

The company's greatest nineteenth-century president was Charles Peter Clark, the New Hampshire native and Dartmouth graduate who succeeded Watrous in 1887. We met him in Chapter Eleven as president of the rival New York & New England Railroad. When not vigorously campaigning for harmony and consolidation between the two big roads, Clark was undertaking such dramatic improvements to the Consolidated as four-tracking its main line between New Haven and New York, integrating electric block signals, funding electric traction projects, eliminating grade crossings, and making a public hit by reducing most passenger train fares. His philosophy? It was best communicated in the Consolidated Annual Report of 1887, in which he stated that "Your Board proposes to so manage your affairs that competition will never come."

Clark completed by acquisition the basic New Haven Railroad system in Connecticut, including the take-overs of the Naugatuck, Stonington, and Housatonic railroads, plus the huge New York & New England (as described in previous chapters). By also acquiring the Old Colony system of lines in southeastern Massachusetts and Rhode Island, he achieved for the Consolidated a formal entrance into Boston proper, a monopoly of railroad operations in "Little Rhody," plus control of the New Bedford and Fall River steamboat lines. The latter joined the Norwich and Stonington line fleets in giving the New Haven control of almost all Long Island Sound steamboating. To Clark also went the credit for opening the immense and much needed South Station terminal in downtown Boston. His record as a leader was an enviable one and his list of successes never endangered the Consolidated's treasury. Stockholders were duly grateful.

Obtaining these new additions did require huge amounts of money, stock swaps, and the proper legislative approvals. A $35,000,000 security issue was floated, and Connecticut lawmakers finally permitted the Consolidated to hold stock of other railroads—essentially creating a holding company.[4] In the early 1890s, authorized stock capitalization grew to the unheard amount of $100,000,000. (It was not all issued, of course, but ready if needed.) The Company now operated more than five hundred miles of lines, took in slightly more than $100,000,000 in revenues annually, and paid 10 percent dividends. Four thousand employees were needed to run Clark's corporation; twelve million people rode the line in a year. Coal and lumber were the biggest freight manifests moved over the Consolidated network. The combined roster of engines, cars, and other rolling stock numbered almost six thousand pieces, something like three times the equipment with which Amtrak today serves all of America.

During the Clark tenure J. Pierpont Morgan and William D. Rockefeller, brother of John, the dime-giver, joined the Consolidated's board of directors. This was a plain sign that New York money was more than casually interested in the prospering line. Nearly twenty other men of considerable business and financial fame filled the directorate (See Appendix), in what soon became a most exclusive club. Clark staffed only the finest legal and operating men, among them Vice Presidents John M. Hall and Charles S. Mellen. Both would become future presidents. After the New York & New England lease was written in 1898, the Consolidated completed railroad coverage of Connecticut by obtaining the little Shepaug, Litchfield & Northern, and the Middletown, Meriden & Waterbury railroads. It extended the Norwich & Worcester main line south from Allyn's Point (Gales Ferry) to Groton. In 1899 a weary C. P. Clark resigned the presidency and was succeeded by Vice President Hall, a Yale graduate, Willimantic attorney, and later state justice. Improvements and maintenance slowed. The Hall tenure was a quiet one—he did not rock the boat—and his legal expertise and political connections at first proved useful to the Morgan group which now was dictating corporate policy. But the golden age was ending.

It was Morgan, obsessed with the possibilities of having his Consolidated control all modes of transportation in New England, and finding Hall too mild and cautious, who chose as the next president his carefully trained adjutant, Charles Sanger Mellen. Mellen genuinely thought as Morgan did, and the two collaborated on plans, beginning in 1903 when Mellen was transferred from his presidential position on the Northern Pacific Railroad to the same spot on the Consolidated. Mellen recalled:

> I suppose that there is more or less prejudice against me because I wear the Morgan collar, but I am proud of it. When I was on the Northern Pacific Railroad I frequently had many differences of opinion with J. Pierpont Morgan, but I was informed by mutual friends that old man Morgan was camping on my trail. At one of the Northern Pacific directors' meetings, Mr. Morgan made a side remark to the effect that I could kick up more damn trouble than any man he knew of. I knew then that there was trouble brewing, and I went straight to Morgan's New York City office. He received me in his usual cold, austere, autocratic manner. I told him certain things he did not know, and we left each other with a better understanding of each other's position. It wasn't long after this that I was told by Mr. Morgan that he wanted me to be President of the New York, New Haven and Hartford Railroad.[5]

Mellen, the expansionist and unifier, knew what he thought needed to be done in his New England homeland. In his mind there existed too many railroad companies in such a compact geographical area. The region was ripe for consolidation, and soon. Reared in Concord, New Hampshire, Mellen never attended college but had eagerly and patiently trained in the hard school of northern New England railroading. He possessed analytical abilities, and a keenness for mathematics, finding it easy to recall mountains of numbers and facts. On top of that he exhibited oratorical skills that could be variously dry, devastating or Homeric. After cutting his teeth on

Almost every freight train had a home-on-wheels.

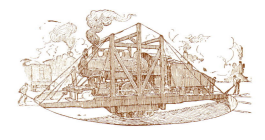

This turntable was operated by muscle power.

Side-dump cars really helped do a job.

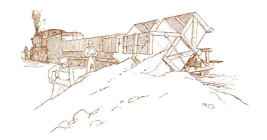

212

[ABOVE] People make a railroad go, too. The men gathered here are part of yard switching crews. An official, likely the yardmaster, stands on the ladder. The ornate New Haven script on the box car was applied to countless cars and engines.

213

several clerical and superintendency positions, he had been promoted to management and then helped reshape the railroad map of New Hampshire. In 1888 he went west to serve as purchasing agent of the Union Pacific, and four years later returned as general manager of the fast-crumbling New York & New England Railroad. His not inconsiderable assignment was to effect a reorganization and restore solvency. Mellen attacked the work in earnest and was soon achieving such rapid results that even his great competitor, the Consolidated, had to take note. President C. P. Clark informed his New Haven board that Mellen's progress was so intense and complete that, if they did not attempt to hire him away, "Mellen and the New York & New England will get us."[7]

Clark made an offer, and Mellen jumped horses in midstream to join the New Haven as a vice president. This brought him under the eye of Morgan, but his aggressive and outspoken manner annoyed Clark and caused conflict with the conservative Connecticut board. It should be remembered that Morgan and other New Yorkers were still not in the majority. Morgan, aware of the rift, nevertheless saw great potential in the man and subsequently offered him the presidential job out on the Northern Pacific Railroad, a new Morgan toy. A gruff telephone call confirmed the offer and acceptance:

Morgan: Is that you, Mr. Mellen?
 Mellen: Yes.
Morgan: Anybody hear what we say?
 Mellen: No.
Morgan: Will you take the Northern Pacific?
 Mellen: Yes.
Morgan: Will you leave it all to me?
 Mellen: Yes.
Morgan: Good-bye.[8]

By that piece of head-hunting Morgan hired an up-and-coming executive who, with surgical skill, ultimately reorganized the valuable but bankrupt property.

Eugene V. Debs had been secretary of the Brotherhood of Locomotive Firemen but it was not militant enough for him. He formed the short-lived American Railway Union and led it into the violent and disastrous Pullman strike of 1894. Subsequently he was five times Socialist candidate for president. Here he is spellbinding a sea of Connecticut derbys sometime in 1912.
BROWN BROTHERS

A great many people, of both sexes, were required to clean and provision the New Haven's passenger cars, especially in the days of steam. Nothing was overlooked.
R & LHS

214

With walking stick and cigar, the greatest of all American bankers, J. Pierpont Morgan, leaves his office. It bothered the master to have people stare at his unsightly nose.

Northern Pacific stock, depressed at $17 a share, grew handsomely to $130 within six years; net revenues jumped by a whopping 228 percent. Mellen's accomplishments drew attention in national railroad circles. He rubbed elbows with celebrities and important business figures of the West, and loved it. He made friends with at least one New York politician whose ranch was nearby. Theodore Roosevelt would later consult this rising railroad executive and crib from the polished Mellen speeches. Less-distinguished folk also enjoyed the Mellen friendship, including "Diamond Jim" Brady, the extravagant railway equipment salesman and beau of Lillian Russell who enjoyed favoring Mrs. Mellen with occasional pieces of precious jewelry.

215

Justifying railroad consolidation in New England was a topic dear to Mellen, and one about which he could speak convincingly. He knew intimately the strengths and weaknesses of every line. He knew too of their reliance upon the various trunk railroads that brought traffic to and from the western markets of America. Mellen felt unification could provide many benefits to both shipper and traveller; efficiency and economy would become watchwords. For instance, if the New England lines united they could purchase expensive materials and supplies in volume at large savings. Yards, facilities, and ships would be reduced to a minimum for maximum productivity. Redundant lines would be eliminated, while favorable rates would prevail on highly utilized routes. Further, New England would speak with one voice to the outside trunk lines, and this would mean competitive, uniform rate structures. And, where virtually dozens of conflicting arrival and departure times and missed traffic exchanges occurred, there would be the promise of an orderly blending of schedules among the different lines.

Mellen's monopolistic ideas certainly had logic and appeal, but how a railroad master and his board would achieve such a model environment, and especially at what cost, was a matter for conjecture. About this time Americans in general were looking with distaste upon "the trusts," that is, big businesses—especially the railroad business. Scandals had overwhelmed many western railroads. The age of the robber baron was not over. Many felt that Washington should be doing more to stop violators, even though the Interstate Commerce and Sherman Anti-Trust acts were on the federal books.

Charles Sanger Mellen

WHITE HOUSE,
  WASHINGTON.
  Personal.

                                 February 10, 1904.

My dear Mr. Mellen:

      It seems to me that in your speech at Hartford on January

21st, a copy of which Garfield has given me, you stated the

case as to the proper attitude of corporations and their mana-

gers better than I have known it elsewhere to be stated. I

intend to crib from your address for my message to Congress

next year.

      With high regard,

            Sincerely yours,

                  Theodore Roosevelt

Mr. C. S. Mellen,
     President, N.Y.,N.H.& H.R.R.,
          New Haven, Conn.

William Rockefeller

The New York, New Haven & Hartford distinguished itself in a number of electrification projects, the greatest being the four-track electrification program between New Haven and New York. Steam engines formerly working the line were photographed (below), stored at Bridgeport.

COLLECTION OF THOMAS McNAMARA

Because ex-President Hall had limited plant improvements, Mellen arrived fresh from his Northern Pacific triumphs to discover that the New Haven Railroad was in need of much physical attention. "I came to the New Haven with the idea that I was going to operate a railroad. I find that I have got to build one instead." [9] And over the next six years Mellen proceeded to modernize the line. His work in Connecticut included rebuilding the Cedar Hill (New Haven) and Waterbury yard complexes; double tracking the Naugatuck Division; building a new passenger depot at Danbury; inaugurating a huge new yard and engine facilities at Midway (Groton);

217

The enormous, $27,000,000 Hell Gate Bridge, begun in Mellen years with the Pennsylvania Railroad, opened in 1917. It allowed New Haven trains to enter Pennsylvania Station and go on to southern destinations. Amtrak uses it today. [BELOW] The New Haven also tried electrified third rail operations from Hartford to Bristol and Berlin, where this car-set sits. They resemble oversize open trolley cars, and did a rather similar local business. People and livestock, though, strayed on the "live" third rail; experiments ended.

installing new drawbridges with electric operation at Cos Cob, Devon, Westport, and Old Saybrook; upgrading the vital freight line from Devon to the Poughkeepsie Bridge and Maybrook, New York; reworking the track layout at Hawleyville to ease grades; electrifying the popular New Canaan Branch; and initiating an electrification project from New Haven west to New York. The latter received nationwide recognition and was a tremendous credit to Mellen's engineering department. The cost of all these improvements? Nearly $116,000,000.[10] Accompanying these expensive achievements were Morgan and Mellen's controversial acquisitions of other railroads, trolleys, and steamboat lines. Financial justification could be made for most of the physical improvements; however, the treasury would reel while try-

ing to underwrite the acquisition strategy, largely inspired by Morgan but dutifully carried out by a subservient Mellen.

Morgan's first directive to President Mellen was to get the Consolidated linked with the coal-hauling railroads emanating from Pennsylvania. The most northeasterly point of the coal lines terminated in the vicinity of Campbell Hall and Maybrook, New York. To reach them Mellen obtained a stock control of the Central New England Railway; its main line ran west from Hartford to New York via Tariffville, Winsted, and Canaan, and eventually crossed the Hudson River by a high bridge at Poughkeepsie. This coup took Mellen a mere sixty days to achieve and something over $5,000,000 in securities. Interestingly enough, Mellen had advocated this acquisition long ago when he served under President Clark. Yet Clark, and Hall, deferred action. In Mellen's surviving correspondence is a letter to Hall underscoring his view:

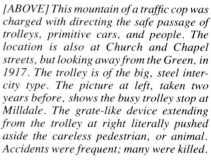

[ABOVE] This mountain of a traffic cop was charged with directing the safe passage of trolleys, primitive cars, and people. The location is also at Church and Chapel streets, but looking away from the Green, in 1917. The trolley is of the big, steel intercity type. The picture at left, taken two years before, shows the busy trolley stop at Milldale. The grate-like device extending from the trolley at right literally pushed aside the careless pedestrian, or animal. Accidents were frequent; many were killed.

NEW HAVEN COLONY HISTORICAL SOCIETY

220

During the Mellen administration, the New Haven decided to allow street cars to operate on certain steam railroad tracks, by merely installing an overhead trolley wire. The subject of this two-page spread is the section between Taftville ("Taft's") and Central Village via Plainfield. In the picture at right, a train from Providence halts at Plainfield, while the trolley from Central Village comes to her station stop. Later, this southbound car will go down to Taft's, whereupon a crew member will throw the switch allowing the car to leave the old Norwich & Worcester main line, then proceed down the "real" trolley track to Franklin Square in Norwich. The panoramic photograph below shows an idyllic Quinebaug River, Taft's station with the steam railroad track in front, and the trolley track in foreground. But the careful observer will note in the very right immediate foreground is the quaint trolley line that ran from Norwich to Willimantic, by way of Taftville and Baltic. It did not use any steam railroad track. The New Haven ran the combination service because it tapped dense population areas (at times!) and the trolley was cheaper to run than a steam train with cars.

BOTH: COLLECTION OF OLIVER JENSEN

Is it wise, when you know so much depends upon the maintenance of your monopoly, not to take in what you know you must eventually have when the opportunity offers; even at a moderate advance over and above what you estimate the value of such an acquisition to be at the time?[11]

With the Central New England controlled, the Consolidated then snapped up the New York, Ontario & Western, which extended the New Haven tentacles all the way to Lake Ontario and down into the anthracite region of Pennsylvania. The ore, mineral, and coal markets were the impetus as well as the passenger attractions of

the Catskills and Lake Oneida. Much later Morgan would delicately relieve the New York Central of its one-half controlling interest in the Rutland Railroad in Vermont, and that meant a Canadian connection as well.

Although the trolley car might seem for the present generation an article for museums—if it has seen one at all—it was, at the opening of the twentieth century, a serious competitor to railroads across America. The trolley has a unique chapter in our nation's transportation history. It arrived after the steam train and lasted until America became hopelessly infatuated with the automobile. Trolley lines were fairly cheap to construct, their cars were generally well equipped and a lot cleaner than steam trains, and service was more frequent and convenient. More than one stopped for a straw hat that blew off a passenger's head. Soon many city and rural lines began linking up. Connecticut was heavily stricken with "trolley fever" and many competed with services offered by the Consolidated. In the nighttime, trolleys even carried freight to the doors of businessmen, and this was another steam-railroad loss. At one brief time, about 1922, there were sixteen hundred miles of electric railways in the state to about one thousand of steam roads.

Previously, under presidents Clark and Hall, the New Haven Railroad had acquired some trolley companies and even undertook several trolley line experiments. Mellen, however, insisted that all lines in the Consolidated's territory must be controlled. And most of them were. They were acquired during the years 1904-1907 at the fantastic cost of nearly $92,000,000[12]—in bonds, of course, not in cash. A good many of them were superfluous or in poor financial shape; most waited for the Consolidated to show an interest, whereupon price tags were quickly jacked up. Indeed, the sellers were fortunate to get out when they did, for the trolley era was short-lived; most of the electric lines coasted to financial ruin. Through a New Haven Railroad subsidiary—the Consolidated Railway Company—nearly all trol-

A lonely trolley car edges past Lily Pond in Jewett City en route (on New Haven steam railroad) between Taft's and Central Village. The railroad installed similar operations on its Berlin to Middletown line; Middletown-Cromwell; and East Hartford to Vernon, Rockville and Melrose. All used six-hundred-volt, direct current. Trolley poles and wires were installed, except that the stretch Burnside-Vernon had catenary.

222

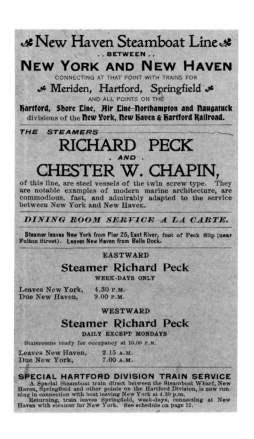

without legislative approval.) Overall, the Mellen plan to buy trolley companies *ad infinitum* proved a financial disaster. The companies never made the return anticipated, and the bond interest on them was crippling.

While Mellen was busy buying trolleys, Morgan mesmerized the board into purchasing a bevy of steamboat companies. Just as the modern generation may not fully appreciate trolley mania, it may also not grasp the immense—often romantic—popularity that the great palace steamboats enjoyed from the Civil War era up to the Great Depression. Service was year-round, and the vessels boasted all the latest amenities, including sumptuous staterooms, a fine table, and roving orchestras. Most navigated through the scenic and sheltered waters of Long Island Sound. For some travellers a trip was relief from stifling city air. Supplementing passenger revenues earned by the boats were those generated from transporting freight, of which a major item was cotton, to feed the hungry New England textile mills. Overall, steamboat firms generally provided a reasonable return to investors, and the Consolidated was definitely an investor.

Perceptive President Clark had previously secured the Stonington and Norwich lines of steamboats along with those of the famous Fall River Line and the local boats for New York City which sailed from New Haven and Bridgeport. Morgan's maritime endeavors had already organized the big International Mercantile Marine Trust, and he found it easy work to pick up for the railroad the Narragansett Bay Line; the New London Steamboat Company that served Block Island and proper Watch Hill; the Joy Line out of Providence; the Hartford & New York Transportation Company, which worked the Connecticut River; the Maine Steamship Company; the lines serving Martha's Vineyard and Nantucket; plus others. Complex and secret accounting procedures shielded the public from knowing the real steamboat portfolio of the railroad. None were bargains, and with the expensive trolley purchases they sent the railroad's funded debt to new heights. For the steamboat adventures the railroad organized the New England Navigation Company as the catch-all subsidiary.* Later the trolley subsidiary operated the boats and, still later, the New England Steamship Company was formed for the same ostensible purpose. Whatever Morgan wanted he got, so Mellen said:

> I took orders from J. Pierpont Morgan. I did as I was told, and when Morgan, who always sat at my left hand in the meetings of the Board, desired the approval of his directors, he got it, and don't you think he didn't! When he wanted their negative vote he got that just as quick![13]

Because so many valuable company records have vanished—conveniently or not—and the leading figures of the day are long dead, many details of the Morgan-Mellen regime will never be fully known or documented. Perhaps there are still some who like things that way. We do know that Morgan and Mellen attempted a transportation monopoly of New England and came very close to achieving it. One barometer of how the corporation grew is the figure of stock capitalization. Stock could be advantageously exchanged to purchase assets. Within Mellen's brief decade it soared by $324,000,000. That is what it took to underwrite the physical improvements and acquisitions. In an Interstate Commerce Commission report many years later it would be stated that about $200,000,000 of that figure was "invested in enterprises and corporations not directly involved in transportation operations."[14] For sure this included superfluous trolley and steamboat companies, investments in other railroads not needed, real estate, and gas and power utilities, not to mention payoffs and bribes. Those were the big-ticket items. At the other end of the spectrum were lesser spoils such as Pavilion Park at Savin Rock in New Haven and shellfish beds near Niantic, Connecticut. At one point Morgan insisted that the railroad attempt to buy the Cape Cod Canal.[15]

*First known as the Colonial Commercial Company. Organized at New London, Connecticut, in 1903; name changed in 1904. Among its charter clauses was the amazing right to purchase, hold, and sell stocks and other securities of any kind of corporation it desired.

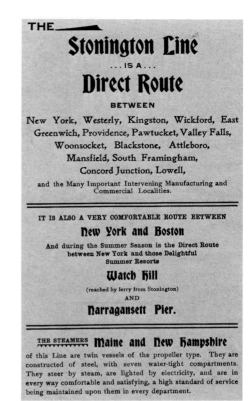

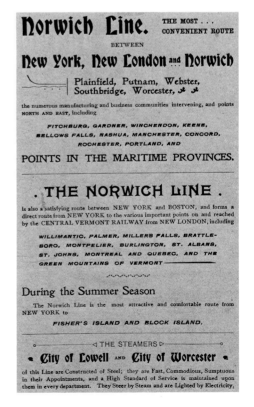

The · Hartford Courant

Fair today and probably to-morrow.
(Weather Report on Page 3.)

PRICE 3 CENTS.

Established 1764. VOL. (DAILY EDITION) LXXVII.   HARTFORD, CONN., WEDNESDAY MORNING, SEPTEMBER 3, 1913.—22 PAGES.

21 Dead, 50 Injured in Wreck Near North Haven When Engineer of White Mountain Train Runs by Signal in Fog and Smashes Two Wooden Pullmans of Bar Harbor Express.

Bodies Hurled Into Nearby Melon Patch

SCENE HEARTRENDING

One Woman's Body On Top of Locomotive

TWO BOY CAMPERS DEAD

Jewelry and Money Hurled About Tracks

VICTIMS IN NIGHT CLOTHES.

Locomotive of the White Mountain train and third coach of the Bar Harbor express, in which boy campers were. The wreckage in the foreground is all that is left of the two wooden Pullmans that were smashed like eggshells.

"Banjo" Signals Are Blamed For The Wreck

SYSTEM CONDEMNED

Meriden Physician Tells a Graphic Story

50,000 SEE THE RUINS

Wreckage Burned — Orders To Stop It

STATEMENT BY ELLIOTT.

COLLECTION OF CONNECTICUT HISTORICAL SOCIETY/ROBERT J. BITONDI PHOTOGRAPH

Occasionally one of Mellen's own board members would question the cost and integrity of a purchase, but, to be sure, not often. What gave rise to one such inquiry were the scandalous costs surrounding the $36,000,000 investment in the now-defunct New York, Westchester & Boston, a commuter railroad in and near Westchester County and New York City. It boasted only eighteen miles of track, making it one of the most expensive to build in America. A curious director, William Skinner, a prominent silk manufacturer of Holyoke, Massachusetts, confronted Mellen early on about the exorbitant costs. "Holy Caesarea Philippi, what in the world have you been doing with eleven million dollars?" A cool and collected Mellen offered to appoint Mr. Skinner a committee of one to get some answers. But a smarter Mr. Skinner replied, "Not on your life."[16]

If the Westchester investment had no apparent justification, then nothing redeeming could be found in the Morgan and Mellen take-over of the Boston & Maine Railroad, the Consolidated's sprawling sister to the north which, at that hour, legally controlled the Maine Central. The Boston & Maine was as dear to Bay State men as the Consolidated was to Nutmeggers. Mellen secretly bought large blocks of Boston & Maine stock through the New England Navigation Company, hoping a majority would complete a railroad monopoly in five of the six New England states. (The Smith family of St. Albans, Vermont, controlled the Central Vermont Railroad kingdom.) Massachusetts ultimately declared Mellen's Boston & Maine trolley purchases illegal, even though some legislators felt his plans had merit. Mellen fumed, and still countered that his Connecticut charter allowed him all the purchase authority he needed. Moreover, he insisted that if the New Haven Railroad did not buy the Boston & Maine stock some foreign interest would—like Vanderbilt's New York Central system or railway magnate Edward H. Harriman. The Consolidated later agreed to divest itself of the Boston & Maine stock, but how Mellen did it was characteristic: he hired a "front man" to buy it, hold it, then secretly sell it back. Of course for these favors the front man would receive a small fee.

The ghastly New Haven Railroad train wreck at North Haven in 1913. Twenty-one people perished in this rear-end collision. Public outcry reverberated throughout the state, but this was only one of a long series of disasters that struck the New Haven during this era. Many blamed Charles Mellen, because he slashed preventive maintenance budgets and failed to install safer signal systems. Mellen was indicted for manslaughter, but was never tried. The smashed locomotive at the top of the page is the same one, seen on page 1 of the Courant. *It was attached to the* White Mountain Express.

226

Mexican Situation
Nearing a Crisis

The Hartford Courant

Rain, Maybe Snow
Today, Fair
Tomorrow
(Weather Report on Page 8.)

Established 1764. VOL. (DAILY EDITION) LXXVII.   HARTFORD, CONN., MONDAY MORNING, NOVEMBER 10, 1913—20 PAGES.   PRICE 3 CENTS.

NO VERDICT GIVEN
IN TRIAL AT KIEV

$1,600,000 IS GIVEN
TO COLUMBIA IN YEAR
President Butler Speaks of Changing
Relation of Public To University.
New York, Nov. —

STORM HITS EAST
WITH GREAT FOR

ITALIAN CITIES HONOR
TARS OF AMERICAN NAVY

CLIMAX IS NEAR

MAKE NOVEL PLANS FOR
RED CROSS SEAL SALE

WHAT MELLEN DID;
WHAT HE OPPOSED

"New Haven" Road
Management Scored by
Commerce Commission

The Hartford Courant

Probably Showers To-
day; Fair Tomorrow
(Weather Report on Page 8.)

PRICE 3 CENTS.

Established 1764. VOL. (DAILY EDITION) LXXVIII.   HARTFORD, CONN., TUESDAY MORNING, JULY 14, 1914.—20 PAGES.

700 MARINES FOR SERVICE IN HAITI AND SAN DOMINGO

Force Ordered Assembled At Guantanamo Ready to Protect U. S. Interests.

MANY APPEALS FROM AMERICANS

Proximity a Warning to Rebel Leaders—Machias With Other Ships.

Washington, July 13.—Seven hundred marines today were ordered assembled at Guantanamo, Cuba, to be held in readiness for service in population-torn Haiti and San Domingo.

Croker Coming to Renew Fight Against Murphy

New York, July 13.—Richard Croker will return to New York from his island next September and seek to oust Charles F. Murphy from the leadership of Tammany Hall, according to Harry W. Walker, confident of Croker, who reached here today from a visit to Croker in Ireland.

CLEAR UP MOHAWK MURDER MYSTERY

Police Expect to Make Arrest In Twenty-Four Hours—Suspect a Russian.

WOMAN PROBABLY SLAIN IN SHACK

Murderer Had Boarded With Victim and Husband In New York.

United States Army Officers And General Staff Officers Of C. N. G. Who Take Care Of State's Soldiers At Camp Baldwin

Standing—Major George A. Cornell, Quartermaster Corps, C. N. G.; Major Joseph H. Townsend, Chief Surgeon,— ; (5) Captain E. S. Harishorn, Third Infantry, U. S. A., camp adjutant; Major Edward S. Shut-tleworth, U. S. A., Inspector-Instructor of C. N. G.; Second Lieutenant James A. Crawford, C. A. C., U. S. A. Camp Quartermaster.

Sitting—Major Michael J. Wise, Assistant Chief Quartermaster, C. N. G.; Colonel A. P. Buffington, Third Infantry, C. N. G.; Major Thomas J. Kirkpatrick, Medical Corps, U. S. A.; Colonel Calvin D. Cowles, U. S. A. retired; Major Thomas J. Kirkpatrick, Medical Corps, U. S. A.

(Special Dispatch From Camp Baldwin On Page 12.)

Management of "New Haven" Under Mellen Scored As "Reckless and Profligate"—Directors Blamed

Summary of Alleged "New Haven" Losses

(From the Interstate Commerce Commission's Report On Its Investigation of Affairs of the New York, New Haven & Hartford Railroad.)

Interstate Commerce Commission Says the Railroad Has Lost From $65,000,000 to $90,000,000 Through "Maladministration" of Which Possibly $8,000,000 May Be Recovered By Proper Action—Says Directors Knew They Were "Perfecting An Illegal Combine."

Ten Held In $133,000 Bail for Kidnapping

New York, July 13.—Nine men and a woman, all foreigners, were held today under bail totaling $133,000 on alleged kidnappers of eight-years-old Frank Longo, son of a prosperous baker.

UNDUE INFLUENCE NOT PROVEN IN HILLS WILL CASE

Error Found By Supreme Court and Judgment Is Reversed.

NEW TRIAL ORDERED IN NOTED CONTEST

Testimony Showed That Will Probated Expressed Hartford Woman's Wishes.

PLAN TRANSFER OF AUTHORITY AT MEXICO CITY

Brazilian Minister Says Huerta Is Expected to Resign Today Or Tomorrow.

CARRANZA WON'T DEAL WITH CARBAJAL

Guarantees Protection If Huerta Forces Surrender Unconditionally.

WHAT MELLEN DID; WHAT HE OPPOSED

Tells "Boston Sunday Post" Reporter All About His Ten Years At the Head of the "New Haven" Transportation System—Morgan's Dominance of Its Financial Policy.

PULLING THE WIRES FROM SPIDER'S WEB

Pays Respects to Boston Capitalists Who Desire to "Help" "New Haven" By Taking Over Its Trolley Lines, Which They Want Because There Is Money In Them—Opposed Owning Steamships.

Charles S. Mellen, former president of the New York, New Haven & Hartford Railroad Company, tells the people through the "Boston Sunday Post" of his stewardship while at the head of this great transportation system.

THIS MORNING'S NEWS.

GENERAL

"New Haven" management scored by commerce commission—civil and criminal action recommended—1.
Huerta ready to transfer power—1.
700 Marines for Haiti service—1.
Boyle Day without disorder—16.
Foreman before grand jury today—17.
Coal roads indicted—1.
Steamship arrivals—17.

STATE

Lawyer Alling's car hits man—8.
Bartenders fines in Meriden—13.
Brison circus bars constables—13.
Moorhouse selectmen act—13.
Rock rolls on Torrington man—13.

CITY

Err in Hills will case—1.
E. O. Whitmore's title matter—5.
Bulldog for past six months—5.

THE SUNDAY "COURANT"

Such a man was found in the person of John L. Billard, an unknown coal merchant of Meriden, Connecticut, supposedly worth about $30,000. However, Billard conveniently came up with nearly $14,000,000 to buy the stock, thanks to "special" loans that were arranged for by Morgan at the National City Bank. When the Consolidated, by another maneuver, legally established its control of the Boston & Maine the services of Billard were terminated. Billard had bought the stock at $125 a share. He sold it back for $150 and realized, without investing a nickel, nearly $3,000,000 in profit. The transaction was more profitable than selling coal. Mellen, on the Interstate Commerce Commission witness stand years later, provided a cameo of Billard to Commissioner Folk, its chief counsel.

> Folk: What kind of man is Mr. Billard; is he a good business man or otherwise?
> Mellen: Well . . . if I am trading with him, I don't look in any other direction than right in his eyes.[17]

Mellen coaxed Billard to reduce his heavy "fee" for the services rendered, but the thrifty Yankee said nothing doing, or he would talk.

Fortunately, there were some people who felt that the real financial condition of the great New York, New Haven & Hartford was being seriously strained. Many of the deceptions were slowly brought to light by a probing Boston attorney and later U.S. Supreme Court justice, Louis D. Brandeis. In 1907, through intensive private investigation at his own cost, he produced a significant report in which he stated his opinion that the New Haven Railroad was on the brink of financial disaster. Brandeis said that its securities were overvalued, losing money, and that many of the investments made by Morgan and Mellen were illegal. The report rocked New England—and the nation at large—and the sensational allegations were hastily denied by the Consolidated management. Mellen immediately called in his political friends, along with newspaper and magazine publishers. A positive publicity campaign went forward. Mellen, who still clung to a friendship with Theodore Roosevelt, immediately launched letters to the president advising him that accusations of late upon his road were unfounded and that in no way was he conducting monopolistic or fraudulent activities.[18]

The 1907 panic had a chilling effect on New England business. Mellen was concerned with how the economic conditions of the time might affect the railroad's dividend. Maintaining the huge Consolidated system was frightfully expensive. The cost of debt to buy lines was escalating, and huge investments were still required for the new Grand Central Station and Hell Gate Bridge projects in New York City. Unfortunately, many of the Morgan-Mellen acquisitions were not bringing the expected returns and were showing steady losses. In 1911 traffic conditions

Louis Brandeis unequivocally believed that the "real" financial posture of the New York, New Haven & Hartford had to be told. He personally undertook the challenge and devoted years to investigative research. Brandeis produced a seventy-seven-page report that underscored his belief that, if not corrected, financial ruin lay ahead for the big concern. From thereon, he became a great enemy of the New Haven, though the latter could never fully silence the man's annoying activities.

Until 1899, there existed no railway track on the east side of the Thames from Gales Ferry south to Groton. The New Haven completed the link, and the first train "up" from Groton is seen here, in star-spangled dress, easing past Laurel Hill in Norwich. Yale-Harvard Regatta trains used the link.

again slumped, and New Haven stock, just as Brandeis had predicted, began to slip. Economies became the order of the day, and an "axe" committee was formed to trim waste and reduce the workforce.

In their glory days Morgan and Mellen commanded the New Haven, Boston & Maine, Maine Central, trolley companies, steamboat firms, and a host of other businesses. Revenues flowed in, money flowed out, and lots of securities were issued to buy things. Many historians believe that Morgan even used the New Haven treasury to bail out friends, banks, and corporations that were in trouble during the 1907 panic—some so important that their demise might have triggered wide business failure, in domino-effect fashion, all across America. The railroad and Morgan's banking house maintained "special accounts" for these delicate situations. Sometimes the transactions involved innocent players. An obscure Yankee handyman named Grover Richards was one day taken to New York and ushered inside the impressive Bank of Manhattan. He met James Hemingway, a New Haven Railroad director. Richards was handed a check—made out to him—for $3,000,000. He was then asked to endorse it over, on the spot, to a Hartford attorney, who then took it to a teller's window. Then, two more large checks were made out to Richards for endorsement. Richards asked no questions, and the next day he went back home with a new suit of clothes for his troubles.[19] Morgan's power could never be underestimated, according to Mellen, who said later:

> I regarded Mr. Morgan, and I think we all did on the board, as a man of very great experience, very great energy, very great capacity, and we naturally looked up to him. There were strong men on the New Haven board other than Mr. Morgan. But I do not recall anything where Mr. Morgan was determined, emphatic, insistent, in which he did not have his own way.[20]

With most of New England railroading controlled, it seemed incredible to Morgan and Mellen that a Canadian firm would decide in 1910 to invade the sacrosanct empire of the New Haven. Yet one did. The aggressive president of the British-owned Grand Trunk Railroad of Canada, Charles Melville Hays, wanted very much a deep, ice-free port in southern New England. Already in his combine was the Central Vermont Railway. One of its leased lines sliced down through Massachusetts to reach New London, Connecticut, where boats and docks already existed. But Hays sensed a far greater potential in the highly industrial city of Providence, Rhode Island. The plan was simple: the "Southern New England Railroad" would be built from Palmer, Massachusetts (a Central Vermont junction point) to Providence by way of Southbridge and Webster, Massachusetts. Canadian roads offered lower rates than American trunk lines on western traffic, and that fact alone delighted Providence businessmen, who had always been at the mercy of the New Haven rate structure. An anxious city of Providence spent $500,000 on a Grand Trunk route through the city to her docks. The Central Vermont boatline ordered two new steamships for the new service between Providence and New York City from Harlan & Hollingsworth in Delaware.

Mellen did everything possible to delay the Southern New England, and even bought farm properties which lay in the railroad's path. but tragedy occurred. While returning in 1912 from a London directors meeting, Hays perished in the sinking of the *Titanic*. Edson J. Chamberlin succeeded Hays; he was a boyhood friend of Mellen. Despite tremendous business and public pressure to finish the line, Chamberlin abandoned it—deep cuts, embankments, and trestle work are still visible today along the route. The track was almost all laid but never used. Mellen was ultimately indicted for violating the Sherman Anti-Trust Act. Had this line been built Connecticut railroad history would likely have been very different, for the Southern New England had eventually planned to construct branches off its new line into eastern Connecticut, competition for the Consolidated.

The Grand Trunk affair did not sit well with the press and public, nor did the announcement that the Interstate Commerce Commission would start investigating complaints from shippers. An irrepressible Louis Brandeis still buzzed away, waging his one-man campaign against the monopoly. Had the New York, New Haven & Hartford grown beyond practical limits? Many said yes.

While the Interstate Commerce Commission inquiry went forward there unfolded a different kind of chapter that tragically involved human life. The loss of business, starting in 1911, had forced Mellen to cut manpower and make reductions in maintenance. These factors contributed to a long series of often deadly train wrecks. One after another they occurred—at Fairfield, Greens Farms, Bridgeport, Middletown, Stonington, Berlin, Westport, and Putnam. Rather than accept some company blame, Mellen attributed almost every wreck or derailment to employee carelessness. Two hundred employees were killed in 1913 and three thousand injured; more than thirty-seven passengers lost their lives in the same year and more than eight hundred received injuries. Soon Mellen himself was indicted for manslaughter.

As 1913 wore on the New Haven colossus finally began to crack. The Boston & Maine skipped its dividend, followed by the startling news that the New Haven's would be dropped from 8 down to 6 percent. Suddenly, Morgan died in Rome, having only recently appeared before the noted Pujo Congressional Committee to deny he ran America's "Money Trust." The loss of the great financier was a blow to the New Haven board and to his adjutant, Mellen. Now pushing for the latter's exit was Morgan's son, who upon the father's demise became the new board chairman. Mellen reluctantly resigned.

> Morgan, Jr. wanted to know if I would step down and out if I was given a retainer of $30,000 a year for five years. I told him in the presence of the other directors that I was not a charity patient, that I was not asking and would receive no gratuities from their hands unless I could give value received.[21]

There was no question Mellen had gravely erred in judgement and instigated many of the company's problems. He and Morgan together were, as one observer put it, like "dynamite and gunpowder in spending money."[22] On the day of Mellen's resignation the Interstate Commerce Commission handed down its first report. A perturbed United States Senate then ordered a more comprehensive investigation to determine if parties connected with the frauds were punishable. To avoid prosecution, Mellen agreed to give testimony, and his disclosures ultimately implicated national and political figures of the day. Said Mellen: "I told young Morgan that I intended to stand out on the firing line and take all that was coming to the road. I

Description of Equipment — Entire Line.

Item.	Number on June 30, 1909.	Number added during year.	Number retired during year.	Number on June 30, 1910.	No. fitted with train brake.	No. fitted with automatic coupler.
Locomotives — owned or leased:						
Passenger,	533	1	6	528	528	528
Freight,	453	......	2	451	451	451
Switching,	199	......	2	197	197	197
Electric,	43	1	......	44	44	44
Total Locomotives in Service,	1,228	2	10	1,220	1,220	1,220
Less Locomotives Leased,	159	......	5	154	154	154
Total Locomotives owned,	1,069	2	5	1,066	1,066	1,066
Cars Owned or Leased:						
In Passenger Service —						
First class cars,	1,490	2	25	1,467	1,467	1,467
Combination cars,	294	......	3	291	291	291
Dining cars,	19	......	......	19	19	19
Parlor cars,	163	......	4	159	159	159
Sleeping cars,	49	......	......	49	49	49
Baggage, Express, and Postal cars,	322	5	4	323	323	323
Other cars in Passenger Service,	100	114	......	214	214	214
Total,	2,437	121	36	2,522	2,522	2,522
In Freight Service —						
Box cars,	21,120	2,419	511	23,028	23,028	23,028
Flat cars,	2,684	......	119	2,565	2,565	2,565
Stock cars,	1	......	......	1	1	1
Coal cars,	9,878	1	257	9,622	9,622	9,622
Refrigerator cars,	501	......	1	500	500	500
Total,	34,184	2,420	888	35,716	35,716	35,716
In Company's Service —						
Officers' and pay cars,	15	1	......	16	16	16
Gravel cars,	305	......	2	303	298	303
Derrick cars,	48	2	......	50	37	50
Caboose cars,	335	20	15	340	336	340
Other road cars,	510	13	53	470	434	470
Total,	1,213	36	70	1,179	1,121	1,179
Total Cars in Service,	37,834	2,577	994	39,417	39,359	39,417
Less Cars Leased,	1,345	......	208	1,137	......	......
Total Cars Owned,	36,489	2,577	786	38,280	......	......

How much equipment did it take to run Mr. Morgan's New Haven? The interesting tally here was printed in the 1910 Annual Report of the Connecticut railroad commissioners.

continued to do so, notwithstanding that all sorts of threats, even against my life, had been made."[23] He explained to the tribunal that it was really Morgan who had masterminded most of the controversial plans. Mellen was never found guilty, nor did he profit illegally from any of the schemes. Unscathed, Mellen then left his Whitney Avenue home in New Haven for his farm in Stockbridge, Massachusetts. He died in 1927 at Concord, New Hampshire, the town he was raised in and where his railroad career began as a lowly clerk on the Northern Railroad at $25 a month. Historians have had trouble judging him personally, but it is certain that with his departure a deplorable chapter in American railroad history came to a close.

Chapter Twelve Footnotes

1 James Bryce, *The American Commonwealth* (New York: MacMillan & Company, 1891), 530.

2 *Hartford Courant*, 8 June 1869, 3 March 1880.

3 *Annual Report of the New York, New Haven & Hartford Railroad Company for the Year 1887* (New York: William W. Clark, 1887), 11.

4 Connecticut General Assembly, Special Acts and Resolutions of the State of Connecticut, Volume IX, X, pp. 1298-1300.

5 Arthur Pound and Samuel T. Moore, eds., *More They Told Barron* (New York: Harper & Brothers, 1931), 153.

6 H. H. Metcalf, "Charles Sanger Mellen," *Granite Monthly,* XLV (January 1913): 5.

7 Burton C. Hendrick, "Bottling Up New England," *McClure's Magazine,* XXXIX (September 1912): 548.

8 Oliver Jensen, *American Heritage History of Railroads In America* (New York: American Heritage Publishing Company, Inc., 1975), 148.

9 Hendrick, "Bottling Up New England," 550.

10 Sylvester Baxter, "Remaking a Railway, A Study In Efficiency," *The Outlook,* XCIII (December 25, 1909), passim.

11 Charles S. Mellen to John M. Hall, May 30, 1900, Mellen Papers, New Hampshire Historical Society, Concord, New Hampshire.

12 John L. Weller, *The New Haven Railroad—Its Rise and Fall* (New York: Hastings House, Publishers, 1969), 68.

13 Pound and Moore, eds., *More They Told Barron,* 168.

14 *Investigation of the New York, New Haven & Hartford Railroad Company,* 220 I.C.C. 505 and 506 (1937)

15 Pound and Moore, eds., *More They Told Barron,* 165.

16 Henry Lee Staples and Alpheus Thomas Mason, *The Fall Of A Railroad Empire*, (Syracuse, NY: Syracuse University Press, 1947), 167.

17 U.S. Senate, 63rd Cong., 2nd sess., 1914, S. Doc. 543, I: 1099.

18 Charles S. Mellen to President Theodore Roosevelt, n.d., Mellen Papers, New Hampshire Historical Society, Concord, New Hampshire.

19 Jensen, *Railroads In America,* 155.

20 Ibid., 155.

21 Pound and Moore, eds., *More They Told Barron,* 167.

22 Ibid., 169.

23 Ibid., 167.

EAMES VACUUM BRAKE CO.,
115 BROADWAY,
NEW YORK.

With exhaust smoke and steam beautifully suspended in mid-air, a local New Haven Railroad freight departs Highland Junction in Waterbury for Bristol, winter, 1948. The picture was taken by the late Kent Cochrane.

COLLECTION OF THOMAS McNAMARA

Chapter Thirteen

Halcyon Days on the New Haven

Besides the railroad of mergers, investigations, and boardroom battles there is always a very different one. This is the working, physical railroad, constantly in motion, managed and supplied and maintained by thousands of people, the railroad of passengers and shippers. What the financiers toyed with was a vital public institution, a useful and bustling presence in the Connecticut of only a few decades ago, when city stations and country depots alike hummed with activity. Passenger trains brought in mail, express parcels, and newspapers in great bundles; freight cars were dropped off or picked up at hundreds of now-vanished sidings, carrying lumber and feed and coal and produce, not to mention the manufactured goods that nowadays speed by on the interstate highways. Most of those who used and worked for the institution knew little and cared less about the faraway railroad of finance and scandal.

Despite its troubles, the New York, New Haven & Hartford Railroad in the period between the two world wars—the actual, physical organization—became a model of management and service. It was widely regarded as one of the best in the United States, especially from the passenger standpoint. Commuters on other lines regarded the crowds pouring off the New Haven with envy, and the intercity trains were frequent and famous. This is a time better recorded in photographs than any other before it, and we interrupt our main narrative here with a chapter which is really a picture album on how the New Haven operated and maintained itself in those halcyon, bygone days.

233

Just how comfortably one might travel in the first decade of this century is demonstrated in this sharp, clear photograph of the somewhat overblown interior of a Pullman chair car: all shining ornate fixtures, fancy curtains, upholstered wicker chairs. There are few such pictures surviving, but what rivets the eye here is the party of middle-aged but rather sporty gentlemen, the two little girls, the attending staff of three at the rear. The pencilled caption reads: "Special train: Hartford men on their way to see a gold mine." A gold mine? In these clothes? Who are they? Any reader who can identify any of these unsmiling voyagers is begged to send us the pertinent details.

[OVERLEAF FOLLOWING] This is Regatta Day at New London, in 1909. Excitement fills the air as the Yale-Harvard Boat Train prepares to leave. Alumni sport boaters; ladies and their escorts scurry aboard. The bleacher-like seats are filled and within minutes the train will head for Groton and up the Thames River bank to parallel the annual four-mile crew race. The photograph, by T.S. Bronson, marvellously captures the style and spirit of this famous New Haven Railroad train (Imagine maintaining a long string of special cars like this for use one or two days a year!— but those were spacious days.) Note the announcer with his megaphone, the balloon hawker, the newsboy, and the banner beneath the massive station canopy ("Restrooms for Ladies & Escorts on 2nd Floor of Station"). Oh, carpe diem!

235

Massive Cedar Hill freight yard at New Haven classified (that is, sorted out) cars for all destinations, "humping" them downhill from the high point in the foreground. Trains came and went, activity hummed around the clock, seven days a week. Huge engine facilities fed and cared for motive power, others for passenger equipment; only vestiges remain. In wartime [RIGHT] the New Haven sent state boys to Mexico, hauled heavy artillery, and carried the lion's share of all goods and people. In another war, it could not likely be done again. Too many tracks and facilities have been abandoned.

COLLECTION OF THOMAS McNAMARA/ KENT COCHRANE PHOTOGRAPH

Days of Steam

From the earliest beginnings, when wood was placed in the fireboxes piece by piece and light ahead was furnished at night by pushing a handcar with a little fire on it, there have been all manner of steam locomotives on Connecticut railroads. Here we present a mere sampling of those that hauled New Haven trains in their greatest days. As early as 1904, with that company near its largest extent, there were almost exactly one thousand locomotives in service, a few of them hand-me-downs but most bought by the New Haven for the many, varied purposes of a major system. This is not a technical book, and those who wish the intricate details of weight, stroke, valve gear and the like must look to engineering works, or to the members or journals of the New Haven Railroad Historical and Technical Association.

COLLECTION OF THOMAS McNAMARA/KENT COCHRANE PHOTOGRAPH

COLLECTION OF THOMAS McNAMARA/ KENT COCHRANE PHOTOGRAPH

Tank engine 2305 (0-6-0 wheel arrangement) carried its own water and was ideal for switching and yard work. To her right, and at work in 1947 in East Hartford, is 3433 which was an 0-8-0, good for yard and main line assignment. "Consolidation" class (2-8-0), like New Haven 153, is below.

COLLECTION OF CHARLES B. GUNN

Rail buffs line the turntable at Cedar Hill Yards in 1935. Interestingly, the engines are arranged almost in ascending order of power from left to right.

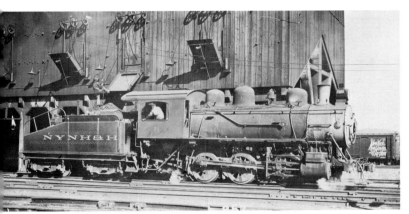

Unlike the 0-6-0 on the opposite page, 2426 boasted a slope-back tender. The fireman has just topped off with coal. This engine had cylinders 19" × 26" and driving wheels 51" high. A 2-6-0 is know as a "Mogul," and No. 276 at right was built by Baldwin in 1907. Driving wheels were 62" high.

The "Mikado" class of steam engine appeared around 1900 and some were sold to Japan, whence the nickname originated. The 2-8-2, with its wide firebox, was a highly successful freight engine. A smaller "Mike" runs today at the Valley line in Essex. She hauled freight and passenger trains.

242

The "Mountain" class of freight engine, a 4-8-2, had a huge boiler, a superheater to boost the temperature and energy of its steam, a mechanical stoker, and fine adhesion qualities. As its forward-moving plume of smoke reveals, the one above is backing down after giving a healthy push to an outbound freight at Airline Junction. [BELOW] The greatest passenger steam locomotive on the New Haven, the last model, was the streamlined, bullet-nosed I-5, built by Baldwin on 4-6-4 configuration. It weighed with tender 348 tons. No. 1407, received in 1937, is getting tender care at Cedar Hill; such sleek monsters pulled Shore Line trains at eighty miles per hour until replaced by diesels over thirty years ago. Not one survives in a museum.

The mammoth "Santa Fe" class with its ten drivers (2-10-2) was the biggest freight steam power ever to run on the New Haven. Built by the American Locomotive Works, it aimed at an extra high 77,800 pounds of tractive effort with a relatively low loading per axle over its many wheels. These muscular giants slugged it out over the Poughkeepsie Bridge route, hauling train after train to and from the other big New Haven yard at Maybrook, New York. With the exception of one pre-Civil War locomotive, the Daniel Nason, which state officials recently let get sold away to a railroad museum in St. Louis, Missouri, not one of the great New Haven—or even Connecticut—steam locomotives remains in existence to celebrate the railroads' role in building the state. (The half dozen steamers at the Valley Railroad in Essex were built for and collected from other states.) [BELOW] The scrap line at Readville, Massachusetts, was for years the elephant graveyard where New Haven locomotives awaited the torch. They were sold, by the pound, for scrap.

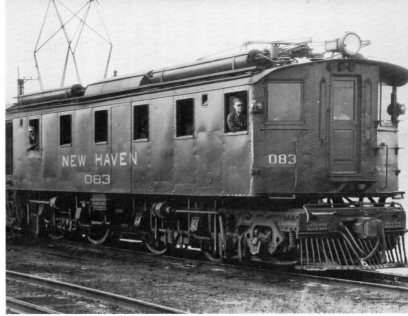

Electric engine No. 5, of the B-1 class, weighed fifty tons and was built by Baldwin-Westinghouse in 1924. She ran on six hundred volts of direct current, like a trolley (observe her trolley pole), and could haul freight on street-car tracks. The New Haven soon turned to the use of eleven thousand volts of alternating current, and bought "Cigar Box Motors" like 083 at right, an EF-1. You could team up as many as you needed.

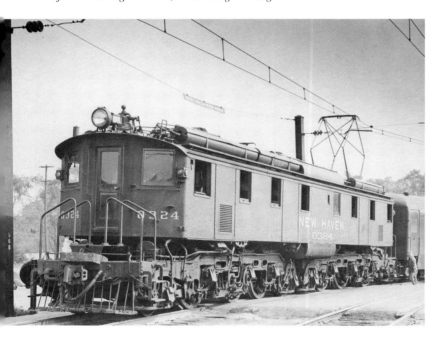

Electrics like No. 0324, of the powerful EP-2 series of the 1920s, with great blowers to dissipate the intense heat they generated at 1,680 horsepower, were familiar to generations of Fairfield County commuters. In the McGinnis days on the New Haven they burst out of their drab green into bright red, white and black, like No. 322 at right. EP-2s were 68½ feet long. [BELOW] The famous streamlined EP-5s began to arrive in 1954. "Jets" had four thousand horsepower and could work off both the pantograph overhead or a third-rail "shoe" as required in approaching New York.

Electric Power Appears

If electricity could move a street car, as was demonstrated in the late 1880s, it would move trains. Electric power was infinitely cleaner around cities, and essential in tunnels like that long one approaching down Park Avenue to Grand Central Terminal. The New Haven Road was an early experimenter in electric running, from New York to Stamford, and later on to New Haven. Its former four-track main line still carries electric-powered Amtrak and Metro North commuter trains.

The spotless, four-track main line, probably near Greens Farms, takes on EP-4 No. 0361, a thirty-six-hundred-horsepower workhorse from General Electric. These engines were known as the "Streamliners." The mixed bag of coaches characterized the declining New Haven of the 1950s and 1960s. [BELOW LEFT] The EF-3, similar in appearance to the EP-4, developed 4,860 horsepower and was used for freight. [BELOW RIGHT] Electric freight locomotive No. 304, Class EF-4, was purchased used from the Virginian Railway, a coal road. Lionel toy train company produced a replica of it.

246

Early diesel 0900 was built by Alco-General Electric and arrived in 1931; it had six hundred horsepower and no elegance. At right, No. 0906 was bigger and better. It appeared in 1936. Both were used as switchers, but never ran on main lines. The diesel drives a generator, which energizes a traction motor.

The engineer peers from the fireman's door on a pair of DL-9s built by Alco, the first road diesels. They arrived in 1941. The gearing allowed them to go as fast as eighty miles an hour. [BOTTOM LEFT] No. 0605 was an S-1, which came in 1944. [BOTTOM RIGHT] Little 0801, of forty-four tons and only 380 horsepower, got light duties. General Electric produced quantities of them. Many industrial plants spoke well of their versatility.

No. 644, an SW-2, could perform both yard and local freight train work; she was two-way radio equipped. General Motors' Electro Motive Division built her in 1956. [RIGHT] No. 560, built in 1952, pulled freight drags all around the state and was generally regarded as a real workhorse.

Stepping through Berlin in 1953 is high-nosed No. 790 with a passenger train. The twenty-five-hundred-horsepower engine, a "C-Liner," was built by Fairbanks Morse. [BELOW] Alco-built "FA" engines of 1947 worked in units; each added fifteen hundred horsepower.

The Diesel Takes Over

Dr. Rudolph Diesel, a French-born German engineer, devised the engine that bears his name in the 1890s; General Electric, by combining it with traction motors to create the diesel-electric, made it practical. It is three times more efficient with fuel than steam, starts quickly, and is cleaner and easier to maintain; it swept the great steam engines into the discard in a few decades, although not without tears in some quarters. Here is a sampling of diesels as they came to the New Haven.

248

A model LD-198 diesel, with sixteen hundred horsepower, appears below in a photograph by the builders, Fairbanks Morse. Such engines were used for both yard and road service, and were frequently coupled together.

These interior cab photographs contrast the task of the steam engineer below with that of the diesel engineer on the opposite page. The steam man has more valves, gauges and controls to cope with—mostly left-handed—and the place is hot, dirty and apt to fill up with smoke or steam. The diesel chap has fewer items to watch, and the work is a lot easier and cleaner. Old-time railroad work clothes and caps are disappearing among the new generation of diesel men. The fireman has very little to do, and in some parts of the country his hard job has simply ceased to exist.

BOTH, COLLECTION OF CHARLES B. GUNN

General Motors GP-9 units were fit for freight or passenger work; they arrived in late 1950s.

Alco workhorse 1408, an RS-11 built 1956, was one of fifteen. Its 1,800-horsepower engine could throw up a lot of smoke.

Railroad tracks crossing Asylum Street in Hartford, near station, were first at street level, but later raised when the current station was built. In the scene below, three forms of New Haven Railroad transportation are present: steam train on Asylum Street girder bridge, city trolley cars, and New England Transportation bus, which frequented light density areas too expensive to serve by passenger trains. The Hartford station is to be renovated.

Photographer Fielding L. Bowman of New Canaan journeyed, in 1951, to just over the state line to compose this New York scene. The place is Woodlawn Junction, where many New Haven Railroad trains enter tracks of the New York Central's Harlem Division. The Central's are used to reach Grand Central Terminal, an arrangement dating back to the early days of the New York & New Haven Railroad. Electric engine No. 307, with pantographs down and "trolley shoe" picking up D.C. voltage from the mini-third rail near the track, "flies" through the junction en route New Haven to Manhattan. Trains coming up from the Terminal use tracks at far right. The New York Central and the New Haven used different electric current and voltages; New Haven engines therefore had to be dual-equipped. Minimal train service goes forward in 1985. Trains now operate under the Metro North Railroad banner.

Aside from those-in-the-know, few people comprehend what it took to feed and care for a company like the New Haven. The next few pages remind us, thanks to a superb photograph scrapbook loaned to us by Lester Smith of Suffield. A member of his family, Charles Edward Smith, was a prominent New Haven Railroad executive.

In the Montowese area of the Cedar Hill yards stood mountains of "black diamonds." Mega-tons were always required in the days of steam. It came by the carloads, and was dumped or scooped into mini-mountains. The biggest consumers were locomotives, but rations were also sent to heat depots, shops, signal towers, bridge tenders, crossing-gate keepers, cabooses, etc. Imagine the costs today!

Having dried in the open air, seasoned railroad ties are bundled and set upon cars of electric tramway. In the next step (at bottom) ties are inserted into creosote treating cylinder. The heat lets the goo permeate every crack and crevice. After removal and drying, they are ready for installation. The bottom right scene gives some idea of the ordering scale, just for shovels. And shovels were used by firemen, track workers, laborers, maintenance people, etc.

Deft hands and a sharp pike maneuver slippery chunks of ice at a special plant in the Maybrook, New York, yards of the New Haven Railroad. The product was made at the lower level, whisked up to workmen by conveyor, and slid outdoors to hatch openings of "reefer" cars full of meat, or produce.

Vast parts inventories had to be maintained for cars and engines, all before the days of computers. At left is a selection of pipe fittings. Some items could be stored outside, such as heavy car couplers at right. Keeping track of what was on hand was the job for storekeepers.

Huge repair and rebuilding shops of the New Haven were situated in Readville, Massachusetts, outside Boston. Two important items kept here were steel wheels and wheel sets. Far lighter were cartons upon cartons of sanitary drinking cups and seen below in New Haven, Conn., storekeeping rooms.

Housewives (and husbands, too) may fret at the cost of new china, but imagine the cost of this purchase in order for dining cars to be properly furnished. And this was only three rows! Recently railway china has become an expensive, desirable collector's item. Many buy and trade at shows.

[BELOW] Putting aboard fresh dining car provisions was overseen by both the store-keeper and steward. Produce was super-fresh. Franklin Roosevelt once declared that dining car meals on crisp white linen were one of the great pleasures of life.

Not only were cartons of china required, but the dining car storehouse also supplied pots and pans for the kitchens, along with table and cooking utensils, glassware, coffee urns, condiment holders, and numerous other items. All this, so the scene below could take place in the dining car.

"There isn't a train I wouldn't take. No matter where it's going." So wrote Edna St. Vincent Millay. Relaxing in a parlor car like Wallingford, *above, and enjoying an unfolding panorama mesmerized more than one New Haven passenger. Today, the car is restored as above and in use on the Valley Railroad in Essex. The automobile or airplane seat cannot compare for comfort.*

Effective February 11, 1934

The New York, New Haven and Hartford RAILROAD CO.

Time Tables

Aristocrat of Trains
The Yankee Clipper

Form 200

The Merchants Limited was one of the star, extra-fare flyers of the late New Haven Railroad. In 1913, ten parlor cars and a diner made up the elite train, with not a lowly coach to be found. According to Arthur D. Dubin of Chicago, doyen of passenger train historians, "patronage was largely masculine. Ladies were rarely seen except in private staterooms." The Merchants' "Dollar Dinner" was equally legendary. A generous martini would cost only 20¢. Stock quotations were posted en route. The train's popularity suffered a little when, in 1930, the crack and sumptuous Yankee Clipper joined up on the New Haven's Shore Line Route. But in 1949, the grand dame was fitted anew with stainless-steel streamlining, and even a coach or two. Business jumped. The Merchants will be remembered by discriminating travellers as the last daily all-parlor-car train in the United States.

Chapter Fourteen

Decline And Fall

"It wasn't worth it."

—deathbed comment of Frederic C. Dumaine, Sr.

The death of J.P. Morgan the Elder* and the precipitous exit of Charles Mellen left the New York, New Haven & Hartford Railroad Company a very sick as well as leaderless corporation, and one that needed a massive and speedy injection of reform. The position vacated by Mellen packed every conceivable challenge and problem that any incoming executive could possibly encounter. Such was the job that fifty-three-year-old Howard Elliot faced in September 1913. In fact, his very first day had an incredibly tragic start when Elliot had to contend with one of the railroad's worst train wrecks: the fancy *Bar Harbour Express*, which had stopped in North Haven, Connecticut, was rear-ended by a speeding *White Mountain Express*, killing twenty-one people, including many children returning from summer camps, and injuring no fewer than fifty others. It was an inexcusable tragedy. On board one of the first trains able to get around the wreck site—standing on an open platform at the rear—was a stern and highly disturbed President Woodrow Wilson.

Elliot's appointment as chairman was arranged by Morgan the Younger, who brought the seasoned executive off of the Northern Pacific Railroad—ironically from the same job and line whence Mellen had come a decade before. Most of the Morgan cronies whom the Elder had appointed still sat around the board table, with the addition of Arthur Twining Hadley. Considered a railroad expert, Mr. Hadley was president of Yale, and his appointment by the young Morgan, was to create—supposedly—a new dimension of earnestness and probity in the boardroom. Elliot plowed into a work pile that included bad morale, a treasury fast running out of cash, and charges that were being handed down by the Interstate Commerce Commission and the Justice Department. In December 1913 the New Haven would pass its much-revered dividend for the first time in forty years.

The Wilson administration, working with Elliot and a conciliatory board, now ordered the resignation of Morgan the Younger and the Elder's old colleagues. In addition, and as a result of hearings and trials beginning in 1914 and lasting

*So inadequate have the terms "senior" and "junior" seemed for this austere and powerful father and son that many historians still fall back on labelling them, like the Catos and the Pitts, as "The Elder" and "The Younger." We follow the tradition.

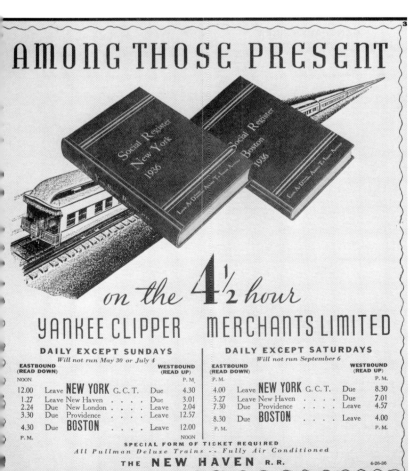

262

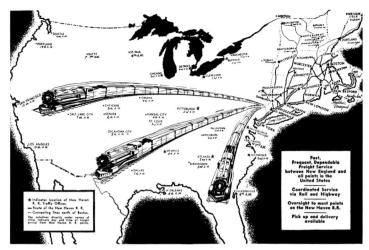

SOUTHERN NEW ENGLAND—*the logical location for America's postwar industry!*

Your plant location is only as good as its transportation facilities. And your transportation system, like a chain, is only as strong as its weakest link. The New Haven System—with its comprehensive network of track... and many freight gateways...insures a continual influx of raw materials... and a steady flow of manufactured products to the world's waiting markets.

The Industrial Development Department of the New Haven Railroad is thoroughly familiar with the real estate market throughout Southern New England and parts of New York State served by the New Haven Railroad. It is your most logical source of confidential information about factories and warehouses that will become available in the postwar period.

Correspondence is welcomed and will be kept in strict confidence. Contact or address any District Traffic Office listed on page 1 of this time table.

The postwar economy was booming along when this plea appeared in 1945. The New Haven's industrial department was eager to have new manufacturing plants locate along the rail route. Many actually did.

The New Haven Railroad was equally at home in moving vast amounts of freight, baggage and mail. The trio of 1948 scenes below attest to that: Engine No. 1337 steams north of Naugatuck for Waterbury with more baggage cars than coaches; parcels and baggage are readied for an incoming train in

OUR PLACE IN THE **AIR FUTURE** OF SOUTHERN NEW ENGLAND

Continually threatened by auto, truck and airplane competition, the New Haven responded with aplomb to the latter: it sought, as the advertisement says, to establish a "coordination of interests." The spirit was marvelously prophetic. In 1985, the major freight railroads of America were snapping up other transportation modes.

rural Pomfret; and Number 1305 eases out of Hartford for her Boston trek. The train has an equal number of coaches and baggage cars. Most of this valuable business succumbed to trucks.
[ALL] COLLECTION OF THOMAS McNAMARA/KENT COCHRANE PHOTOGRAPHS

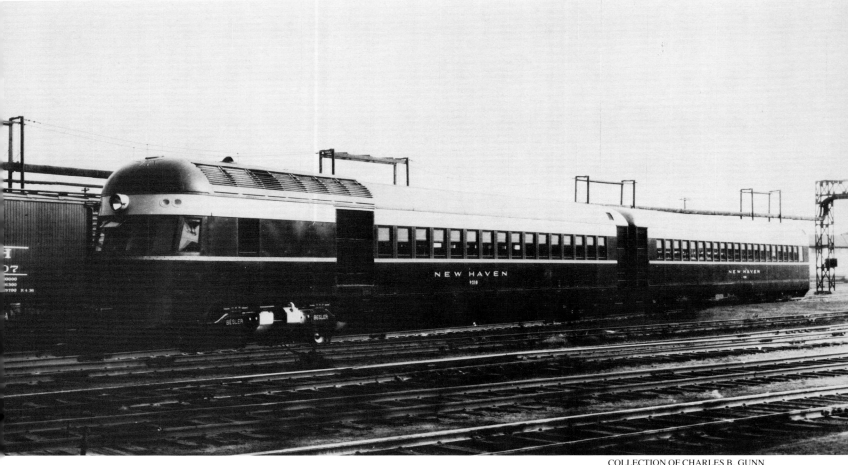

[ABOVE] America was being swept into streamlined trains in the 1930s; the New Haven got caught up in the fever, too. There arrived in 1936, The Blue Goose, built by Besler. The train consisted of two New Haven cars, rebuilt and streamlined, with a power plant that burned fuel oil and fired-up a steam engine. The paint scheme was royal blue up to the letterboard, which was finished in aluminum, while the roof was a darker shade of blue. Blue, deep-plush upholstered tubular seat frames gave patrons a comfortable ride. The Budd Company did the actual construction work. The Goose saw service on the Naugatuck Division.

[OPPOSITE PAGE] In 1935, the New Haven previewed train Comet, another bold approach to streamlining. Built by Goodyear Zeppelin Corporation in Akron, Ohio, the train was powered by Westinghouse diesel engines. Maximum speed was 110 miles per hour. Comet toured Connecticut but served Boston-Providence.

for some time afterwards, the railroad had to divest itself of certain holdings—all under the watchful eye of trustees. Criminal indictments were later obtained against many of the Morgan directors,—including banker George Baker; William Rockefeller; John L. Billard, the coal dealer from Meriden, Connecticut; Theodore Vail, president of American Telephone and Telegraph; Charles Brooker, president of the American Brass Company; Lewis Cass Ledyard, the cagey attorney of Morgan the Elder; and others. They were accused of violating the Sherman Anti-Trust Act and other infractions of law. All posted bail. The conspiracy trial lasted a full three months, Mellen himself taking the witness stand for thirty-one days. The jury ultimately came in with a split decision. Those who were found guilty were to be retried, but they never were. Suits for restitution, however, were brought by stockholders. One was aimed at Billard, who eventually surrendered about half of his $3,000,000 "commission." The Grand Trunk Railroad indictments against Mellen were dropped, as were the manslaughter suits growing out of the wrecks. Nothing was ever done to recover the scandalous losses associated with the New York, Westchester & Boston Railroad.

President Elliot helped secure a $45,000,000 loan from the federal government, but this proved to be just a drop in the bucket. In 1917 he returned to the Northern Pacific. Edward J. Pearson, a Cornell University engineering graduate with a fine reputation in western railroading, then came to the helm. A renaissance of sorts ensued. Shortly after his arrival America entered the first World War. The government now stepped in and took control of the nation's railroads; Pearson was named federal manager of the New Haven. Wartime traffic soared on the line, and Washington provided funds for much-needed supplies and equipment. When the road was returned to private operation in 1920, the line was badly worn, but it had performed a superb job in moving munitions, supplies, and troops.

265

The decade of the 1920s began slowly, but thanks to rate increases and a postwar economy zipping along in the "roaring twenties," the picture brightened, even though the automobile was making itself a strong competitor to the railroads. In 1925 the New Haven responded by organizing its own New England Transportation Company, whose buses replaced certain lightly patronized passenger trains while its fleet of motor trucks brought freight, mail and express from station freight houses to business doors. As the decade closed, Pearson even unveiled the railroad's most up-to-the minute development in passenger train luxury: the elegant *Yankee Clipper* and *The Senator*. Travel time between Boston and Manhattan was now cut to four hours and forty-five minutes, thanks to the new flyers. But looming on the track ahead was the Great Depression, which would slice New Haven Railroad revenues in half. Pearson died in office in 1928, and the task with all its new headaches fell into the lap of John J. Pelley, a former president of the Central of Georgia Railroad. Pelley lasted six years and miraculously kept the railroad from going under, thanks to efficient, cost-saving measures and a heavy dose of belt-tightening. Then Pelley left to become the first president of the new Association of American Railroads in Washington.

The New Haven board next called up its own vice president and controller, Howard S. Palmer, to be the new president. A succession of short-term loans kept the road going, but it must be remembered that because it had escaped a deserved bankruptcy in 1913 and 1914, the dwindling empire was still encumbered with the great debt that Morgan and Mellen created. Not even a generous $16,000,000 loan that Palmer got from the Reconstruction Finance Corporation could wipe the slate clean. In October 1935 the railroad finally went to the wall. The bankruptcy court appointed trustees, leaving the day-to-day activities to principal trustee Palmer. A twelve-year reorganization period followed.

Howard S. Palmer oversaw the New Haven Railroad's extended receivership. Inherited debt had forced the line into bankruptcy. The entire railroad was pared down, then overhauled thanks to loan programs.

Hurricane and Flood Strike the New Haven

When the great Hurricane of 1938 struck Connecticut, the New Haven's exposed Shore Line route took a heavy pounding, especially from New London eastward to Stonington. Train No. 14, The Bostonian, was fighting through wind and waves, at a crawl, on the causeway leading into Stonington, the storm rising steadily in fury. Engineer Harry Easton, realizing the cars would soon go over, had everyone aboard moved into the first coaches, uncoupled the rest of the train, and thus lightened, pulled safely ahead into Stonington.

Stonington was hard hit but New London was devastated by the 1938 storm, and its fatal tidal wave. Part of the city burned, and down at the railroad the New Haven had to contend with lightship tender Tulip, *which had slammed up on the Shore Line Route of tracks. Riggers, jacks, tow boats with lines, and high tides helped re-launch the vessel. The steamboat docks near the depot were also ravaged.*

Floods in Connecticut have also taken their tolls over the decades. In the spring of 1936, the Connecticut River rose very high, and this scene at Deep River was repeated up and down the river valley. The New Haven's Valley Division track is not to be seen. A boxcar, though, can be spotted just beyond the freight house. President Palmer's administration ably handled disaster.

268

With hands on the table, Frederick C. Dumaine poses with his board of directors shortly after his take-over of the New Haven. The Appendix of this book lists at least one slate of his colleagues and peers. Huge parcels of real estate were subsequently sold off for profit, but even so revenues began to slip in 1949. The late John L. Weller, noted New Haven historian, stated that "Dumaine conducted a reign of terror, dismissing or forcing to resign at least sixteen of the company's top executives. His rule was reported to be that anyone earning more than $10,000 per year should be eliminated." Later, about two thousand other employees were slashed from the payroll. Dumaine had actually proposed replacing the road's chief operating officer with, of all things, the company's chief storekeeper.

During this court-protected time, the New Haven Railroad suspended crippling interest payments. More than $300,000,000 was allocated to buy new locomotives and cars, and to modernize track, facilities, and structures. Bankruptcy proceedings forced the trustees to wipe out $200,000,000 dollars worth of stock. Crew strikes in 1937, despite sober warnings from the company to the union, shut down forever the last of the railroad's steamboat operations on Long Island Sound, which had started losing money in the Depression. The huge, comfortable boats were broken up. (One can only imagine the money they would be making in our own free-spending days!) The trolleys had long since left the fold of the New York, New Haven & Hartford, and had been abandoned except in New Haven, where they lingered through 1948. Palmer was allowed to dispose of many unprofitable properties and terminate several expensive leases. In 1947 a reorganized New York, New Haven & Hartford Railroad Company emerged from bankruptcy spic and span. A new morale prevailed; managers spoke with cautious optimism. Looking back, Palmer's work force had ably responded to two great floods in 1936, and a hurricane in 1938 that overwhelmed many parts of the still large system. A superb effort was made by the railroad in World War II. Palmer's engineering forces had successfully experimented with America's first piggyback operations (truck trailers riding on railroad flat cars) and had ushered in the era of diesel locomotives.

The big and optimistic 1947 annual report of the line described at length the excellent condition of the road. A freight rate increase had been granted, passenger fares were raised, and expenses, for the most part, were under control. But seven weeks after the report was released came the astounding news that a Massachusetts speculator and industrialist, Frederick C. Dumaine, had obtained working control of the

Although many were ordered in the previous Palmer administration, the New Haven received during the Dumaine period some of its long-awaited stainless-steel fleet of coaches, parlor cars, dining cars, and sleepers. The prototypes were the prewar "American Flyer" series cars—so called because a New Haven toy manufacturer by that name produced replicas. The new cars were handsome, shiny-sided, and equipped with better glass. They had fluorescent lighting, mechanical water coolers, and improved seats. Almost all had pneumatically operated doors, panoramic windows and smoking areas. The more elaborate cars were attached to the Merchants Limited, Yankee Clipper, Patriot, and Colonial. A few additions were purchased by the Dumaine administration, 1949-50.

railroad (through its preferred stock), along with one Patrick McGinnis. Critics were immediately suspicious as to what the eighty-two-year-old New Haven director Dumaine wanted other than personal gain. *Fortune* magazine would later describe the coup, and how Dumaine had previously profited at the expense of the Amoskeag Mills and the Waltham Watch Company[1]. The Dumaine gang came on board, ordered expenditures reduced, sold off real estate, and halted recently instituted policies of preventive maintenance. Of course, preferred stock dividends were always paid. When the economic recession of that period set in, and revenues began to slip, the Dumaine administration wantonly fired executives, rolled back

McGinnis was eager for streamlined trains. The Daniel Webster *[ABOVE] was the New Haven's version of* Train X *bought by the New York Central. It had Baldwin-Lima-Hamilton one-thousand horsepower engines on either end. It was painted gray and white; doors were orange. [BELOW] In 1957, the* John Quincy Adams *arrived. It was modeled on the Spanish Talgo articulated system.*

the work force, and slashed costs. Public distaste with late and shabby trains mounted in a hurry.[2] In 1951 Dumaine died and was replaced by F.C. "Buck" Dumaine, Jr. Though criticized for being too aggressive and impulsive, the son introduced several imaginative operations and performed much overdue maintenance.[3] Revenues on the road brightened as a result of rate increases. There were heavy freight movements owing to the Korean conflict. Dividends on preferred stock were ever-present, but the brief prosperity allowed for the purchase of newer equipment, cars, and engines. Even passenger train service was restored on certain lines (like the New London to Worcester segment) using novel, self-propelled pas-

Pat McGinnis alights from his Cadillac-on-railroad wheels.

BOTH: COLLECTION OF CHARLES B. GUNN

American Car & Foundry built three Talgo train sets; the cars were articulated. The experimental one above stands at Old Saybrook. McGinnis's fever for them likely sprung from this model. Below is Roger Williams, *a six-car train of modified Budd rail diesel cars.*

senger cars built by the Budd Company. But Patrick McGinnis, architect of the New Haven take-over with the elder Dumaine, was not in favor of these policies of the son. He opposed so much reinvestment of earnings in capital improvements. To McGinnis, dividends were more important: they kept stock unrealistically high, a practice very useful to traders and insiders.

A nasty proxy fight erupted in 1954. An exasperating, forty-one-hour stockholders' meeting finally revealed McGinnis as the winner; his group then named eleven of the twenty-one directors, and young Dumaine was ousted. McGinnis, something of a railroad reorganization expert, had previously conducted some financial antics with the Norfolk Southern (a southern railroad not to be confused with the modern Norfolk Southern) and the Central of Georgia Railroad. In the course of these adventures he generously awarded himself and certain friends extravagant salaries, bonuses, and excessive dividends. It didn't take the Interstate Commerce Commission long to find out what he was up to. Later he was indicted for violating the Clayton Act.[4] The hapless New Haven was his next target.

The McGinnis administration was vivid but brief. At the outset there was the bad hurricane in 1954, an economic recession the following year, and a severe flood in 1955. The business strategy of McGinnis was simple: slash maintenance, manipulate financial records, advertise that the New Haven would be "a railroad of tomorrow," and insure that preferred stock dividends would always be declared. As the

(Continued on Page 278)

[ABOVE] A glib tongue and plenty of press pictures characterized the McGinnis style. When not touting the "New Haven of Tomorrow" to a listening ear, he was on the property eager to be photographed.

ALL PICTURES THESE TWO PAGES: COLLECTION OF CHARLES B. GUNN

[RIGHT] McGinnis drives home the last spike that completed a welded rail program between Boston and New Haven. The occasion, in the early 1950s, took place at Branford, and when it was over he reached into his public relations bag and gave each attendee a gold painted spike as a commemorative. Chief engineer Peter Polson watches.

[ABOVE] Specimens from the Bronx Zoo ride with young passengers on McGinnis-inspired Zoo Trains. [BELOW] New Haven "snow train" time at Grand Central. The specials ran to the Housatonic and Berkshire hill towns of western New England.

It is not so many years since the New Haven road ran large crowds to winter sports. This is an ice-skating train, parked on a siding by a pond at South Kent for the day. Warm cars were handy for chilled skaters, and a dining car provided food and drink. The trains were well-patronized, but the automobile won out in the end.

COLLECTION OF ERIC F. BEERWALD

At West Cornwall, Connecticut, the station has just received a visit from a Budd Rail Diesel Car. In September 1966, the depot and grounds look quite respectable. Fifteen years later, after service abandonment, trees spring up from the ties. Fortunately, the Housatonic Railroad—a tourist operation—has now surfaced, and in 1985 all's well once again at scenic West Cornwall.

COLLECTION OF FIELDING L. BOWMAN

277

witty historian Peter Lyon, describes it, "the 'special situation' men moved in, licking their lips, and whetting their knives to strip the carcass. [McGinnis] . . . . . paid himself first fifty, then seventy-five thousand dollars a year; he went on the payrolls of subsidiary companies; he was also paid 'expenses' at the rate of forty thousand dollars a year. He maintained a suite of rooms in two different New York hotels simultaneously; the decoration of his executive offices in the Grand Central Terminal cost the company one hundred and twenty thousand dollars."[5] There was other folly as well: a typical McGinnis mistake was the purchase of three stream-lined, articulated train sets—a $5,000,000 purchase that would supposedly "revo-lutionize" passenger service. The problem was that none of the streamliners ever worked very well. One actually caught fire on its inaugural run. McGinnis made enemies by trying to charge Fairfield County commuters a monthly parking fee for the privilege of leaving their cars at stations. Frequently, he would be seen touring the railroad network, stopping here and there to urge employees to be thrifty with supplies and to cut back where possible on purchases. After such cost-saving lec-tures he would climb into his own company vehicle, a Cadillac motor car mounted on railroad wheels. Irate stockholders ousted McGinnis in 1956, and on the day he left he became president of the Boston & Maine Railroad. His activities there later sent him to the Federal penitentiary in Danbury, Connecticut.

George Alpert, a shrewd Boston attorney and former New Haven director, took on the presidency. Like others before him, he got off to a rocky start. Business

When a line is abandoned, a railroad com-pany will frequently reclaim valuable rails, reusable ties, and steel used on bridge work. That is precisely what is occurring in the scene below as New Haven workers per-form their tasks on the Housatonic River bridge near Sandy Hook. The Interstate Commerce Commission sanctioned the nine mile abandonment, between Southbury and Hawleyville, back in 1948. The line was part of the old New York & New England.

George Alpert

[BELOW] *The old and decrepit Central New England track in Collinsville, 1941; station is at left. Collinsville Branch of Canal Railroad used the bridges in back.*

slumped because of intense truck competition, severe weather plagued the line, the steel industry went on strike in 1956, strikes erupted on the neighboring Long Island and Pennsylvania railroads, and the big Connecticut Turnpike was built, paralleling the railroad's main line. The great project generated a steady flow of highway construction supplies by rail, but, when it was finished, the long concrete alley siphoned off valuable commuter and freight revenues. Alpert could also not meet the spiraling tax bills. As Lyon informs us, "Alpert's function with the New Haven was that of undertaker, and for the job he was paid sixty thousand a year under a contract that expired June 1, 1961. His contract also provided that he was to receive twenty-five thousand a year for the subsequent twelve years as severance pay or as deferred compensation."[6] When the federal and state governments refused further loans, Alpert had no choice but to allow the line to slip again into bankruptcy—this time on July 7, 1961. The great ship began to founder.

The bankruptcy court named to the railroad several trustees to manage its crumbling affairs. As it turned out their primary task was to insert the unwanted, unloved New Haven into the proposed merger of the New York Central and Pennsylvania railroads, to be called the Penn Central Transportation Company. A nod of approval came from the Interstate Commerce Commission in 1967. On February 1, 1968 the great merger became a reality. The life of the New York, New Haven & Hartford Railroad Company was over, and its future was entrusted to a highballing Penn Central express, on which no one, apparently, was watching the signals.

Chapter Fourteen Footnotes

A tired and unloved New Haven Railroad quietly slipped away in the late 1960s. Employees were also tired. Tired of misadventures, a bad press, and the financial disgrace. The forlorn bridge tender at Middletown, seen above, could likely have told us about far better times.

1. *Fortune Magazine.* April, 1949, 184.

2. *Business Week,* 2 September 1950, 64-68.

3. *Business Week,* 14 March 1953.

4. Duncan Norton-Taylor, "The McGinnis Express," *Fortune Magazine,* April 1955, 148.

5. Peter Lyon, *To Hell In A Day Coach* (Philadelphia and New York: J.B. Lippincott Company, 1968), 291.

6. Ibid, p. 292.

In 1965, the Federal government passed the U.S. High Speed Ground Transportation Act. Its "Demonstration II" project (in modern bureaucratic jargon) involved the Boston-New York corridor. Washington leased two new train sets for the scenic Shore Line Route through Connecticut. United Aircraft designed and owned the TurboTrains (first known as Turboliners), and they were built in Chicago by Pullman-Standard. They were powered by aircraft-type, gas-turbine engines, plus two traction motors for electric operation in New York tunnels. Service began April 8, 1969. At first they proved popular, though mechanical problems crept in. Ridership dropped when service cutbacks occurred. The set at right sits in the New Haven yards. Penn Central's best schedule times with Turbo service is reflected on the opposite page.

Few moments in American railway history have been as discouraging as the Penn Central debacle. Many counted on the huge company to reconcile New Haven Railroad problems once and for all. It didn't. The Penn Central logo was seen in Connecticut for a few brief years. It appears on engine No. 5533 below, which is hauling, in 1973, a caboose and cars on the old South Manchester Railroad branch. But on careful scrutiny it can be determined that the caboose is derailed on account of packed ice and snow on the Woodland Street crossing. Soon, the infamous Penn Central derailed.

S.E. OFIARA/MANCHESTER EVENING HERALD

Chapter Fifteen

Survivors

"The Americans are alone in assuming that railroads have to be profitable."

—*The Economist, August 24, 1985*

A glimmer of hope arose for the New Haven when the $4,000,000,000 Penn Central Transportation Company was ordered by the court to take in the skeletal remains of the New Haven. Of course, they did not want it, and had never wanted it ever since the first discussions in 1957 looking to a merger of the New York Central and Pennsylvania railroads. As former Penn Central President Alfred Perlman stated on July 29, 1970, in bankruptcy testimony before the U.S. Senate Commerce Committee, "We recognized almost from the beginning that we would have to pay certain penalties as a price for the Penn Central merger. We were required to take over, at a fantastic cost, the bankrupt New Haven Railroad, which had shown a $22,000,000 deficit the previous year."

Within three years of its creation, huge, unwieldly, run-down Penn Central crashed as America's worst business bankruptcy. Certainly no restorative balm was brought to the hapless New Haven. The windows got dirtier, cracked, and often milky-opaque; seats were torn and shabby; trains arrived ever later. All that was frequent were firings, service reductions and track abandonments, Most of the same problems that derailed Penn Central had also afflicted the New Haven: bad management, disappearing industries, intense trucker and highway competition, profitless train operations, inherited debt, lack of sufficient loan programs and credit lines, union problems, runaway diversification, excessive regulation, poor rate structures, deteriorating tracks, and undermaintained fleets of obsolete engines and cars. Sometimes bigger is not better.

The ruined giant, once boasting nearly twenty thousand miles of railroad, was subsequently placed under the protection of court-appointed trustees. Unpaid creditors hastened to the doorstep and slapped judgements upon the company's diversified holdings. Even if the railroad was hopeless, almost penniless, however, it still owned much prime real estate, hotels, oil and gas pipelines, jet aircraft, amusement parks, and even sports teams. Its high executives did not stint themselves. In their revealing 1971 book, *The Wreck of the Penn Central*, authors Joseph Daughen and Peter Blinzen obtained an interesting cameo of the times from the late Connecticut insurance executive, E. Clayton Gengras, a Penn Central director:

> After the first board meeting I attended in Philadelphia, I got in the car to drive home and I was sick. At a board meeting you talk about operating the business. It lasts three

Connecticut briefly witnessed Conrail operating the commuter train business. Later the firm was relieved of such burdensome and money-losing responsibilities. In the picture above, Conrail engine No. 5040 hauls a train away from the main line at South Norwalk, to Danbury. The date is June 9, 1978. "Berkshire" interlocking tower is at left, and the operator within controls switch and signal activity for trains in this immediate area. The branch up to Danbury was once electrified by the New Haven Railroad, but the wires were later dismantled. Diesel powered trains of Metro North now do the honors on the Danbury Branch.

or four hours and you find out what's wrong and do something about it. You don't spend all your time talking about stock options for the executives. But, they sat up there on the eighteenth floor in those big chairs with the name plates on them and they were a bunch of, well, I'd better not say it. The Board was definitely responsible for the trouble.

The short life of the Penn Central was an expensive and tragic example of gross mismanagement. Over and again the public wondered how it could have happened. Were its senior executives so completely devoid of any sense of public service? Of foresight? Of wisdom? Apparently many of them were. The federal government, uncharacteristically generous to the Highway Trust, listened but ultimately refused to bail out Penn Central, and perhaps with good reason. Yet it would respond with hands stuffed with money to a huge and sick Chrysler Corporation years later.

It is another curious fact that Penn Central would later emerge from bankruptcy no longer a railroad operator, although it still owns certain lines of track, abandoned or in service, including until recently those now used by the Metro North Commuter Railroad. In October, 1985, that busy, four-track, commuter line was purchased by the Connecticut Department of Transportation. The new, present-day Penn Central Corporation is a kind of conglomerate of choice real estate and other holdings and has done very well financially, thanks in no small part to its ability to write off taxes on its current profits against the huge backlog of inherited losses.

At this juncture, the reader might be reminded that railroads *can* be properly run. Protracted struggles tend to make people overlook the fundamental assets of railroads: their ability to move huge numbers of people and to haul vast tonnages of freight. They do that, often with great efficiency and with little environmental harm. Some also forget the worth of our railroads during times of war, natural disasters, energy crisis, and when other transport modes break down or fail. They also can handily get commuters in and out of many congested urban centers of America. And to dispel a widespread myth, trucks and truckers simply cannot move everything that American industry needs or ships every day. They do not approach, for instance, the sheer practicality of a one-hundred-car, unit coal train moving that resource from minehead to public utility; or, that of a double-decker trainload of new automobiles arriving in New England; or truck trailers that have been "piggybacked" on special railway flat cars across the country.

Railroads were partners to every industrial success story of the last century. Today that partnership is far more selective. Railroading in the Northeast is in an unprecedented hour of restructure. New corporations have emerged, joining old firms in fine-tuning what remains of the rail systems and lopping off little-used trackage. Big rebuilding programs are going forward; government funding and invervention are involved. A few lines are going to survive.

After the federal government had allowed the Penn Central bankruptcy to happen, the decaying railroad picture in the Northeast prompted President Nixon, in 1973, to sign the Regional Rail Reorganization Act. This created the United States Railway Association, out of whose pool of expertise came plans for a replacement company. By taking rail properties linked with Penn Central and combining them with other lines which it decided could not be reorganized or rescued separately,* the Association created, in 1976, the vast Consolidated Rail Corporation—Conrail for short. Nearly $4,000,000,000 was eventually pumped into the new system with the aim of making it self-supporting and then selling it to a suitable purchaser. The Conrail system, almost thirty-four thousand track miles, stretches from the Atlantic Ocean to St. Louis, and from the Ohio River to Montreal. Approximately 55 percent of all American manufacturing plants are situated somewhere along its tracks.

But Philadelphia-based Conrail had a very bumpy start. Computers did not accurately forecast what troubles in the economy might do to the line or its finances. Federal cash was loaned steadily. Unprofitable lines were severed, the work force was whittled down, and new agreements were ironed out with unions. Such cost-saving measures began to take effect, and the company started to show earnings instead of losses. In 1984 net income stood at a remarkable $500,000,000. As this

*The Reading Railroad, Central Railroad of New Jersey, Erie-Lackawanna, Lehigh Valley, Lehigh & Hudson, and, for a period, the Ann Arbor.

Conrail's principal revenues are derived from the movement of freight. As this book is written, it is still the largest rail hauler in the state. Virtually every day one of its freight trains rolls. The one below was at work near a snow-laden Brookfield, 1978.

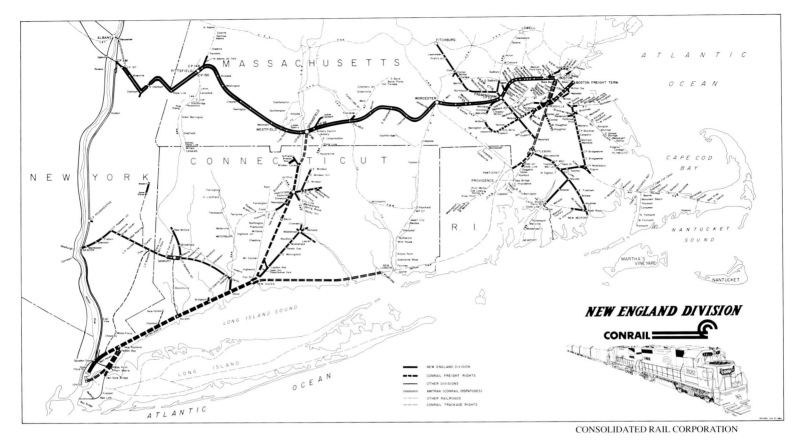

The map above charts where Conrail goes in the New England area. The company's president, L. Stanley Crane, is pictured below. Mr. Crane previously distinguished himself on the hugely successful Southern Railway. He supports the idea of Conrail being owned by employees and investors.

book is written the ultimate purchaser of Conrail is yet to be chosen. The leading contenders include the Norfolk Southern Corporation (made up, in part, of the Norfolk & Western and Southern railways); the CSX Corporation (an acronym for the Chessie Systems of Railroads and related companies, of which the Chesapeake & Ohio, Baltimore & Ohio, Seaboard and other famous old railroads are parts); and a consortium of investors who are linked with Conrail employees. Wealthy and able Norfolk Southern is the preferred choice of Elizabeth Dole, the nation's current Secretary of Transportation, though final approval rests with the Congress.

Although it is the largest railroad company operating in Connecticut today, Conrail is represented within the state only by local trainmasters; regional officers are situated in Springfield, Masssachusetts, in old Boston & Albany Railroad buildings. Almost all freight shipments destined to and from New England pass through Conrail's computerized Selkirk, New York, classification yard near Albany. This gateway has been used since Penn Central days instead of the once all-important Poughkeepsie Bridge.* A terminal for "piggyback" shipments, that is, truck trailers or containers riding on special railroad flat cars, is located at Cedar Hill yard in North Haven, conveniently serving truckers who come off Interstate 95. At Hartford the railroad maintains a terminal that transfers dry and liquid commodities like bulk cement from cavernous rail hopper cars to waiting trucks. The accompanying map shows where the blue and white Conrail engines go in Connecticut.

The Washington-based National Railroad Passenger Corporation is better known to the average rider as Amtrak, and was authorized in 1970, by the Rail Passenger Service Act. The following year experimental work began, all in response to the nation's ailing passenger train business. There still remains a genuine requirement

*That massive Hudson River structure—still standing silent as this is written—was used for decades by the New Haven Railroad for its connection with the west via Maybrook, New York, and Cedar Hill yard in New Haven. It caught fire in Penn Central days, and was never repaired.

285

Financial Highlights ($ In Millions Except Per Share)

	1984	1983	1982	1981	1980	1979	1978	1977	1976*
Revenues—Freight	$ 3,379	$ 3,076	$ 2,999	$ 3,557	$ 3,368	$ 3,436	$ 3,057	$ 2,881	$ 2,105
—Passenger	—	—	618	644	614	515	448	407	339
Income (Loss) from Operations	466	288	49	66	(187)	(178)	(386)	(361)	(173)
Net Income (Loss)	500	313	174	39	(244)	(221)	(430)	(412)	(246)
Net Income (Loss) Per Common Share— Fully Diluted	18.50	11.73	6.59	1.42	(9.84)	(8.94)	(17.27)	(16.46)	(9.83)
Capital Additions									
Roadway	400	336	329	321	331	502	457	382	277
Equipment	156	119	32	64	143	339	376	189	28
Average Number of Employees**	39,044	39,820	57,704	70,264	79,574	87,511	91,318	94,605	99,827
At December 31									
Current Assets	$ 1,516	$ 1,170	$ 1,151	$ 1,371	$ 1,323	$ 1,283	$ 1,156	$ 967	$ 817
Current Liabilities	929	859	957	1,166	1,172	1,202	1,179	967	864
Working Capital	587	311	194	205	151	81	(23)	—	(47)
Total Assets	6,236	5,703	5,505	5,705	5,628	5,426	4,823	4,406	3,761
Long-Term Debt (Net of Current Maturities)	1,711	1,679	1,691	1,866	2,069	2,109	2,023	2,120	1,341
Redeemable Preferred Stock	2,317	2,311	2,307	2,303	2,164	1,668	936	157	—

*Nine Months
**Company Only, Including Passenger Employees 1976-1982

CONSOLIDATED RAIL CORPORATION

for passenger trains in America, as most civilized societies have learned. A successful trial period for Amtrak led to expanded authority and service beginning in 1971.

What passenger railroad service survives in Connecticut in 1985 is divided between Amtrak and the Metro North Commuter Railroad, on the theory devised by Congress that the former should provide "inter-city" service, while state and local authorities should look after the short runs "into cities." As is customary in Washington, however, there are exceptions, and little attention is paid to whether an arrangement is basically efficient. In this case both systems use the same electrified main line between New Haven and New Rochelle, New York, where Amtrak trains turn south toward the Hell Gate Bridge route into Penn Station (for Philadelphia and Washington) while Metro North's continue on the old New York, New Haven & Hartford route into Grand Central Station. Making connections between the two systems is difficult, both in terms of separate timetables and separate ticketing.

Metro North also serves three branch lines, one from Stamford to New Canaan, another from South Norwalk to Danbury, and a third from Bridgeport to Waterbury. Connecticut and New York's Metropolitan Transit Authority (MTA) contract

[ABOVE] Comparative financial data of Conrail for the years 1976 (at the time of its inception) to 1985. Substantial losses preceded Crane; financial stability followed.

[BELOW] Amtrak train No. 473 rolls across the Connecticut River bridge at Enfield, September 30, 1984. This train, and others like it, provide frequent service from New Haven northward to Springfield.

COLLECTION OF SCOTT HARTLEY

An Amtrak Washington-Boston train pauses at New London's historic depot, designed by Henry Hobson Richardson and in continuous use since 1888. Amtrak's "Shore Line" service is popular; trains run full. Some of the firm's finest equipment is used in Connecticut. In 1975-1976, the station was completely renovated by Anderson, Notter, Finegold, Inc., of Boston. It was first built at a cost of $76,300. It is called a "union" station, although no other railroad joins Amtrak in using it. Contrary to belief, the New Haven Railroad did not build the structure; it was put up by the New London Northern, later the Central Vermont. Back in those days it was a true Union Station.

jointly with Metro North Commuter Railroad (an MTA subsidiary) to supply all the services. Most main line equipment consists of multiple-unit, subway-style electric cars (i.e., without locomotives) that seat five persons across on cramped seats—passengers hemmed in tightly three on one side of the aisle and two on the other. Large Urban Mass Transit grants help keep the lines in a medium state of repair, but stations, tracks, and cars are often littered with trash and paper in a way no European railroad would permit.

Amtrak operates two main routes in Connecticut: the famous Shore Line from New York to Boston via New Haven (where it still changes locomotives, from electric to diesel), and from New Haven to Hartford and Springfield. At Springfield the *Montrealer* goes on to the north, and another service turns east to Boston. There is also a daily budget of self-propelled cars furnishing a good commuting service with nine stops up that industrial spine, made possible under a cost-sharing arrangement between the state and Amtrak. The frequency of service on the old Shore Line, now limited to six stops in Connecticut, is about half of what it was before Amtrak, but the streamlined cars run full and are much more clean and comfortable than those of Metro North, with just four seats across. There are sleepers, extra-fare "club cars" (three across), and "snack bars" for so-called "fast food," but the parlor cars (two across) and elegant diners of the old Shore Line service have disappeared.

As this book is written, question marks still gather over the future of Amtrak. In the course of federal budget debates many assaults have been made on the whole national passenger railroad system; in the most recent it narrowly survived an administration attempt to kill its entire subsidy, of $684,000,000, which amounts to about 40 percent of its income—despite the fact that an aggressive management has been steadily improving its ridership, equipment, and earnings in the last few years. The company is approaching the break-even point on the Northeast Corridor routes. Amtrak President E. Graham Claytor has made it clear, however, that an Amtrak reduced only to the Corridor could not survive. Some of the fine old stations have been restored, with local help, notably in New London and New Haven.

Its major problem, of course, is that it began life in 1971 with rattletrap equipment, broken-down structures, and worn-out tracks. There was ludicrously insufficient starting capital from the Congress, which is not noted for its business acumen. Could intercity railroad passenger service simply disappear? Could America become the only modern country in the world without long-distance trains? It seems impossible to believe, but it seemed equally impossible, in 1937, that all the great palace steamers, still crowded with travellers, could suddenly vanish from the waters of Long Island Sound. But they did.

Besides Conrail and Amtrak, there exist other federal programs from which Connecticut railroads have drawn profit. Since 1976 significant rehabilitation has occurred to the vital shore-line route of tracks, thanks to the Northeast Corridor Improvement Project. Concrete ties and welded rail now make up most of this route, all with an eye towards high-speed train service. Many bridges have been rebuilt or replaced, such as the drawbridges at Shaw's Cove in New London and

COLLECTION OF TOM NELLIGAN

[ABOVE LEFT] Amtrak train No. 12 crosses the new Shaw's Cove drawbridge at New London in October, 1985. Baggage cars at end carry Boston mail. At right, a Metro North train, using a single Amtrak rail diesel car, departs Waterbury and eases over the Naugatuck River also in 1985.

COLLECTION OF SCOTT HARTLEY

[BELOW] Amtrak engine No. 207 easily leads her train of three coaches over the lovely old stone viaduct at Windsor. Sheets of ice enhance the Farmington River below.

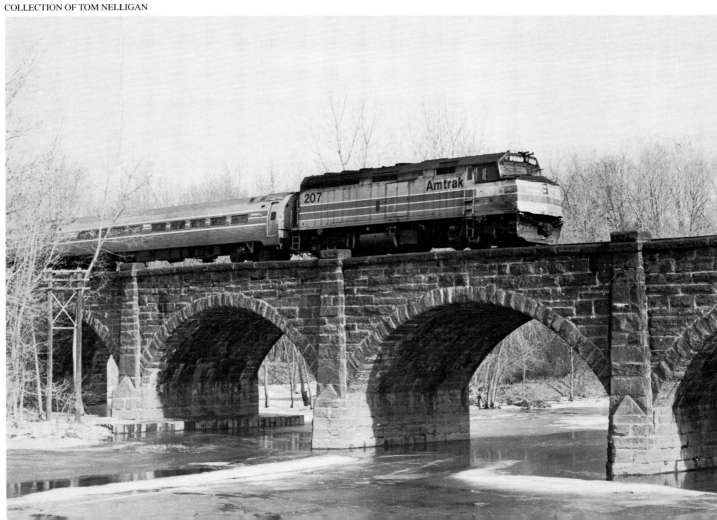

Kill Off Passenger Trains, Treasured by Other Countries?

By OLIVER JENSEN

Full of bounce and metaphor, David A. Stockman, the Administration's boy budget director, bobbed up again last week to tell a Senate subcommittee to "pull the plug" on Amtrak and let the 23,000-mile passenger railroad system die. Get rid of this "mobile money-burning machine," he said, and save its $684-million subsidy. It costs $35 each time a passenger gets aboard, he adds. Swinging his slingshot like his Biblical namesake, Stockman warned the lawmakers that what they do about trains will be a "litmus indicator" as to whether they really mean to cut the federal deficit, a Goliath now estimated at $200 billion.

If Stockman manages to brainwash Congress this time, we can score a funny sort of "first." We can be the first country in the civilized world without a passenger railroad system. And we can win this deplorable distinction at the very moment that Canada, Japan, France and even the Soviet Union are pouring new money and new technology into theirs.

There's no question that some big cuts must be made in the budget, and they have to stick through assaults of special interests. But young David isn't swinging at the right giant, merely at a pygmy. If he had done his homework he would know that killing Amtrak, far from saving money, would actually add to the deficit—this year, next year and for some years to come.

Chemists know that litmus paper changes color, depending on the concoction that it's exposed to. This Amtrak "saving" would not turn a good Tory blue, not when you would be forced to offset that $684 million with certain unavoidable costs. For instance, there are contractual "labor protection" guarantees that Congress bestowed on the 25,000 Amtrak workers when it set up the system in 1971. The costs in fiscal 1986 would come to $800 million. The guarantees run for six years, and would be expected to total $2.1 billion—for which no one would lift a hand or turn a wheel. This would turn the "saving" into $116-million loss.

Since Amtrak owns and maintains the Northeast corridor system, other freight and commuter railroads using it would have to carry all its costs. These other railroads are already beneficiaries of a congressional "back-door subsidy" that Amtrak has to pay by not charging them their real cost. That comes to $50 million annually; with Amtrak gone, it would reach an estimated $212 million. Add that

to the other figure above, and the fiscal 1986 deficit would grow by $328 million. The litmus paper would turn red.

These figures don't even count the various penalties for broken contracts and canceled leases on vehicles, Metroliners and Amtrak's new supercomputer for reservations. There also would be the cost of liquidation, handled no doubt by a corps of bureaucrats hidden in some other department's budget. You can forget all about the net capital loss—the government doesn't keep a capital budget—but Uncle Sam nevertheless would be kissing goodby an equipment, track and real-estate investment, reckoned with full depreciation, of $3.1 billion.

As for the $35 that it costs the government each time someone gets on a train—this is hocus-pocus. The $35 (actually nearer $34) includes not only the per-rider

share of the subsidy but also the loss to the Treasury for all rail trips deducted from income taxes for business travel. Using that method to figure each airline traveler's much higher subsidy, the tax deduction *alone* is $33, before the air controllers and other subsidies are added.

The real capital Goliath of the federal transportation budget for fiscal 1986 is the figure approved for highways: $15 billion. That would support 22 Amtraks. Goliath Jr. is aviation, which is getting $5 billion, or seven Amtraks. With tempting targets like these, why take aim at a relatively puny passenger railroad system that serves a mere 20 million riders a year? Because hit men always pick a weak target.

Stockman is going to have to hustle, however, because Amtrak, in its maddening way, is doing better every year. In the last four years it has increased its revenues

and cut costs by 26.6%. Riding its rising efficiency curve, it could, in a few years, become self-supporting. Despite its handicaps, built in by Congress, and despite insufficient capital at the start, it has converted itself from an inherited rattletrap into an cleaned-up, almost-brand-new affair—a little proletarian, perhaps, when compared to the grand old days of the "20th Century Limited," but the best way to see America, cheaper than flying in any similar comfort, serving many places that you can't get to by bus or air. Maybe Stockman is getting shrill when he thinks of a *profitable* Amtrak. After all, you can't kick a dog that's up.

Oliver Jensen is senior editor of American Heritage Magazine and chairman of the board of Valley Railroad Co., an unsubsidized steam tourist railroad in Essex, Conn.

Amtrak Is Pleasant but Non-Essential

By JAMES J. KILPATRICK

The future of Amtrak is not one of those cosmic matters, in a class with "Star Wars" and Social Security, on which the fate of nations and politicians may depend. Relatively speaking, the cost of maintaining passenger rail service is small potatoes. Even so, the debate over Amtrak offers a fine example of the problems that Congress must face in cutting our federal deficit.

These are among the arguments advanced by Amtrak's proponents: All forms of commercial transportation are federally subsidized in some degree. The President has said that taxpayers have to pungle up a subsidy of $35 for every Amtrak ticket sold, but, if the cost of maintaining highways, airports and air-traffic controllers were similarly apportioned, the per-passenger subsidy for Amtrak would not be out of line.

Further, Amtrak trains serve 19 million passengers a year, including 17,500 a day between Washington and New York. Chaotic conditions will be created in the whole Northeast corridor if Amtrak is abandoned.

Still further, to let Amtrak go into bankruptcy would be to toss its $3 billion in rolling stock onto a scrap heap. Cessation would trigger costs running into the billions to cover contracts with rail unions. The savings claimed by the Office of Management and Budget would be more than offset by these liabilities. Amtrak's ratio of revenues to costs is improving. While passenger service never can be wholly self-supporting, the mere existence of passenger cars could have great value if the nation again had to move great numbers of troops within the United States.

To these arguments Budget Director David A. Stockman responds: The overarching issue has to do with reducing the federal deficit as a whole. That need is so urgent that only the

most necessary government outlays should be continued. Amtrak is not necessary: "In a budget that must be pared back drastically, it ranks near the bottom of the program priority-scale."

As for subsidies to the other commercial carriers, at least bus and air travelers pay special taxes; rail passengers pay none. Amtrak's agreement with the rail unions provides that, if it goes under, every worker with at least six years' seniority must receive full pay for six years. But this contingent liability is not the government's $2-billion liability; it is Amtrak's $2-billion liability.

In any event, Amtrak is not without salable assets. Canada might buy some of the rolling stock; the company owns such valuable properties as Penn Station in Manhattan. New operators might be found for the Northeast corridor.

In our total transportation picture Amtrak's role is minuscule. On a given day, airports in Atlanta and Chicago each will board as many passengers as the entire Amtrak system boards. Only 14 of Amtrak's 500 stations board more than 500 passengers a day. If such expenses as interest and depreciation were properly included, the per-ticket subsidy would not be $35; it would be closer to $60. The time has come, after 12 years of losses and $9 billion in investment, to give up.

The proponents' arguments are persuasive. They are not convincing. On this issue Stockman clearly has the better case: If these appalling deficits ever are to be reduced, many pleasant but non-essential services will have to be abandoned. Amtrak is among them.

James J. Kilpatrick is a syndicated columnist in Washington.

---

over the Mystic River. Better signalling apparatus and communications have been integrated, but the plan to moderate certain curves and to electrify tracks east of New Haven to Boston seems in doubt owing to reductions in available capital funds. In the 1960s President Johnson's administration helped finance the introduction of "Turbo Train" service along parts of the Corridor, though it did not prove successful. United Aircraft, a Connecticut supplier, built the units, but advanced as they were, the scenic, winding route of shore line tracks held down operating speeds. Mechanical problems also plagued their operation; as one wag remarked to the author, "No other train in the world goes seventy miles an hour forward and forty sideways, all at the same time."

In addition to funding physical improvements, Washington also addressed the issue of excessive government regulation. One of the most important moves of the times occurred in 1980, when the famed Staggers Act was passed. It allowed the nation's freight railroads to set their own rates and institute long-term, special contracts with shippers.

The reader may recall that the federal government had to give Conrail a second helping hand in the early 1980s. The company was not showing a profit; it was also too large and unable to absorb losses on less-used lines. The Northeast Rail Service Act of 1981 halted federal subsidies to money-losing lines and allowed Conrail to transfer certain operations to other carriers. It also extended the time for Conrail to become profitable. Conrail commuter train operations in Connecticut were later

COLLECTION OF SCOTT HARTLEY

Metro-North Commuter Railroad

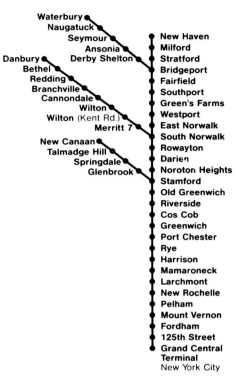

Waterbury
Naugatuck
Seymour
Ansonia
Danbury
Derby Shelton
Bethel
Redding
Branchville
Cannondale
Wilton
Wilton (Kent Rd.)
Merritt 7
New Canaan
Talmadge Hill
Springdale
Glenbrook

New Haven
Milford
Stratford
Bridgeport
Fairfield
Southport
Green's Farms
Westport
East Norwalk
South Norwalk
Rowayton
Darien
Noroton Heights
Stamford
Old Greenwich
Riverside
Cos Cob
Greenwich
Port Chester
Rye
Harrison
Mamaroneck
Larchmont
New Rochelle
Pelham
Mount Vernon
Fordham
125th Street
Grand Central
Terminal
New York City

When not riding Amtrak, Connecticut commuters turn to trains of Metro North, such as this electrified one on the New Canaan Branch. This particular train is designated by timetable as Number 1996, and we observe her, having departed Stamford, near Springdale Cemetery, summer of 1984.

Amtrak trains are hauled by both diesel and electric locomotives. Engine No. 904 was built by the Electro Motive Division of General Motors. The powerful AEM-7 can develop seven thousand horsepower. Here, she hauls the Bay State *across the Pequonnock River drawbridge at Bridgeport in June, 1985. "Peck" signal tower is at right.*

[BELOW] *Providence & Worcester engine No. 1801, a U18A built by General Electric, emerges from the ancient tunnel at Taftville. Because of narrow clearances, engineers must reduce train speed as they pass through. The tunnel was originally blasted for the old Norwich & Worcester.*

COLLECTION OF SGT. WILLIAM HALLENE

[RIGHT] *A commanding view of the big feed facility that the Providence & Worcester serves at Wauregan. Farming still goes on in the "Quiet Corner" of Connecticut. By purchasing basic feed ingredients, operators can mix feed for a variety of requirements. They reach many farms via trucks.*

COLLECTION OF SCOTT HARTLEY

passed along to Metro North, while certain freight routes were divided between the Providence & Worcester and the Boston & Maine railroads.

The Providence & Worcester, based in Woonsocket, is an old Rhode Island railroad company with considerable real estate interests in the capital city. Long ago it had a history of leasing itself to bigger lines, and when Penn Central defaulted on lease payments it decided to go independent again. In 1976 the Providence & Worcester ran its first freight train of modern times over the old Norwich & Worcester Railroad (Chapter Three) between Worcester and Plainfield, Connecticut; by state authority it was allowed to go west to Willimantic. Four years later it was providing service south of Plainfield to Groton thanks to a purchase arrangement with Conrail. When Conrail gave up certain freight lines in Connecticut, the Providence & Worcester enlarged its territory a step further in 1982. It now services customers west of Groton along the shore line to Westbrook, and east of Groton all the way to

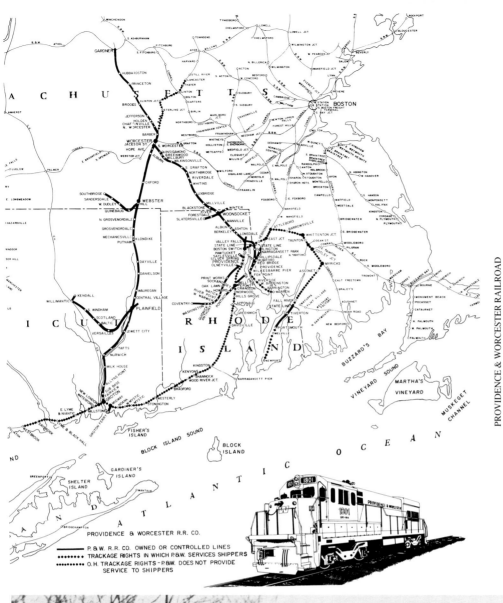

PROVIDENCE & WORCESTER R.R. CO.

—— P. & W. R.R. CO. OWNED OR CONTROLLED LINES
••••••• TRACKAGE RIGHTS IN WHICH P.&W. SERVICES SHIPPERS
••••••• O.H. TRACKAGE RIGHTS - P.&W. DOES NOT PROVIDE
        SERVICE TO SHIPPERS

Plainfield, Connecticut, can be located on the Providence & Worcester corporate map at left. Engine No. 2001 has just departed the town and is headed for the Worcester yards. This 2,000 horsepower engine was built by the Montreal Locomotive Works in Canada. From Plainfield, there stems the branch track to Willimantic, a fragment of the old Hartford, Providence & Fishkill.

COLLECTION OF SCOTT HARTLEY

An official business car of the Delaware & Hudson Railroad, now owned by Guilford Transportation Industries, helps make up the first Boston & Maine Connecticut train, between Waterbury and Torrington. She stands near the famous Waterbury station and tower, June 2, 1982. Officials and dignitaries were entertained aboard the car.

Timothy Mellon

Stonington and Providence. It also runs an occasional passsenger excursion train, with coaches and a parlor-observation car, around its lines. Company stock is publicly held.

The Boston & Maine did not operate in Connecticut until the summer of 1982; it did so by assuming certain lines of Conrail. The Boston & Maine is a unit of Guilford Transportation Industries, as are the Maine Central and the Delaware & Hudson railroads. Guilford—organized by Timothy Mellon, a member of the Pittsburgh family of bankers—has sought to create a profitable, unified railroad system of his own in the Northeast. Boston & Maine is based in North Billerica, Massachusetts, and operates only freight services in Connecticut, depicted in the accompanying map. Though it was invited to do so, the Boston & Maine had previously elected not to be part of Conrail.

Chapter Five traces the evolution of the Central Vermont story in Connecticut. Company headquarters are still in the old railroad town of St. Albans, Vermont, while area offices remain at the foot of Fourth Street in East New London. Only sixty miles of Central Vermont main line track is in Connecticut, but it is some of the

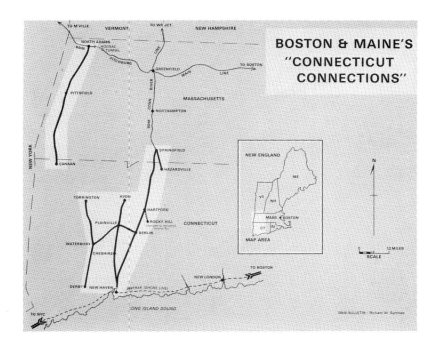

BOSTON & MAINE'S "CONNECTICUT CONNECTIONS"

The map at left was prepared by Richard W. Symmes of the Boston & Maine Railroad Historical Society. The company's Connecticut operations are clearly shown. In the picture below, photographer Tom Nelligan recorded local freight train WA-1 (Waterbury-Derby) rolling through Naugatuck in August 1984. Note this is a caboose-less train. Manufacturing and chemical companies still dot this important river valley.

Central Vermont engine No. 4548 pauses in front of the Mansfield depot, now a fine restaurant. Highway Route 44 crosses in back.

Old maple-leaf insignia (above) contrasts to modern "noodle" of Central Vermont, seen on engines below. Diesels powered a special passenger train excursion from Stafford to New London and return in 1981. The train had just left Amtrak's New London station when photographer Scott Hartley leaned out to catch the Winthrop Cove view.

best maintained in New England. Forest and agricultural products are the company's biggest freight manifests. Operating revenues from 1980 have hovered just above the $20,000,000 mark. Much traffic from Canada flows down the Central Vermont, whose parent is Canadian National Railways. Central Vermont management reports directly to that conglomerate's American affiliate, the Grand Trunk Corporation in Detroit, Michigan. Concern over its earnings record and the competitiveness favoring an encroaching Guilford Transportation Industries prompted Detroit and Montreal to announce, in the early 1980s, that its Central Vermont unit

Five-year facts	1984	1983	1982	1981	1980
Financial (Dollars in millions)*					
Forest products	$ 11.5	$ 10.6	$ 10.7	$ 11.1	$ 8.7
Agricultural products	2.6	3.3	3.3	4.3	4.2
Construction materials	1.7	1.3	1.4	1.5	1.4
Fuel and chemicals	1.4	2.2	2.5	2.9	2.0
Ores and metals	1.3	1.0	1.7	1.2	1.3
Intermodal	.4	1.1	1.5	1.2	.5
All other	2.0	1.7	2.3	2.3	2.7
Railway operating revenues	20.9	21.2	23.4	24.5	20.8
Railway operating expenses	22.0	21.3	23.8	18.3	18.0
Operating income	(1.1)	(.1)	(.4)	6.2	2.8
Other net	.6	.5	.6	1.1	.3
Income (loss) before income taxes and extraordinary item	(.5)	.4	.2	7.3	3.1
Income taxes				2.5	1.1
Income (loss) before loss on planned disposal	(.5)	.4	.2	4.8	2.0
Adjustment of carrying value of assets and liabilities of Central Vermont Railway, Inc.		1.9	(30.7)		
Net Income (loss)	$ (.5)	$ 2.3	$ (30.5)	$ 4.8	$ 2.0
Revenue ton miles (millions)	477	445	392	376	302
Revenue per ton mile	4.1ȼ	4.5ȼ	5.6ȼ	6.3ȼ	6.3ȼ
Revenue carloads (000's)	42	48	53	61	57
Capital expenditures / plant improvements					
Roadway	$ .4	$ .6	$ 1.1	$ 4.3	$ 2.6
Equipment	.1	.2	.1	.2	.1
Total	$ .5	$ .8	$ 1.2	$ 4.5	$ 2.7
Number of ties laid (000's)	6	6	33	35	34
Miles of welded rail laid on main line	.6	2.3	4.2	21.6	19.4
Physical plant – year-end					
Miles of road operated	375	377	377	377	377
Number of locomotives	27	24	24	24	19
Number of freight cars	226	352	1,294	1,304	1,284
Employees					
Average number	308	320	373	409	412

GRAND TRUNK CORPORATION

A lash-up of three Central Vermont diesel units haul their consist through Stafford Springs proper. Station roof silhouettes third engine; town hall looms over station.

[LEFT] A five-year fact sheet of the Central Vermont. Unstable net income has been attributed to a faulty economy and heavy competition from neighboring railways.

A festive mood permeates the air as the first Valley Railroad passenger excursion train rolls north out of Essex, July 29, 1971. Flags bedeck engine No. 103, built by the Baldwin Locomotive Works in Philadelphia in 1925. She was first purchased by the Sumter & Choctaw Railway, an Alabama logging road. She arrived in Essex, Connecticut, in 1970, and was a regular locomotive for several seasons. Attentive hands keep her preserved. Other steam engines operate Valley trains; diesels do too.

was for sale. Later, the decision was withdrawn. Apparently a young and aggressive Central Vermont management is going to try to stem the tide.

Most readers, if asked, can readily confirm that Connecticut is home for two "tourist" railroads:* the ever-popular Valley Railroad in Essex, and the newly inaugurated Housatonic Railroad over at Canaan. Promoters of the Valley gathered as early as 1969, among them Oliver Jensen, who edited this book. They sought to operate steam-hauled trains up the very scenic but abandoned and overgrown track of the lower half of the old Valley Division of the New Haven Railroad (see Chapter Ten.) Sure enough, they succeeded. On July 29, 1971, the first train chuffed out of Essex—exactly one century after the very first train ran on the Connecticut Valley Railroad. The Valley currently leases twenty-two miles of track from the state, the latter having bought it from Penn Central with federal assistance. Trains in 1985 can operate from Old Saybrook (an Amtrak stop) but generally start from Essex

*Connecticut is also home for two trolley museum operations: one at Branford and another at Warehouse Point.

297

north to Chester; except in winter they connect at Deep River with Connecticut River cruise boats, in a kind of re-creation of the days when New York, New Haven & Hartford trains also met Sound and river steamers. The line is an operating museum of Connecticut transportation sixty and seventy years ago. There is authentic parlor-car and private-car service in the old style of heavy-weight steel Pullmans. Haddam will be reached soon—opposite the confection of Victoriana at Goodspeed's—and one day the management hopes to have its trains whistle into Middletown, or Hartford, and to operate freight service. At Essex historic preservation of cars and engines goes forward by members of the Connecticut Valley Railroad Museum. During weekday operations, mainly paid hands keep the trains rolling at the Valley Railroad Company, and on weekends dedicated volunteers appear. Often they are the same persons.

Tourists and residents enamored of the beautiful Litchfield Hills and Housatonic River can now enjoy them from the window of a Housatonic Railroad train. It runs over an old route by the same name (see Chapter Four) that became part of the

Boats and trains along the Connecticut River were a familiar sight a century ago. Today, Valley Railroad patrons can get a steam train ride, then board a waiting river cruise boat opposite the Deep River stop. Here Point Gammon *prepares for departure as Engine No. 97 readies for the return trip to Essex. The transfer to the boat has just been made. Since this was photographed in the early 1970s, a more elaborate dock structure has been erected, called, fittingly enough, Deep River Landing.*

The Branford Steam Railroad is one of the largest industrial railroads in New England. Modern diesel-powered trains, such as above, carry quarry products south from North Branford to Stony Creek. Their crushed rock is famous, and used by railroads everywhere for ballast between ties.

illustrious Berkshire Division of the New Haven Railroad. The rich and famous once travelled along this way to get to their rural seats dotting the Berkshire chain of mountains. Ski trains, camp specials, and service to Lenox and Tanglewood were also popular. But in the 1970s the track was overgrown in vegetation between Canaan and Boardman's Bridge in New Milford. The potential of this section as a tourist line inspired a Fairfield engineer-businessman, John Hanlon, into action. A company was formed, the line was leased from the state, studies were made, and volunteers began to clear the line. The Remington Arms Company of Bridgeport donated a used industrial diesel engine; six used passenger cars were hunted down. By November 29, 1984, the first revenue train was under way south from Canaan to Falls Village. West Cornwall was reached in 1985, and eventually patrons will be able to alight in smart Kent and New Milford.

The nine-mile long Branford Steam Railroad does not any longer, as its name implies, operate steam trains, nor in fact does it serve the public.* However, as an industrial short line it ably serves the Tilcon-Tomasso Company. Its diesel engines haul drags of stone-laden cars from the company's traprock quarries in North Branford south to Juniper Point near Stony Creek. If Conrail or Amtrak work trains do not take the cars away, the contents are swiftly unloaded into barges for transshipment. Traprock is that durable crushed blue-gray stone most frequently found under and between ties of railroad track.

Back in 1969 Connecticut organized its first Department of Transportation with the purpose of achieving within the state a balanced system of transportation. It jointly purchased electric cars for the "West End" (or New Haven Line) commuter sector and has made commitments to modernize other cars and to rebuild several maintenance facilities. Eventually, that line's ancient generating plant at Cos Cob will be

*The name did differentiate it from the Branford Electric Railway, the old local trolley line restored since World War II as the Branford Trolley Museum, running out of East Haven.

phased out and modern signal systems will be installed. Important studies go forward by the department determining the future rail needs and responses of the state. Many dangerous grade crossings have been eliminated thanks to their work. The state has "rail-banked" certain railroad rights of way that have been abandoned, and has purchased several small lines now in use by other railroads. State subsidies keep several less-used lines open, but the modern formula is for towns and rail users to absorb the costs. Inventories of vacant but valuable railway parcels have been made by the department, hoping that such data will aid their redevelopment by municipalities or private investors. Several capital improvement projects to Connecticut railroad companies have occurred as a result of state funding. A feasibility study of restored rail passenger service between Waterbury and Hartford is now being conducted.

Nevertheless, as we conclude this book at the end of 1985, over a century and a half since Connecticut granted its first railroad charters, it is hard to say whether the decline of railroading is continuing, or whether it has reached bottom. There is less service than in 1852. Further abandonments are threatened on a few weed-grown lines, where poor service almost seems to be a deliberate device to hasten an unnecessary end. The state, and many of its citizens, still entertain the idea that railroads—unlike highways, or airports, or waterways—must show a profit or perish. That it might be wiser to support them as freight carriers than to keep on building and widening highways—cheaper and easier and safer where motorists are concerned—is not widely perceived. That the railroad, if reasonably maintained and operated, is a valuable alternative means of transport in a dangerous age is also true, for, as Lewis Mumford observed a long time ago, if the railroads disappear it will be necessary to re-invent them. A historian can only wish he might live to see how Connecticut's network, once so thick and now so thin, will look in another century, and what manner of devices will run along the tracks.

A newcomer to the tourist railroad business, Housatonic Railroad train No. 1, with a used General Electric (eighty-ton) diesel engine, prepares to leave the beautiful and historic depot at Canaan. Ridership has been brisk, and it is likely this tourist operation will grow in popularity. The rails often parallel the highly scenic Housatonic River.

COLLECTION OF SCOTT HARTLEY

Track Laying.

Appendix

TYPES OF STEAM LOCOMOTIVES

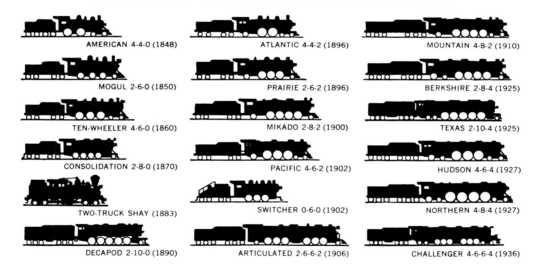

AMERICAN 4-4-0 (1848)

ATLANTIC 4-4-2 (1896)

MOUNTAIN 4-8-2 (1910)

MOGUL 2-6-0 (1850)

PRAIRIE 2-6-2 (1896)

BERKSHIRE 2-8-4 (1925)

TEN-WHEELER 4-6-0 (1860)

MIKADO 2-8-2 (1900)

TEXAS 2-10-4 (1925)

CONSOLIDATION 2-8-0 (1870)

PACIFIC 4-6-2 (1902)

HUDSON 4-6-4 (1927)

TWO-TRUCK SHAY (1883)

SWITCHER 0-6-0 (1902)

NORTHERN 4-8-4 (1927)

DECAPOD 2-10-0 (1890)

ARTICULATED 2-6-6-2 (1906)

CHALLENGER 4-6-6-4 (1936)

[OPPOSITE PAGE] A popular New Haven diesel was the General Motors-built model FL-9 series, which could also collect electric power from a third rail shoe when in New York tunnels. Metro North inherited several such units; most sport the old New Haven color scheme.

A railroad map of Connecticut showing the principal railway lines and their opening dates. Prepared by Sidney Withington, Electrical Engineer of the New York, New Haven & Hartford Railroad Company, for use in The First Twenty Years of Railroads in Connecticut, a booklet issued as part of a series marking the Tercentenary of the state, 1935.

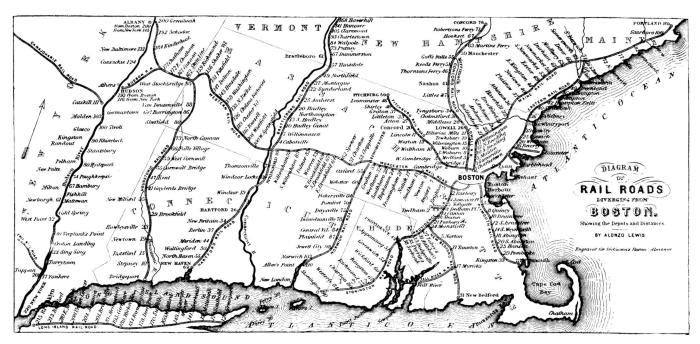

A railway map by Alonzo Lewis which appeared in Dickinson's Boston Almanac, *ca. 1840. Though the western half of Connecticut is somewhat distorted, the map clearly shows how several pioneer roads depended upon the Western Railroad in Massachusetts for a northern connection. All four—the Stonington, Norwich & Worcester, Hartford & New Haven, and Housatonic—located their southern terminals on or near Long Island Sound, and from here boats plied to New York City.*

A railway map drawn by the late Richard Shelton Kirby, P.E., Associate Professor of Engineering Drawing at Yale University. The map, prepared for a booklet presented by the author in 1935 for the 51st Annual Meeting, Connecticut Society of Civil Engineers, locates a number of Connecticut railway routes chartered but ultimately aborted. In a few cases, some work occurred.

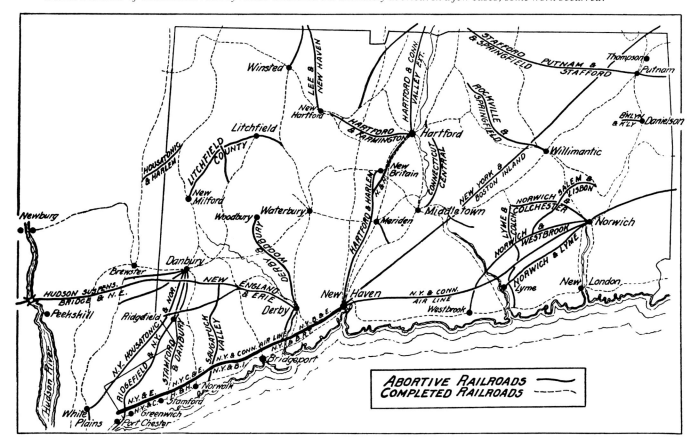

Names of Connecticut Railroad Commissioners from 1853, when the commission was first formed, to 1911, when it was absorbed by the state's Public Utilities Commission. Taken from the 1911 Annual Report of the railway commissioners.

Names of Railroad Commissioners, Commencement of Term, and Residence.

Name	Residence	Year	Note
Zaccheus W. Bissell,*	Sharon,	1853	
Moses B. Harvey,*	Stafford,	1853	
John Sewart,*	Chatham,	1853	resigned.
James N. Palmer,*	New Haven,	1854	to fill vacancy.
John Gould,*	Fairfield,	1854	
John S. Jewett,*	Sharon,	1855	
Henry Hammond,*	Killingly,	1856	
Patten Fitch,*	Bolton,	1857	
John Gould,*	Fairfield,	1858	
George D. Wadhams,*	Torrington,	1859	
Henry Hammond,*	Killingly,	1860	
Joseph W. Dudley,*	Madison,	1861	
John J. Jacques,*	Waterbury,	1862	to fill vacancy.
Abel Scranton,*	Madison,	1862	
Samuel Fitch,*	Stafford,	1863	
Abel Scranton,*	Madison,	1864	
William A. Cummings,*	Darien,	1865	
Samuel Fitch,*	Stafford,	1866	
Albert Austin,*	Suffield,	1867	
James Pike,*	Sterling,	1868	
Charles H. Denison,*	Stonington,	1869	resigned.
Simeon Gallup,*	Groton,	1870	to fill vacancy.
John I. Hutchinson,	Essex,	1870	
James Pike,*	Sterling,	1871	resigned.
Simeon Gallup,*	Groton,	1872	to fill vacancy.
Andrew Northrop,*	Brookfield,	1872	
Charles W. Scott,*	Sprague,	1873	to fill vacancy.
George W. Arnold,*	Haddam,	1873	
George M. Woodruff,	Litchfield,	1874	
Minott A. Osborn,*	New Haven,	1875	
George W. Arnold,*	Haddam,	1876	
George M. Woodruff,	Litchfield,	1877	
John W. Bacon,*	Danbury,	1877	to fill vacancy.
John W. Bacon,*	Danbury,	1878	
Francis A. Walker,*	New Haven,	1879	resigned Nov.
William H. Hayward,*	Colchester,	1880	to fill vacancy.
George M. Woodruff,	Litchfield,	1880	
John W. Bacon,*	Danbury,	1881	
William H. Hayward,*	Colchester,	1882	
George M. Woodruff,.	Litchfield,	1883	
John W. Bacon,*	Danbury,	1884	
William H. Hayward,*	Colchester,	1885	
George M. Woodruff,	Litchfield,	1886	
William O. Seymour,*	Ridgefield,	1887	
George M. Woodruff,	Litchfield,	1889	
William H Hayward,*	Colchester,	1889	
William O. Seymour,*	Ridgefield,	1891	
George M. Woodruff,	Litchfield,	1893	
Alex. C. Robertson,*	Montville,	1893	
William O. Seymour,*	Ridgefield,	1895	
Orsamus R. Fyler,*	Torrington,	1897	
Washington F. Willcox,*	Chester,	1897	
William O. Seymour,*	Ridgefield,	1899	
Orsamus R. Fyler,*	Torrington,	1901	
Washington F. Willcox,*	Chester,	1901	
William O. Seymour,*	Ridgefield	1903	
Andrew F. Gates,	Hartford,	1905	
Orsamus R. Fyler,*	Torrington,	1905	
William O. Seymour,*	Ridgfield,	1907	
E. J. Doolittle,	Meriden,	1909	to fill vacancy.
Andrew F. Gates,	Hartford,	1909	res'd Oct. 1, 1910.
Richard T. Higgins,	Winsted,	1910	to fill vacancy.
Theodore B. Ford,	Bridgeport,	1911	to fill vacancy.

Clerk,..............HENRY F. BILLINGS,

HARTFORD, CONN,

OFFICE, Nos. 41 and 43 State Capitol, Hartford.

* Deceased.

List of principal railway stations in Connecticut showing their rail mileage distance to Hartford using the shortest possible routes in 1883. From the Annual Report *of the railway commissioners for that year. Today the bound reports are collectors' items.*

STATEMENT.

SHOWING THE SHORTEST DISTANCE BY RAILROAD FROM HARTFORD TO THE VARIOUS STATIONS IN CONNECTICUT.

Station	Dist.	Station	Dist.	Station	Dist.
Abington,	49.	Clinton,	50.6	Goodspeed's,	29.75
Allyn's Point,	54.2	Cobalt,	20.95	Granby,	19.83
Andover,	22.5	Colchester,	38.85	Judd's Bridge,	71.35
Ansonia,	48.9	Colebrook,	38.	Grant's,	41.25
Arnold's,	27.25	Collinsville,	24.64	Greeneville,	49.2
Avon,	19.62	Conn. River,	43.67	Green's Farms,	62.47
Baltic,	41.9	Cos Cob,	79.86	Greenwich,	81.46
Bantam,	85.86	Cottage Grove,	4.	Grosvernordale,	60.2
Bartlett's,	56.	Cook's,	11.7	Groton,	61.75
Beacon Falls,	41.39	Crescent Beach,	53.17	Guilford,	52.47
Beckleys,	13.125	Cromwell,	12.75	Haddam,	26.5
Berlin,	10.625	Cornwall Bridge,	70.75	Hampton,	43.3
Bethel,	62.6	Danbury,	63.	Hancock,	26.1
Birmingham,	47.16	Danielsonville,	64.	Harrison's,	59.4
Blackhall,	45.75	Darien,	71.61	Hayden's,	9.
Bloomfield,	5.5	Dayville,	61.2	Hawleyville,	56.6
Bolton,	16.6	Deep River,	34.5	Hazardville,	19.6
Botsford,	64.6	Derby,	46.62	Higganum,	24.
Branchville,	70.48	Eagleville,	38.5	HighRockGrove,	40.39
Branford,	44.61	East Berlin,	15.625	Hitchcock's,	21.5
Bridgeport,	53.81	East Canaan,	52.25	Hoadley's,	27.8
Bristol,	17.9	East Hampton,	24.25	Hop River,	26.3
Broad Brook,	14.6	East Hartford,	2.7	Hoskins',	13.5
Brookfield,	62.6	East Haven,	41.51	Jewett City,	47.4
Brookfield Junc.,	60.6	East Lyme,	54.17	Kent,	79.75
Brookside Park,	65.6	East River,	54.59	Lakeville,	64.
Buckland,	7.5	East Thompson,	64.6	Lanesville,	65.6
Burlington,	22.78	East Windsor,	8.8	Lebanon,	38.2
Burnham's,	4.7	Ellithorpe,	52.8	Leete's Island,	49.62
Burnside,	4.1	Ellington,	19.3	Leonard's Br'ge,	37.95
Burrville,	39.5	Elliott,	49.2	Liberty Hill,	36.3
Campville,	47.14	Elmwood,	3.7	Lime Rock,	62.75
Canaan,	54.75	Enfield Bridge,	15.5	Litchfield,	47.7
Cannon's,	74.31	Essex,	38.	Long Hill,	61.81
Canterbury,	50.2	Fairfield,	58.88	Lyman Viaduct,	27.45
Canton,	21.5	Fair Haven,	38.9	Lyme,	44.11
Central Village,	57.6	Fall Village,	60.75	Madison,	54.15
Centreville,	35.44	Farmington,	16.99	Manchester,	8.7
Chapinville,	59.5	Fenwick,	45.	Mansfield,	40.4
Charter Oak Park,	3.	Five Mile River,	70.3	Maromas,	20.5
Cherry Brook,	25.	Forestville,	15.5	Massapeag,	53.3
Cheshire,	25.63	Franklin,	41.	Mechanicsville,	58.2
Chester,	33.5	Georgetown,	71.72	Melrose,	16.3
Chewink,	38.3	Glen Brook,	74.8	Meriden,	18.
Clayton,	6.6	Goshen,	39.9	Merrow,	42.
				Merwinsville,	75.6
				Middlefield,	21.25
				Middlef'd Centre,	20.25

Station	Dist.	Station	Dist.	Station	Dist.
Middletown,	15.25	Ridgefield,	74.48	Thompson,	60.2
Milford,	46.07	Riverside,	79.47	Thompsonville,	17.375
Mill Plain,	67.6	Rockfall,	18.65	Tolland,	46.
Mohegan,	51.4	Rocky Hill,	7.5	Tolles,	24.9
Montowese,	35.25	Rockville,	16.7	Towantic,	40.6
Montville,	55.2	Romford,	80.54	Torrington,	44.84
Moosup,	57.7	Roxbury,	68.8	Trumbull C'h,	58.81
Morris,	82.55	Roxbury Falls,	65.07	Turnerville,	35.25
Mt. Carmel,	32.63	Sadd's Mills,	18.	Twin Lakes,	57.5
Mystic,	69.5	Salisbury,	62.25	Tyler City,	40.88
Naugatuck,	37.45	Sandy Hook,	51.4	Union City,	35.7
New Britain,	9.1	Sanford's,	68.08	Union C'y,(Naug)	36.54
New Canaan,	84.55	Saybrook Junc.,	42.25	Unionville,	19.86
New Hartford,	27.79	Saybrook Point,	44.	Vernon,	12.3
New Haven,	36.5	Scotland,(H. & C. W.)	9.5	Versailles,	44.7
Newington,	5.	Scotl'd,(N.Y.& N.E.)	38.5	Yalesville,	20.5
New London,	61.	Seymour,	48.49	Yantic,	44.2
New Milford,	68.6	Shaker Station,	21.6	Wallingford,	24.
New Preston,	76.85	Shepaug,	61.44	Walkley Hill,	25.25
Newtown,	60.6	Simsbury,	15.	Warehouse P't,	13.5
Noank,	67.	Sound Beach,	78.25	Washington,	75.67
Norfolk,	45.25	South Coventry,	36.8	Waterford,(S.L.)	57.92
Noroton,	72.9	Southbury,	46.9	Watertown,	38.13
North Cromwell,	11.5	Southford,	43.9	Waterville,	29.9
Northford,	31.55	Southington,	19.04	Waterbury,	32.4
N. Grosvern'dale	61.7	South Kent,	78.6	Wauregan,	59.
North Haven,	29.625	South Lyme,	50.03	Weatogue,	16.86
North Windham,	35.8	S. Manchester,	10.95	Westbrook,	46.12
Norwalk,	69.69	South Norwalk,	68.19	Westchester,	30.45
Norwich,	47.9	Southport,	60.45	West Cornwall,	66.75
Norwich Town,	46.2	S. Wethersfield,	5.5	Westfield,	17.625
Oakville,	35.9	S. Willington,	44.25	West Haven,	38.91
Oneco,	62.9	South Wilton,	76.36	West Mystic,	68.5
Orange,	42.69	S. Windham,	34.9	West Norfolk,	48.
Orcutt's,	54.1	South Windsor,	6.2	Westport,	65.25
Ore Hill,	66.	Springdale,	81.25	West Street,	15.5
Osborn,	12.9	Stafford,	51.9	West Thompson,	58.6
Packerville,	52.5	Stamford,	76.25	West Winsted,	36.25
Parkville,	1.6	State Line,(N. L. N.)	50.1	Wethersfield,	3.75
Pine Meadow,	27.04	Steele's,	18.3	Wheaton's,	27.1
Plainfield,	54.5	Stepney,	63.81	Whiting River,	50.25
Plainville,	13.7	Sterling,	61.1	Willimantic,	31.5
Plantsville,	19.75	Stoney Creek,	48.11	Wilson's, (H.& N.H.)	3.5
Pomfret,	51.3	Stonington,	73.	Wilson's (N. & W.)	63.8
Pomperaug V'y,	46.9	Stratford,	50.59	Wilson's Point,	70.84
Portland,	16.25	Stratton Brook,	17.5	Wilton,	75.82
Poquonnock,	64.	Summit,	43.5	Windermere,	17.6
Pratt's,	7.4	Taftville,	51.	Windsor,	6.375
Putnam,	56.1	Talcottville,	11.3	Windsor Locks,	12.
Quinnipiack,	33.	Talmadge Hill,	83.	Winnipauk,	71.37
Quinnebaug,	71.1	Tariffville,	11.5	Winsted,	35.5
Reading,	65.99	Terryville,	22.2	Woodland,	5.1
		Thamesville,	49.	Wolcottville,	44.84
		Thomaston,	41.82	Woodmont,	42.46

List of Directors and Officers of the New York, New Haven & Hartford Railroad Company in 1911, at the height of the Morgan-Mellen era.

1911.] NEW YORK, NEW HAVEN AND HARTFORD RAILROAD.

Directors.

Name.	Post office address.	Date of expiration of term
WILLIAM ROCKEFELLER,	New York, N. Y.,	4th Wednesday in October.
J. PIERPONT MORGAN,	New York, N. Y.,	" "
GEO. MACCULLOCH MILLER.	New York, N. Y.,	" "
CHARLES F. BROOKER,	Ansonia, Conn.,	" "
GEORGE J. BRUSH,	New Haven, Conn.,	" "
I. DE VER WARNER,	Bridgeport, Conn.	" "
EDWIN MILNER,	Moosup, Conn.,	" "
WILLIAM SKINNER,	Holyoke, Mass.,	" "
D. NEWTON BARNEY,	Farmington, Conn.,	" "
CHARLES S. MELLEN,	New Haven, Conn.,	" "
ROBERT W. TAFT,	Providence, R. I.,	" "
JAMES S. ELTON,	Waterbury, Conn.,	" "
JAMES S. HEMINGWAY,	New Haven, Conn.,	" "
JAMES McCREA,	Philadelphia, Pa.,	" "
A. HEATON ROBERTSON,	New Haven, Conn.,	" "
FREDERICK F. BREWSTER,	New Haven, Conn.,	" "
HENRY K. McHARG,	Stamford, Conn.,	" "
LEWIS CASS LEDYARD,	New York, N. Y.,	" "
CHARLES M. PRATT,	New York, N. Y.,	" "
AMORY A. LAWRENCE,	Boston, Mass.,	" "
ALEXANDER COCHRANE,	Boston, Mass.,	" "
JOHN L. BILLARD,	Meriden, Conn.,	" "
GEORGE F. BAKER,	New York, N. Y.,	4th Wednesday in October.
THOMAS DeWITT CUYLER,	Philadelphia, Pa.,	" "
THEODORE N. VAIL,	Boston, Mass.,	" "
EDWARD MILLIGAN,	Hartford, Conn.,	" "
FRANCIS T. MAXWELL,	Rockville, Conn.,	" "

Principal Officers.

Title.	Name.	Official address.
Chairman of the Board,	C. S. MELLEN,	New Haven, Conn.
President,	C. S. MELLEN,	New Haven, Conn.
Vice-President,	T. E. BYRNES,	Boston, Mass.
Vice-President,	H. M. KOCHERSPERGER,	New Haven, Conn.
Vice-President,	E. H. McHENRY,	New Haven, Conn.
Vice-President,	E. G. BUCKLAND,	New Haven, Conn.
Vice-President,	B. CAMPBELL,	New Haven, Conn.
Assistant to the President,	H. J. HORN,	New Haven, Conn.
Secretary,	A. E. CLARK,	New Haven, Conn.
Treasurer,	A. S. MAY,	New Haven, Conn.
General Counsel,	E. D. ROBBINS,	New Haven, Conn.
General Auditor,	J. M. TOMLINSON,	New Haven, Conn.
General Managers,	S. HIGGINS,	New Haven, Conn.
Chief Engineer,	EDWARD GAGEL,	New Haven, Conn.
General Superintendent,	B. R. POLLOCK,	New Haven, Conn.
Freight Traffic Manager,	R. T. HASKINS,	New York, N. Y.
General Freight Agent,	L. H. KENTFIELD,	New Haven, Conn.
General Passenger Agent,	A. B. SMITH,	New Haven, Conn.
Commissioner,	A. A. MAXWELL,	New Haven, Conn.
Manager of Purchases and Supplies,	H. A. FABIAN,	Boston, Mass.

The New York, New Haven and Hartford Railroad Company
DIRECTORS

CHARLES FRANCIS ADAMS   Concord, Mass.
Chairman, State Street Trust Company, Boston, Mass.

CHARLES ULRICK BAY   New York, N. Y.
Ambassador to Norway
President, Connecticut Railway and Lighting Company, Bridgeport, Conn.

*FREDERICK S. BLACKALL, jr.   Cumberland Hill, R. I.
President and Treasurer, The Taft-Peirce Manufacturing Company, Woonsocket, R. I.

CHARLES PREVOST BOYCE   Baltimore, Md.
Senior Partner, Stein Bros. & Boyce, Baltimore, Md.

MORGAN B. BRAINARD   Hartford, Conn.
President, Aetna Life Insurance Company, Hartford, Conn.

*ALLERTON F. BROOKS   Hamden, Conn.
President, The Southern New England Telephone Company, New Haven, Conn.

*FREDERIC C. DUMAINE   Groton, Mass.
Chairman, Amoskeag Company, Boston, Mass.

*HARVEY D. GIBSON   Locust Valley, N. Y.
President, Manufacturers Trust Company, New York, N. Y.

JOHN L. HALL   Boston, Mass.
Senior Partner, Choate, Hall & Stewart, Boston, Mass.

JOHN A. HARTFORD   Valhalla, N. Y.
President, Great Atlantic & Pacific Tea Company, New York, N. Y.

MILTON P. HIGGINS   Worcester, Mass.
President, Norton Company, Worcester, Mass.

RUSSELL MAKEPEACE   Marion, Mass.
President, A. D. Makepeace Company, Wareham, Mass.

*WILLIAM B. SNOW, Jr.   Brookline, Mass.
President, Suffolk Savings Bank for Seamen and Others, Boston, Mass.
President, Amoskeag Company, Boston, Mass.

RUPERT CAMPBELL THOMPSON, Jr.   Providence, R. I.
President, Providence National Bank, Providence, R. I.

*LAURENCE F. WHITTEMORE   Pembroke, N. H.
President, The New York, New Haven and Hartford R. R. Co., New Haven, Conn.

EDWARD F. WILLIAMS   West Newton, Mass.
Resident Manager, Assabet Mills, American Woolen Company, Maynard, Mass.

*Member of Executive Committee.

OFFICERS
(As of February 1, 1949)

Chairman of the Board	FREDERIC C. DUMAINE
President	LAURENCE F. WHITTEMORE
Vice-President and Executive Assistant	GEORGE T. CARMICHAEL
Vice-President—Purchases and Stores	CHARLES E. SMITH
Vice-President and General Counsel	HERMON J. WELLS
Vice-President and Assistant to President	ERNEST C. NICKERSON
Vice-President—Operation, Maintenance and Engineering	J. FRANK DOOLAN
Vice-President—Traffic	HENRY F. McCARTHY
Assistant to President	HOWARD F. FRITCH
Comptroller	LEO V. SULLIVAN
Secretary	WILLIAM H. ROWLAND
Treasurer	WILLIAM R. BENJAMIN

ANNUAL REPORT 1955

BOARD OF DIRECTORS

JOHN E. SLATER, *Chairman*	Essex Fells, N. J.
GEORGE ALPERT	Newton Centre, Mass.
GEORGE T. CARMICHAEL	Hamden, Conn.
HOWARD G. CUSHING	Newport, R. I.
FREDERIC C. DUMAINE, JR.	Weston, Mass.
HARRY L. FILER	Hamden, Conn.
HORACE C. FLANIGAN	Purchase, N. Y.
ROY W. FREEBURNE	Hamilton, Ontario
WILLIAM M. GOSS	Waterbury, Conn.
WILLIAM K. JACOBS, JR.	New York, N. Y.
FRANCIS S. LEVIEN	Stamford, Conn.
PATRICK F. McDONALD	Brookline, Mass.
PATRICK B. McGINNIS	New York, N. Y.
EDWARD A. MERKLE	Haworth, N. J.
FREDERICK R. MURGATROYD	Burlington, Ontario
EDWARD F. O'BRIEN	Worcester, Mass.
JEREMIAH J. O'NEILL	Orange, Conn.
PAUL A. RUST	Fairfield, Conn.
WILLIAM B. SNOW	Brookline, Mass.
HOMER O. WHITMAN	Boston, Mass.
EDWARD F. WILLIAMS	West Newton, Mass.

OFFICERS

JOHN E. SLATER	*Chairman of the Board*
PATRICK B. McGINNIS	*President*
GEORGE T. CARMICHAEL	*Senior Vice President*
WILLIAM T. GRIFFIN	*Vice President – Law*
JOHN P. RUTHERFURD	*Vice President – Real Estate*
PAUL R. GOULETT	*Vice President – Operations*
WILLIAM K. TATE	*Vice President – Freight Traffic*
JEREMIAH J. O'NEILL	*Comptroller*
HARRY L. FILER	*General Counsel*
FREDERICK J. ORNER	*General Manager*
JOHN F. LARKIN	*Secretary*
REGINALD H. BREITENSTEIN	*Treasurer*

Selected Bibliography

AMERICAN RAILROADS:

Armstrong, John H. *The Railroad—What It Is, What It Does*. Bristol, CT: Simmons-Boardman, 1978

Holbrook, Stewart H. *The Story of American Railroads*. New York: Bonanza Books, 1947

Hubbard, Freeman. *Encylopedia of North American Railroading*. New York: McGraw-Hill, 1981

Jensen, Oliver. *The American Heritage History of Railroads in America*. New York: American Heritage, 1975

Lyon, Peter. *To Hell in a Day Coach*, Philadelphia: J.B. Lippincott, 1968

Nock, Oswald S. *Railways of the USA*. New York: Hastings House, 1979

Ogburn, Charlton. *Railroads: The Great American Adventure*. Washington, D.C.: National Geographic Society, 1977

HISTORY OF NEW ENGLAND RAILROADS:

Baker, George Pierce. *The Formation of the New England Railroad Systems*. Cambridge, MA: Harvard University Press, 1937

Harlow, Alvin F. *Steelways of New England*. New York: Creative Age, 1946

Kirkland, Edward Chase. *Men, Cities and Transportation*. Cambridge, MA: Harvard University Press, 1948

CONNECTICUT RAILROADS:

Beaudette, Edward H. *Central Vermont Railway, Operations in the Mid-Twentieth Century*. Newton, NJ: Carstens Publishers, Inc., 1982

Daughen, Joseph R., and Peter Binzen. *The Wreck of the Penn Central*. Waltham, MA: Little, Brown & Co., 1971

Farnham, Elmer F. *The Quickest Route*. Chester, CT: Pequot Press, 1973

Jones, Robert C. *The Central Vermont Railway*. 6 vols. Silverton, CO: Sundance Publishers, Ltd., 1981

Lewis, Thomas R., Jr. *Silk Along Steel*. Chester, CT: Pequot Press, 1976

Nelligan, Tom. *The Valley Railroad Story*. New York: Quadrant Press, 1983

Pavlucik, Andrew J. *The New Haven Railroad, A Fond Look Back*. New Haven: Pershing Press, 1978

Staples, Henry Lee, and Alpheus Thomas Mason. *The Fall of A Railroad Empire*. Syracuse, NY: Syracuse University Press, 1947

Weller, John L. *The New Haven Railroad, Its Rise and Fall*. New York: Hastings House, 1969

Withington, Sidney. *The First Twenty Years of Railroads in Connecticut*. Tercentenary Commission, State of Connecticut, New Haven: Yale University Press, 1935

INDEX

Compiled by Frances Alida Hoxie, research associate, The Connecticut Historical Society

312

Author GREGG TURNER, a life-long railway enthusiast, is a former researcher and a national director of the Railway & Locomotive Historical Society at Harvard Business School. A Waterford, Connecticut, native who lives in Mansfield Center, he writes and lectures frequently on Connecticut railway history. He owns and operates the Connecticut and Western Massachusetts agency of Allen Church Organs.

Editor OLIVER JENSEN, was a writer/editor for *Life* magazine; he was also one of the founders, and editor for 22 years, of *American Heritage*. He is author of the *American Heritage History of Railroads in America*, among many other books. A resident of Old Saybrook, Connecticut, he is chairman of the Valley Railroad, a restored tourist steam rail line in Essex, Connecticut.

Designer-illustrator E.J. McLAUGHLIN operates his own graphic arts business in his home town of Washingtonville, New York. A railway buff, he has worked in the art department of *Railway Age* magazine, and was art director for the McCall Corporation and for Grolier.

MASSACHUSETTS

NEW YORK

TO PITTSFIELD

B&M

CANAAN

FALLS VILLAGE

HOUSATONIC R.R.

WEST CORNWALL

(H.R.R.)

KENT

(H.R.R.)

NEW MILFORD

TO BEACON

CONRAIL

CR

HAWLEYVILLE

BERKSHIRE JCT.

DANBURY

CONRAIL

BETHEL

BOTSFORD

REDDING

BRANCHVILLE

GEORGETOWN

METRO NORTH – CONRAIL

WILTON

NEW CANAAN

TALMADGE HILL

NORWALK

SPRINGDALE

MN CR

S. NORWALK

GLENBROOK

STAMFORD

GREENWICH

WESTPORT

FAIRFIELD

BRIDGEPORT

STRATFORD

DEVON

SHELTON

BRIDGE OUT

DERBY JCT.

CR-MN

MILFORD

NEW HAVEN

SEYMOUR

ANSONIA

HAMDEN

MONTOWESE

N. BRANFORD

B5RR

PINE ORCHARD

GUIL

TORRINGTON

BOSTON & MAINE

THOMASTON

B&A

WATERBURY

METRO NORTH – B&M

NAUGATUCK

BOSTON & MAINE

CHESHIRE

BRIDGE OUT

BRISTOL

PLAINVILLE

FARMINGTON

AVON

B&M

B&M

HARTFORD

BLOOMFIELD

WINS

BRADLEY SPUR

SP

SU

NEWINGTON

NEW BRITAIN

B&M

H&B

BERLIN

SOUTHINGTON

BOSTON & MAINE

MERIDEN

AMTRAK – BOSTON&MAINE, CONRAIL

WALLINGFORD

CONRAIL

EAST WALLINGFO

MIDDLETOW

YAR

MID

AMTRAK – CONRAIL (

LONG ISLAND SOUND

AMTRAK – METRO NORTH-CONRAIL (GREENWICH TO NEW HAVEN)